Chrislam:
How Missionaries Are Promoting An Islamized Gospel

Revised edition

Chrislam:
How Missionaries Are Promoting An Islamized Gospel

Revised edition

Edited by
Joshua Lingel
Jeff Morton
Bill Nikides

i2 Ministries Publications

Unless otherwise indicated, Scripture quotations are taken from the *New International Version*, Copyright © 1984 by the International Bible Society, used by permission. All rights reserved.

Scripture quotations taken from the *English Standard Version,* Copyright © 2001 by Crossway, a ministry of Good News Publishers, used by permission. All rights reserved.

Scripture quotations taken from the *New American Standard Bible,* Copyright © 1960, 1962, 1963, 1968, 1971, 1972, 1973, 1975, 1977, 1995 by The Lockman Foundation, used by permission. All rights reserved. (www.Lockman.org)

Scripture quotations taken from the *New King James Version*, Copyright © 1982 by Thomas Nelson, Inc., used by permission. All rights reserved.

First edition 2011
Revised edition 2012

i2 Ministries Publishing © 2011
Garden Grove, CA
Printed in Canada

DEDICATION

*To our Christian brothers and sisters
who have courageously come out of Islam…
and with prayers for those who want to.*

CONTENTS

Foreword vii
Preface and Acknowledgements ix
Introduction 1

Insiders' Perspectives 11

1.1 The Inside Story: Theology
   Bill Nikides 12
   The proponents of IM provide biblical support for the movement.

1.2 The Inside Story: Missiology
   Jeff Morton 23
   The advocates define IM, look at Islam as a culture and religion, and explain how they understand Judaism, Christianity, and the Church.

1.3 The Inside Story: Translation
   Joshua Lingel 38
   A presentation of the rationale for the removal of filial language by one of SIL's leading translation consultants.

IM and Hermeneutic Problems 43

2.1 Lost in Translation: Insider Movements and Biblical Interpretation
   Bill Nikides 44
   A critique of the some of the more problematic hermeneutical principles employed within IM.

2.2 Would Paul Become Muslim to Muslims?
   Georges Houssney 62
   A proper exegesis of 1 Cor 9:19-23, which is a significant passage used by IM to support insider decontextualization.

2.3 The Confusion of Kingdom Circles: a Clarification
   John Span 77
   A critique of the kingdom circles paradigm that explains how Muslims come to Christ without the need of coming through the church or Christianity.

Missiology of IM 87

3.1 Moving On from the C1-C6 Spectrum
    Roger Dixon 88
    The inadequacies of the Spectrum are clarified in this thorough explanation by a missionary with more than 30 years experience with Muslims.

3.2 Pagan Religious Practices and Heretical Teaching: What Is to Be Our Attitude? Gleanings from the Old and New Testaments
    David Talley 100
    A detailed look at what Old Testament says about God's view of other religions and the serious implications for the insider movements.

3.3 Theology of Religions: Would Jesus Be Caught Dead Working in Islam?
    Jeff Morton 116
    A biblical theology of religions must conclude that Islam is a religion of bondage and ultimately demonic in its origin.

3.4 Dhimmitude, Muslim Replacement Theology, the Stockholm Syndrome and the Insider Movements
    Roger Dixon 126
    This is an ingenious examination of power relationships and its impact upon the missionaries who advocate for IM.

3.5 IM: Inappropriate Missiology?
    Jeff Morton 132
    Relying too heavily on social sciences, IM's missiology is more reliant upon the observations of the anthropologist than the teachings of scripture.

3.6 Insider Movements' Equivalent of Limbo: The CAMEL Method
>	*Emir Caner* *145*
>	A serous examination of a method of evangelism, some troubling assumptions about Islam, the Qur'an, and the prophethood of Muhammad.

IM and Translation Problems 155

4.1 Islamizing the Bible: Insider Movements and Scripture Translations
>	*Joshua Lingel* *156*
>	SIL's vexing Muslim compliant translation principles and practices are given a critical look resulting in some very troubling implications.

4.2 A World of Riches
>	*David B. Garner* *173*
>	A very detailed inspection of the biblical, theological, and historical importance of the title *son of God*.

4.3 Jesus the Eternal Son of God
>	*David Abernathy* *181*
>	A very detailed inspection of the biblical, theological, and historical importance of the title *son of God*.

4.4 How Insider Movements Affect Ministry: Personal Reflections
>	*Adam Simnowitz* *199*
>	An essay of personal experiences, it shows how the removal of filial language from the Bible, among other matters, creates friction among field missionaries.

IM Inside Out 227

5.1 Interview of a Former Insider, Anwar Hossein
>	*Bill Nikides* *228*
>	Pastor Anwar Hussein relates his own story of being an insider in Bangladesh, how and why he left, and the situation in his country today.

5.2 Flirting with Frankenstein: Insider Movements from the Inside
    Abdu Murray 238
    A young Lebanese Muslim tells his story of coming to faith in Christ while attempting to amalgamate Islam and Christianity, then realizing the monster he created.

5.3 Observations and Reactions to Christians Involved in a New Approach to Mission
    Edward Ayub 250
    A Bengali pastor speaks out about the division brought to the church by IM. He calls for unity in the church by guarding the true teachings of Jesus.

5.4 Islamization of the Gospel
    Elijah Abraham 262
    Insights of a Christian from an Iraqi Muslim family who sees IM as a absolute betrayal of the true gospel.

5.5 The New Christians of North Africa and Insider Movements
    Bassam Madany 267
    The Christians of Algeria, converts from Islam, are happy to identify themselves as Christians, and thankful to be considered worthy of persecution.

5.6 Insider Movements: a Critique by an Iranian Convert
    Sasan Tavassoli 274
    An essay by a highly educated Iranian convert reveals his incredulity that IM is considered genuine evangelism.

IM, the Past and Present 277
6.1 An Assessment of IM's Principle Paradigms
    Jay Smith 278
    The leadership of the Common Ground conference engaged with the author's questions for them, allowing him to produce this detailed critique of Common Ground and the principles of IM.

6.2 Can Christians Be Muslims?
David Cook *297*
   History shows us that Christians who attempt to be hidden Christians within Islam end up as Muslims.

6.3 A Word to Secret Believers...
Samuel Zwemer *307*
   This final chapter is a word of caution and encouragement to secret Christians; it cannot last and you will not grow.

Appendixes..311
Appendix 1. A letter to Lausanne Leadership *311*
Appendix 2. My experience with *Common Ground*: Hilki Berisha *312*
Appendix 3. Questions for *Common Ground* leadership *315*

Selected Bibliography: Advocates of Insider Movements 317

IM Websites and Blogs 321

Selected Bibliography: Historical Perspective 325

Historical Perspective Websites....................................328

Index..329

Scripture References 335

Qur'anic References 341

Abbreviations

BECNT (Baker Exegetical Commentary on the New Testament)

EBC (The Expositor's Bible Commentary)

EMQ (*Evangelical Missions Quarterly*)

IB (*International Bulletin*)

ICC (International Critical Commentary)

IJFM (*International Journal of Frontier Missions*)

JETS (*Journal of the Evangelical Theological Society*)

MF (*Mission Frontiers*)

Missiology (*Missiology: An International Review*)

NAC (New American Commentary)

NCBC (New Century Bible Commentary)

NIBC (New International Bible Commentary)

NICNT (New International Commentary on the New Testament)

NIGTC (New International Greek Testament Commentary)

NTC (New Testament Commentary)

PNTCS (Pillar New Testament Commentary Series)

SFM (*St. Francis Magazine*)

TNTC (Tyndale New Testament Commentary)

WBC (Word Biblical Commentary)

Foreword

The book you hold in your hands, *Chrislam: How Missionaries Are Promoting an Islamized Gospel,* is an important study. It engages the question of how much one can and should remain connected to one's Muslim heritage as that Muslim comes to embrace Christ. What should we teach others to do in a Muslim context and how should we translate the Scripture for them so the message of the New Testament is clear? On analogy with the Messianic movement, the claim is that the ability exists to extensively keep both relationships. This impacts translation and practice. It is a significant claim that needs careful assessment.

On one level, the comparison to messianism with its Jewish roots is flawed. Old Testament faith preceded Christian belief, and the Hebrew Scripture was accepted as canon by the movement Jesus started. No such connection exists from a Christian perspective to the sacred text of Islam. The one point of connection is an affirmation of monotheism in a world where many gods can be worshipped. Second, the conception of God and his attributes in Islam differs significantly to the Christian faith (and from Judaism). The personal nature of God in his relationships is an emphasis that is diminished in the Islamic view of God. Third, even in the case of the analogy with Judaism, it is clear that Jesus and the apostles sometimes chose to confront the religious views they had emerged from in making their case for why Jesus was necessary. When practices did not matter substantively, people of that background could choose to retain such practices; but where they made a theological difference, they were strenuously opposed and avoided. To do less than this risked making Jesus more of an add-on than a real source of religious transformation. The shame of the cross and the offense of Jesus' exaltation to God's right hand stood as obstacles to previous Jewish understanding, but the apostles preached these themes nonetheless. The books of Galatians, Colossians and Hebrews warned about any practices, including core practices like circumcision or sacrifices, that suggested Jesus alone was not enough for salvation. In authentic religious discussion, it is differentiation that makes for clarity in understanding why faiths differ. The doctrine of God as Father and Jesus' unique relationship to the Father in the Christian faith are central to affirming who Jesus is, what he has done, and why. Appreciating the Bible as unique revelation from God means being clear about how it differs from other religious works.

The concern the authors of *Chrislam* have is that insider movements risk underestimating the impact of failing to differentiate enough in translation and practice between Christianity and Islam. Although insiders are often well meaning in attempting to reach out to Muslims, the manner of their doing so may actually compromise the ultimate result they seek, making effective followers of Jesus out of those who come out of a Muslim background. In the effort to keep people connected to their cultural roots, there may be a real loss of the religious distinctive that was the real reason for a coming to faith in Jesus. Confusion rather than clarity may be the result.

Now there are real questions about how to stay connected to one's past culture. It is important to learn how to separate translations and practices that matter from those where there is room for discussion. Those in the insider movements have made their case for why they practice as they do. The goal of this book is to help people see which moves may really matter, assess the claims of those who think there is more cultural room, and make a case why more differentiation is important to maintain. In an increasingly diverse world, where encounters with those of other faiths are going to multiply, this kind of reflective discussion becomes more necessary as people wrestle with the theological and sociological questions raised by differing faiths. So take advantage of the reflection this book will inevitably raise. Compare the views. Read the Scripture. Ask yourself which views really matter and differentiate, and how does one show such distinctiveness. I think this book will send you in a helpful direction to begin making such assessments.

Darrell L. Bock

Preface to the Revised Edition

Three things characterize this revised edition of *Chrislam*. First, we corrected typographical and formatting errors. Second, the Table of Contents now has a brief description for each article. Third, this new preface is meant to make clear the major issues and biases of the book.

This book is a critique of Insider Movements. It is written in a forthright, unapologetic tone; neither the editors nor the individual authors have pulled their punches. The premise of this work is that insider movements must not be seen as a viable strategy for Evangelical missions to Muslims.

The following themes will become evident throughout the book:
What do we think about the religion of Islam?

- Islam is not a religion that can be adopted or adapted by Christians. It is a false religion with a false view of deity (Allah), a false prophet (Muhammad), and false scriptures (Qur'an).
- Allah of the Qur'an is unknown and unknowable. Allah has never spoken directly to a man. He sends angels, messengers, and books to humanity demanding submission to Allah's will and law (*sharia*). Allah is completely transcendent, never immanent. Allah is not a God that has revealed himself personally to humanity as a unity in Trinity: Father, Son and Holy Spirit. Allah has not revealed anything about himself; he has only revealed his will, a will that states Islam is the chosen religion for mankind (for his friends, i. e., Muslims) except those Allah leads astray (his enemies, i. e., non-Muslims). Allah's relationship to the Muslim is as a master to a slave, certainly not a personal God in relationship or covenant with his people, a father with a child, a crucified incarnate savior, or Son of God who suffered on the cross in order to die for sinners. Christians must not align themselves with this false God (Allah).[1]
- Muhammad is a false prophet. He denied the fatherhood of God, the sonship of Jesus, the crucifixion, resurrection, and Trinity—not to mention other Christian beliefs. Christians are not able to accept Muhammad as a prophet.
- Christians must not call themselves Muslim. Islam has defined a Muslim as one who is submitted to Allah and Muhammad, the prophet of Allah. Muslims cannot be Christians nor can Christians be Muslims.

What do we think about Muslim practices and behaviors?
- The *shahada* is the Muslim confession of faith: "There is only one

---

[1] This is not an argument that Arabic speaking Christians must stop calling the God of the Bible Allah. Our argument is that Allah of the Qur'an ought not to be confused with Yahweh (or Allah) of the Bible.

God Allah and Muhammad is the Messenger of Allah." A Christian cannot say this and be faithful to Jesus or biblical, historical Christianity.
- Christians should neither be part of a mosque nor pray (*salat*) in the direction of Mecca for this Islamic form was delivered to the prophet of Islam as a divinely prescribed form of worship.
- Christians must not go to Mecca on the *hajj* or pilgrimage.

What is our view of missionaries and new converts vis-à-vis Islam?
- Christians must not ask new converts to Christianity to remain in Islam, to call themselves *Muslims*, to stay in the mosque, or to recite the *shahada*. Instead, new Christians from Islam must be discipled to turn to Christ and away from their previous religion.
- Bible translations that obfuscate or miscommunicate the sonship of Christ by not accurately translating the Greek and Hebrew terms of *Son, Son of God, Son of Man,* or *Father* must stop.
- Christians must not use the Qur'an as scripture. The truth about Jesus is found in the Bible; the qur'anic statements about Jesus are untrustworthy, incomplete, and confusing. Furthermore, Christianizing the Qur'an by reinterpretation is inappropriate for Christian evangelization.
- It is our conviction that Christians are baptized by the Spirit of God into the Body of Christ (1 Cor 12:12-14 and Eph 4:4). Further it is our conviction that Christians be identified with the visible church (Rom 12:4-6; 1 Cor 10:17; 12:25). It is in the Body of Christ the individual believer is discipled. Insider movements do not identify themselves with the local, visible Christian church, in many cases actually preventing believers from associating with visible Christians, thus limiting the believer's growth in Christ.

Our first edition contained an error on p. 172. A copyediting error dropped the remainder of the Philippians 2:11 in Malaysian: *Isa al-Masih adalah Junjungan Yang Esa, untuk mendatangkan kemuliaan kepada Allah Bapa* (Jesus the Messiah/Isa al Masih is the only Divine Glorious One, to bring glory to God the Father), thus changing the entire understanding of the verse. We sincerely apologize for our mistake and the confusion it may have caused. We have removed this passage from this revision.

The editors
February 2012

Acknowledgements

In a book this size there are numerous people to thank. It is our desire not to forget anyone, but if we have forgotten you, please accept our sincerest apologies—and call Joshua; he will buy you a cup of coffee and a bagel (Bill and Jeff are too cheap).

First, we are very grateful to Ayub, Anwar and the visible churches of Bangladesh for standing for God—no matter the cost.

Our thanks to Jos Strengholt, editor of St. Francis Magazine for allowing us to use and edit articles from the site.

We deeply appreciate Scott Seaton for taking these matters to the American churches; and Brian Lenney, who when he recognized the problems of IM in the church, did something about it. Thanks.

We are very thankful to people like David Abernathy who courageously stood in the face of much opposition as he challenged the new movement in translation circles.

Paul Schultheis, David Benware, David Harriman and others of SRG: thank you for your help, encouragement and tangible support.

Elizabeth Drury, Dean Merrill, Eddy and Paul, thanks for your input toward the readability of the book.

Thanks to Alfred Poirier and Jim Routson of Rocky Mountain Community Church for the church's unwavering support in this effort, especially toward Bill.

To Phil Dehart for teaching me, Bill; thank you.

Our gratitude goes to Dr. Mike Milton, RTS, for his commitment to ensure the next generation stands with the church.

We are happy to be associated with Emily Belz of *World*; thanks for your courage to witness for the Gospel and to stand against insider movements.

For the i2 Ministries global staff: i2 Ministries Brazil (M3), Maisel and Marcia Rocha; i2 Nigeria, Moses Gbenu; i2 India, Sudhakar and Santhi Mondithoka; i2 England, Jay Smith; and all those working with them.

Thanks to Ergun Caner and Liberty University for hosting our 2010 conference, from which many of these chapters originated.

We are grateful to Pastor Daniel Ho, Pastor Sameh Maurice, Elias Dantes, and Mike Bickle for their love of the Gospel and the stand they have taken on insider movements.

The encouragement and friendship of Steve Strang of Charisma Magazine to Joshua is deeply appreciated.

Thanks to Pastor Edmund Chan and staff in support of i2 Ministries training.

Pastor Bob Hasty, Francis Anfuso, Chris Manginelli, Don Cain, and Jay Hoff for their support.

Our great appreciation to Stuart McAllister, Ravi Zacharias and SWAD; we need a group of like-minded scholars and friends to complete this mission.

Thanks to Pastor Jack Hibbs and Dave Ringoen for their encouragement and "atta boys."

Especially to Casey and Erica Wilson and Ona Azimioara of i2/USA for their input on the cover, logistical support for the *Insider Movements: A Critical Assessment Conferences.* Muchas gracias.

Finally, to our wives: Cheryl, Debbie, and Sara; thank you for your patience and giving up your husbands for such an extended length of time to accomplish this goal. Without your support, the project would not have moved beyond the *what if* stage.

Joshua Lingel
Jeff Morton
Bill Nikides
4 September 2011

Introduction

Just a few questions

A bright, young, enthusiastic couple has recently returned from their church planting ministry among Muslims. Their prayer letters of the past three years have shared the wonderful things God has been doing. You are on the missions committee, and after some introductions, they begin their story. They tell of many believers, new churches, and scores being trained for ministry—it all seems too good to believe. But before you can ask your first question, another of the committee members begins asking a string of intriguing questions.

"Is it alright for the new believers to say that Muhammad is the prophet of God as long as they believe in their hearts that Muhammad led to their belief in Christ?"

"Do you believe the best way to share the Gospel with Muslims is to use the Qur'an?"

"What are your thoughts about a New Testament that substitutes the original Greek *Son of God* and *Father* for words and phrases that are more acceptable to a Muslim audience?"

The committee member stops to take a breath. You can see she is not angry, but she is serious; then looking over the top of her glasses, she continues.

"Do you pray in the mosque or encourage Muslim converts to pray in the mosque?"

"Are the believers who have come out of Islam calling themselves Messianic Muslims, followers of *Isa al Masih* or maybe even Muslims?"

"Are the new believers congregating as a church for fellowship, the breaking of bread, prayer and the teaching of the apostles or have they stayed in the mosque?"

The young couple looks at each other; they are silent.

And then the committee member says, "Take your time. We have all night."

What answers would you have expected from your missionaries? By the time you have finished this book, we believe you will know the answers.

Our purpose

This book is about **insider movements** (IM).[1] Perhaps you have not heard of it. Is it something someone made up? No, it is real—all too real.

---

[1] Insider movements are polyvocal, so our use of the plural *movements* is deliberate; there are similar insider movements among Buddhists and Hindus. We use the term *insiders* to designate new Christians from Islam practicing an amalgam of Christianity and Islam or *Chrislam*. Any proponent of insider movements, mostly Western missionaries, is called a pro-IMer, proponent or advocate of IM, pro-insiders or just IMers. These terms may soon fade from use as some IMers are beginning to call themselves "alongsiders."

The initial three chapters of the book are the proponents of IM telling us what IM is. We have taken special care to be fair and honest with their views, in fact, we invited four advocates in the movement to read the chapters and to help us maintain an unbiased presentation. The rest of the book critiques the advocates of insider movements' methods, theology, and goals.

Our purpose is twofold: first, to educate the Church concerning missions, especially about missionaries that look evangelical, but act quite differently; and second, to help the next generation of missionaries think clearly about reaching Muslims in a biblical, holistic, critical and Spirit-led manner.

During the past thirty years the discussion about IM has been mostly limited to its advocacy. With little give-and-take between the two sides, the situation is something like the long-married couple that never argued. When asked the secret to their marital bliss they said, "We share the same hearing aid." The discussions of IM have been much the same: one-sided. One side has been talking; the other has not been listening.

For too long proponents of IM had their views published in both pro-IM journals (*International Journal of Frontier Missions* and *Mission Frontiers*) and a neutral journal, *Evangelical Missions Quarterly*. IM gained legitimacy as a mission methodology to Islam through the activities of some untamed Frontiers missionaries, and possibly due to the publication of the book, *From Seed to Fruit*.[2] IM was further validated at Lausanne, South Africa (2010),[3] as just another one of God's methodologies. Only recently has the Historical[4] approach found its voice in *St. Francis Magazine,* although pro-IM articles are also there. Now *Chrislam* can be added to the short list of those speaking out against IM.

Insider movements did not materialize out of thin air. As part of our introduction, we want to take you on a kind of safari to discover its beginnings. To do that we thought it best to compare the known (the emergent church) with the unknown (IM). The two, while not identical twins, are curiously related. Letting the former air out in the sunshine helps us see the stains on the latter. We trust it will become clear that what the emergent church is to the church in the United States, insider movements is to the Church at large.

---

[2] An interesting phenomenon of the book is the absence of references to *insider movements* in either the table of contents or index. IM is mentioned only once—and that is in a footnote; however, the book includes well-known IM proponents giving the book an IM *feel* without the label.

[3] See Appendix 1 for an example of IM's inroads as an acceptable—though protested—methodology.

[4] We use *Historical* because it best captures the essence of our foundation: biblical methodologies practiced by missionaries throughout *history*, such as John of Damascus, Raymond Lull, Samuel Zwemer, Carl Pfander, Sir Arthur Jeffery, et al. Those opposed to IM are not yet agreed that *Historical* is the appropriate sobriquet, but it serves the purpose of not being the inelegant *Those-Opposed-To-IM* (TOTI)!

Emergence of insider movements

Getting underneath the skin of insider movements, moving beyond the anecdotes and hype is no easy task. Shrouded in mystery, accompanied by hushed tones—as if the telling of its stories puts *real* people in danger—trying to get under its outer layer is a bit like Rudyard Kipling's blind men fumbling to describe an elephant. It seems too big, too diverse to have a coherent picture. Insider movements grew in the dark. Most of us in the West never knew they existed for decades; but when the various parts of the Church began to enquire, we were met with missionary success stories from unknown locations recounted by people with pseudonyms.

We believe that insider movements **are** understandable. Looking at insider movements as extensions of American evangelical expressions can help us understand them. One recent strand of contemporary evangelicalism, the emergent church movement, stands out as an interesting study.

It is said if you want to eat an elephant, you first need to recognize that such an enormous meal can only be consumed one bite at a time; and second, you need a plan. A bit of elephant anatomy helps; and so it is with insider movements. Many people and ideas shaped its thinking. More importantly, many people and ideas shaped its thinkers; however, before we can connect the emergent and IM, we need to look at a few things that helped create both.

Getting ready to eat an elephant

A good place to start is with a bit of prehistory. This is a book about missions, but we often err by not looking outside the box of missions to understand what is in the box. For example, Erich Kahler, literary critic and scholar, noted changes in American and European worldviews after the Second World War,

> We live in an era of transition, on which age-old modes of existence, and with them old concepts and structures, are breaking up, while new ones are not as yet clearly recognisable. In such a state of flux . . . concepts like wholeness, like coherence, like history are widely discredited . . . Not only are they felt to be encumbering the freedom of new ventures, they are considered obsolete and invalid. The repudiation of all these concepts implies a discarding of form, for . . . wholeness, coherence, history are inherent in the concept of form. They all mean and constitute identity. Indeed, form may be plainly understood as identity. . . . losing form is equivalent to losing identity.[5]

---

[5] Erich Kahler (1968). *The Disintegration of Form in the Arts* (21). New York, NY: George Braziller.

Kahler noticed a growing trend among the thinkers to discard traditions for the sake of *new ventures* designed to maximize freedom. People wanted freedom from constraint even at the risk of losing coherence.

Zygmunt Bauman, a highly influential sociologist, has made a career of understanding postmodernism; he concluded that it was not much *post* anything. Postmodernism is just an accelerated version of everything that was taking place within modernism. He coined the term *liquid modernism*: as we discard old forms for new ones, social forms and institutions cannot keep their shape for long.[6] The things we thought solid liquefy as we move forward with fluidity.

In the brave new world of rapid change, the first "sacreds to be profaned" is traditional obligations. Bauman noted that the power to create had to be free of barriers; so, intense social bonds were cleared away.[7] Mainline churches were in massive decline throughout most of the twentieth century, but filling the void was a neo-evangelicalism that both repudiated the insularity and perceived backwardness of fundamentalism. It was time to engage the world and in so doing, rebuild the face of Western Christianity.

In the early days of the nascent evangelicalism, the vast majority of evangelical leadership maintained a close watch on core doctrinal commitments. But, the engagement with the world outside the Church cut both ways. It allowed believers to engage the world on its terms. It also created a bridge to thinking in the outside world that would threaten the Church's original commitments. The bridge builder does not control who drives on his bridge; and an ever-increasing gap began to grow between different wings within evangelicalism. One could see it coming in the late 60's and 70's with movements such as the Jesus People: Christians fiercely mono-generational, experiential and anti-historical.[8]

Recently Gerald McDermott described the two main wings of evangelicals as the Meliorists and the Traditionalists.[9] Reformational and conservative Christians align with McDermott's Traditionalists. On the one hand, traditionalists believe they are in continuity with the early church, maintaining Scripture, espousing biblical doctrine, and believing the *forms* of Church and office are not culturally conditioned options, but necessary for God's people.

On the other hand, many within the emergent church are Meliorists, who, according to McDermott, think that conservatives pay too much

---

[6] Zygmunt Bauman (2007). *Liquid Times: Living in An Age of Uncertainty* (1ff). Cambridge: Polity.
[7] Zygmunt Bauman (2000). *Liquid Modernity* (3-14). Cambridge: Polity.
[8] Kevin DeYoung and Ted Kluck (2009). *Why We Love the Church: In Praise of Institutions and Organised Religion* (92). Chicago, IL: Moody.
[9] Gerald McDermott, "Evangelicals Divided" *First Things* 21(2): 45-50. *Meliorists* generally emphasize the important role that humans play in improving the world.
http://www.firstthings.com/article/2011/03/evangelicals-divided (accessed 4/1/11).

attention to tradition. For two reasons: either conservatives are simple-minded biblicists or they are paleo-orthodox, unable to face the modern world. For many Meliorists, biblical inspiration means the authors of Scripture were inspired, but the words were not. The logic of the Meliorists leads them to proclaim Scripture's authority while rejecting the Church's historical understanding of it, making a theologian "just another culture-bound interpreter of spiritual experience." Out go the theologians; in come the anthropologists.

If McDermott has his categories correct—and we think he does—the emergent church and insider movements are a kind of Meliorism.

The elephant's anatomy

With some bite-sized morsels taken care of, we need to examine the emergent structure a bit more closely. Sam Storms lists a number of emergent distinctives, including:
1. Journey vs. Destination;
2. Belonging then believing vs. believing then belonging;
3. Inclusion vs. exclusion;
4. Corporate vs. individual;
5. Incarnational vs. attractional;
6. Fluid ecclesiology vs. fixed ecclesiology.[10]

The list is helpful in seeing the conceptual overlaps between emergents and insiders. Take the first distinctive: journey vs. destination. Is this not analogous to the definition of insider movements as *movements to Christ* rather than as movements in Christ? This concept allows for the rest of the distinctives to take place. Someone in the insider milieu can remain a Muslim member of the mosque because he or she is on the way to Jesus, not the Church. As it is with the proponents of IM,[11] so it is with the emergents.

Bosch and others warn of syncretism in light of culture, but both insiders and emergents seem to pay little attention. It is as though the culture is the ultimate, irreducible reality. Leonard Sweet, an emergent guru, talks about doing church in a way that is biblically absolute, but culturally relative. Speaking for postmodern believers, he states, "Postmoderns have had it with religion. They want no part of obedience to sets of propositions and rules required by some *officialdom somewhere.*"[12]

Rob Bell, an emergent rock star, explains Church:

> Jesus is supracultural. He is present within all cultures, and yet outside of all cultures. He is for all people, and yet he refuses to be

---

[10] Sam Storms, "The Emerging/Emergent Church: Observations and Analysis" www.samstorms.com.

[11] Cf. Rebecca Lewis, "Promoting Movements to Christ Within Natural Communities" *IJFM* 24(2): 75-6.

[12] Leonard Sweet (2000). *Post-Modern Pilgrims* (112). Nashville, TN: B & H.

co-opted or owned by any one culture. That includes the Christian culture. Any denomination. Any church. Any theological system.[13]

The point that emergent thinkers and the proponents of the insider movements make is that the Church is not the sole proprietor of Christ, so it is completely appropriate to find him embraced by Muslims and Hindus. Whereas emergents see the organized Church as hopelessly corrupt, they find the kingdom compelling.[14] Emergent leader, Erwin McManus, states that his goal is to "destroy Christianity as a world religion and be a recatalyst for the movement of Jesus Christ."[15]

Both movements are broadly open to other religions.[16] Semir Selmanovic, pastor of Church of the Advent Hope in Manhattan, notes approvingly that many emergents have eschewed Christian identity. Emergents are moving beyond that identity in order to live a "Christ-like life" as Hindus and Native Americans.[17]

Lloyd Chia recounts a night out with four others: Eliacin, Raul, Felipe, and Brian McLaren.[18] McLaren had been at a conference where he advocated dual-identity in religion. Felipe was perplexed. "How can I be a Christian if I can't draw a clear line between myself and a non-Christian?"

McLaren explained to Felipe that he could maintain a deep commitment to his faith without having insider-outsider boundaries. He then told stories of people that had come through other religions to Jesus.

Eliacin recounted a minister who told him recently of his study of the Qur'an. The minister concluded, "I think Islam is making me a better Christian."

---

[13] Rob Bell (2011). *Love Wins: A Book about Heaven, Hell and the Fate of Every Person That Ever Lived* (153). New York, NY: HarperOne. The prevailing way of understanding religion for emergents and insiders is as an expression of culture. The editors also believe Jesus is supracultural, but this does not mean Jesus is in every culture. *Supra* means above or over, not limited to, but not "within all cultures;" in other words, Christ is in culture where his Church is found in its variegated forms.

[14] DeYoung and Kluck, *Why We Love the Church* 17. See Jonathan Bonk, "Salvation, Other Religions, and Asian Mission" *Asian Missiology* 2(1): 112. Bonk seems to believe that insider movements are the best way to preserve biblical faith, as opposed to visible churches. See Stuart Caldwell, "Jesus in Samaria: A Paradigm for Church Planting Among Muslims" *IJFM* 17(1): 29f. He also promotes kingdom over church.

[15] Quoted in Richard Bennett, "Hazards Unfolded By Emerging Church Leaders" www.bereanbeacon.org.

[16] See Abdul Asad, "Rethinking the Insider Movement Debate: Global Historical Insights toward an Appropriate Transitional Model of C5" *SFM* 5.4 (August 2009) 151. Asad, a pen name for an American missionary, proposes turning insider movements into a sect of Sufi Islam. Cf.

[17] Tyson Dauer and Cecilia Pick, "Re-Emerging Pietism: The Emerging Church as Postmodern Pietism" *Journal of Undergraduate Research* 8 (1 September 2008) 32. Compare Kevin Higgins, "Beyond Christianity: Insider Movements and the Place of the Bible and the Body of Christ in New Movements to Jesus" *MF* (July-August 2010).

[18] Lloyd Chia (2010). *Emerging Faith Boundaries: Bridge-building, Inclusion, and the Emerging Church Movement in America* (263ff). PhD Dissertation, University of Missouri-Columbia.

In terms of a theology of religions, one can clearly see the overlapping perspectives of insiders and emergents.[19]

Another emergent feature is the nature of their interaction in the world of ideas. According to Scott Clark, both liquid modernity and the emergent church find critique fairly unwelcome. Arguing over truth claims is considered an especially unwelcome intrusion. It is old-speak after all.[20] Consider the following emergent response to D.A. Carson's Reclaiming the Centre, proposing establishing rules of engagement:

1. Respect for boundaries and difference: "You do it one way, we do it another."
2. A commitment to dialogic engagement instead of *one-way* criticism.
3. Responsible critique that includes not perpetuating second-hand critique.
4. The necessity of personal encounters, or *get to know us*.
5. Establishing a realistic sense of *scope*: "We ask our critics to remember that we cannot be held responsible for everything said and done by people using the terms *emergent* or *emerging church*, anymore than our critics would like to be held responsible for everything said or done by those claiming to be *evangelical* or *born-again*."[21]

We see the same pattern of inclusion and exclusion occurring today with regard to conversations about insider movements—just plug in *insider movements* for *emergent* in the list above. If you are going to interact, you will have to play by their rules. Anything else will be deemed an occasion for conflict resolution.

Finally Michael Frost and Alan Hirsch's seminal book on the emergent movement must be mentioned: *The Shaping of Things to Come: Innovation and Mission for the 21st-Century Church*. Explicitly interacting with insider literature, the authors lean repeatedly on the incarnation as a model for contextualizing the Gospel. They delve into the contextual approaches of both Charles Kraft and Orlando Costas. They interact with Phil Parshall

---

[19] Cf. Bernard Dutch, "Should Muslims Become 'Christians'?" *IJFM* 17(1); Joseph Cumming, "Muslim Followers of Jesus?" www.christianitytoday.com; Rebecca Lewis, "The Integrity of the Gospel and Insider Movements" *IJFM* 27(1); Rebecca Lewis, "Insider Movements: Honoring God-Given Identity and Community" *IJFM* 26(1); Kevin Higgins, "Identity, Integrity and Insider Movements" *IJFM* 23(3;) John J. Travis and J. Dudley Woodberry, "When God's Kingdom Grows Like Yeast: Frequently-Asked Questions About Jesus Movements Within Muslim Communities" *MF* (July-August) 27. The funny thing is that such an inclusive attitude creates a boundary of exclusion; that is, the view that *few are as inclusive us* is, in itself, an excluding barrier.

[20] R. Scott Clark, (2008). "Whosoever Will Be Saved: Emerging Church, Meet Christian Dogma" (115). In Gary L. W. Johnson and Ronald N. Gleason (Eds.). *Reforming or Conforming: Post-Conservative Evangelicals and the Emerging Church*. Wheaton, IL: Crossway.

[21] Chia, *Emerging Faith* 290ff. Joshua Massey exhorts both proponents and critics of insider movements to "accept God's diversity in drawing Muslims to Christ" ("God's Amazing Diversity in Drawing Muslims to Christ" *IJFM* 17(1):11). See also Kevin Higgins, "Speaking the Truth about Insider Movements" *SFM* 5.6 (December 2009) for an insider parallel.

and his communities of "Messianic Muslims." Then they get into the heart of insider movements with a brief survey of John Travis's C1-C6 scale.[22] Interestingly, they posit the usefulness of its application to a distinctively Western context. What better evidence of shared ideas and perspectives can one have? Frost and Hirsch conclude their investigation of insider movements with a brief exhortation:

> How can the church in the West, while recognizing that it is now operating within a post-Christian mission field, not take steps to move toward deeper levels of critical contextualization! Since the church in the West is likewise operating in a post-Christian mission field, we need to work toward something between C4 and C5 levels of critical contextualization.[23]

The plan

There is purpose to this madness: the comparison of two present day movements helps us take one bite at a time. Both the emergent church and insider movements are worthy of our deliberations. One is local (generally in North America), the other global (on several continents), but both have lumbered out from the same jungle. The two movements have a similar anatomy: a thin hide (and ability to hide!) and a tail (or is that a tale?). Both movements crash through the undergrowth foraging in the tall trees of postmodernism the rest of us thought best to avoid. And perhaps more soberingly, both emergents and insider proponents have been nourished from the same contaminated spring of water.

Finally, we want to move the insider movements out of the world of abstract ideas and into the everyday world. We know of no better way than telling a story—yes, we have our own tale to tell. We believe the following will help you begin to see the elephant for what it is.

The tale

Tahwil and Jim were on the way to the market. Tahwil, a recent convert from Islam, was being discipled by Jim, a missionary from the United States.

Jim said, "How has your family been taking your decision to follow Jesus?"

"I really haven't told them . . . yet," Tahwil replied. He shook his head, looking at the ground. "They know something is different, but I haven't said anything. How can I tell my family I am not a Muslim but a Christian? It'll break their hearts and . . . " Tahwil paused, "and my older brothers, Hojar and Sakhra, if they ever found out, they would beat me

---

[22] John Travis invented a scale that purports to describe the levels of contextualization within different "Christ-centered communities."

[23] Michael Frost and Alan Hirsch (2003). *The Shaping of Things to Come: Innovation and Mission for the 21st-Century Church* (93). Peabody, MA: Hendrickson.

until I came back to Islam."

Jim smiled. "There may be another way." Tahwil looked up.

"I've been reading and thinking a lot lately," Jim continued, "about how to overcome this very problem. I have a solution that might just work."

Tahwil was very interested. He was tired of hiding his decision to follow *Isa al masih* from everyone he knew. Maybe Jim did have the answer.

Stopping, Jim said, "Look, the real problem is not that you love *Isa, but* that if you tell your family you're a Christian, they'll think the worst of you, right?"

Tahwil nodded. "Yes. My uncle is always cursing Christians. He calls them swine-eating Zionists. I can't tell my family I'm Christian, even though I know they don't understand what a Christian is."

Jim laughed. "That's right! They don't! That's my point."

Tahwil shook his head and shrugged his shoulders, thoroughly confused at Jim's riddle.

"You don't have to tell your family you're a Christian. You aren't a Christian! You're a follower of *al masih*.[24] How are you any different than the Jews we've been reading about in Acts? They remained Jews when they chose to identify themselves with *Isa*, right? It's as if you're . . . well, a Messianic Muslim."

Jim smiled, letting Tahwil think about that. Then he said with emphasis, "Tahwil, **you are not a Christian.** You're a follower of *Isa bin Maryam al masih*.[25] *Isa* doesn't want you to stop being a Muslim because . . . because . . . now you've discovered what true Islam is all about. Just as *Isa* came and fulfilled the law—remember, he didn't abolish it—so he also came and showed us how to live in our family situations. When did Jesus ever ask a Jew to stop being a Jew? When did Jesus ever ask the Samaritans to stop being Samaritans? When did he demand Gentiles become Jews? What you've done is **not** become a Christian, but you are a Muslim who loves *Isa*!"

Tahwil was overwhelmed. He remembered his talks with Matt, another missionary. He said to Jim, "But Matt said I am a Christian and should think about my place in the body of Christ; that I am no longer a Muslim, but I am in Christ. And now you tell me this? I'm confused."

Jim could see his confusion and said, "Look, Matt operates one way and I work another. We have agreed to disagree. Your decision how to follow *Isa* is not Matt's, but yours."

Tahwil thought this seemed right, and somehow strange at the same time.

The two began walking toward the market again.

"Let me see if I understand you," Tahwil said. "I can continue being a

---

[24] *Arabic*, Messiah.
[25] This is Jesus, son of Mary, the Messiah, the Qur'anic name of Jesus.

Muslim and a Christian at the same time?"

Jim interrupted him. "No, I'm not saying **that**. Don't think like a Westerner! You're a Muslim who is following *Isa*, period. Finished. Done. That's all there is to it. You're not a Christian. The word *Christian* is full of bad connotations for Muslims. You're not a Christian, but a Muslim following *al masih*. What could be simpler?"

Tahwil shrugged.

After some time they passed a masjid on their right. Looking at his watch, Jim said, "It's about time for *Asr*."[26] He looked hard at Tahwil.

Tahwil stopped. Jim stopped. Tahwil looked at his watch. He nodded and said, "Yes, it's almost time for *namaz*."[27]

Jim looked first to the masjid, then back to Tahwil. "If you were to go into the masjid, perform *salat* to *Isa*, no one in the masjid would know you were anything but a Muslim."

Tahwil was taken aback. Pray in the masjid? He hadn't done that since he had became a Christian—or was he now a Messianic Muslim? He wasn't quite sure at this point. And Jim wanted him to go into the masjid and pray? It was all so confusing.

Jim could see the wheels of Tahwil's mind spinning. Finally, he said, "Tahwil, you don't have to go into the masjid to pray. You are free of course to pray whenever and wherever you are. But think of this: if you return to the masjid, you aren't simply another Muslim performing *namaz*, rather you're a Muslim who loves *Isa* and is submitted to Allah. You don't have to leave your family or Islam. Stay in your family. Let the light of the Gospel shine from you in your family, in the masjid, at the *madrassa*,[28] and during *namaz*."

Tahwil looked at his watch, to the masjid and then back to Jim. What should he do?

By the time you have finished this book, it is our hope you would be able to help Tahwil make a decision that is appropriate, wise and biblically informed.[29]

And what about that young missionary couple? Our prayer is you'll be able to help them, too.

May God help us all.

---

[26] *Asr* is the third prayer of the day, performed after noon but before sunset.
[27] *Namaz* is another word for *salat*, the five-times daily performance of Islamic worship.
[28] An Islamic school.
[29] This story does not represent the views of every proponent of IM.

1

Insiders' Perspectives

1.1 The Inside Story: Theology[1]

Bill Nikides

Bill is a minister with the Presbyterian Church of America (PCA). He served Muslim background congregations in the Middle East, Europe and East Asia for the last twelve years, after having worked in the Middle East and Persian Gulf. He has an MDiv and is writing a PhD dissertation on the role of the Trinity in the Mission of the Church. He is conducting a systematic first-hand study of insider movements in Asia, and has made more than two hundred interviews with insiders and former insiders directly within their home communities. Bill works with ANM as missionary-at-large and i2 Ministries as Director of SE Asian training and publishing on insider movements.

Introduction

Where else should one begin but with the topic of Scripture and theology? And so that we are not accused of building a straw man case, why not let the proponents of these new ideas, theologies and excursions into God's word speak for themselves?

What is the role of theology and doctrine?
What is necessary for salvation in terms of belief?

- *Brown*: It could be said that the Gospel's message concerning getting saved is very simple and does not require one to have a great depth of theological understanding. That may come afterwards, but it is not a prerequisite for salvation. What is required is simply to put one's faith personally in **Jesus as the Christ, the Messiah,** meaning **one's Lord and Savior.** Saving faith, in both its propositional and relational aspects, is simply saying "Yes" to Jesus. After that there can be growth in the Christian life and understanding.[2]

---

[1] To help us capture an objective presentation of IM views, three of the major advocates of insider movements' principles saw the first two chapters; one who writes extensively about translation issues for SIL, read the first three chapters. Most of their comments were requests to add more to the quotation for the benefit of the context; we agreed to the requests. We have also noted a few of their comments in the footnotes for clarity. Our position is to honestly and accurately state the facts; only then should we offer an opinion.

[2] Rick Brown, "What Must One Believe About Jesus for Salvation?" *IJFM* 17(4): 20 (the online version has no original publication page numbers). For a fuller understanding of how Brown explains doctrine to Muslims, cf. "Presenting the Deity of Christ from the Bible" *IJFM* 19(1):20–27; "Muslim Worldviews and the Bible: Bridges and Barriers" *IJFM* 23(1)(2) and (3); "Biblical Muslims" *IJFM* 24(2): 65–74; "Contextualization Without Syncretism" *IJFM* 23(3):127-133. Brown told us: "Citing only bits of *What Must One Believe*, gives the impression that I advocate teaching the minimum for salvation." The following lengthy quote shows misdirection was not our intention.

- *Brown*: While Evangelicals are basically united in their proclamation of salvation by grace through faith. . . . For surprisingly many people, saving faith is a belief in the vicarious substitutionary punishment of Christ, i.e., Anselm's theory of the atonement. If one accepts this doctrine, one is saved, otherwise one is lost. . . . Although this doctrine can be fully justified from Scripture, it wasn't developed until the 11th century, and it is not part of the public proclamation of the Gospel recorded in the Bible. If belief in it were essential to salvation, then the Apostles failed to preach the Gospel and no one was saved until Archbishop Anselm propagated this doctrine in the Church. . . .

    These doctrines about the deity of Jesus and his substitutionary punishment are wonderful parts of the Good News, and it is worthwhile discussing them with seekers, as Paul demonstrated in Romans. But the overwhelming biblical witness is that although these doctrines are important for the disciple to understand, an understanding of them is not required for salvation.

    . . . The reader can see that salvation is offered to those who put their faith in Jesus as their Lord Messiah, the Christ, where 'Christ' means the Savior-King sent by God. Their faith in Jesus as their Lord the Christ can be expressed using a number of different Messianic titles. These include the Christ, the Son of God, he who is coming into the world, the son of Man, the Lord, and others. There is no statement that one must believe Jesus is the Lamb of God or Image or Word or Wisdom of God incarnate or even that he is God himself incarnate.

    There is no requirement for belief in the virgin birth nor the Trinity or other such teachings. These other doctrines although true and important can make the Gospel more appealing in many cases, but we should not confuse importance with necessity. . . .

    I am not suggesting that we should not present the whole work and person of Christ, only that we should not tell people that they cannot be saved until they understand and accept it all. . . . As they attend to the cross and prayer and fellowship, the Holy Spirit opens their eyes to an increasing understanding and belief in the more difficult doctrine. . . .

    It could be said that the Gospel's message concerning getting saved is very simple and does not require one to have a great depth of theological understanding. That may come afterwards, but it is not a prerequisite for salvation. What is required is simply to put one's faith personally in Jesus, as the Christ, the Messiah, meaning one's Lord and Savior. Saving faith, in both its propositional and relational aspects, is simply saying 'Yes' to Jesus. After that there can be growth in the Christian life and understanding. . . .

There is no verse that says one must understand the divinity of Jesus to be saved.[3]

- *Talman*: Our doctrines of the Trinity and hypostatic union of the divine and human natures of Christ are theological formulations of biblical data that were the result of the Western (Greek) philosophical mindset and language prevalent in the early centuries of the Church. Though I can accept these doctrines, they are scandalously incomprehensible to the Muslim mind.[4]

What is the biblical support for insider movements?
Genesis 17:20 and 21:20

- *Culver:* I propose that there is also a significant element of divine involvement in the remote origins of Islam, beginning with Hagar and Ishmael. Genesis 17:20 and 21:20 characterize this involvement as divine providence, a special kind of common grace granted to the other seed of Abraham (Gen 21:13). I believe it is this divine providence, which has sustained the rise of Ishmael's descendants, culminating in the worldwide Muslim community. God graciously blessed Ishmael because of Abraham's great concern for his firstborn. Through this blessing God also intends to redeem Ishmaelite culture to glorify His name in this age and in the eschatological age to come (Is 60:6-7). Matthew 2:1-12 reiterates this Isaianic theme in his account of the Magi (most likely Ishmaelite Arabs) who worshipped the Christ child. Taken together, Genesis 17, Isaiah 60 and Matthew 2 reveal important data to support a "Muslims for *Isa*" contextual approach.[5]

Isaiah 60:6-7 and Psalm 72:9-11

- *Culver:* The Magi's offering of gold, frankincense and myrrh is clearly reminiscent of the gifts offered by the non-covenant Abrahamic nations in Isaiah 60:6-7. . . . A number of authorities have acknowledged this (cf. Brueggemann 1998:205-206; Gundry 1967:206-211; Davies and Allison 1988:250-251; Hengel and Merkel 1973:140-142; 154-155). . . . One cannot fail to notice that

---

[3] Rick Brown, "What Must One Believe" 1, 3, 5, 6, 8, and 12. Brown told us: "Faith is not relationship alone, with no cognitive content; the whole point of the article was to ask what that content is. I answered that it is to believe that Jesus is Christ, the Lord and Savior, who was crucified, died, and rose again on the third day, in accord with the Scriptures. The relational part is to receive him as one's Lord and Savior, without which one cannot be saved."

[4] Harley Talman, "Comprehensive Contextualization" *IJFM* 21(1): 9f. The trinity as the historic church understands it, is not strictly biblical; it is, rather, the product of interaction in the early church with Greek philosophy.

[5] Jonathan Culver, "The Ishmael Promise and Contextualization Among Muslims" *IJFM* 17(1): 61.

Isaiah 60:6-7 and Psalm 72:9-11 contain parallels to Matthew 2:11 in terms of the gifts offered and the submission of the nations to a *King*. We must further notice, however, that all these Old Testament references cite the submission of Arabian nations. Therefore, it would seem inconsistent for Matthew to have understood the Magi to be anything other than ethnic Arabs. The problem with an Arabian identity of the Magi is that it conflicts with the traditional view that they were Persian or Babylonian. Matthew only tells us the Magi "came from the east." In short, we have no reason to reject the possibility that the Magi were ethnic Arabs.[6]

Melchizedek
- *Higgins*: The pluralist position can point to examples such as Melchizedek in which the Canaanite *El* and the Jewish *Yahweh* are recognized by Abraham as the same Being. However, the pluralist conclusion that therefore all religions are leading in the same direction breaks down on the wealth of biblical material we have also cited to the contrary.[7]

Numbers 22-24
- *Higgins*: The pagan prophet Balaam used omens and divination as a seer but communicated directly with, and heard directly from Yahweh (Num 22 through 24). He is in relationship with Yahweh, and this relationship is actually facilitated by his practice of divination (Num 23:1ff.).[8]

2 Kings 5
- *Higgins*: The text is an example of a follower of another religion who becomes a believer in the true God and yet continues to worship the true God within the religious life and practices of his prior religion. Not only is it a description, but also the text includes the clear blessing of the prophet upon the practice. In this text we find at least one case where God blesses *remaining inside*.[9]

- *Higgins:* In Naaman we see a complex situation. Some of his beliefs and behaviors change while others remain the same. At the level of belonging, he seems to have continued just as before. This should

---

[6] Culver, "Ishmael" 67. Therefore, the magians represent one of the earliest NT insider movements.

[7] Kevin Higgins, "Inside What? Church, Culture, Religion, and Culture in Biblical Perspective" *IJFM* 5(4): 87.

[8] Higgins, "Inside What" 85.

[9] Kevin Higgins, "The Key to Insider Movements: The 'Devoteds' in Acts" *IJFM* 21(4): 158.

sensitize us to the possibility that our wisest response in some situations could be the same as that in 2 Kings 5:19, 'Go in peace.'[10]

- *Travis*: I have known some C5 believers who attend prayers in the mosque, some who only attend occasionally and some who never go at all. In much of the Muslim world, there are many nominal Muslims who seldom attend the mosque anyway. Returning again to Gilliland and Hiebert's emphasis on process and direction, mosque attendance may only be a transitional part of some C5 believers' spiritual journey. For others, they may attend with the mindset of Naaman in 2 Kings 5:18, where he asked Elijah's permission to still enter the temple of Rimmon in his home country. Still other C5 believers may attend the mosque like evangelical Catholics who attend mass but no longer pray to saints or exalt Mary. On the other hand, it is not unusual for some C5 believers to avoid mosque attendance all together, especially if they did not attend prior to following Christ.[11]

Jonah

- *Higgins*: In the book of Jonah it is ironically not the Hebrew Jonah who hears and obeys God. In addition, it is the pagan sailors' prayers that are heard by Yahweh. When they cast lots, it is Yahweh who directs the answer. They are in relationship with Yahweh.[12]

John 4

- *Higgins*: After their conversion recorded in John 4, they worshipped in spirit and in truth. But they did so in Samaria (in their prior place of worship) just as Jesus worshipped the Father in spirit and in truth in Jerusalem, in the Temple. That this episode is an example of an Insider Movement is further suggested by a second feature of the passage. After Jesus spends two days in the Samaritan village, the villagers affirm that they now believe Jesus is the Savior of the world. Then Jesus leaves. What does He leave behind? A group of believers.[13]

- *Caldwell*: After acknowledging Jesus was a prophet, the Samaritan woman's first comment resembles Islamic regard for place in worship. . . As we seek to reach Muslims, this same issue of place for true worship emerges. . . .

---

[10] Kevin Higgins, "Inside What?" 85.
[11] John Travis, "Messianic Muslim Followers of Isa" *IJFM* 17(1): 55.
[12] Higgins, "Inside What" 85.
[13] Higgins, "The Key" 159

Outside of Jesus' instructions to the woman at the well, Scripture is silent about what Jesus taught these Samaritans during those two days. However, his Jewish followers, having heard him say 'neither in Jerusalem,' continued to worship in Jerusalem since they understood the real meaning of his teaching. Therefore, it seems reasonable to assume Samaritan believers also understood Jesus' teaching and continued to worship in spirit and truth on Gerizim. . . .

Historical evidence is scant to prove Samaritan believers continued to worship within the Samaritan religious system, but if they did not, there is a strange silence about this in Acts 8 where the Apostles do not mention a 'proper place' for worship, or an alternative to Samaritan religion. We see instead a believing, Spirit-filled community apparently within Samaritan society. Why don't we see the Apostles extracting believers out of Samaritanism? . . .

Jesus simply avoided direct confrontation about her concept of Scripture, though he alluded to the superiority of Jewish Scripture when saying, "salvation is from the Jews" (Jn. 4:22). . . . we have no evidence that denigration of Samaritan Scripture was ever part of Jesus' ministry. . . .

Forming a community of believers within the religio-cultural world of Muslims will include Islamic places and patterns of worship. This is what happened in Samaria (Jn. 4; Acts 8), and it seems to be what Jesus expected when he taught about Kingdom sowing in parables, especially the parables of the yeast in the dough and the wheat and the tares.[14]

- *Lewis*: The woman at the well in John 4 at first refused Jesus' offer of eternal life because, as a Samaritan, she followed an Abrahamic religion that the Jews reviled as corrupt. As a result, she could not go to the temple or become a Jew. But Jesus distinguished **true faith from religious affiliation**, saying God was seeking "true worshipers who worship the Father in spirit and truth" (vv. 19-24). Realizing that Jesus was "the Savior of the world" (v. 42), **not just of the Jews**, many Samaritans in her town believed. Later in Acts we see that Samaritan believers remained in their own communities and retained their Samaritan identity (Acts 8:14-17). But at first the disciples did not understand that just as they could **remain Jews** and follow Jesus, the Samaritans could also **remain Samaritan**.[15]

John 17

---

[14] Stuart Caldwell, "Jesus in Samaria: A Paradigm for Church Planting Among Muslims" *IJFM* 17(1): 25-27, 31.
[15] Rebecca Lewis, "Insider Movements: Honoring God-Given Identity and Community" *IJFM* 26(1): 17.

- *Massey*: Because Jesus' humanity is often eclipsed by our focus on his divine glory, we often miss the profound implication of his prayer in John 17, where he appears to expect the self-revelation of God to similarly occur in us, even as it did in him—because we are **in him** and he is **in us**. *Even as thou, Father, art in me, and I in thee, that they also may be in us, so that the world may believe that thou hast sent me"* (17:21). Jesus proceeds to explain how this mind-boggling translation can possibly occur, *The glory which thou hast given me I have given to them, that they may be one even as we are one, I in them and thou in me. . .* (17:22–23). . . . we cannot help but hearken back to John's usage of the term in his prologue, *and the Word became flesh and dwelt among us. . . we have beheld his glory, glory as of the only Son from the Father* (1:14). The Greek here for **'dwelt'** is connected with the word **'tabernacle'**, so that early Jewish readers of John would almost certainly be reminded of the Tent of Meeting, which was filled with God's **glory** (Ex 40:34–35). God wants to reveal himself to the nations by tabernacling in those whose hearts are fully his. Clearly then, one does not need to be pre-existent to be **indwelt** by God, or for his word and wisdom to **become flesh**. . . . If the word of God became flesh today not as a Hebrew– and Aramaic–speaking Jew of Palestine, but as a - speaking of (fill in the blanks for your context), what would he say to Muslims? How would he live? How would he dress? How would he teach? What words would he use to describe Kingdom realities?[16]

Acts 15

- *Woodberry*: If Paul were retracing his missionary journeys today, would he add, 'To the Muslim I became a Muslim'? Or would he and the Jerusalem Council endorse Muslims being free to follow Jesus while retaining, to the extent that this commitment allows, Muslim identity and practices . . .

    To answer these questions, we shall look through the biblical lens of the Incarnation. . . .

    At the Jerusalem Council, Peter noted that God testified to the inclusion of the Gentiles in the Church by giving them the Holy Spirit (Acts 15:8) . . . . Many of those that I have met in insider movements have evidenced by the fruit of the spirit, wisdom, and devotion the indwelling Spirit of God. Because of the limitation of formal training opportunities for the believers in insider movements, they are highly dependent on the Bible as interpreted and applied by the Holy Spirit to them. But my questioning of numbers of them and the reports of others I that trust lead me to conclude that, although they are different from

---

[16] Joshua Massey, "Living Like Jesus, a Torah Observant Jew" Part II *IJFM* 21(2): 56f.

traditional Christians, they certainly evidence the guidance of the Bible and the Spirit.[17]

- *Wiarda:* When the Judaizers insisted that Gentiles needed to be circumcised, they were in effect demanding that Gentiles submit to *cultural conversion.*[18]

- *Dutch:* Judaizers wanted Gentiles believers to make a complete break from their pagan traditions by embracing Judaism along with Jesus . . . This all must have seemed to have clear biblical support. The Jerusalem Council discussed the matter at great length. Finally, James articulated their decision of the early church . . . Gentile believers were not required to join the Jewish community, attend synagogue services, become circumcised, change their names, or maintain the ritual cleanliness prescribed by the Law.[19]

- *Travis:* My daughter, who loves our neighbors dearly, asked one day, "Daddy, can a Muslim go to heaven?" I responded with an Acts 15:11-type "yes": "If a Muslim has accepted *Isa* (Jesus) the Messiah as Savior and Lord, he or she is saved, just as we are." We affirmed that people are saved by faith in Christ, not by religious affiliation. Muslim followers of Christ (i.e., C5 believers) are our brothers and sisters in the Lord, even though they do not change religions.[20]

- *Lewis:* In Antioch, Jewish believers were telling Gentile believers they must become Jews to be fully acceptable to God. Paul disagreed and brought the issue to the lead apostles in Jerusalem. The issue was hotly debated . . . But the Holy Spirit showed the Jewish apostles they should not *burden* Gentile followers of Christ with their religious traditions and forms (Acts 15:19, 28). If we use the same two criteria today, insider movements affirm that people do not even have to go through the **religion** of Christianity, but only through Jesus Christ, to enter God's family. Thus, the Gospel reveals that a person can gain a new spiritual identity **without** leaving one's birth identity, and without taking on a new socio-religious label or going through the religion of either Judaism or

---

[17] Dudley Woodberry, "To the Muslim I Became a Muslim" Don McClure Lectures, Pittsburg Theological Seminary 2008.
[18] Timothy Wiarda, "The Jerusalem Council and the Theological Task" *JETS* 46:2: http://findarticles.com/p/articles/mi_qa3817/is_200306/ai_n9243951/?tag=content;col1 (accessed 4/3/11).
[19] Bernard Dutch, "Should Muslims Become 'Christians'?" *IJFM* 17(1): 17f.
[20] John Travis, "Must All Muslims Leave 'Islam' to Follow Jesus?" *EMQ* 34(4): 860. http://paul-timothy.net/pages/perspectives/lesson_14_readings.pdf (accessed 3/16/11).

Christianity.[21]

- *Massey*: The intensity of his debate with these brothers is clearly seen years earlier in his rather harsh comments about Judaizers, "As for those agitators, I wish they would go the whole way and emasculate themselves!" (Gal. 5:12). So if we find ourselves agitated and perhaps even upset at dogmatic Christians who condemn our freedoms to reach Muslims, let us remember that the Apostle Paul wrestled with similar issues. . . .

    We can be confident that many Judaizers loved the Lord Jesus deeply (Acts 21:20), but wouldn't it have been better if they could have acknowledged God's diversity in drawing Gentiles to Christ and then responded to contextualizers like Paul in an entirely different manner?[22]

- *Brown*: Acts 15 tells how God showed James and the Apostles, through key Scriptures and the evident work of the Holy Spirit, that Gentile believers should follow the customs of their own culture rather than adopting Jewish culture (although they would need to shun some bad practices). The result of this revelation was that Church life for Greek disciples was different from Church life for Jewish disciples, and each of these believer subcultures was appropriate for the culture in which it was embedded. A further result was that the cultural differences that exist between Jewish believers and other believers no longer formed a barrier preventing fellowship between them.[23]

Acts 17

- *Higgins*: Contextualization . . . does not imply that the missionary or 'insider' leader assumes everything in a culture is pleasing to God. Acts 17 forces us to wrestle with the issue of sin and darkness in other cultures and religions, including our own. . . .

    Paul begins by affirming what he can truly and honestly affirm: "I see that in every way you are very religious . . . I even found an altar . . . TO AN UNKNOWN GOD" (vv. 22, 23). . . .

    A Jewish monotheist (Paul) is using a pagan altar as a sign that the people he addresses are religious and that they have in fact been worshipping the true God without knowing it. This is not the same thing as saying that this *anonymous worship* is salvific. I am not arguing that, nor do I believe it. But Paul *is* assuming they have been worshipping the true God without knowing Him.

---

[21] Lewis, "Insider Movements" 18.
[22] Joshua Massey, "God's Amazing Diversity *IJFM* 17(1): 10-11.
[23] Rick Brown, "Contextualization Without Syncretism" *IJFM* 23(3): 128.

From the altar Paul moves to creation. . . . although he clearly sees the altar as **preparing** the Athenians for his message about the true God, he does not take that to mean that everything in their religion and culture is **preparation** that can be fulfilled. Some things will need to be corrected or discarded, polytheism being an obvious example. . . .

It is interesting to note that while Paul never cites Scripture directly in this encounter, he does speak biblical truth, using poets and writers to support the biblical truths he proclaims. . . .

Based upon this reading of Paul's message to the Athenians, it is biblical to speak of the Gospel as a fulfillment of the 'seeking, feeling and finding' process in every culture and religion. This is true not only in the Jewish religion (where we can point to direct Old Testament prophecies and *types* that are fulfilled in Christ) but also in a pagan religious culture such as that found in Athens. Thus, insider movements can be said to relate to their religious context from this perspective of fulfillment, as well as from the perspective that the Gospel will correct and change the culture.

Paul's teaching indicates that he believed God had actually designed the locations and times and indeed cultures in which people lived so that they could seek God and find Him. There was an intentional design on God's part. . . .

Implication: Missionaries among peoples of other religions can and should approach their work with the same expectations Paul had. I should expect, in my work among Muslims, that I will find in the Quran, the Hadith, worship in the mosque, and indeed in the Hajj itself the Islamic equivalents of *altars to an unknown god* and *poets* that I can quote to proclaim biblical truth. This is true of Islam generally, but would have additional *altars* and *poets* in each of the widely varying cultural expressions of Islam. These things are not accidents; they are there by God's design. They are, we might say, the fingerprints of God within the religions of the world.[24]

- *Dutch*: After noting their altar to "an Unknown God," Paul pronounced, "Now what you worship as something unknown I am going to proclaim to you" (Acts 17:23 NIV). He then proceeded to use quotes from their pagan poets (including a hymn to Zeus) as stepping-stones to the Gospel.[25]

1Cor 7:17-20
- *Massey*: The greater context of marriage in 1Cor 7, they say,

---

[24] Higgins, "The Key" 161-2.
[25] Dutch, "Should Muslims" 17.

disallows application to C5-related issues. However, any Jew familiar with the rites of passage for Gentile conversion cannot miss the implications of disallowing circumcision.[26]

1Co 8-10

- *Higgins*: In some passages religion is said to involve the activity of demons and demonic bondage. 1 Cor 8-10 builds the case that although idols themselves are nothing, idol worship involves the worship of demons.[27]

---

[26] Joshua Massey, "Misunderstanding C5" *EMQ* 40(3): 297.
[27] Higgins, "Inside What" 85.

1.2 The Inside Story: Missiology

Jeff Morton

Jeff took both his MDiv and DMiss from Biola University where he is also an adjunct professor of intercultural studies. The author of several articles on Islam, he recently wrote *Two Messiahs* (Biblica). He worked in West Africa for nine years with SIM and personally discovered the problems of decontextualizing the Gospel. Jeff works with i2 Ministries in curriculum development and helps organize *Insider Movements: A Critical Assessment* Conferences.

An interview with an insider?

Missiology is the critical study of missions involving theology, Church history, and the social sciences. In this chapter we want to present clearly and accurately the missiology and missiological premises of many IM proponents.

If I could sit down and interview proponents of IM in order to elucidate the essential understandings of IM, what would I ask? This chapter serves the purpose of an interview. There are no critiques or assessments offered at any point. I want the proponents of IM to be heard clearly and on their own terms.[1]

The areas of discussion include the following:

a) What are the basics?
- How do proponents of insider movements define IM?
- What is the IM understanding of religions?
- What are the foundational assumptions of IM?

b) What is the IM view of Islam?
- Is it a culture or religion?
- How are Judaism and Islam comparable?
- How do IM proponents understand the Kingdom of God?
- What forms can be carried over from Islam into Christianity?

c) How do proponents of IM view Judaism and Christianity?
- What is the relationship between the two religions?
- What is Christianity?
- What do insiders think of the Church?

What are the basics?

What are insider movements?

---

[1] There are a few occasions when I ask more pointed questions that have, of course, no reply, but these will be found as a footnote.

- *Higgins*: As I use it, the phrase *Insider Movements* encompasses not only these earlier descriptions of people movements but adds *religion* to the above list of aspects of *togetherness* or unity. In other words, I suggest that followers of Jesus can continue to embrace at least some of their people's religious life, history, and practice without compromising the Gospel or falling into syncretism.[2]

- *Rebecca Lewis*: An "insider movement" is any movement to faith in Christ where a) the Gospel flows through pre-existing communities and social networks, and where b) believing families, as valid expressions of the Body of Christ, remain inside their socioreligious communities, retaining their identity as members of that community while living under the Lordship of Jesus Christ and the authority of the Bible.[3]

- *People of the Book*: The People of the Book is taking an *insider* approach to working with Muslims. . . . We do not want to extract them from their family and culture. We want them to come to saving faith in Christ, but stay inside their culture to be able to share Christ with family, friends and the rest of the Muslim world. . . . It is based on biblical principles and practices, and expressed through the pre-existing local community . . . It must also guard against any form of syncretism.[4]

- *Decker*: These *insider movements* are not intended to hide a believer's spiritual identity, but rather to enable those within the movement to go deeper into the cultural community—be it Islamic, Hindu, or Buddhist—and be witnesses for Jesus within the context of that culture. In some countries, such movements are just getting started. In other places, estimates of adherents are in the hundreds of thousands.[5]

- *Mallouhi*: And the only thing that is required of me to stay inside is to not be against my Islamic heritage.[6]

- *Travis*: Some Muslims who receive Christ as Savior deliberately choose a C5 [spectrum attempting to illustrate various expressions

---

[2] Kevin Higgins, "The Key to Insider Movements: The 'Devoteds' in Acts" *IJFM* 21(4): 156.

[3] Rebecca Lewis, "Promoting Movements to Christ within Natural Communities." *IJFM* 24(2): 75.

[4] Introductory statement from The People of Book website: http://www.ThePeopleOfTheBook.org/strategy.html (accessed 3/15/11).

[5] Frank Decker, "When Christian Does Not Translate" *MF* (September-October 2005) 8.

[6] Mazhar Mallouhi, "Comments on the Insider Movement" *SFM* 5(5): 9.

of a Christ-centeredness] expression of faith.[7]

- *Travis and Woodberry*: In another Jesus movement, a young Muslim man boarded with a Christian family, and came to faith as he joined them in their daily reading of the Bible. He came from an influential family and, once saved, committed himself to sharing the Gospel with family members in a way they would understand, Muslim follower of Jesus to Muslim. The entire family accepted Jesus as Lord and Savior, and through them the Gospel spread to in-laws and distant family members. These Jesus following Muslims gather regularly in their homes to study the New Testament.[8]

What are religions?
- *Lewis*: The new spiritual identity of believing families in insider movements is in being followers of Jesus Christ and members of His global kingdom, not necessarily in being affiliated with or accepted by the institutional forms of Christianity that are associated with traditionally Christian cultures. They retain their temporal identity in their natural socio-religious community, while living transformed lives due to their faith in Christ.[9]

- *Travis and Woodberry*: How do movements remain faithful to Jesus and the Bible when Islam contains teachings that are not compatible with biblical revelation? Among groups of Muslims who follow Jesus, a three-fold pattern is observed: they reject certain traditional beliefs and practices that are contrary to the Bible; they reinterpret others in accordance with the Bible; and they minimize others." [10]

- *Higgins*: We may speak of religion as a cultural sub-system [that comprises] . . . beliefs, behaviors and belonging.[11]

---

[7] C5 or insider movements are, among other things, an expression of faith. Cf. John Travis, "Messianic Muslim Followers of Isa" *IJFM* 17(1): 58.

[8] John Travis and Dudley Woodberry, "When God's Kingdom Grows Like Yeast: Frequently Asked Questions About Jesus Movements Within Muslim Communities" *MF* (July-Aug 2010) 25. IM is a movement to Jesus. It is therefore not a movement proceeding from within Jesus, but is moving toward him.

[9] Lewis, "Promoting" 76. Lewis contrasts the personal, spiritual emphasis and natural *socio-religious* context of insider movements to institutional forms of Christianity (expressions of historic Christianity in Muslim areas) with its inherited traditional Christian cultural forms.

[10] Travis and Woodberry, "When God's Kingdom" 26. How can genuine believers follow Jesus in accordance with certain practices of Islam if it is, at its core, anti-Christ in its teachings? How can anything of Islam mesh with Scripture if Islam is not from Yahweh?

[11] Kevin Higgins, "Inside What? Church, Culture, Religion, and Culture in Biblical Perspective" *IJFM* 5(4): 83.

- *Kraft*: Does God intend Christianity to be simply a set of cultural forms that we call a religion or did He intend something more?[12]

What are the premises of the insider movements?
- *John and Anna Travis speak of these premises:*[13]
  1. For Muslims, culture, politics and religion are nearly inseparable, making changing religions a total break with society.
  2. Salvation is by grace along through relationship/allegiance to Jesus Christ. Changing religions is not a prerequisite for nor a guarantee of salvation.
  3. Jesus' primary concern was the establishment of the Kingdom of God, not the founding a new religion.
  4. The very term 'Christian' is often misleading – not all called Christian are in Christ and not all in Christ are called Christian.
  5. Often gaps exist between what people actually believe and what their religion or group officially teaches.
  6. Some Islamic beliefs and practices are in keeping with the Word of God; some are not.
  7. Salvation involves a process. Often the exact point of transfer from the kingdom of darkness to the Kingdom of Light is not known.
  8. A follower of Christ needs to be set free by Jesus from spiritual bondages in order to thrive in his/her life with Him.
  9. Due to the lack of Church structure and organization, C5 movements must have an exceptionally high reliance on the Spirit and the Word as their primary source of instruction.
  10. A contextual theology can only properly be developed through a dynamic interaction of actual ministry experience, the specific leading of the Spirit and the study of the Word of God.

What are the "gaps" (number 5 above) and why are they important?
- *Travises*: Many Muslims hold to personal beliefs religiously at odds with Islam . . . Marantika estimates that thirty percent of the [Indonesia] nation's Muslim community observes "the rituals of Islam, but are not personally committed to its teachings" (1989:218). This gap between personal commitment and official theology is one of the things that allows for some Muslims to remain a part of their community and still follow Jesus as Lord and Savior.[14]

---

[12] Charles H. Kraft (2005). "Is Christianity a Religion or a Faith?" In Charles H. Kraft (Ed.)., *Appropriate Christianity* (83). Pasadena, CA: William Carey Library,

[13] John and Anna Travis, "Appropriate Approaches in Muslim Contexts." In *Appropriate Christianity* (397-414).

[14] Travises, "Appropriate" 405. To press the point a bit more, if both terms, *Christian* and *Muslim* are used so loosely by so many of each religion's adherents, why does saying one is a

Why should Muslims remain in their Islamic culture?
- *Mallouhi*: If I were a Jewish believer continuing to call myself a Jew and remaining inside my Jewish community, I would be lauded by most of the Christian West. My experience is that most Jewish ideology rejects the entirety of the New Testament and often reviles our Lord; yet even with those obstacles, believers that remain inside Judaism do not undergo the same scrutiny by Christians.[15]

- *Lewis*: When the Gospel is implanted in this way, the families and clans that God created are *redeemed* and *transformed* instead of broken apart . . . The Gospel is not seen as a threat to the community, and an insider movement develops as the Gospel flows into neighboring relational networks. Because believers remain in their families and networks, insider movements honor God-given community. . . . the Gospel reveals that a person can gain a new spiritual identity without leaving one's birth identity, and without taking on a new socio-religious label or going through the religion of either Judaism or Christianity.[16]

What is the IM view of Islam?

What do insiders think of Islam?
- *Dutch*: When a Muslim comes to faith in Christ as his savior, he knows he is making a religious change. . . . Muslim background believers do not perceive themselves as Muslim reformers following a *purified Islam*. . . . A true Islamic perspective would hold that the religion revealed by all prophets (e.g., Abraham, Moses, David, Jesus, and Muhammad) was originally the same, but later changed by Jews and Christians. . . . Some Muslim background believers could possibly consider that they are returning to the 'true Islam' as revealed through Jesus. . . . It would be understood that this 'true Islam' is what real Christians believe.[17]

- *Travises*: Even nominal Muslims tend to see Islam as a single fabric

---

Muslim who follows Jesus, a biblical Muslim or Messianic Muslim make the situation better? Are you not defeating what you want to accomplish—blurring the lines of identity by using terms that carry such baggage?

[15] Mallouhi, "Comments" 7.
[16] Rebecca Lewis, "Insider Movements: Honoring God-Given Identity and Community" *IJFM* 26(1): 17.
[17] Bernard Dutch, "Should Muslims Become 'Christians'?" *IJFM* 17(1): 17. For some insiders, following Jesus equates to returning to genuine Islam.

weaving together tradition, culture, and customs related to dress, diet, family life, morality, worship, and in some contexts, even economics and politics.[18]

- *Travis and Woodberry*: Over time this Muslim leader felt God was calling him to follow Jesus. He did not believe, however, that God was calling him to change his religious community. . . .

  Retaining a social and/or cultural Muslim identity means that followers of Jesus see themselves, and are seen by others in society, as Muslim. . . . They clearly hold some new values and beliefs not shared by all their neighbors. . . . Many Muslims lean toward belief systems technically incompatible with Islam, such as secularism, communism, occultism or even agnosticism. Yet they identify with the Muslim community and are considered full members of it.[19]

Is Islam a culture?
- *Rick Brown*: For many Muslims, being a Muslim is an inseparable part of their self-identity, their background, their family, their community, and their cultural heritage, regardless of what they actually believe about God.[20]

- *John Travis*: How they [Muslim converts to Jesus] view Islam is not prescribed by us, but left to them as they are guided by the Word and the indwelling Spirit.[21]

- *Mallouhi*: An *insider* believer is someone, like me, who comes from a family and country that is Muslim and chooses to maintain their culture after being irretrievably changed by the transforming power of our Lord. . . . The kind of witness that will birth productive communities doesn't require us to compromise our beliefs, only change our attitudes. . . . Islam is my heritage and Christ is my inheritance.[22]

If Islam is a culture, is there no conversion out of Islam?
- *Higgins*: We need to hold firmly to a biblical understanding of *conversion* as the reorientation of the heart and mind (e.g. Rom 12:1ff.), rather than as an institutional transfer of religious

---

[18] John Travis, "Messianic Muslim Followers of Isa" *IJFM* 17(1): 3. Islam is a complete way of life. It is their social and religious context.

[19] Travis and Woodberry, "When God's Kingdom" 24, 27. Following Jesus in faith does not entail changing religions. Therefore, insider followers of Jesus think of themselves as Muslims rather than Christians or some other category.

[20] Rick Brown, "Biblical Muslims" *IJFM* 24(2): 65.

[21] Travis, "Messianic" 53.

[22] Mallouhi, "Comments" 3, 9 and 14.

affiliation.[23]

- *Kraft*: People may be able to become Christian while retaining as secondary and tertiary allegiances their relationships to cultures, including their traditional religious structures. . . . since God adapts to people within their cultures, **this equivalence should be in meaning, function or dynamic, not merely in form.**[24]

- *Jameson and Scalevich*: Twentieth-century Muslims are forging an identity for themselves within Islam. . . .They have become 'new creations.' However, most of them never considered changing their religion. Some of their leaders, who also became followers of the Straight Way, taught them to remain in their Islamic heritage. After all, the Qur'an teaches that followers of *Isa* are Muslim (5:111). They are new creations within their old religious environment. Conversion is primarily a change of allegiance in which a Muslim becomes a follower of Jesus while retaining various Islamic forms that are given new meaning.[25]

Is there a biblical analogy to help us understand your perspective on Islam?

- *Higgins*: "We see in Acts that although the Church developed the kind of structures we just noted in Acts 14, members also remained within the religious expressions of the people of Israel, continuing to attend the Temple and synagogues."[26]

- *Jameson and Scalevich*: "The New Testament reveals great similarities between Judaism as practiced in the first century and modern Islam. The pillars of Islamic religion and the pillars of Islamic faith parallel basic tenets of first-century Judaism. . . . Jesus speaks directly about three of the five pillars in the Sermon on the Mount: giving, *zakat* (Mt 6:2-4); prayers, *salat* (Mt 6:5-7); and fasting, *sawm* (Mt 6:16-18). . . . We have been amazed at the parallels between the emerging Muslim believing community of today and the Palestinian believing Jewish community of the first century."[27]

If Muslims are not changing religions, but entering the kingdom of God, what does that look like?

---

[23] Higgins, "Inside What?" 89.
[24] Charles H. Kraft (1996). *Anthropology for Christian Witness* (201, 455). New York, NY: Orbis.
[25] Richard Jameson and Nick Scalevich, "First Century Jews and Twentieth Century Muslims" *IJFM* 17(1): 34.
[26] Kevin Higgins, "Inside What?" 77-8.
[27] Jameson and Scalevich, "First Century" 33.

- *Higgins*: The kingdom of God includes the Church, but is bigger than the Church. The kingdom refers to the whole range of God's exercise of His reign and rule in the universe. This includes religions.[28]

- *Higgins*: Men and women enter the kingdom directly, on the basis of what the King has done for them and through faith in Him, without passing through Christianity. There are movements around the world taking place *beyond Christianity*. But such movements are inside the kingdom and under the leadership of the King.[29]

- *Lewis*: Over the centuries, "Christianity" has become a socio-religious system encompassing much more than simply faith in Christ. It involves various cultural traditions, religious forms, and ethnic or political associations. While many people who call themselves Christians have truly believed in Christ and entered the Kingdom of God, others have not, though they may attend church. The Acts 15 question is still relevant today: Must people with a distinctly non-Christian (especially non-Western) identity "go through" the socio-religious systems of "Christianity" in order to become part of God's Kingdom? Or can they enter the Kingdom of God through faith in the Lord Jesus Christ alone and gain a new spiritual identity while retaining their own community and socio-religious identity?[30]

- *Timmons*: The building and expansion of little local kingdoms called churches has replaced genuine transformation through the good news of Jesus and the kingdom. Christianity . . . has placed the emphasis in the wrong place . . . Spiritual transformation can only happen through the power of Jesus, not Christianity. The emphasis must be upon Jesus and the kingdom and churches/fellowships gathering in the name of Jesus to teach and practice the kingdom lifestyle.[31]

- *Travis and Woodberry*: Scripture teaches that in Christ we are "one

---

[28] Higgins, "Inside What?" 89. Higgins commented: "I believe the context would have made clear that I am **not** saying that all religions and everything in a religion is part of the Kingdom or part of His reign. My article in fact tried to highlight the reality of the need for transformation under the light of biblical, Gospel truth. . . . religions are under the sovereignty of God even when they do and express and teach things that are not in keeping with His truth and will."

[29] Kevin Higgins, "Beyond Christianity" *MF* (July-August 2010) 13.

[30] Lewis, "Insider Movements" 18.

[31] Tim Timmons, "Christianity Isn't the Way – Jesus Is" *IJFM* 23(5): 159.

body" (Eph 4:4-6). . . . We can affirm that the great majority of Jesus-following Muslims view all people who are truly submitted to God through Christ . . . as fellow members of the kingdom of God.[32]

- *Travises*: Due to the overtly demonic nature of most of these folk Islamic practices, unless a new believer renounces them and is set free by Jesus, he is likely to fall back into the occult, becoming hamstrung in his spiritual growth.[33]

What forms in Islam are keeping with the Word of God?
- *Kraft*: Their background would lead them to want to face in the direction of Mecca (and Jerusalem). They would probably be inclined to pray five times a day with particular postures at specified ties. They would probably continue to recognize Muhammad as a prophet, worship (without songs) at a mosque, and so on. I doubt that any of these things would bother God (though honor given to Muhammad would probably bother many Christians, since we have usually seen Muhammad and Christ, contrary to the Koran's portrayal, as competitors).[34]

So the forms of Islam can be filled with new meaning?
- *Travises*: Woodberry showed "that most Islamic religious forms, even those involving the five Pillars, are actually borrowed from the practices of seventh century Middle Eastern Jews and Christians."[35]

- *Jamie Winship*: People always ask me, when a Muslim comes to faith, what do they give up? They have prayer, do they give that up? No. They give, do they give that up? No. They follow the law, do they give that up? No. There's nothing they give up. Instead, everything they do becomes not a form of duty, but an act of worship.[36]

- *Woodberry*: Although there are some differences, much of Islamic Law is similar to Mosaic Law and can be internalized and interpreted as fulfilled in Christ.[37]

---

[32] Travis and Woodberry, "When God's Kingdom" 28. Insiders see themselves as part of the same spiritual body as Christians but do not believe that necessitates joining churches or demonstrating visible, formal unity. What matters most is the mutual, indwelling Spirit of God.
[33] Travises, "Appropriate" 408.
[34] Kraft, *Anthropology* 213-4.
[35] Travises, "Appropriate" 398.
[36] Jamie Winship, "From Bandung to Baghdad: A Journey to the Inside" IJFM 25(4): 198.
[37] J. Dudley Woodberry, "To the Muslim I Became a Muslim?" IJFM 24(1): 24.

- *Mallouhi*: However, although I am born a Muslim, I am not obligated to practice all of the customs of Islam, nor am I obligated to believe all of its religious doctrines. But the day I reject Islam outright, I disavow myself of my culture, my family, my community and my people. There are many ways to bring the Gospel into this confessional home, and as mentioned earlier vocabulary is important: the words I use to describe a life-changing relationship with God through Christ and my attitude will determine how the community understands and reacts to my journey.[38]

What role does the Qur'an have?
- *Winship*: It's a pointer to the Gospel.[39]

- *Patricia Bailey*: I use their own book of precepts to validate the authenticity of Christ . . . If Muslims embrace the Qur'an as their holy book, then it is the ultimate tool to reach them and at least to provoke them to question what is written in their own book of the law. The Qur'an makes references to the Bible. The Bible never refers to the Qur'an for truth or authenticity.[40]

- *Jameson and Scalevich*: Both Jewish believers of the first century and Muslim believers of the twentieth defend their faith with their traditional Holy Book. Moreover, both communities radically reinterpret these writings based upon their knowledge of God through Jesus Christ.[41]

Can Muslims who follow Christ say the *shahada*?
- *Brown*: Personally I think the second half of the shahada should be avoided whenever possible and said only under duress with an interpretation that is compatible with the Bible. . . . I know godly, biblical Muslims, highly blessed in their ministry . . . who think saying the shahada has no negative consequence.[42]

---

[38] Mallouhi, "Comments" 8.
[39] Winship, "From Bandung" 196, 198. If I could ask a follow-up question: Is this not *cherry picking* the evidence? Is not the Qur'an just as much a pointer away from the truths of the Bible? Does not the Qur'an tell us Jesus is not the Son of God, was not crucified, did not rise from the dead, and that he performed an extra-biblical miracle taken from a pseudopigraphical book?
[40] "Evangelists Use the Qur'an as a Tool to Preach Jesus Among Muslims" http://www.charismamag.com/index.php/component/content/article/268-people-and-events/10266-evangelists-use-the-quran-as-a-tool-to-preach-jesus-among-muslims (accessed 3/15/11).
[41] Jameson and Scalevich, "First Century" 36.
[42] Brown, "Biblical Muslims" 73.

- *Travises*: Some C5 believers still repeat the creed ("There is no god but God and Muhammad is his prophet"); some do not. Others have modified it to exalt the name of Jesus. We have heard some C5 believers say that they can accept Muhammad as a *prophet* in that he pointed his people to the one true God and spoke highly of Jesus in the Qur'an. They are quick to add, however, that Muhammad is neither divine nor a savior.[43]

What should followers of *Isa* think about Muhammad?
- *Brown*: Saying that Muhammad is a prophet does not mean that Jesus is not the Messiah and the Lord. It also does not mean that Muhammad is Messiah or Lord. Muhammad never claimed that. So someone can say the shahada and at the same time can believe in Jesus as his Savior and Lord.[44]

- *Higgins*: One possible instance that gives some believers grounds for seeing Muhammad as continuing his role as one who called people back to the Books—and indeed, even back to Jesus himself—is an incident related by Ishaq in his *Sirat Rasul Allah* (Life of the Messenger). In Guillaume's translation we find the story of Muhammad's return to Mecca . . . He went to the Ka'aba and cleaned out all the pictures and idols except a picture portraying Jesus and Mary. That picture was allowed to remain inside the Ka'aba itself. For some this indicates Muhammad's intention that Jesus be the center of Islamic devotion.[45]

Are you saying one may be a Christian Muslim or Muslim Christian?
- *Woodberry*: The Qur'an also speaks of certain individuals who received the book before the Qur'an who said, "We were Muslims before it" (28:52–53). Muslim Qur'anic commentators say that some or all of those individuals were Christians (McAuliffe 1991, 240–246). Thus there is at least some textual rationale for disciples of Christ from Muslim contexts to continue to include Muslim in their identity.[46]

- *Brown*: They become what we could call *Messianic Muslims*. In their own opinion, however, they are simply being better Muslims by submitting to the Messiah whom God sent to guide and save them.[47]

---

[43] Travises, "Appropriate" 407.
[44] Brown, "Biblical Muslims" 73.
[45] Kevin Higgins, "Identity, Integrity and Insider Movements: A Brief Paper Inspired by Timothy Tennent's Critique of C-5 Thinking" *IJFM* 23(3): 117.
[46] Woodberry, "To the Muslim" 25.
[47] Brown, "Biblical Muslims" 67.

- *Winter*: In some places thousands of people who consider themselves Muslims are nevertheless heart-and-soul followers of Jesus Christ who carry the New Testament with them into the mosques.[48]

- *Travises*: Due to the overtly demonic nature of most of these folk Islamic practices, unless a new believer renounces them and is set free by Jesus, he is likely to fall back into the occult, becoming hamstrung in his spiritual growth.[49]

How do proponents of IM view Judaism and Christianity?

What is the relationship between Christianity, Judaism, and Islam?
- *Jameson and Scalevich*: Some argue, "How can you compare Judaism of the first century with Islam of the twentieth century? The former was a religion received from the true God, whereas the latter is not."

    The New Testament reveals great similarities between Judaism as practiced in the first century and modern Islam. The pillars of Islamic religion and the pillars of Islamic faith parallel basic tenets of first-century Judaism. . . . The basic tenets of faith are also common to both religions: Belief in One God, angels, Holy Writings, prophets, and final judgment based on a man's deeds. . .

    Paul is identifying himself as a Jew to other Jews. He will not even concede that he is a part of a *sect*, though he acknowledges Jewish leaders think of Jesus' followers in this way. It would be more accurate to say that Paul and his Jewish background believing friends saw themselves as the only proper expression of Judaism. Similarly, twentieth-century Muslims are forging an identity for themselves within Islam.[50]

What do proponents of IM and insiders think of Christianity?
- *Travises*: The term *Christian*, when coined 2000 years ago in Antioch, originally meant "those belonging to Christ" (Barker 1995). . . . To American evangelicals, *Christian* is a positive word meaning one who knows or is committed to Christ. More than mere religious affiliation, this term describes one's heart-faith and relationship with God. Therefore, it is not uncommon for evangelicals to say, "I went to Church regularly as a child, but became a Christian in high school." Here "becoming Christian" refers to the time he experienced salvation and life-changing faith

---

[48] Ralph Winter, "Editorial Comment" *MF* (September-October 2005) 5.
[49] Travises, "Appropriate" 408.
[50] Jameson and Scalevich, "First Century" 33.

in Christ.[51]

- *Travis and Woodberry*: Numbers of Muslims accepting Christ leave Islam and take on a Christian religious identity. For many, however, religious identity is strongly linked with all other aspects of life, so that a change of identity would make it nearly impossible to remain a part of their own family and community.[52]

- *Brown*: Paul Hiebert (1994) distinguished these two missiological viewpoints in terms of *bounded sets* versus *centered sets*. Hiebert applies this to believers in Jesus Christ. Bounded-set Christians define themselves as people who meet the boundary criteria of assenting to the same traditional creeds and religious practices . . . people with this view work hard to maintain conformity to these boundary markers and reject non-conformists as non-Christians or heretics. Centered-set Christians define themselves in proximity to the central exemplar . . . a model provided by Jesus himself. . . . Another way to put this is that traditional bounded set Christians define themselves in terms of a recognizable socio-religious category, whereas centered-set Christians define themselves in terms of discipleship to Jesus Christ. . . . Hiebert's point was that the New Testament presents a centered-set view of mission and holiness, in which the task of mission is to call and disciple people to Christ rather than promote a particular religious tradition in opposition to all others.[53]

How do Muslims understand the word *Christian*?

- *Dutch*: To the average Muslim here, *Christian* means someone who worships three gods, believes Jesus is the product of a sexual liaison between God and Mary, drinks wine, eats pork, defiles himself with ritually unclean habits, betrays his cultural heritage, and uses religion to procure assistance from Westerners.[54]

- *Lewis*: In many countries today, it is almost impossible for a new follower of Christ to remain in vital relationship with their

---

[51] Travis, "Muslim Followers" 54. Western evangelical Christians equate their religion with a personal relationship to God rather than with outward institutions such as Church.

[52] Travis and Woodberry, "When God's Kingdom" 25. Christianity is, for Muslim followers of Jesus, a foreign cultural identity that forces them away from their families and communities.

[53] Rick Brown, "Muslims Who Believe the Bible" *MF* (July-Aug 2008) 22. Traditional Christians are wedded to cultural practices, traditions, and external forms while insiders wed themselves to the essence of faith, Jesus Christ. Christianity is an outward creation that focuses on maintaining outward conformity, but insiders focus on spiritual realities, the essence of faith.

[54] Dutch, "Should Muslims" 16.

community without also retaining their socio-religious identity. In these places, the term *Christian* does not mean a sincere believer in Jesus Christ. In India, for example, *Christian* has become a socio-religious-political category (like Muslim, Hindu, Tribal, etc.) written on one's identity card at birth.[55]

How do insiders view the Church's role and purpose?

- *Higgins*: Church is made up of believers who have been saved by grace through faith[56] (Eph 2:8-10). . . the Church's ultimate purpose is to participate in, and be the first fruits of the transformation of the universe under the headship of Jesus Christ. The Church's primary strategy' to fulfill its purpose is to multiply itself through functions such as those listed in Acts 14:21-28. . . . Those same biblical functions can take place as an insider movement albeit with altered forms and vocabulary. . . . Members also remained within the religious expressions of the people of Israel, continuing to attend the Temple and synagogues. . . . There was a dual identity. . . .

    The biblical definition of Church does not necessarily refer to a bounded or closed set social grouping which prevents a member of His Body, the Church, from also being a *member* of another social or even religious structure or expression."[57]

- *Lewis*: In *insider movements* . . . there is no attempt to form neo communities of *believers-only* that compete with the family network . . . instead, *insider movements* consist of believers remaining in and transforming their own pre-existing family networks, minimally disrupting their families and communities. . . They do not need to adopt the meeting and program structures common in Western aggregate churches. . . . Just as the Apostles freed the Gentiles from any perceived need to convert to the Jewish religion, today we should likewise free people groups from the counter-productive burden of socio-religious conversion and the constraints of affiliation with the term *Christianity* and with various religious institutions and traditions of Christendom.[58]

---

[55] Lewis, "Insider Movements" 17.

[56] The true church is inward and spiritual. Therefore one can have that inward identity and still retain membership in another outward community. A follower of Jesus can have two religious identities without compromising faith.

[57] Higgins, "Inside What?" 77-79. Jewish believers remained within the Jewish religion without compromising their new faith in Jesus. The word *church* does not require specific outward structures and identity, so it is possible to embed faith in Christ within another religion.

[58] Rebecca Lewis, "Promoting Movements to Christ Within Natural Communities" *IJFM* 24(2):76. In other words, an outward change of identity and alignment with a new, non-Muslim believing community is an unnecessary and destructive measure. Changing from a

- *Lewis*: A church is *implanted* when the Gospel takes root within a **pre-existing** community and, like yeast, spreads **within** that community. No longer does a **new** group try to become like a family; instead, the God-given family or social group becomes the church. . . .

    This type of church . . . was birthed in many households in Acts. . . The redemption of pre-existing communities is a fulfillment of God's promise to Abraham that all the families of the earth would be blessed (Gen 12:3; 28:14). When the Gospel is implanted in this manner, the families and clans that God created are **redeemed and transformed**, instead of broken apart. The larger community and society are also blessed in significant ways. . . The Gospel is not seen as a threat to the community, and an insider movement develops as the Gospel flows into neighboring relational networks. Because believers **remain** in their families and networks, insider movements honor God-given community.[59]

- *Mallouhi*: Muslim insiders are being transformed by the same Holy Spirit that transforms all of us. We read the same Holy Bible that all Christians throughout the centuries have read. Our respect for and familiarity with God's Word varies, but it varies in the exact same way that it varies in other parts of the Church. Shouldn't we allow the Holy Spirit to show us if we need to re-learn how to pray or change our forms and customs?[60]

- *Travises*: These C5 groups are **maximizing the Bible!** In contrast to traditional churches which normally enjoy regular preaching, worship services with theologically rich hymns, the recitation of creeds and any number of other beneficial activities, these C5 believers have no materials to study other than the Bible. Their growth depends almost solely on inductive Bible study, prayer and small group interaction with other C5 believers.[61]

Muslim community identity to a Christian community identity is simply an unnecessary and culturally inappropriate separation from one's people (this statement reflects Lewis's comments).

[59] Lewis, "Insider Movements" 17.
[60] Mallouhi, "Comments" 10.
[61] John Travis, "Maximizing the Bible!: Glimpses From Our Context" *MF* (January-February 2006) 22.

1.3 The Inside Story: Translation

Joshua Lingel

Joshua Lingel is the president of i2 Ministries, apologist and trainer for numerous catalytic movements in Asia, Africa and South America with the *Mission Muslim World University* video curriculum for church based training. Since 1999, Lingel has been an adjunct professor at Biola University teaching *Christian Apologetics to Islam*. He has served as co-director & academic mentor for SWAD, a Ravi Zacharias International Ministries program for PhD students in Islamic Studies. Joshua has MA's in Philosophy of Religion and Ethics (Talbot School of Theology), and in Islamic Societies and Cultures (SOAS at University of London). He is the founder of the *Insider Movements: A Critical Assessment* conferences.

Rick Brown, an apologist for the followers of Jesus who remain cultural Muslims, has also been an advocate for translation of the *Son of God* in a non-gender format (while retaining the word-for-word translation in the introduction and notes). The purpose of his translation principles is to minimize the Muslim misunderstanding of God being sexually active.[1] This substitution is justified by Brown and others primarily on the basis of linguistic and semantic considerations, but theological and missiological justifications are also offered. In this essay I summarize his arguments and understanding.

Linguistic and semantic justifications

In the minds of many Muslims, *Son of God* evokes an emotional response. Christians are charged with blasphemy because the language of sonship is completely counterintuitive to their understanding of Allah. Their minds are made up: *Son of God* is a linguistic stumbling block that cannot be overcome.[2] In some languages it is not possible for the term to have any meaning other than a biological one.[3] No amount of explaining will supplant the negative semantic and affective meaning attached to it.[4] The problem, Brown says, is not the theological objections Muslims have with the idea,[5] but to the wording itself: it is taboo.[6] When we call Jesus the

---

[1] Most of his work on the subject can be found in *IJFM*, with at least one other appearing in *EMQ*. An additional article by Rick Brown, John Penny, and Leith Grey can be found in the December 2009 issue of *SFM*. Brown reminded us his principles of translation are found in *IJFM* 22(4):138.
[2] Rick Brown, "Explaining the Biblical Term 'Son(s) of God' in Muslim Contexts" *IJFM* 22(3): 93 and "Translating the Biblical Term 'Son(s) of God' in Muslim Contexts" *IJFM* 22(4): 135.
[3] Rick Brown, "'The Son of God:' Understanding the Messianic Titles of Jesus" *IJFM* 17(4): 41; "Why Muslims Are Repelled by the Term Son of God." *EMQ* 43(4): 423.
[4] Brown, "Why Muslims" 423-4.
[5] Brown, "Translating" 137; "Why Muslims" 424-5.

Son of God, we create a linguistic and cultural wall, a barrier preventing Muslim readers from understanding the Gospel.[7] If Muslims are going to hear and understand the Gospel message, some other wording must be chosen. Fortunately, since *Messiah* and *Son of God* have roughly equivalent semantic content,[8] the latter term can be changed without any significant loss of meaning.

According to Jewish usage in the first century, *Son of God* was a metaphor that described the Messiah;[9] a synonym for *Christ* or *Messiah*.[10] This would presumably hold true for statements made in the Gospel accounts by both Jewish and non-Jewish speakers, and even for supernatural speakers such as God the Father at Jesus' baptism and the transfiguration, Satan at the temptation, the angel at the annunciation, or demons who were being exorcised. In other words, when the Gospel writers used *Son of God* they meant *Messiah*.[11] This is also true for Paul's use of the term in his epistles to Gentile audiences[12]

The New Testament term, *Son of God*, is a reference to Jesus' post-incarnate role as *Messiah*, though there are times it is applied to his pre-incarnate state in a referential sense. The referential sense means that writers employ Son of God as understood post-incarnationally, but are referring to Jesus' existence prior to the Incarnation. They do this without implying he was the eternal son.[13] This understanding, Brown asserts, represents the consensus among conservative scholars.[14]

In the past, Brown suggested Muslim target translations could substitute *Christ sent from God* for *Son of God*, providing the notes explain the meaning.[15] He believes translators ought to explain the meaning of *Son of God* as Messianic when scholars agree it is Messianic.[16] This provides transparency, he explains, and thus is not misleading.[17] This helps avoid the charge that translators are actually changing the Bible, a claim many

---

[6] Brown, "Why Muslims" 424; "The Son of God" 50.

[7] Brown, Rick, John Penny and Leith Gray, "Muslim-Idiom Bible Translation: Claims and Facts" *SFM* 5(6): 88, and "Why Muslims" 426.

[8] Brown, "Explaining" 94-5.

[9] Brown, "Explaining" 93; Brown, "Translating" 141; Brown, "Why Muslims" 429.

[10] Brown, "Translating" 139; Brown, "The Son of God" 45, 48-9, 51.

[11] Brown, "Explaining" 94, 96, Brown, "Translating" 140-1. We also assume this means they expected their reading audiences, whether Gentile or Jewish, to understand it this way as well.

[12] Brown, "Explaining" 94.

[13] Brown, Penny and Gray, "Muslim Idiom" 103. On page 102, the authors offer this example of referential use: a man will commonly say, "'My wife was born in such-and-such a place,' even though she was not yet his wife when she was born."

[14] Brown, "Translating" 143.

[15] Brown commented on this: "*Christ sent from God* has not been used in approved translations of straight text, because better solutions have been found, and I no longer support its use." It would be appropriate for Brown to make this publicly known in an article and to retract all such articles that originally supported the practice.

[16] Brown, Penny and Gray "Muslim Idiom" 90-1; Brown, "Why Muslims" 426.

[17] Brown, Penny and Gray, "Muslim Idiom" 93.

Muslims have long maintained against Christians.

Theological justifications

Moving away from the linguistic and cultural issues, there are also theological reasons that allow the conscientious translator to substitute for the troublesome term, *Son of God*. Frequently the New Testament shows us the Trinity as God, his Word, and his Spirit.[18] The eternal identity of the second person of the Trinity as understood by all the New Testament writers is as the Word of God.[19] Although *Son of God* is roughly equivalent to *Messiah* and can be used interchangeably with it, it is sometimes used referentially to describe the eternal Word's Incarnation at his birth in Bethlehem.[20] Those who object to removing Son of God from the text because this diminishes the testimony of Christ's deity will find their objections invalidated when it is understood that his identity as eternal deity is not tied the title *Son of God*.[21] Substituting *Messiah* in the place of *Son of God* is not a theological compromise, but an adaptation to a culturally entrenched emotional response.[22] Because Christ's deity can be adequately established from other biblical texts without the loss of theological content, the metaphor can legitimately be changed.[23]

Missiological justifications

Although Brown offers linguistic and theological justifications for not using *Son of God* in New Testaments produced for Muslim readers, it appears that it is a missiological premise that drives the practice. From a pragmatic perspective, Brown points out that no translator wants to see his or her long hours and years of linguistic work remain unread and neglected, the people for which it was meant remaining untouched by the Gospel message. It is unthinkable that the work remains unappreciated because a blasphemous term is present. In order for the Gospel to be heard and for it to be effective, Brown says, translators must remove offensive terms that are stumbling blocks to understanding. If they do not, access to the Gospel is cut off for Muslim readers before they ever have a chance to understand it.[24] Once a Muslim is a born-again believer, the Holy Spirit can provide a fuller understanding of who Christ is.[25] Subsequent to receiving Christ personally as Lord and Messiah, and following regeneration, the Holy Spirit

---

[18] Rick Brown, "Presenting the Deity of Christ from the Bible" *IJFM* 19(1): 26.
[19] Brown, "Presenting" 24; Brown, "Explaining" 95.
[20] Brown, Penny and Gray "Muslim Idiom" 103.
[21] Brown, "Explaining" 95. Brown explained this: "What I recommend to translators . . . which was agreed at Houghton: Some translations retain the sonship image but use a wording that is not a simile but differs enough in other ways from the taboo term that it is not regarded as a blasphemy."
[22] Brown, "Why Muslims" 428.
[23] Brown, "Translating" 143; Brown, "Why Muslims" 428-9.
[24] Brown, "Explaining" 92-3; Brown, "Why Muslims" 426.
[25] Rick Brown, "What Must One Believe about Jesus for Salvation" *IJFM* 17(4): 15, 18.

comes alongside the believer helping him to recognize Jesus' divinity.[26] Ultimately the strategy proposed by Brown and others is an attempt to get a hearing for the Gospel in the difficult work of Bible translation.[27]

---

[26] Brown, "Presenting" 26; Brown, "Why Muslims" 424.

[27] Brown commented: "The problem translators are addressing is not with theology but is concerned primarily with how to convey the meaning accurately in a combination of text and paratext." This is an artificial separation of text from theology when, in fact, the meaning of the text is primarily theological.

IM and Hermeneutic Problems

2.1 Lost in Translation: Insider Movements and Biblical Interpretation

Bill Nikides

People of the Book

We are all privileged and perplexed to live in interesting times. So much has changed already in my half-century. When I came to Christ in 1973 the one and only thing I did not expect to shift from under my feet was my grasp of God. I had searched for so long, endured disappointments and disillusion along the way. But now, with Jesus, I could rest. For the first time I knew what the world really looked like. How foolish. But then I, like many of you, was restless and lost. I needed the shalom that only God in Christ can give.

I did not know that I was entering God's kingdom in the midst of revolution. So much has changed in terms of how we understand ourselves, God and his work in the world. Much has been exciting and soul-feeding. God is alive and he is very much on the move. I am particularly thankful for the explosion of growth in the Church outside of the West, often deep in the guarded heartland of the enemies of the Gospel. There is shalom for certain, but also a cacophony of voices, all of which militate for new ministries, new directions and new ideas stoking the fires of evangelism and kingdom growth. This is not really new, but how it was at the beginning of the Gospel age.

Some of this chaotic activity is a very positive sign of God's love because it means that God is moving out in many ways and many directions. But sometimes, and I think perhaps this time, there are serious problems that do not simply stem from God's incomprehensible grace assaulting our limited understanding. I think this time we have taken his wonderful provision and injected, with the best of intentions and full of faith, ideas that are not worthy of him. We listen to God as hard as we can and sometimes we just get it wrong. But because our zeal is real and our faith all-consuming, we do not like to admit it.

I am taking a course in Peacemaking. It is a timely provision. We touched last week on the primary need for Christians to confess their sins and faults. So far so good, but the difficulty is in the details. We admit being flawed in general, but when it comes down to specifics, confession eludes us. We are so sure of what we have seen and tasted that we cannot consider being wrong about this or that specific idea or ministry. It is understandable; we have invested our whole beings into our ministries, so both good and bad ideas stubbornly stick to us.

Even though we sinners go astray, God provides us an irreducible standard, a plumb line and gauge that remains beyond our prejudice: the

Word of God, perfect, complete, and infallible. Of course we tinker with it. We apply layers, glosses and accretions on it, ostensibly to better explain it, but often to bend it to our wills. Try as we might to make it say what we want, it always comes back home to God's original design for it. No one can ultimately destroy the Word of God, though I do think we can manage to hide or obscure its meaning in our efforts to make it more useful. That is something of what the Reformers called the perspicuity of Scripture. It means that the Scripture is simple and clear enough to be understood even by the simplest of us (and the distance from the simplest to the cleverest of us is not far in God's eyes). It also has another side. It means that no matter how much we tamper with its intended meaning, God's intentions survive to reassert themselves. In other words, no matter how hard we try to make it say what we want, the truth of its words survive to triumph in God's visible people, the Church. Even when we bury it, it finds its way back into the light.

This purpose of this chapter is to consider one of the most exciting and most contentious ideas in ministry: insider movements (IM). Survey the literature, popular or academic; analytical or anecdotal and you will see disagreement, not simply with regard to peripheral matters, but concerning the basics of what we believe and how we express it. Every side of this issue is presented. The experts, the bystanders, the outside observers, the participants, and I will assert, the victims all testify. How then do we then consider this? I propose that there is no better way to proceed than with Bibles in hand. As a follower of Jesus, a Christian, I believe that the key to IM's viability is not in four Scriptures, one of which is the *Injil*, but in the one and only one authoritative text, the Bible. Everything stands or falls on that.

This brings us back in a circle to where we started. Everyone involved in this issue leans on the Word for justification. Nevertheless, I think our best hope is to examine IM proponent's scriptural foundations carefully and in detail. What Scriptures do insider thinkers use, and how? What Scriptures do they omit? I think as we look at all of these angles, we will learn more about what they are thinking and why. As we offer our observations and critique, our own presuppositions and prejudices are also revealed. Let me be very clear before we dive into the meat of this. I strongly believe that IM represents a fundamentally flawed initiative, based on a fatally deficient understanding of Scripture, but I do not assume a place of privilege or power in saying this. I know that I can be just as wrong or deceived as the next human being. My ideas should be judged just as theirs. I simply propose taking a good look at a wide range of IM writing in order to see what provides for scriptural justification. Achieving this is no simple task and requires us to consider many factors. Some of these are relatively straightforward; others are riskier and should be considered hesitatingly. What I mean by the latter is the possible sources of someone's hermeneutic, the lens through which one interprets Scripture. Since they do not reveal these things directly in their writing, we cannot assert them except reflectively and suggestively.

One last preliminary point: I see two principle issues involved in the insider use of Scripture. The first is their interpretation of the Bible as a central foundation for their methodology. The second is the issue of how they treat the Bible in translation. We will focus on only the first of these tasks. Having set the table, let us proceed to the meal.

How firm a foundation?

What texts and what interpretation do pro-insiders use in order to explain and justify their thinking? Most who are laboring in the field and favorable to IM, whether that means indigenous insiders professing Christ, missionaries, or professors teaching it, do not leave audit trails explaining how they justify their ministry with Scripture. We have to rely on the writing available from missiologists, researchers, missions directors, teachers and the like. In order to prepare this chapter, I read everything I could get my hands on. I have included a list of sources consulted in the written transcript of this address. The only exceptions are observations gleaned from having interviewed scores of insiders directly in the field on two continents. My regret is that I do not have space enough to address every passage cited. I have other papers that address some of these in greater detail.

My first observation is that the overwhelming majority of biblical texts cited are narrative. That should not be a surprise in one sense. Almost 40 percent of the Bible's content is narrative. This means taking special care whenever we try to derive doctrine or practice from narrative since teaching points, if any, generally are not unambiguously stated (but more on this later).[1] Second, insider writers appear to be extremely selective in which stories they use. A number of these stand out because they are so often presented. Third, the selection of texts appears to be based on how well the story illustrates the presence of either IM or at the very least insider thinking supportive of IM. Finally considerable effort is made by pro-IMers not only to justify these movements biblically, but also to locate IM within the Bible itself. This merits careful consideration. It is one thing to find biblical justification for something you wish to attempt in the here and now. It is quite another to locate it verbatim in the there and then, too.

Kevin Higgins profiles the pagan prophet Balaam being in a relationship with Yahweh (2 Kgs 5). Though he practiced divination as a pagan, he communicated directly with Yahweh. Higgins concludes from

---

[1] Kevin Higgins rightly pointed out to me that narrative can indeed be a source of teaching. See "Speaking the Truth About Insider Movements" *SFM* 5(6). My concern in highlighting such a strong reliance on narrative was that it made interpretation of the teaching points far more tenuous and less reliable when not also paired with more clearly didactic passages. Nevertheless, his point is taken.

this that they were in relationship.² This is an especially popular insider text proving that God approves of people living as believers inside their home cultures and religions. Higgins writes,

> The text is an example of a follower of another religion who becomes a believer in the true God and yet continues to worship the true God within the religious life and practices of his prior religion. Not only is it a description, but also the text includes the clear blessing of the prophet upon the practice. In this text we find at least one case where God blesses 'remaining inside.'³

Higgins also states that Naaman gives us

> a complex situation. Some of his beliefs and behaviors change while others remain the same. At the level of belonging, he seems to have continued just as before. This should sensitize us to the possibility that our wisest response in some situations could be the same as that in 2 Kings 5:19, 'Go in peace.'⁴

Higgins also contrasts the unbelief of the Hebrew prophet Jonah with the faith of the pagan sailors that throw him overboard. He characterizes the fact that the terrified sailors prayed to Yahweh as if they were "in relationship to Yahweh."⁵

Within the Gospels, Higgins takes us to John 4 and the Samaritans are also mentioned several times, particularly by Higgins. "After their conversion recorded in John 4, they worshipped in spirit and in truth. But they did so in Samaria (in their prior place of worship) just as Jesus worshipped the Father in spirit and in truth in Jerusalem, in the Temple."⁶ In another piece, he elaborates again on this theme and relates it even more tightly to insider movements and Muslims.

> That this episode is an example of an Insider Movement is further suggested by a second feature of the passage. After Jesus spends two days in the Samaritan village, the villagers affirm that they now believe Jesus is the Savior of the world. Then Jesus leaves. What does He leave behind?
>
> A group of believers.⁷

---

² Kevin Higgins, "Inside What? Church, Culture, Religion and Insider Movements in Biblical Perspective" *SFM* 5(4). Reference is to Numbers 22-24.

³ Kevin Higgins, "The Key to Insider Movements: The Devoted's of Acts" *IJFM* 21(4): 158.

⁴ Higgins, "Inside What?" 85.

⁵ Higgins, "Inside What?" 85.

⁶ Higgins, "The Key" 159.

⁷ Higgins, "The Key" 159.

Within the New Testament, Acts is referred to most often with three texts highlighted for the most extensive treatment: Peter and Cornelius (Acts 10-11), the Council of Jerusalem (Acts 15) and Paul in Athens (Acts 17). Higgins beyond all other insider champions has a great deal to say concerning them.

IM proponents see the Council of Jerusalem as a model of contextualization fundamentally dealing with issues of identity and practice.[8] Therefore the decision to absolve Gentile believers from the burden of circumcision is a matter of freeing them from the burden of Jewish cultural baggage. Similarly as "Messianic" Muslims, Jewish followers of Jesus could maintain most of their outward Jewish forms.[9] This, in turn, is universalized into a rule, or at least a set of principles that should be followed when Christian teaching crosses ethnic-cultural boundaries.[10] "The principles debated at the Council of Jerusalem . . . are as applicable today as they were then-converts can follow Christ without abandoning their culture for that of another."[11] The implications of this are that circumcision and the Law of Moses are primarily concerned with matters of Jewish culture. Charles Kraft asserts that "When the Judaizers insisted that Gentiles needed to be circumcised, they were in effect demanding that Gentiles submit to "cultural conversion."[12]

John Ridgway has an interesting take on the actions surrounding the council. He believes that it demonstrates that every religious community is susceptible to syncretism. He refers to the imposition of what he believes were Levitical prohibitions against drinking blood. This is then equated to Western syncretism such as churches employing marketing methods. His point, believing it to be Luke's point, is clear: every religion is syncretistic and there is no reason to either impose on or exchange one brand of syncretism for another. What matters is that we work as salt and light where we are, within our own community.[13]

With regard to Paul on the Areopagus (Acts 17), Higgins launches into his explanation by reassuring us he knows that Paul is not happy with the religious worldview of the Athenians. The way he does so is interesting: "Contextualization . . . does not imply that the missionary or 'insider' leader

---

[8] Matthew H. Lumpkin, "The Call of Christ and Religious Identity: A Theology of Religions Analysis of C5 'Insider Movements'" Fuller Theological Seminary, www.scribd.com. Lumpkin here refers to the approach adopted by Kevin Higgins.
[9] John Travis, "Messianic Muslim Followers of Isa: A Closer Look at C5 Believers and Congregations" *IJFM* 17.(1):54f.
[10] Timothy Wiarda, "The Jerusalem Council and the Theological Task" *JETS* 46(2): 233f.
[11] Wiarda, "Jerusalem" 234.
[12] Charles H. Kraft, "Christianity in Culture: A Study in Dynamic Biblical Theologizing in Cross-Cultural Perspective" (340–41). Cited in Wiarda, "Jerusalem" 234.
[13] Basil Grafas, "Evaluation of Scriptural Support for Insider Movements: Critique of John Ridgway's 'The Movement of the Gospel in New Testament Times With Special Reference to Insider Movements'" *SFM* 4(2).

assumes everything in a culture is pleasing to God. Acts 17 forces us to wrestle with the issue of sin and darkness in other cultures and religions, including our own."[14] Nevertheless, Higgins sees Paul's actions as an affirmation both of the Athenians' religiosity. Higgins notes their faith is imperfect, but he sees their understanding in positive terms. "Acts 17 describes God's sovereign design of the times and places in which humans are born. The intention of God behind this is that men and women would seek after Him and actually find Him (see 17:27)."[15] He concludes:

> This implies that people in other religions can be in relationship to the true God." Finally he concludes Paul's teaching indicates that he believed God had actually designed the locations and times and indeed cultures in which people lived so that they could seek God and find Him. There was an intentional design on God's part. . . . we should conclude that God's own hand was involved in the Athenians making that altar and that He did so in order that they would seek and question and someday find Him.[16]

He appears to justify finding such truths in the Qur'an by noting that, "while Paul never cites Scripture directly in this encounter, he does speak biblical truth, using [pagan] poets and writers to support the biblical doctrines he proclaims."[17] According to Higgins there is truth from God in Islam and in Muslim culture; that is what Acts 17 proves.[18] His point is not that paganism could save its adherents; nor can Islam. Nevertheless he believes that Christ can build on the truths found in other religions and transform people without removing them from these faith systems.[19] We must keep in mind that he bases his opinions on these specific Scriptures. So too does Bernard Dutch. As far as he is concerned, what Paul did was build a bridge for the Gospel "with redeemable elements of Athenian paganism."[20]

The fundamental gloss for every text in Acts, according to many in the IM, appears to be cultural. Rebecca Lewis bridges from a description of the Samaritans in John: "in Acts we see the Samaritan believers remained in their own communities and retained their Samaritan identity (Acts 8:14-17). But at first the disciples did not understand that just as they could remain Jews and follow Jesus, the Samaritans could also remain Samaritan."[21] Why

---

[14] Higgins, "The Key" 160.
[15] Higgins, "Inside What?" 86.
[16] Higgins, "The Key" 161.
[17] Higgins, "The Key" 161. The brackets around pagan are mine.
[18] Higgins, "The Key" 161f.
[19] Higgins, "Inside What?"
[20] Bernard Dutch, "Should Muslims Become Christians?" *IJFM* 17(1): 17.
[21] Rebecca Lewis, "Insider Movements: Honoring God-Given Identity and Community" *IJFM* 26(1): 17.

could they do so? Because, as she notes, "The Gospel is not seen as a threat to the community, and an insider movement develops as the Gospel flows into neighboring relational networks. Because believers remain in their families and networks, insider movements honor God-given community."[22] Bernard Dutch accuses modern Protestants of forgetting the lessons learned in Jerusalem. "After 2000 years and a Protestant ethos that emphasizes theology over community, it is easy to think in only theological terms and completely overlook the massive communal identity issues being addressed in the Jerusalem Council decision."[23] Is that what really happened? Did theology triumph over Scripture? Have we missed the point to which the council pointed? We will come back to that soon.

They are digging in the wrong place (Raiders of the Lost Ark)

What can we conclude from all this? Have advocates of IM proven their case? Are there actually insider movements in the Bible? In my opinion, they have neither proved the existence of biblical insider movements nor justified the current practice from biblical proofs. First, let us look at Scripture and particularly the genre of narrative and address commonly accepted practices for interpreting biblical texts. Then we will revisit some of the passages briefly and present alternative interpretations. Let us see if we can understand why the two versions differ so strongly. What, in other words, are the bases of the different views? Unfortunately we cannot look in depth at each passage cited by some proponents of IM or give an exhaustive treatment to their exposition. We can however highlight key passages, focus on the degree of validity of their expositions, and compare their results to the most commonly accepted practices for biblical interpretation.

This of course does not mean that everyone does not have his own experts and it cannot guarantee that experts have it right anyway. I simply want us to connect to generally accepted practices adopted by evangelical believers from a wide variety of traditions. These also contain warnings concerning interpretive practices to avoid. For example, Don Carson cautions us about a "selective and
prejudicial use of evidence."[24] In other words, do not **just** use verses or passages that support the point. Consider all of the texts that relate to the matter. Likewise, do not use the text in a way to which it was not intended. It fits within a context that follows the redemptive flow of the whole Bible. How do you know whether you are doing that or not? Take a big picture look at the terrain. See where the text fits in the larger scheme of things. If you are trying to take your smaller Scripture stream and divert it so that it now flows up hill, you are going in the wrong direction. Then there is what

---

[22] Lewis, "Insider Movement" 17.
[23] Dutch, "Should Muslims" 18.
[24] D.A. Carson (1984). *Exegetical Fallacies* (54, 98). Grand Rapids, MI: Baker.

he terms, "world view confusion," something that takes place when you inappropriately allow your own present experience to distort the meaning of the ancient text.[25] Consider *conceptual parallelomania*: what happens when an expert in a specialized field such as psychology, sociology etc., examines texts and believes he has a firmer grasp of Scripture based on his of speciality. "Many of the specialists who fall into these fallacies are devout believers who want to relate the Bible to their discipline. They think they have a much firmer grasp of Scripture than they do; the result is frequently appalling nonsense."[26]

Having created my own nonsense from time to time, I take his point. Graeme Goldsworthy points to a problem that should caution all of us. He calls it "evangelical pragmatism:" the case of taking "good and important truths" and letting them crowd out "the central truths of the historic events of the Gospel." This happens when the present experience of a Christian, rather than the finished work of Jesus becomes the hermeneutical norm. The result is that whenever we experience success, we conclude that we must be acting biblically.[27] T. Norton Sterrett cautions against formulating doctrines by inference. Make sure that you have a considerable weight of clear instruction, rather than murky passages or stories where you are uncertain of the central point before you build a doctrine. Along with this, have a healthy skepticism concerning your own speculation.[28]

Fee and Stuart give advice for handling narratives. They note that Old Testament narratives do not usually teach doctrine. What they typically do is illustrate a doctrine taught somewhere else. When they do look for doctrine in the story itself, they are, to use Indiana Jones words, "digging in the wrong place." If you think the story is pointing to a doctrine, do not build your foundation there; find the better ground.[29] Be cautious in your approach. Really grasp the context surrounding the story, but make sure that you start with the story in order to understand it, not outside elements. Start with the immediate context. Beginning from the other side of it, Dennis Bratcher warns, "Actions of biblical characters do not directly present us with norms for our behavior today, although they may illustrate the consequences of a particular behavior."[30] Excepting Jesus in the statement, I see wisdom in his care.

I take as a final caution the words of Gerald Bray: "In the early church there were many who tried to use the Bible for their own purposes and who contextualized it in the culture of their time. Today these people are lumped

---

[25] Carson, *Exegetical* 105.
[26] Carson, *Exegetical* 136.
[27] Graeme Goldsworthy (2006). *Gospel-Centered Hermeneutics: Foundations of Evangelical Biblical Interpretation* (179). Downers Grove, IL: InterVarsity Academic.
[28] T. Norton Sterrett (1974). *How to Understand Your Bible* (151-55). Downers Grove, IL: InterVarsity.
[29] Gordon D. Fee and Douglas Stuart (1982). *How to Read the Bible For All It's Worth* (78). Grand Rapids, MI: Zondervan.
[30] Dennis Bratcher, "Guidelines for Interpreting Biblical Narrative" *The Voice* (2010).

together as 'gnostics.'" Bray goes on to exhort readers of the Word to pay attention to what the text really says, seeking to understand it thoroughly in terms of what its original writers, hearers and readers understood.[31]

Consider Balaam and Balak of Numbers 22-24. Balak is the son of Zippor, king of Moab. Balak, fearing Israel's encroachment on his land, ordered Balaam, to curse the Israelites. Contrary to Balak's plan, however, Balaam is compelled by God to testify in Israel's favor. Even when Balaam determined to disobey God's instructions, his donkey would not allow him. Eventually Balaam saw that it was no mere animal standing in his way, but the angel of the Lord who corrected Balaam and set him on a path to testify to the pagan king of God's judgment on Moab and favor for Israel.

Is this an endorsement of a peace treaty between Yahweh and pagan religion? Can we say that Balaam is a faithful follower of Yahweh though he remains formally within paganism? He respects the true God, saying the Lord spoke to him (Num 22:8) and that he could not go beyond Yahweh's command (Num 22:18). However, the Bible judges him as a false prophet (Num 31:16) because he caused Israel to act treacherously with Yahweh. He is a self-serving opportunist who sought to benefit from his disobedience to God (2 Pet 2:15; Jude 11). Jude lumps Balaam with Cain and Korah; not the company pro-insiders strive to keep I hope. Interestingly, it is only Origen in ancient tradition that gives his life a positive spin, seeing him as an ancestor of the magi. By contrast, most early Christian interpretation identifies him as a forefather of the Libertines and Nicolaitans.[32] Surely the text's principle purpose is, rather than demonstrating some strange approval of Balaam's religion, to clearly celebrate the inability of the nations to hinder God's purposes lived out in Israel. Everything that transpired in Numbers cascades from the promises made by God to Abraham.

A favorite Old Testament story of IM advocates is Naaman and the temple of Rimmon (2 Kgs 5). Is the point that one can and should worship the true, triune God from within his non-covenantally based religion as IM suggests? The background of the passage immediately militates against the IM interpretation. Rather than concerning itself with a generous God who countenances Naaman remaining within paganism, the context concerns Israel's serial prostitution with pagan gods. Their unbelief is contrasted to the covenant-keeping nature of the God they ignore. Naaman unambiguously embraces faith in the covenant God of Israel, so we know that he is no syncretist. He is not asking for permission to worship Rimmon. Naaman appears to be asking permission to enter the temple as his master's aid-de-camp.[33] God does indeed address the nations in the

---

[31] Gerald Bray, "The Challenge and Promise of Biblical Interpretation Today" *The Jordanstown Lectures,* www.latimertrust.org (2007).

[32] Philip J. Budd (1984). *Numbers* (272f). WBC Waco, TX: Word. See also Dennis R. Cole (2000). *Numbers* (367). NAC Nashville, TN: B & H.

[33] Richard Nelson (1987). *First and Second Kings* (179). Louisville, KY: John Knox.

text, but with a twist: he will deliver the nations from slavery to sin, bringing triumph, that is, shalom, over moral and physical consequences. In this sense Elisha sends Naaman as a forerunner into enemy territory, secure with the knowledge that God is with him.

The context helps explain Elisha's shalom. God is not approving of Naaman's remaining within paganism. Naaman asks for forgiveness, knowing he will probably never return to Israel. He recognizes he will have no opportunity to worship in a covenantal community. Naaman is in a difficult place and he has a tender conscience. As Paul House recognizes, Elisha decides not to heap more guilt on Naaman for his present circumstances.[34] Gary Corwin suggests that it more appropriately points to a long-standing principle within non-C5 convert communities that time and certain compromises are expected in the transition to a new identity that is located outside of Islam. Corwin notes, however, the insider community's ignoring of God's expectation of exclusive outward as well as inward reverence.[35] This is a vital context omitted that alters the whole direction of the text.

What of the sailors praying to God during Jonah's disobedience? Was God approving of their genuine faith? We know the sailors fear the god Yahweh (Jonah 1). They call on him to not punish them for the sins of Jonah. They throw Jonah into the sea and, when things calm down, offer sacrifice to the Lord and make vows. Higgins theorizes the sailors have personal relationship with God. Are they religious dual citizens? Rather than reading anything into the story, consider the facts. Their actions prove they are religious, believing that Jonah's powerful god, Yahweh, exists. "This does not imply that they had suddenly become monotheists. There is nothing at all in the text to indicate that they did any more than add Yahweh to the number of gods to which they sacrificed."[36]

Moving to the New Testament, what about the Council of Jerusalem and the Gentiles? Who are the participants who made the decisions? What was the main issue in play? Was it fundamentally an issue related to contextualization or did something else dominate? As for background, we get a sense of who the players were when we read Acts 15 and its backdrop: Peter's visit to Cornelius, his consequent conviction that God redefined the people of God to include the Gentiles, and the Galatians episode that describes the opponents to including the Gentiles without requiring covenant circumcision. We discover they are not Pharisee Background Believers (PBB), as Brian K. Petersen names them, a curiously anachronistic term, or even just "Jewish believers." Many IM proponents obscure the

---

[34] Paul R. House (2002). *1, 2 Kings*. NAC (electronic ed.). Nashville, TN: B & H. Cited in John Span, "God Saves ... Go in Peace: Wholeness Affirmed or Promotion Piece?" *SFM* 6(1): 219.

[35] Gary Corwin, "A Humble Appeal to C5/Insider Movement Muslim Ministry Advocates to Consider Ten Questions" *IJFM* 24(1): 16.

[36] Bill Nikides, "A Response to Kevin Higgins's 'Inside What?'" *SFM* 5(4).

intention of the passage by popularizing these terms in their literature. Paul simply refers to them as the circumcision party because they located the core of the faith in circumcision rather than faith in Christ. They promoted circumcision as a ground or condition of salvation. John Stott's point is decisive. These Judaizers believed "they must let Moses complete what Jesus had begun."[37] In other words, they had everything backwards. They even had Christ pointing away from himself to something greater: salvation in a covenant identity as the visible, physical, material Israel of God. In this scheme Christ facilitated their entrance into the realized Jewish nation.

The Council of Jerusalem responded to this as a renunciation of genuine faith, not a mere Torah-observant expression of it. It was, to be blunt, false religion, a cul-de-sac, a dead end, a counterfeit, and a fatal one at that. Paul condemned them, not as weak believers, but rather as "sham-Christians; people that presented themselves as believers but whose actions put the lie to their claims (Gal 2:4).[38] They were false brothers who were not what they seemed to be; who were secretly trying to destroy the work of the Gospel, and doing it deliberately. Their fruit was heresy.[39] These were the people that forced the glorious, prophetically-fulfilled, Church-wide decision in Acts 15 to admit Gentile believers with baptism, but without circumcision. The only additional requirement was four Jewish prohibitions probably associated with pagan religious practice, similar to the advice Paul gave the Corinthians.[40]

This formed the backdrop to the momentous, one-of-a-kind decision. This was no intramural debate between genuine believers about contextual tactics. This meeting and Pentecost were the defining moments in the universalization of the Gospel. The flower bloomed. It also asserted that the spread of the Gospel by the one, visible, united, covenantal family of God would be its defining mission; the very principle foundation for ecumenism. Timothy George summarizes this point: "Paul would not work together with false brothers, even though they claimed to be fellow Christians, because their theological position was antithetical to the Gospel message itself."[41]

Timothy Wiarda asks two diagnostic questions regarding this text. First, to what extent did any of the participants in the debate view circumcision and the Mosaic Law as matters of culture? Second, was the council's theological decision conceived as universal (applicable for all peoples, both Jews and Gentiles) or local (restricted to one cultural

---

[37] John R.W. Stott (1990). *The Message of Acts: The Spirit, the Church & the World* (243). Leicester: InterVarsity.
[38] Ronald Y.K. Fung (1988). *The Epistle to the Galatians* (93f). Grand Rapids, MI: William B. Eerdmans.
[39] Timothy George, (1994). *Galatians*. NAC Nashville, TN: B & H.
[40] David Peterson (2009). *The Acts of the Apostles* (433) PNTCS Grand Rapids, MI: Eerdmans. Peterson cites Witherington in support.
[41] George, *Galatians* 167.

community)?

In answer to the first question, circumcision was tightly linked to the Jewish nation and the relationship to their covenantal God. Circumcision was not just an ethnic boundary marker. It was a historical sign and seal of promised blessings found exclusively within that covenant. It was therefore considered redemptive, a matter of life or death. In the second case, the fact that Peter proclaimed the law was a yoke that "neither we nor our fathers have been able to bear," suggests the council's discussion was not principally one of developing a culturally specific or customized local theology. This is a far cry from the mere cultural, contextual debate embraced by IM. Nor does it present a cookie cutter pattern for diversity that includes world religions. It is the trumpeting of salvation by Christ in faith alone exclusively in one people according to the Scriptures. The council's decision does not justify people loving Jesus and remaining in their non- or unbiblical religions. Beyond this is a supreme irony. In using Acts, pro-insiders chose a text that showed the Church's commitment to removing barriers, not to contextualization within religions, but to table fellowship. I find this ironic because the methodology they champion erects barriers preventing fellowship.

What about Paul's Mars Hill address in Athens in Acts 17? Is it proof that God erects Gospel bridges using pagan material? Is it an affirmation that pagans know God really, if imperfectly? Can it legitimately be used as a justification for using the Qur'an to explain Christ? Higgins appears to believe that Paul quotes Gentile philosophers as a tacit approval of their genuine belief, thereby justifying Messianic Muslims remaining within Islam.

Even though Paul proclaims the universal ancestry of humankind, he moves from there to proclaiming this world will be judged according to its relationship to the resurrected Jesus. Paul is not using his reference to Greek philosophy as a way of accepting non-covenantal religion or to say one can be saved regardless of religious affiliation. Rather, he clearly uses a local reference to communicate the exclusive claim of the Gospel. And it works! The Greeks clearly understand what Paul is up to. We know because they react to his idea with either derision or genuine interest. When they heard of the resurrection of the dead, some mocked, but others said, "We will hear you again about this" (Acts 17:32). Greek religion or philosophy could never lead to salvation. It was headed on the wrong road. Rather than allowing these pagans to continue on their road to ruin, Paul intercepted them at the crossroads, trying to persuade them to follow the path to life.[42]

The dog that did not bark in the nighttime

At the conclusion of the Sherlock Holmes short story, "Silver Blaze," Holmes is asked how he solved the seemingly insoluble theft of a

---

[42] See Nikides, "A Response" 109-110.

disappearing horse. Holmes replies that it was the barking dog that gave the criminal away. When Dr. Watson noted there was no barking dog, Holmes replied that it was the absence of a dog barking in the nighttime that gave him the clue to unlock the mystery. It was not what he saw or heard that convinced him; it was what he **did not** hear. Similarly, we must note the texts left out by the pro-insiders' attempts to justify their perceptions. Though it is characteristic for those of us engaged in missiology to wrangle over the interpretation of passages put forth by advocates of IM justifying their positions, the wrangling often diverts our attention from noting what texts are left out. Proponents of IM may claim this is an unfair demand since the Bible talks about so may things; there is no way to harmonize an idea with all of them. True enough, but altogether unnecessary.

I suggest there are a great many neglected passages that bear directly on this matter. If we seriously wish to ascertain whether or not IM is a biblically justifiable construct, we need to examine a great deal more Scriptures than supplied by its proponents. Those of us who write in the fields of theology, biblical studies and missiology, know our work is judged academically credible on the basis of our objectivity and fairness. In order to do that, we have to look at things from many angles, to include the vantage points of our critics and texts that can militate against our positions. This is a serious and perhaps egregious omission of pro-IM literature. We should hear barking dogs, but we do not. That should alert us.

Who are some of these mute canines? They would include texts and trajectories that place the isolated narratives in larger perspective. If the Bible really is one story and not simply the collation of fragmented ideas presented by liberal theologians, like piles of paper stacked up neatly in front of a giant shredder, then it should have themes uniting all of the narratives into one narrative, one river from the confluence of its many streams. Is not redemption in Christ the grand scheme that unites the stories? This theme dominates the Acts 15 and John 4 stories. Can we seriously believe that cross-cultural understanding of religion is intended as the heart of these passages? Is not the bigger picture and clearer picture the redemptive story? Likewise, my survey of insider literature testifies to an almost complete absence of texts referring to the mechanism recognized in both Testaments as the vehicle for bringing the truth to the world, the idea of covenant.

In my opinion, the absence of covenant is fatal to IM. Its absence undergirds so much of the misinterpretation of texts. The reason pro-insiders believe Acts defines the people of God as transcending historic Israel by means of a cross-cultural dynamic (allowing for Muslims to drop into the dynamic) is IM's lack of appreciation for covenant as the defining paradigm of Scripture. Associated with this is IM's neglect of passages focusing on the core sin of idolatry. Why does the Bible devote so much effort on idolatry from Genesis to Revelation? Read the text; it is not just because people are a little ignorant about God. Rather, it is because people are made in God's image, but are fallen. Because they reflect God, they create. We are also relational because the triune God is relational; we reflect that to one another. We do all of this as fallen sinners. It means that we do craft things, but the things we build are not alive and they do not bring glory to the God who is there, to quote Francis Schaeffer.

We are so good at manufacturing counterfeits we must have a direct revelation from God to move us away from our impulse to move away from God. In the Bible, this takes the form of the covenant that outlines the one true way that people can relate to God and each other through him. So often when we think and talk about IM, we speak of false religion and fallenness as extreme expressions. Our ancestors in the early church have much to say to us about this. They recognized better than we that bad ideas are the worst when they look very much like good ideas. The early church recognized these as ideological "angels of light," not to be dialogued with, but spurned. They had to be rejected, not because there was no truth in them, but because we sinners latch onto the false parts that corrupt our faith, just as bits of Canaanite pagan religion eventually corrupted the Israelites. They also knew that big ideas have cores; the externals could look good and familiar, but at their hearts were wicked and deceitful things. The Bible is a story of truth in a people, a family and its relationship to God. That relationship was the one thing that preserved the truth from a universe of counterfeits, signposts all pointing to the wrong destination. So God gathered a people for himself; a family that he chose to love. And it was in the fullness of time that it brought us to the point of it all, Jesus Christ our Lord. That would have been good enough, but God even trumped himself. In the fullness of time, he expanded his family so much so that it wrapped itself around the world. This is the idea of covenant in the light of the resurrection and it does not harmonize with insider movements and their fragmented stories. This is also why my greatest desire in this matter is not to extend the olive branch to those with whom I disagree. Rather, it is to invite them to fully identify themselves with God's visible family, his olive tree, his people, the Church of Jesus Christ.

Advocates of IM highlight biblical stories that suggest God's working in the world among the nations, but they overlook the vast and overwhelming part of the Bible that equates religion outside of the covenant with wilderness, exile and death, not light. This may be the result of an inclusivist theology of religions, in turn the result of reading the Bible in fragments rather than as a whole. Outsiders are indeed honored in the Bible: Rahab sides with God's anointed covenant people, but she becomes one of them, adopted into the covenant. The Jews had trouble grappling with the idea that the land, the Law, and their ethnicity were not the prizes to which the covenant pointed. They were waypoints, pointing beyond themselves to the Lordship of Christ and their own membership in the global family that united with him. The end game was not the Law, but everlasting life in Christ as part of his resurrected, renewed, recreated family. The mistake Judaizers made was in focusing on the means (the covenant and its outward forms) rather than the end (union with Christ as part of his body). This family is what our older, more distant relatives called the One, Holy, Catholic, and Apostolic Church. It is one because Christ only has one body, a fact we remember whenever we celebrate the Supper together. It is holy because it is a family distinct from all others; distinct in its covenantal self-identity, its ethics and its unique relationship to the head of the household. It is catholic, both because it extended all over the world and through time. It is apostolic because it carried the exclusively divinely revealed words of life from its savior to the world without addition or subtraction.

I like the way Tom Wright tells the story:

> In the Christian canonical Bible there is a single over-arching narrative. It is story which runs from creation to new creation. The great bulk of the story focuses quite narrowly on the fortunes of a single family in the Middle East. They are described as the people through whom the creator God will act to rescue the whole world. The choice of this particular family does not imply that the creator has lost interest in other human beings or the cosmos at large; on the contrary, it is because he wishes to address them with his active and rescuing purposes that he has chosen this one family in the first place.[43]

This I believe highlights the heart of the matter regarding IM's poor hermeneutic. On reflection, I think two factors account both for the crystallization of insider methodology and the strained manner with which they treat Scripture. These two are the immediacy of life-changing personal experience and IM's interaction with popular notions of missiology, social science in general, history, and theology. To put it simply, insider movements are the product, in my opinion, of immediate personal religious experience and contemporary ideas. To make the point even more strongly, both poles of opinion in this matter gravitate around these two factors. It is not simply a matter of one group being open to ideas and the other not, any more than it is the fact that one group uses the Bible or prays and the other does not. Nor is it primarily an issue of Christian peacemaking, though enough sin exists on all sides that we probably have plenty to repent of. The issue is saturated with intelligent, creative people on all sides of the issues. No one's response is the symptom of a brain drain. I think the heart of this seeming morass is exegetical, hermeneutical and theological. We cannot be either helped or hindered by each others' personal experiences and

---

[43] N.T. Wright, "The Book and the Story." In *The Bible in TransMission* (Summer 1997). http://www.biblesociety.org.uk/products/295/49/summer_1997_the_book_and_the_story/ (accessed 3/25/11).

observations enough to resolve any of this.

My plea is that we sit down, not in intimate enclaves in order to attempt conflict resolution, though that can be done as a way of developing better relationships; but that should not divert us from an even larger task. Our differences are fundamentally theological and doctrinal, regardless of how we understand the motives or circumstances that shaped them. The early church set a pattern for such difficulties, as we see in Acts and later in the early period of Church patristics. Diverse parts of the visible church gathered together to debate and decide key matters of doctrine in open sessions. Read the eyewitness reports about these gatherings. They were not pretty, to be sure, but they did focus on a close examination of the Word. They addressed how to read, understand, and apply biblical texts to ministry. Do not let Adolf Harnack or other modernist historians fool you, these gathering were not philosophy-dominated tragedies showcasing the triumph of Greek ideas over Hebrew revelation. They were serious (in the best sense of the word) gatherings saturated with Scripture. I do not know what that sort of thing would look like in our world. We have no Emperor moderating. We are children of our past and that means that we are products of theological family divorces or estrangements. We represent, sad to say for me a champion of the Reformation, a fracturing of the body. Nevertheless, we must focus on the word. "There is one body and one Spirit—just as you were called to the one hope that belongs to your call— one Lord, one faith, one baptism, one God and Father of all, who is over all and through all and in all" (Eph 4:4-6 ESV).

The biblical worldview admits no understanding of religion as a cultural expression, in some sense neutral with regard to truth, or separated from faith and belief. Again, Wright exposes the difference between the world of the Bible and our understanding of religion:

> The biblical metanarrative challenges the view of Christianity, or biblical Judaism, as a 'religion' in the post-enlightenment sense, and I suspect that many Muslims, Hindus and others would want to do the same. Insofar as post-enlightenment thought suggests that truth lies in Deism, and that all 'religions' are different humans expressing their own ideas about or experiences of the one distant and unknowable god, most genuinely religious people and groups are bound to object. Once that point is grasped, it becomes clear that if the biblical narrative is true, the Muslim one is not, and vice versa; and the same for Hinduism, Buddhism and so on.[44]

It is in this respect the omission of didactic passages drumming on idolatry is most felt. Their absence creates a false sense of the drift of Scripture; like biblical theologies that only profile God's love and not his jealousy.

---

[44] Wright, "The Book." n.p.

As far as IM's handling of Scripture, it is hard to avoid seeing personal experience looming above everything else. Over and over we are faced with the overwhelming presence of their conviction, not conviction rooted in Scripture but in the certainty that what the proponent experienced is true. I could be wrong about this, but the writing is insistent that what the IM champion has seen is real and good. The expositing generally appears to follow that. The insider proponents do not simply use Scripture to justify their modern methodologies, they merge Scripture with their experience. Consequently these movements are not similar to biblical examples, they are deemed identical.[45] Consider Woodberry's, "To the Muslim I Became a Muslim." He writes, "If Paul were retracing his missionary journeys today, would he add, 'To the Muslim I became a Muslim?'[46] He equates a modern day Muslim with a first century Jew or Greek. The comparisons are not approximate; they are exact. Kevin Higgins pronounces, "every movement to Jesus is in some way an insider movement. Every movement to Jesus is inside some culture or some aspects of a culture."[47] Jameson and Scalevich introduce us to an insider, Dawud, in a most interesting way. The authors ask, "Was Dawud a first-century Jew or a twentieth-century Muslim?"[48] Petersen, writing primarily about insiders within Hinduism, in describing the Judaizers present at the Council of Jerusalem, refers to them as PBB's, Pharisee Background Believers.[49]

What should we make of this? In one sense, it sounds healthy as it allows us to inhabit another time and space to become part of the Gospel story. Unfortunately by fusing the horizons of the past and present, IM advocates create something far riskier. They equate past with present. I. Howard Marshall advises us not to make the two horizons so distinct that we cannot apply its truth to our situation, but the concept of balance has to reign.[50] The lessons of the past can be applied to another time, but ancient Judaism and the early church must not turn into dramas involving insiders, outsiders or any other social science category. Speaking over ancient voices silences them; it is wrong. By doing this we deny the Scripture its privilege of distance and difference. When we domesticate Scriptures it no longer critiques us. It does not matter that pro-insiders remind us they know mistakes are made in pursuing this course or that each insider community is different. It does not matter because the fusing of horizons always trumps

---

[45] See Basil Grafas, "Evaluation." Ridgeway does not merely see similarities between the Old and New Testament narratives and insider movements, he believes that actual insider movements existed, despite being modern creations.

[46] J. Dudley Woodberry, "To the Muslim I Became a Muslim?" *IJFM* 24(1): 23-7.

[47] Higgins, "The Key" 156.

[48] Richard Jameson and Nick Scalevich, "First Century Jews and Twentieth Century Muslims" *IJFM* 17(1): 33.

[49] Brian K. Petersen, "The Possibility of a 'Hindu Christ-Follower': Hans Staffner's Proposal for the Dual Identity of Disciples of Christ Within High Caste Hindu Communities" *IJFM* 24(2): 88.

[50] I. Howard Marshall, "How Do We Interpret the Bible Today?" *Themelios* 5(2): 8.

the offhand admission of mistakes in execution. Once Abraham, Jesus, Peter, and Paul become insider champions, every criticism becomes noise. The heavy-handed use of narrative that fuses the horizons of the biblical text with experience looks like a validation of ministry, rather than an attempt to build a biblical foundation for ministry.

Since I have already highlighted the dangers of trying too hard to get into someone else's head, I know that as I share this, I have to address others' possible thought worlds and motives tentatively. Therefore I am suggesting pro-insiders consider the process by which they arrived at their biblical interpretation; however, I do not believe it necessary to apologize for suggesting it. In the first place, I suggest this only after an extensive reading of IM literature so that whatever impressions I have come from the writings themselves. Second, I know that what goes around comes around. The same caution applies to us. Let us guard our hearts and check our motives for our positions. Allow the Word and the Spirit at work in us to scrub us clean and fill us with Gospel truth. Amen.

2.2 Would Paul Become Muslim to Muslims?

Georges Houssney

Born and raised in Lebanon, Georges is well known for his work supervising the translation of the Bible into contemporary Arabic and Kurdish. His academic background in psychology, linguistics, and intercultural studies has also contributed to the production of two books in Arabic and the creation of an indigenous Arabic Bible study curriculum in cooperation with David. C. Cook Foundation. For over thirty-five years he has been a critic of the insider movements in its various facets.

Introduction

Before writing this chapter, I asked a few people, "Who wrote the words, 'I became a Jew to the Jews'?" Without hesitation, each of them had the same answer, "Paul." Then I asked, "What else did Paul say in the same passage?" Again, each one answered the same: "I became Greek to the Greeks." Some of them were quite familiar with the passage and were able to complete it by adding, "I have become all things to all men, so that I may save some" (1 Cor 9:19-23).

For several years I have heard those words attributed to Paul, so often that I too was fooled into thinking that Paul said that he became a "Jew to the Jews" and a "Greek to the Greeks." These two popular misconceptions have contributed to many malpractices of missionaries to Muslims. Some have concluded that becoming a Muslim to Muslims is the God-given strategy to win Muslims. A few years ago, the international director of a large mission agency told me personally that if he were asked, "Are you a Muslim?" he would, in good conscience, say, "Yes." His explanation was: "If *Muslim* means one who is submitted to God, then by all means, I am a *Muslim*."

There is confusion on the mission field because of the serious misinterpretation, and the resulting misapplication, of this passage. Let us examine the text to see for ourselves what Paul wrote. We will then apply hermeneutical principles in an attempt to unearth both the explicit and implicit intent of Paul in this text. Here is the text in question:

> Though I am free and belong to no one, I have made myself a slave to everyone, to win as many as possible. To the Jews I became like a Jew, to win the Jews. To those under the law I became like one under the law (though I myself am not under the law), so as to win those under the law. To those not having the law I became like one not having the law (though I am not free from God's law but am under Christ's law), so as to win those not having the law. To the weak I became weak, to win the weak. I have become all things to all people so that by all

possible means I might save some. I do all this for the sake of the Gospel, that I may share in its blessings. (1 Cor 9:19-23)

Upon reading the passage more carefully, you will observe three main things:
- Paul did not say that he became a *Jew to the Jews*. Rather he said: "To the Jews, I became like a Jew."
- Paul did not say that he became *Greek to the Greeks*. He did not mention the Greeks at all in this passage.
- Paul spoke about those who are "under the law" and those "not having the law."

Three principles

Three principles of interpretation are used to help us explore the original intent of this passage.
1) The immediate context: Every text must be interpreted in its immediate context. This passage should be interpreted in view of the three chapters that make up Paul's discourse on the issue of freedom to exercise or not exercise, the Law (1 Cor 8-10).
2) The broader context: Every text must be interpreted in its broader context, by comparing it with other passages throughout the entire Bible that deal with the same issue.
3) The biographical context: Every text must be compared with the patterned lifestyle of the author. The author cannot be made to say something that is inconsistent with his normative teachings and actions.

1) Immediate context

Hermeneutics helps us to see each passage in light of its context. The five verses of 1 Corinthians 9:19-23 must not be interpreted on their own, for they fall in the center of a long discourse encompassing three chapters: 8, 9, and 10. These three chapters must be taken together as a whole, as the immediate context of the passage. Similar to a mosaic that comprises many pieces, Paul's teaching includes various arguments and illustrations that lead to a conclusion. This material is needed to derive the background, the bases, and the concepts that fit together forming the conclusion of the discourse. Our passage is a small part of the discourse, only five verses out of seventy-three. The interpretation of any word, verse, or even all five verses in this passage must agree with, and not contradict, the major theme of the discourse and its conclusion.

Many proponents of insider movements (IM) are desperate to find biblical support for their theories. This passage has been treated as a gold mine. Rick Love calls it "the *Magna Carta* of contextualization."[1] I personally know many of these IM advocates. They may be knowledgeable in the Scriptures, yet they jump to conclusions in their eagerness to prove their position. It is understandable because Paul seems to provide the perfect formula for dealing with people of other cultures; however, if we were to examine the context of the passage rather than coming to the passage with a preconceived idea, we would discover a different meaning altogether. This may come as a surprise to many of my readers: most who reference this passage to support contextualization or the IM have zeroed in on this particular passage on its own, without much consideration to even its immediate context, namely chapters eight to ten.

Can Christians eat food presented to idols?

This question is the major theme of the entire discourse. Paul starts chapter eight with it and concludes with it in chapter ten. The Church in Corinth had many new believers from pagan backgrounds. Idol worship was part of their culture, and pervaded society and industry. Local butchers, vendors, and cooks commonly dedicated their meat to pagan gods and goddesses, which meant that Jews and Christians from both Jewish and pagan backgrounds had tough decisions to make. Where would they get their meat, and how sure of its origins would they have to be? The Church had a mixed response to these issues. Those who were grace oriented emphasized freedom in Christ and did not see this meat as a problem. On the other side were Jewish-background Christians who continued to adhere to the Law of Moses. They were oriented toward a stricter lifestyle, and a kosher diet, so they were not supportive of the practice. This issue became divisive in the Church, necessitating intervention by the Apostle Paul, who founded that church, led it in person for eighteen months, and continued to shepherd it through letters, representatives, and personal visits.

2) Broader context

To rightly interpret 1 Corinthians 9:19-23 not only must we look at its immediate context in 1 Corinthians, but we should also examine the book of Acts and Paul's other epistles. We shall see that neglecting these other texts contributes to misinterpretation of the passage and therefore erroneous conclusions.

"I became like a Jew"

The introduction mentioned the popular misconception that Paul said he became a *Jew to the Jews*. Paul actually wrote, "I became **like** a Jew." [2] Is this significant? By all means. It is well known to students of the Bible that

---

[1] Rick Love (2000). *Muslims, Magic and the Kingdom of God* (50) Pasadena, CA: William Carey Library.
[2] 1 Cor 9:20

Paul had dual citizenship. In reality he was both a Jew and a Greek at the same time. So why would he say that he became "like a Jew"? Is he denying his Jewish identity and saying that he is "like a Jew," but not a true Jew? Certainly not. There has to be a another meaning. Paul had dual identities. He was both a Jew and a Greek biologically speaking. This shows us that when he says "like a Jew" he is not speaking about identity.

When he says "to the Jews," he is referring to the ethnic identity of the Jewish people. When he says, "I became like a Jew," he is speaking not of identity, but of behavior; doing certain things that Jews do. For example, he was willing to circumcise Timothy to avoid unnecessarily offending the Jews.

The meaning of the word *Jew*

What does Paul mean by the word *Jew* and how does he use it in the broader context of his other writings? The Bible frequently uses terms in more than one sense. Paul often uses terminology that is paradoxical or that simply carries different meanings. For example he writes, "Not all who are descended from Israel are Israel" (Rom 9:6). Here he uses the word *Israel* in two senses. In the first sense, Paul refers to the people who have descended from Abraham through Jacob (renamed Israel). The other meaning is spiritual. Paul says in this verse that not all who are from the bloodline of Abraham are children of faith.

In another passage, Paul explained,

> A person is not a Jew who is one only outwardly, nor is circumcision merely outward and physical. No a man is a Jew who is one inwardly; and circumcision is circumcision of the heart, by the Spirit, not by the written code. (Rom 2:28-29)

Here Paul is making the distinction between an ethnic Jew (outward and physical Jewish identity) and the spiritual Jew (inward and spiritual children of God).

The passage we are discussing was addressed to the Corinthians. It would be helpful to look back to Acts 18:1-18, which contains the story of what Paul did in Corinth, where he stayed, and how he served the church for eighteen months. It sheds light on our text. How is the word *Jew* used here?

> Meanwhile a Jew named Apollos, a native of Alexandria, came to Ephesus. He was a learned man, with a thorough knowledge of the Scriptures. He had been instructed in the way of the Lord, and he spoke with great fervor and taught about Jesus accurately. (Acts 18:24-25)

Apollos was a Christian, yet in Acts he is called a Jew. More than once

Paul spoke of himself as a Jew. "I am a Jew, from Tarsus in Cilicia" (Acts 21:39). In both cases Paul is referring to his and Apollos' background as ethnic Jews.

Why then, in 1 Corinthians 9, would he say that he became "like a Jew"? It is obvious he was not speaking about becoming a Jew or taking on the identity of a Jew. He must have been referring to his behavior toward Jews.

Did Paul continue to practice Jewish law after his conversion? Certainly not. Such a conclusion would be a gross generalization. He clearly states in our passage, "I myself am not under the law," and yet he also says, "I am not free from God's law." Is Paul contradicting himself?

In very specific situations, Paul felt it was more expedient to comply with particular Jewish practices to avoid unnecessary confrontations with the Jews. Looking at all the references to such practices, we see they generally pertain to circumcision. Circumcision was a God-ordained practice deeply rooted in Jewish history and theology. There was nothing sinful about it.

The Church was still not sure what to do about circumcision. Paul and Barnabas were sent to Jerusalem to consult with the Apostles, who affirmed their decision not to burden the Greeks with Jewish regulations (Acts 15). Interestingly, Paul returns from Jerusalem with the message that Greeks did not need to be circumcised, yet he went ahead and circumcised Timothy. Paul "circumcised him because of the Jews who lived in that area, for they all knew that his father was a Greek" (Acts 16:3). While Paul was on his way to announce that Greeks did not need to be circumcised, he made an exception in Timothy's case, not because of the Jews in general, but because of the Jews in that particular area. This is because those Jews did not know Paul and his teachings. The decision of the Jerusalem church had not yet been made public. Paul's action was to avoid being a stumbling block to the Jews in the area who knew that Timothy had a Greek father, and would likely reject him altogether if he were not circumcised.

Adhering to permissible Jewish practices was the exception, not the norm. Paul's teaching is clear throughout his epistles: he does not want new believers, whether Jews or Greeks, to return to submission to the law. In fact he calls such submission a curse:

> For all who rely on the works of the Law are under a curse, for it is written: "Cursed is everyone who does not continue to do everything written in the Book of the Law.". . . So the law was our guardian until Christ came that we might be justified by faith. Now that this faith has come, we are no longer under a guardian. (Gal 3:10, 24-25)

But if you are led by the Spirit, you are not under the law. (Gal 5:18)

"To those under the law"

To whom is Paul referring by this phrase? Naturally he is speaking about the Jews who are under the law, as he himself was before meeting Christ. So why is he repeating himself here? Certainly it was not a mistake. Paul was intentional about distinguishing between Jewish ethnic identity ("to the Jews I became . . . ") and Jewish religious practices ("to those under the law").[3] This shows that Paul's intent for this discussion has to do with adherence to religious law, not ethnicity or culture, Jewish or Greek.

Becoming like a Jew and behaving as though he was under the law should not be misconstrued to mean that he had shifted allegiances according to the context or changed his religious status or identity. As Stern says, Paul merely "put himself in their position . . . He entered into their needs and aspirations, their strengths and weaknesses . . . he tried to understand **where they were coming from**. In addition he made a point of doing nothing to offend them"[4] unnecessarily.

"To those not having the law"

Who are those not having the law? Many have interpreted this as a reference to the Greeks. Paul was quite capable of using the phrase *Greek to the Greeks*, but he did not. Paul was dealing with the matter of the law, not about ethnic identity. He wanted to help the believers face the difficult decision of whether or not to eat meat sacrificed to idols. He was not advocating the adoption of a Greek identity, but sensitivity concerning Jewish law. That is exactly why he phrased it in terms of the Law, not in terms of ethnic allegiance.

Paul was willing to practice some aspects of the law to avoid being a stumbling block to the Jews; however, in dealing with those who do not have the Law, he does not find it necessary to go out of his way to observe the Law. While he found it necessary to circumcise Timothy (Acts 16), Paul intentionally did not circumcise Titus (Gal 2:3). He did not try to be like a Jew to the Jews in this case. The difference between those two stories is significant. In the case of Timothy, the Jews of that area had not yet heard the Gospel. Paul was careful not to create an unnecessary offense. But the Jews in the Titus story were teachers who were advocating circumcision as a requirement. MacDonald observes: "Realizing that this was a frontal attack on the Gospel of the grace of God, Paul stoutly refused to have Titus circumcised."[5]

Peter and the law

Again, looking at the broader context, we need to balance the "like a Jew to the Jews" passage in light of Paul's comments in Galatians:

---

[3] William MacDonald (1989). *Believer's Bible Commentary* (1777). Nashville, TN: Thomas Nelson.
[4] David Stern (1992). *Jewish New Testament Commentary* (462-3). Jewish New Testament Publications.
[5] MacDonald, *Believer's Bible* 1777.

> When Cephas came to Antioch, I opposed him to his face, because he stood condemned. For before certain men came from James, he used to eat with the Gentiles. But when they arrived, he began to draw back and separate himself from the Gentiles because he was afraid of those who belonged to the circumcision group. The other Jews joined him in his hypocrisy, so that by their hypocrisy even Barnabas was led astray. (Gal 2:11-13)

This is a challenging passage. **Paul called Peter's accommodation hypocrisy**. What was wrong? If Paul promoted the idea of being a Jew to the Jews, why was he disturbed by Peter's adherence to the practices of the Jews? Eating with uncircumcised men would have clearly violated Jewish religious law. Why was it wrong for Peter to be sensitive to "the circumcision group"? Was he not being a Jew to the Jews and Greek to the Greeks? This passage demonstrates what Paul **did not** mean in 1 Corinthians 9:19-23. He certainly did not mean to be entirely Greek or entirely Jew.

The circumcision group promoted full adherence to the law. They were Christian Jews who had not broken away from their Jewish practices. Peter was being hypocritical, compromising his convictions to please the wrong crowd. We cannot conclude that Paul, in 1 Corinthians 9, did what he emphatically said he would not do in Galatians 2, unless we want to call Paul a hypocrite. He did circumcise Timothy, but not Titus. Why? Timothy, like Paul, was half Jewish, so Paul "circumcised him because of the Jews who lived in that area, for they all knew that his father was a Greek" (Acts 16:3). Paul chose to remove the potential stumbling block that would cause unnecessary controversy among the local Jews. Circumcising Timothy was not a problem because "in Christ Jesus neither circumcision nor uncircumcision has any value. The only thing that counts is faith expressing itself through love" (Gal 5:6). Paul is saying that with or without it, there is no difference. Elsewhere Paul asserts: "Circumcision is nothing and uncircumcision is nothing. Keeping God's commands is what counts" (1 Cor 7:19).

"To the weak I became weak"

What does Paul mean by *weak*? It helps to go back to 1 Corinthians 8. Paul uses the word five times, and in each case refers to new converts who have freshly left idol worship, but have not fully broken away with pagan practices. Paul makes himself weak in the sense that he refrains from eating meat for their sake, even though he himself has no problem eating such meat.

It is clear from chapter 8 that to "become weak" means Paul does not insist on his freedom to conform to the culture in which he ministers. He identifies with the mindset of the weak, as he does with the Greeks and the Jews and acts accordingly. Weak converts cannot handle such freedom while still vulnerable and emotionally tied to the past. Paul is very careful to stay away from the former cultural-religious practices of the weak in their presence. Likewise, it is clear from Galatians 2 that becoming "like a Jew" certainly does not mean conforming to Jewish law and practice. Therefore, it is incorrect to conclude that becoming *like a Muslim to the Muslim* means indulging in Islamic practices.

"All things to all men"

Paul writes, "I have become all things to all men" (1 Cor 9:22). These words have been misquoted and abused to a shocking degree. Did Paul mean literally that he became all things to all men? Would Paul be a prostitute to prostitutes, a Hindu to the Hindus, sorcerer to the sorcerers, or an idolater to idolaters? Absolutely not.

Paul was very specific in this passage. What he wrote must not be interpreted beyond the scope of the context of the passage. "All things to all men" is a generalization that shows Paul's heart: he is willing to deny himself and do anything for the sake of the Gospel. These words must not be taken as though Paul believes the end justifies the means. Paul adds an important qualifier when he writes, "Though I am not free from God's law but am under Christ's law." This means there are limitations to what he would do: he would do anything for Christ as long as it does not violate Christ's law. This statement excludes any act that does not honor God, such as becoming a stumbling block to the weak. This is more about a spirit of humility that desires to win the lost, rather than the literal sense of becoming all things to all men.

3) Biographical context

To fully understand 1 Corinthians 9:19-23, it is necessary to compare Paul's teachings with his lifestyle, which is recorded for us in Acts and in his epistles. Acts provides the background story and the geographical context of the epistles. These books are so intertwined, it is possible to chronologically insert many of the epistles into Acts with a significant level of accuracy.

There are four principles we can learn from Paul's lifestyle that bring clarity to the passage.

a) Paul's identity was clear to all

This was true both before and after he encountered Christ on the road to Damascus. Before his conversion he was an ethnic Jew, "circumcised the eighth day, of the people of Israel, of the tribe of Benjamin, a Hebrew of Hebrews; in regard to the law, a Pharisee" (Phil 3:5).

Paul's conversion changed his primary identity from a Jew to a Christian (*Christianos*). Every one of his thirteen epistles begins with the affirmation, "Paul . . . an apostle (and/or servant or prisoner) of Christ Jesus." He further declares, "For I resolved to know nothing while I was with you except Jesus Christ and him crucified" (1 Cor 2:2), "I am not ashamed of the Gospel" (Rom 1:16), and "I consider everything a loss compared to the surpassing worth of knowing Christ Jesus my Lord, for whose sake I have lost all things. I consider them garbage, that I may gain Christ" (Phil 3:8).

We do not find Paul hiding his identity or pretending to be someone he is not. He did not assume the identity of his audience in such a way as to confuse or deceive them. He completely and unquestionably associated himself with Christ and his body, the Church. This is part of his calling:

> But the Lord said to Ananias, "Go! This man is my chosen instrument to proclaim my name before the Gentiles and their kings and before the people of Israel. I will show him how much he must suffer for my name." (Acts 9:15-16)

The *name* is used extensively in the New Testament referring to Jesus. It is mentioned forty-one times in Acts and the epistles. Ethnic Jews knew full well that Paul was no longer an insider. He had become a member of "the Way," which he had originally set out to persecute and destroy. The pagan Greeks never thought he was one of them, a Greek insider. Greeks did not hear his message and conclude: "He is one of us. He speaks like one of our philosophers." On the contrary, they viewed him as one who "seems to be advocating foreign gods" (Acts 17:18). They told Paul to his face: "You are bringing some strange ideas to our ears, and we would like to know what they mean" (Acts 17:20).

Paul's message was not familiar to either the Jews or the Greeks. It was a different message that left some in his audience confused about what he was advocating, but not confused about his identity. When they finally understood what he was advocating, many Jews and Greeks opposed him vehemently.

b) Paul preached the same message to Jews and Greeks alike

He did not modify his core message to accommodate the needs or wants of his audience. One powerful piece of evidence that demonstrates his uncompromising position is that, "Jews demand miraculous signs and Greeks look for wisdom, but we preach Christ crucified: a stumbling block to Jews and foolishness to Gentiles" (1 Cor 1:22-3).

It is amazing that Paul knew his message was a stumbling block to the Jews; yet he did not water it down to accommodate them. In the same way, he knew the Greeks considered his message foolish because they exalted reason, wisdom, and knowledge. Yet Paul preached "the Gospel—not with wisdom and eloquence, lest the cross of Christ be emptied of its power" (1 Cor 1:17). He did not create a culturally sensitive message to avoid a negative reaction by his hearers. He understood his audience very well. He knew what they wanted to hear, but deliberately did not scratch them where they itched.[6] Why did Paul not try to appease his audience by preaching a culturally sensitive message that would be more likely well received? Let Paul give the answer:

> But to those whom God has called, both Jews and Greeks, Christ the power of God and the wisdom of God. For the foolishness of God is wiser than man's wisdom, and the weakness of God is stronger than human strength. (1 Cor 1:24-5)

For Paul, the Gospel was an absolute that does not change with any context. He knew that accommodating his audience would not improve his results. His missiology divided his audience into two groups: those who are perishing, and those who are being saved. "For the message of the cross is foolishness to those who are perishing, but to us who are being saved it is the power of God" (1 Cor 1:18).

Those called by God will recognize the power of God in the message of the cross. Those who are perishing will find the cross to be a stumbling block or foolishness, no matter how well it is presented. Who could say that Paul did not have the knowledge and the eloquence that would draw people to his message? Yet he emphatically wrote, "When I came to you, I did not come with eloquence and human wisdom as I proclaimed to you the testimony about God" (1 Cor 2:1). He knew that the real power is in the Gospel message, not in the method.

For many years it has been my experience that those who are closed to the Gospel will not be persuaded by any argument or clever technique. On the other hand, those who are open tend to seek Christ with a thirsty heart and can be ushered into the kingdom through a simple witness. Paul understood that it is all about God, not about us. "I planted the seed, Apollos watered it, but God has been making it grow" (1 Cor 3:6).

c) Paul's boldness often caused him persecution

One rationale behind IM is the avoidance of persecution. Conversion is discouraged because of the negative repercussions it could cause on family and social relationships. Paul did not seem to be overly concerned about his safety or the safety of people he preached to. His normative style was not irenic or conciliatory. His message was offensive to the general population. Although many believed, many opposed him, including leaders of the community who brought him to court numerous times. Behind his boldness was a vision of Jesus encouraging him and telling him, "Do not be afraid; keep on speaking, do not be silent" (Acts 18:9).

Paul's attitude toward his imprisonment and suffering is expressed this way: "Now I want you to know, brothers, that what has happened to me

---

[6] 2 Timothy 4:3

has really served to advance the Gospel" (Phil 1:12 ESV). He was not deterred by anything:

> Pray also for me, that whenever I speak, words may be given me so that I will fearlessly make known the mystery of the Gospel, for which I am an ambassador in chains. Pray that I may declare it fearlessly, as I should. (Eph 6:19-20)

d) Paul's missiology was clearly transformational

The epistles are filled with contrasts between the old and the new, reminding us of our new position in Christ. Anyone in Christ is a "new creation; the old is gone, the new has come" (2 Cor 5:17). Therefore, we must "put on the new self, created to be like God in true righteousness and holiness" (Eph 4:24; cf. 2 Cor 3:18). This transformation is expected of all cultures in order to unify all who experience new life in Christ:

> You have taken off your old self with its practices and have put on the new self, which is being renewed in knowledge in the image of its Creator. Here there is no Greek or Jew, circumcised or uncircumcised, barbarian, Scythian, slave or free, but Christ is all, and is in all. (Col 3:9-11)

The cultural issue

Paul understood pagan culture. Corinth was one of the most advanced cities in ancient Greece. The predominant culture was pagan, though there was a small community composed of exiled Jews from Rome (Acts 18:2). Paul alluded to the cultural aspect of idolatry: "Some people are still so accustomed to idols that when they eat such food they think of it as having been sacrificed to an idol, and since their conscience is weak, it is defiled" (1 Cor 8:7). The word *accustomed* indicates the sacrifice became a standard cultural practice.

Those who exercised their freedom to eat meat sacrificed to idols caused those who had a weak conscience to stumble. The strong held that idols were nothing and therefore the sacrifice made no difference to those with solid faith. Paul admonished the strong believers to be sensitive to those with a weak conscience, arguing they had not completely broken away from the associations of their old religious practices. If a mature Christian begins to exercise freedom in Christ, thinking nothing of meat sacrificed to idols (we know that an idol is nothing)[7], the weak brother could easily stumble. To the weak the idol has spiritual power. The association of meat with idol worship remains with them endangering the new Christian's walk.

Does this sound like contextualization? Certainly not. In fact, this is evidence that Paul's sensitivity toward the weak is not an attempt to

---

[7] 1 Cor 8:4

contextualize but rather to decontextualize. He was not asking the weak to join the strong in the practice of eating meat, but the opposite. He asks the strong to refrain; his aim is to give new and vulnerable converts a chance to heal from associating meat with idols. That means he is promoting a healthy distance from former cultural and religious practices so that the weak's allegiances can **shift** completely to Christ. This is contrary to the idea that cultural-religious allegiances should **remain** intact as Christ is introduced into the context.

The theological issue

Though there is a cultural element to this problem, the undergirding issue is theological. It has to do with the law of Moses. Paul is pitting legalism against freedom in Christ. He is defending his right to exercise his freedom in Christ, yet he stresses that our freedom needs to be restrained by our love for those who may stumble by the exercise of our freedom. He appeals to love rather than knowledge (1 Cor 8:1-3), sensitivity rather than freedom: "Be careful, however, that the exercise of your rights does not become a stumbling block to the weak" (1 Cor 8:9). Käsemann comments that, "Paul is illustrating . . . the principle that love sets bounds to Christian freedom."[8]

What is Paul really concerned about in Chapter 8? Is he concerned about protecting cultural practices? Absolutely not. He wanted to do everything in his power to help new converts transition from their old thinking about idols to a new way of thinking, and a new lifestyle. Meat was closely associated with idol worship. If necessary, Paul was willing to give up meat the rest of his life for their sake. "Therefore, if what I eat causes my brother to fall into sin, I will never eat meat again, so that I will not cause him to fall" (1 Cor 8:13).

Fast-forward to Chapter ten where Paul picks up the same argument again. This time he makes it even clearer that these chapters are not about meat, but about the spiritual significance of eating meat sacrificed to idols:

> Do I mean then that food sacrificed to an idol is anything, or that an idol is anything? No, but the sacrifices of pagans are offered to demons, not to God, and I do not want you to be participants with demons. (1 Cor 10:19-20)

It is clear that the problem is spiritual.

Who can question the real intent of Paul's teaching in these three chapters? To the knowledgeable, idols are nothing, but to pagans, idols are deities Paul attributes to the demonic. One is free to eat meat sacrificed to idols if one does not assign it spiritual value. Is there, however, a guarantee

---

[8] Ernst Käsemann, (1969). *NT Questions of Today* (217-8) (W. J. Montague trans.). Minneapolis, MN: Fortress.

new believers will be clear about what they are doing when they eat meat sacrificed to idols? Paul put his foot down and warned: "You cannot drink the cup of the Lord and the cup of demons too; you cannot have a part in both the Lord's table and the table of demons" (1 Cor 10:21). Here we find a core biblical teaching on cultural practices that have a spiritual or religious significance: we cannot separate the secular from the sacred, the cultural from the spiritual, without regard for brothers and sisters of weaker conscience.

Paul concludes his discourse with these words: "'I have the right to do anything,'" you say—but not everything is beneficial. 'I have the right to do anything'—but not everything is constructive" (1 Cor 10:23).

Our freedom must be exercised responsibly toward others who are not yet completely free from their past. Certainly Paul is not promoting cultural sensitivity, but **spiritual sensitivity**. Paul's inspired teaching prohibits practicing things one may have the freedom to practice for the sake of others, who may be damaged by the exercise of our freedom.

How does this understanding apply to Muslim ministry?

If Greeks coming to Christ struggled with meat sacrificed to idols because it reminded them of the old life, what are some practices Muslims associate with their old ways that could cause them to stumble? I am amazed at those who are so insensitive to the fragile new life of converts from Islam that they practice the very things that Paul warned us against. If Paul's message regarding eating meat is clear, why is it not clear that we must keep away from other practices that could cause a new convert to stumble? These include reading the Qur'an with Muslims or new converts from Islam, attending the mosque, using Islamic terminology and calligraphy, prostrating to pray, and displaying pictures of mosques, Mecca or other Islamic symbols. All these can bring negative memories and temptations for a new convert who is trying to break away with his past.

Some missionaries feel they are free to go to the mosque, read and recite the Qur'an, following what they call "biblically permissible Islamic cultural forms."[9] It is not uncommon for some missionaries to even prepare *iftar* meals (breaking the fast) for their Muslim friends or go to their homes to eat it with them. Paul would plead: Do not practice those things. Do not push them in the face of a weak convert. Your knowledge that these practices do not matter to you personally must not to cause your weak brother to stumble (1 Cor 8:11). You did not grow up with these strong associations. You have no idea of the demonic strongholds associated with these practices.

Though many Christians from Muslim backgrounds object to such practices, it is sad that some missionaries insist on continuing to practice

---

[9] John Travis, "The C1 to C6 Spectrum: A Practical Tool for Defining Six Types of 'Christ-Centered Communities' ('C') Found in the Muslim Context" *EMQ* 34(4): 407-408.

them. I have seen converts so hurt and angry, they refused to believe these missionaries were genuine Christians. Others have been pressured by their missionary leaders to return to Islamic practices, thus harming their fragile hearts and minds.

It is all about the glory of God

Paul's primary concern was the glory of God. He did not care what people thought about him, how they felt toward his message or how they received his message: "Am I now trying to win the approval of human beings, or of God? Or am I trying to please people? If I were still trying to please people, I would not be a servant of Christ" (Gal 1:10). Paul's first and foremost concern was the glory of God. He concluded the discourse of 1 Corinthians 8, 9 and 10 with this: "So whether you eat or drink or whatever you do, do it all for the glory of God" (1 Cor 10:31).

Paul stresses that what we do is all about God, not about the culture or anything else. "Do not cause anyone to stumble, whether Jews, Greeks or the Church of God" (1 Cor 10:32). Paul adds to our understanding that our mission is about God:

> We have renounced secret and shameful ways; we do not use deception, nor do we distort the word of God. On the contrary, by setting forth the truth plainly we commend ourselves to every man's conscience in the sight of God. (2 Cor 4:2)

We must not compromise the message. We must allow the Gospel itself to be a stumbling block to Jews and foolishness to Gentiles, but we ourselves must not be the stumbling block or appear foolish for foolishness' sake. It is our responsibility to preach the Gospel clearly while being careful not to cause anyone to stumble by being insensitive to his weaknesses.

Conclusion

The main purpose of Paul's three-chapter discourse in his first epistle to the Corinthians was to warn against causing the weaker brother to stumble. He centers the issue around eating meat sacrificed to idols, instructing the Church in order to help resolve the confusion caused by this conflict. Those of the circumcision group were legalists. They did not want the new Greek believers to eat meat sacrificed to idols because it was opposed to the law of God. The other faction was grace oriented. They believed Christ frees believers from legalism. They contended, "an idol is nothing" (1 Cor 8:4) and therefore, in itself, has no spiritual significance. Paul argues the problem is not with the meat itself or the idol, rather with the spiritual significance of such a practice to the conscience of the weaker believers.

The law dictates not to eat meat sacrificed to idols. Grace gives us the freedom to eat it in good conscience because idols are nothing. So if you eat meat with a brother who does not know the law and is not expecting you to keep it, you may eat that meat. If a Greek brother tells you this meat was sacrificed to idols, then refrain (1 Cor 10:28).

Paul established the argument not to exercise one's freedom when it may cause a weak brother to stumble. He argues believers have freedom; believers have the right to practice certain things, yet for the sake of others, these things are not practiced. He emphatically says: "But I have not used any of these rights" (1 Cor 9:15). Consequently, if we apply this principle to Islamic religious practices, we will refrain from participation with Muslims. The text does not permit us to exercise this freedom for the sake of our weak brothers, who have converted from Islam and are not yet completely freed from their past.

The lesson we take away from this is that we must put ourselves in the shoes of our audience, trying to understand their mentality, their mindset, and how they see things. This will give us the sensitivity to discern the appropriate behavior that enhances rather than hinders the message of the Gospel of grace we want to preach. The purpose is to advance the Gospel, not hinder it; to bring people to a saving knowledge of Christ. This must be done with humility, without violating the integrity of the message or the consciences of those we are reaching.

2.3 The Confusion of Kingdom Circles: a Clarification[1]

John Span

John Span is an ordained missionary with the Christian Reformed Church, working in West Africa, among an unreached people. John is a frequent contributing author to Saint Francis Magazine. He has a MCS from Regent College, Vancouver. He is a great fan of a TV show called *Myth Busters* in which systematic research methods are used to examine what some people think are truths. He approaches missiology is the same manner: careful research leading to conclusions that are not always the ones for which we hoped.

What is the kingdom?

When we speak of the kingdom of God we speak of what might be called the triumph of the Eternal King, and what might be called the area of his rule called his *turf*. These two concepts are found in both the Hebrew Bible by the term by *malkūt* and in the Greek, whether Septuagint or the Greek Testament, *basileia*.

When we think of *turf* or the area, which falls under the rulership of the King, we think of a text like 2 Chronicles 20:30: "And the kingdom (*malkūt*) of Jehoshaphat was at peace, for his God had given him rest on every side" (cf. Esth 3:6; Jer 10:7; Dan 9:1; 11:9).

When we think of the area of dominion or the right to rule, which we have dubbed *triumph*, we think of the Psalms: "They tell of the glory of your kingdom *(malkūt)*, and speak of your might...Your kingdom is an everlasting kingdom, and your dominion endures through all generations" (Ps 145:11, 13). "The LORD has established his throne in heaven, and his kingdom (*malkūt*) rules over all" (Ps 103:19).

The Lord's Prayer nicely combines the two concepts when we pray, "your kingdom come" (Mt 6:10). We pray that God's rule would be manifest in more and more places on the earth, and also that the area of sovereignty, even in his people's hearts, would grow greater and greater. Yet, the reality is that there is a *now* and *not yet* aspect to the kingdom; more on that later.

Three aspects of the kingdom

In order to do justice to the kingdom, we must have a clear biblical

---

[1] This chapter is a condensed and modified version of two papers: "The Critical Kingdom Question: Can One Be Identified with the Kingdom of God and with Islam at the Same Time? (Part 1 of 2) *SFM* 6(2): 296-326 and "Missiological Musings: Putting Last Things First" (Part 2 of 2 of the Critical Kingdom Questions) *SFM* 6(4): 612-629.

definition. One might suggest that there are two kingdom subsets working under the broadest category of the eternal kingdom of God. The subsets that we will define include the mediatorial kingdom of Christ, the kingdom of darkness, and the consummated kingdom. It could be argued the latter is not a subset of the eternal kingdom of God, but I argue it has present implications and is not only for the future.

In order to clarify the interrelationships between the different aspects of the kingdom we will use Palmer Robertson's helpful diagram, which he originally designed to help explain the inter-relationships between the Church and culture with "kingdom involvement."[2] It may not be a perfect model—it has some arbitrary separations—but it is an adequate platform to offer nuanced explanations and implications for IM.

A. The eternal kingdom of God

The eternal kingdom of God encompasses the broadest category and covers God's dominion as rightful King of the Universe throughout time and space (Figure 1). The prophet Zechariah states, "The LORD will be king over all the earth" (14:9). There is nothing, not even the kingdom of darkness that is outside of its control.

Figure 1. The eternal kingdom of God.

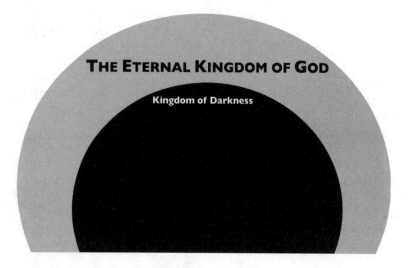

B. The Mediatorial Kingdom of Christ

As Christ was given the task to be the *go-between* for sinful humans and a holy God, Scripture tells us that he has been given the right to rule as the

---

[2] Palmer Robertson, "Toward a Reformational View of Total Christian Involvement," parts 1 and 2, see http://www.ouruf.org/d/cvt_involvement1.pdf (accessed 9/12/10); http://www.ouruf.org/d/cvt_involvement2.pdf.

perfect representative of God on earth—a job that Adam was assigned to do—but miserably failed. In this role Christ exercises the rulership he displayed in his earthly life by his power over nature, over demonic forces, and ultimately over death (Figure 2).

Figure 2. The mediatorial kingdom of Christ.

The cross is front and center in this kingdom and the Church also occupies a conspicuous position (Figure 3); however, in the kingdom circles of IM (Figure 5), the absence of the Church is curious factor.

Furthermore, this kingdom is one of light penetrating the darkness, reaching into areas like education, politics and mission. It is a kingdom that is unstoppable, as the image found in the book of Daniel, which is likened to a stone that demolishes all other kingdoms. This gives us supreme confidence because we know where history is headed.

Figure 3. The Church in relation to the kingdom.

C. The kingdom of darkness

The devil is called the "ruler of the present age," the "ruler of the prince of the air" and the "ruler of this world." He controls the "sons of disobedience" and incites them towards rebellion against God's rightful rule. He uses the religions of this world to deceive people to think that they are somehow doing deeds that might impress the Holy God (Figure 4). As much as we might like to lighten the darkness of this kingdom, we cannot. Ephesians 5:8 goes so far as to describe those who are not in Christ, not as only being in the darkness, but actually contributing to it: "you were once darkness."

The title, "kingdom of darkness" demonstrates the biblical antithesis between Satan's kingdom and the kingdom of light. The postmodern mind detests antithesis; this will become most evident in the kingdom circles diagram that is used by some proponents of the IM.

It should be noted that one of the vectors of darkness extends right into the heart of the Church (Figure 4). This illustrates that if the kingdom of darkness cannot stop the Church by frontal opposition, it may try to subvert it from within.

Figure 4. The all-encompassing eternal kingdom of God.

D. The consummated kingdom

"The kingdom of the world has become the kingdom of our Lord and of his Messiah, and he will reign for ever and ever" (Rev 11:15). Those who are in Christ, in the kingdom of light, can enjoy its present benefits although there is more to come. The consummated kingdom can be diagramed like a cube: it resembles the holy of holies of the Old Testament and is described for us in Revelation 21 and 22. We see its purity, radiance, community, and its intimacy with God. This kingdom in its completeness is what the Church aspires to when Christ hands over his mediatorial kingdom to the Father, and from which it can draw its present power. Thus the Scriptures tell us of those who have tasted the *powers of the age to come*. This is also mentioned in Jesus' ministry. In the consummated kingdom there is no death, no hunger, and no tears. Each of these aspects of the kingdom evidenced in Jesus' ministry can be experienced today.

One final aspect of the consummated kingdom is the two classes of people mentioned in the *vice list* of Revelation 21:8. They are the cowardly and the unfaithful. It is chilling to think that the majority of commentators may be right in telling us that these describe Church members of Revelation 2 and 3. It also should cause us to reflect deeply on whether or not our missiological strategies are actually contributing to those two categories of people who will be found in the lake of fire.

Summary of the biblical view of the kingdom

Here is how we should understand the Kingdom:
- The eternal kingdom of God is all encompassing;
- The cross and the Church are central to the mediatorial kingdom

of Christ;
- The kingdom of darkness is real and very dark;
- The consummated kingdom informs the hopes and gives present power to those in Christ; and
- Religions of this world are located in the kingdom of darkness

Kingdom circles of the IM

For the purposes of this presentation I will employ the model that Jay Smith reported on in his comprehensive analysis of the January 2009 *Common Ground* meetings in Atlanta. He gives a rough sketch of the model that was presented there (Figure 5). The kingdom circle figure reveals several areas in which the IM veers off course.

Figure 5. Depiction of kingdom circles from the *Common Ground* consultation.

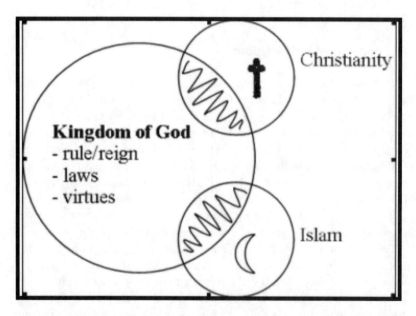

In 2005 Kim Gustafson, who also spoke at Atlanta 2009, gave a presentation at the International Society for Frontier Missiology meetings in Denver, suggesting the kingdom of God is a "more biblical and effective paradigm of mission than *Christianity*." He went on to offer the model of kingdom circles, according to the report on the meeting, "as a practical and productive tool for presenting the central message of Scripture—especially in light of the obstacles presented by traditional paradigms of conversion."[3]

In a nutshell, the idea of the kingdom of God is pitted against Christianity; the kingdom circles are shown as being more in line with the

---

[3] Mack Harling, "ISFM News: ISFM 2005 Shakes the Rockies" *IJFM* 22(4): 134.

central message of Scripture while the Church is not.

Making the kingdom oppose Christianity or the institution of the Church is not a new concept.[4] Another IM proponent, John Ridgway, defends IM's strong kingdom emphasis when he writes, "Spiritual wine must be poured into a spiritual wineskin: the kingdom of God, and not into physical wineskins (Christianity, Islam, Hinduism or any man-made religious system)."[5] Nabil Jabbour confirms Ridgway's thoughts: "The Muslim does not have to change his shape and identity in order to enter the kingdom of God. He can enter directly into the wide gate of the kingdom, rather than through our narrow gate of twenty centuries of Christian identity and tradition."[6]

Rebecca Lewis contributes to the same anti-institutional bent as Ridgway and Jabbour. She furthers the discussion by adding what seems to be the underlying rationale for the kingdom circles diagram: it is a justification for remaining within Islam. It is quite easy to attack the Church; we are an imperfect creation, and Lewis, like Jabbour before her, does just that. She states,

> The new spiritual identity of believing families in insider movements is in being followers of Jesus Christ and members of His global kingdom, not necessarily in being affiliated with or accepted by the institutional forms of Christianity that are associated with traditionally Christian cultures. They retain their temporal identity in their natural socio-religious community, while living transformed lives due to their faith in Christ.[7]

Lewis gives further qualification to her position with a kingdom circle diagram of her own. She describes the same components of the diagram and poses the following rhetorical question:

> Must people with a distinctly non-Christian (especially non-Western) identity *go through* the socio-religious systems of *Christianity* in order to become part of God's kingdom…? Or can they enter the kingdom of God through faith in the Lord Jesus Christ alone and gain a new

---

[4] This is the wrong battle. The real opposition is between the kingdom and Christendom.

[5] John Ridgway, "The Movement of the Gospel in New Testament Times With Special Reference to Insider Movements" ISFM Conference, Atlanta, Georgia (17-18 September 2006), as reported in the *IJFM* 24(2): 81 under the title "Insider Movements in the Gospels and Acts."

[6] Nabil Jabbour (2008). *The Crescent Through the Eyes of the Cross: Insights from an Arab Christian* (240-1). Colorado Springs, CO: NAVPress. [Jabbour's latest edition of *The Crescent* does not use the *wide* and *narrow* language. He told us, "the words 'narrow and wide' are mine and I wrote them in the early edition and have regretted having written them in 2008." – eds.]

[7] Rebecca Lewis, "Insider Movements: The Conversation Continues/Promoting Movements to Christ within Natural Communities" *IJFM* 24(2): 76.

spiritual identity while retaining their own community and socio/religious identity?[8]

Five observations about the kingdom circles of IM

What then are the things we learn from the kingdom circles? Here are my impressions.

- It rightly shows that the kingdom of God comprises both rule and reign. We have called those *turf* and *triumph*, but on this we are agreed: both aspects are important to the kingdom of God.
- As much as rightful prominence is given to the kingdom of God, the kingdom circles diagram fails to differentiate between the mediatorial kingdom of Christ and the eternal kingdom of God. It is not clear to which this illustration refers.
- The kingdom of darkness is curiously absent although one could, with tongue-in-cheek, suggest the intersection of the circles of both Islam and Christianity have a dark area.
- The cross is present in the diagram of Christianity, but the Church is absent.
- Both Islam and Christianity are given equal prominence in the diagram and both are drawn in a manner that suggests they are equally valid options for entering the kingdom of God.

Is there a problem?

The absence of the kingdom of darkness in this diagram might lead us to believe that one can somehow evolve from the area or kingdom of Islam or Christianity into the kingdom of God. The diagram fails to demonstrate the truth of Colossians 1:13: "For he has rescued us from the dominion of darkness and brought us into the kingdom of the Son he loves." The diagram seems to make Islam more benign than it is, whereas it ought to be pictured as a system of rebellion against God—as is every religion. As much as Jesus spent the majority of his time delineating entry requirements for the kingdom of God, the kingdom circles diagram assumes it. Additionally Jabbour completely misunderstands the difference between the wide and narrow entrance gates as Jesus described them.

It is inferred from the circles that apparently Islam is good enough it allow a seeker entrance into heaven; it is somehow compatible with the kingdom of God. This ignores the Scripture: "The LORD detests the sacrifice of the wicked, but the prayer of the upright pleases him" (Pr 15:8), as well as many other biblical descriptions of false religions. These kingdom circles easily lead to an overwhelming confusion of theological terminology. It is technically correct (see Figure 3) in that it makes every religion a part of the eternal kingdom of God, even if it is part of the kingdom of darkness.

---

[8] Rebecca Lewis, "Insider Movements: Honoring God/Given Identity and Community" *IJFM* 26(1): 18.

To suggest, however, that Islam has any part of the mediatorial kingdom of Christ is specious at best, pluralism at worst. The lack of clear terminology gives the kingdom circles diagram a slippery, pluralistic, relativistic, new age feel. One can read into it whatever one wants.

The model appears to communicate the appearance of common terminology between Christianity and Islam. On the contrary Christianity and Islam are nothing alike; we do not share a common philosophy or metanarrative. The kingdom circles present a thoroughly inadequate view of Islam.

The absence of the Church is notable. Whereas the Scriptures tell us this is Christ's chosen vehicle as the embassy of the kingdom, the diagram does not show it. Might there be an anti-ecclesiastical bias that is at work here? This was the conclusion of Basil Grafas in his thorough analysis of Ridgway's paper. He states, "In order to prove that the Gospel does not depend on physical structures and organization, and especially not religion, he [Ridgway] concentrates on kingdom as the fundamental paradigm for the believer in the world."[9] Grafas identifies the pervasive tendency of IM to pit the spiritual against physical. This dualism is highly problematic.

The placement of Islam and Christianity on equal footing is difficult. While it is true the Church comprises sinful human beings, something to which both IMers and Historicals agree, the former have no valid reason to diminish the Church and Christianity as if they were simply man-made. To call the Church "old wineskins" is to forget that Jesus said he would build those "old wineskins;" that he sacrificed his life for those "old wineskins;" that he commissioned those "old wineskins" to make disciples who would in turn, make more disciples who fellowship in those "old wineskins." What other institution is God planning to use to expand the kingdom? No, the equation of Christianity with Islam is equivocation.

The kingdom circles diagram, as explained by Lewis, seems to be less interested in the biblical qualifications for entering and remaining in the kingdom, but more interested in encouraging Muslims to keep their Islamic identity. Regardless of whether they convert or not, identity is the focus. Is it possible that behind the kingdom paradigm is Gustafsen's subtle promise this will deliver more and better results?

Further, the danger of the kingdom of darkness attempting to subvert the Church, and offering a false Gospel, all this is curiously absent in the kingdom circles model. Perhaps the absence of the kingdom of darkness is an indicator of subversion already happening?

Conclusion

Whereas the Palmer Robertson model shows an appreciation for the

---

[9] Basil Grafas, "Evaluation of scriptural Support for Insider Movements: Critique of John Ridgway's "The Movement of the Gospel in New Testament Times with Special Reference to Insider Movements" *SFM* 4(2): 5.

different aspects of the kingdom of God and the interrelationships between the eternal, the mediatorial and the consummated kingdoms, as well as that of the kingdom of darkness, the kingdom circles diagram actually engenders confusion by its lack of theological precision. Its broad strokes leaves it open to suggestion, which may be convenient to proponents of IM, as they can always reply to any critique, "That's not what we meant."

It behooves the body of Christ to use theological precision; no less than a medical journal would be expected to use anatomical precision. How much more important are things eternal?

Finally, one must suppose that some proponents of IM in their attempt to divest themselves of the barnacles of Christendom in order to positively reach out to Muslims, have jettisoned—intentionally or not—the areas of biblical antithesis, the Church and its history, a biblical view of other religions, and theological precision vis-à-vis the kingdom.

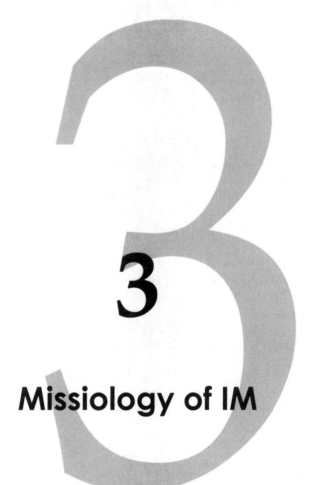

Missiology of IM

3.1 Moving On from the C1-C6 Spectrum

Roger Dixon

As a missionary in Asia for thirty-four years, mostly among Muslim peoples, Roger brings a wealth of experience and wisdom in order to understand the insider movements. Roger was present in Asia when the IM began; he is an eyewitness to its birth and development. He does not write from isolation, but from having lived through IM. Roger took his PhD from Biola University and now serves as consultant with Pioneers.

The first to present his case seems right,
till another comes forward and questions him. (Pr 18:1)

Introduction

New models of work among Muslims have been proliferating over the past twenty years. In general these approaches reflect sympathy for Muslim thought and lifestyle characteristic of the experiences of most workers among Muslims. But it seems there is a dramatic difference in the models: they shift the way missionaries have traditionally understood and presented the person and work of Jesus Christ as the Son of God.

This shift represents a sea change in mission theology. Due to reasons of *security* much of the propaganda disseminated by these practitioners of a new approach to Muslims is not discussed and analyzed by the general missionary community. This lack of exchange has caused leaders of some mission agencies to buy into this new philosophy without really understanding all that it entails. Younger members working among various faith traditions are being indoctrinated in these new methods before they are capable of conceptualizing incisive questions about their intrinsic value. It is vital that everyone hear all sides of the issue. This chapter is an effort to outline some of the critical issues I have observed with an appeal to bring all points of these issues to the worldwide Church for consideration in light of Scripture.

The critical issues

From my perspective, all the primary issues emerge from the lack of theological mooring and consequently the absence of a comprehensive biblical worldview. Illusory models are being developed; the C1-C6 Spectrum is a perfect example. From these models flow methods such as allowing converts to be Muslim and Christian at the same time. Some new Bible translations reconstruct the identity of Jesus in order to support these approaches. Finally, long time mission practices are redesigned as though they are avant-garde creations of this generation. I call these issues into question by revisiting some prominent appraisals of them. This is not to say that I oppose all the ministry of these practitioners. My field experience is not much different from theirs, though longer than most; however, I believe our theology and method differ in significant ways. While their motives are beyond my capacity to judge, their facility in biblical studies and wisdom in the implementation of certain models can be shown to be immature and faulty.

The C1-C6 Spectrum

In 1990 when the C1-C6 Spectrum made its appearance in the Sundanese Muslim situation of West Java, Indonesia, it was promoted as a contextual model even though it had few of the traits normally expected of a contextual model. Although it was obviously the creation of a Western educated thinker, a number of foreign workers among Muslims were fascinated by it and it was widely distributed. In 1998 John Travis (a pseudonym) published this spectrum as a "practical tool for defining six types of Christ-centered communities."[1] In his description, the word "contextualize" only appears under the description of C3 and C4 communities. But the impression is that the other examples in his model (C1, C2, C5, and C6) should also be considered as contextualized models. This impression is reinforced by noted missiologists such as Phil Parshall who consistently refer to it as a model of contextualization.[2]

It is difficult to understand Parshall's meaning here because a model of contextualization normally encompasses a vast array of cultural phenomena. Travis subsequently describes the C1-C6 Spectrum as a "simple chart...to graphically portray these different expressions of faith by MBBs."[3] Due to the confusion that has also emerged in other contexts, my intention is to critique the value of the C1-C6 Spectrum and its impact in mission thinking. While the C1-C6 Spectrum has some diagnostic use, it is important for all workers to see it in perspective. This is partly what I mean by my title: "Moving on from the C1-C6 Spectrum." It may have a limited use, but the understanding of true contextual models goes light years beyond it.

In Colossians 1:24-29 Paul describes the ministry of the Church as the proclamation of Christ while "warning everyone and teaching everyone with all wisdom, that we may present everyone mature in Christ" (v. 28). In passages such as this we comprehend the depth and breadth of our responsibility to envision a ministry of the Church that will affect the broad context of human society and result in mature believers. This covers the philosophy, traditions and structures of a culture. Some examples are the fields of education, politics, law and justice, labor, religion, leadership, economy, kinship relations, domestic activities, and other aspects of social

---

[1] John Travis, 'The C1 to C6 Spectrum" *EMQ* 34(4): 407-408.

[2] See both Phil Parshall, "Danger! New Directions in Contextualization" *EMQ* 34(4): 404, and "Camel Training Manual" *EMQ* 41(3): 385.

[3] John Travis, "Messianic Muslim Followers of Isa: A Closer Look at C5 Believers and Congregation" *IJFM* 17(1): 53.

organization. It takes years of experience, study and close cooperation with national workers to understand and participate in the development of that kind of contextual model.

My other meaning of "moving on" has to do with the way the C1-C6 Spectrum promotes changing traditional Christian missions. By fostering a model of faith that includes both Islamic and Christian worldviews in the same structure, we slide into a liminal category where a traditional understanding of Christian and Muslim is changed. In this special state it is possible that a person would belong to a *new faith tradition* not recognized by its larger society. Neither Christians nor Muslims accept the C5 category. C1-C6 proponents claim this is contextual, but if the society at large does not recognize it as contextual we should not claim it is. We must move on from this type of confusion.

What is the C1-C6 Spectrum?

John Travis authors the most recently published examples of the C1-C6 Spectrum.[4] The later version is more developed than the earlier and arranged in a different manner. By looking at the 1998 version we understand the context for the discussions of recent years. I include an abbreviated schematic showing only the titles of each type but not Travis' explanations (Chart 1). The reader will need to access Travis' full explanation to follow this in detail. However, even without the full Spectrum, the reader will understand my critique.

Chart 1. C1-C6 Spectrum
C1 – Traditional Church using Outsider[5] Language
C2 – Traditional Church using Insider[6] Language
C3 – Contextualized Christ-centered Communities using Insider Language and Religiously Neutral Insider Cultural Forms
C4 – Contextualized Christ-centered Communities using Insider Language and Biblically Permissible Cultural and Islamic Forms
C5 – Christ-centered Communities of *Messianic Muslims* who have accepted Jesus as Lord and Savior
C6 – Small Christ-centered communities of Secret/Underground believers

The illusion of the Spectrum

While Travis' use of the word *spectrum* fits the dictionary definition in a general sense, we normally demand that a spectrum reflect all the variations

---

[4] Travis, "The C1 to C6 Spectrum" 407-408; John and Anna Travis, "Contextualization Among Muslims, Hindus, and Buddhists: A Focus on Insider Movements" *MF* (September-October 2005) 12-15; John and Anna Travis (2005). "Appropriate Approaches in Muslim Contexts" (397-414). In Charles H. Kraft (Ed.). *Appropriate Christianity*. Pasadena, CA: William Carey Library.

[5] Travis says *insider* pertains to the local Muslim population.

[6] Travis says *outsider* pertains to the local non-Muslim population.

that there are in a continuum. When a prism creates a spectrum of colors it does not leave any out. Phil Parshall says that the C1-C6 Spectrum is not an accurate description of the communities. He writes that although the spectrum has some advantages, "a heavy fog has resulted, producing more confusion than clarity."[7] I submit that the spectrum is more accurately identified with the word template. The C1-C6 model has some preliminary use as an instrument to categorize ministries in several general terms such as cultural or religious characteristics. If one were to lay this template over a ministry, a small amount of information would be quickly ascertained, but that information would be severely limited and only useful as a stepping-stone to deeper investigation of the ministry. It is limited in its usefulness due to its one-dimensional nature. Travis admits that it is a "simple chart."[8] It is not only simple; it is also simplistic. While this is probably the attraction to many missiologists, it is also the reason I believe it is doing more harm than good among workers, both new and old. **It creates the illusion of offering insight to ministry while only giving a cursory view.** Inexperienced workers are deluded into thinking the spectrum reveals special insights. New workers are subject to being incorrectly indoctrinated by this tool.

The Spectrum is compartmentalized and divided in a linear manner. The original model was set up in a horizontal mode whereas this later version is vertical. The last publication of this model in *Appropriate Christianity* returns to the linear, horizontal model; however, the principle is the same. This gives away the Spectrum's Western orientation laid over non-Western phenomena—reason enough to use the template with caution. If you trust the template you may miss most of what you ought to see in the situation. The compartments do not reveal the holism of Asian and African societies; these separations do not exist. Where I worked in West Java belief systems operate in a way that shows flow back and forth between all the compartments. I have known numerous believers who fit in the so-called C3 compartment, yet were secret believers to their families and in their communities. They developed elaborate strategies to attend Christian activities without being discovered. This remains common in West Java.

The model depicts an increase of Islamic characteristics; that is, a progressive movement from less Islamic to more. Only Christian and Islamic characteristics are mentioned in the Spectrum; Travis ignores the influence of other belief systems pervading the Islamic and Christian contexts. This is a profound weakness; there are many kinds of practitioners of multiple belief systems influencing the formal religions of Christianity and Islam. Their forms and meanings are woven into the fabric of these religions so that there is no way to develop a contextual approach without understanding these influences. In West Java we have an elaborate shaman

---

[7] Phil Parshall, "Lifting the Fatwa" *EMQ* 40(3): 288.
[8] Travis, "Messianic" 53.

system completely integrated with formal Islamic religious practices. It influences Christianity to a minor degree.

Why we question the C1-C6 Spectrum and its audience

It is naïve for missiologists of this generation to believe they have greater insight than those highly educated, brilliant minds of the past that mastered indigenous theology and culture. While not many indigenous workers or their missionary counterparts will jettison established and proven theology and strategy in favor of a new fad, this new philosophy of ministry has had a significant impact in some quarters. This is not to say that C1-C6 missiologists are all wrong and others all right. Openness to new ideas is necessary because outreach to Muslims has not been successful in many places.

But new ideas require rigorous questioning and testing; many C1-C6 advocates do not appear to be willing to face that. In the past whenever a challenge has been made to their claims, they frequently declined to consult or have revised their position slightly to avoid disapproval. It seems information is shared on a *need to know* basis. They even withdraw into protective enclaves as constructed by Joshua Massey.[9] Massey compares criticism of his ideas and approach to that of the Judaizers whom Paul opposed in Galatia. He sets up a frightening scenario where anyone questioning new approaches to Muslims is condemning their freedom in Christ. These practitioners may not be aware of their immaturity, but others are. The apostles and disciples did not denounce those who criticized their methods. They only warned about criticism of motives, of judging the heart.

Every premise and strategy of Christian ministry must be based on biblical principles. These should be clear for the observer as well as for the practitioner, but C1-C6 practitioners have not made this information available. Evaluation is made nearly impossible. This kind of secrecy is not characteristic of the Church and should be avoided by missiologists. I have some material produced by those espousing radical Islamic contextualization that I am not at liberty to reveal in print. I honor that commitment and am discussing nothing in this chapter that has not already been published. However, I do not agree with concealing information from any relevant population. There are doubtless volumes of similar material to which I have no access. In any social science such as missiology, research must be available for testing. One has to be able to replicate results by following the scientific method described. Reports and surveys of the C1-C6 methods and related Islamic contextualization are frequently not available for testing.

Furthermore we do not know who many of these practitioners are,

---

[9] Joshua Massey, "God's Amazing Diversity in Drawing Muslims to Christ" *IJFM* 17(1): 10.

where they work, or where they trained. Like Joshua Massey and John Travis, they use pseudonyms and report from unknown places on the earth about anonymous people. They quote what they consider significant reports proving their theories, but the reports are only accessible to a few. An example is a major survey made of what is called "Islampur" people. It is noted in journals but not revealed.[10] We are at the mercy of the interpretation of a few who do not allow other missiologists to peruse the full text. I understand the need for security and it is not necessary to reveal the location where the survey was made, but we should have access to the developmental research sequence showing how and why the survey was constructed, its explicit purpose, questions asked, how answers were tabulated, and other aspects of social science research. It is not legitimate for C1-C6 advocates to castigate those who will not blindly accept their interpretation of facts.

The lack of a theological base

The most serious weakness of the C1-C6 Spectrum is a fatal one in my judgment: there is no theological base. When Shoki Coe first presented the idea of contextualization to a 1972 World Council of Churches consultation, he brought the Church new insight. Ray Wheeler wrote: "His approach was to allow the text (Scripture) to provide the vocabulary and the perspective needed to wrestle with a changing context."[11] This message is abbreviated as "faithful to the text, relevant to the context."[12] In contrast, the C1-C6 Spectrum begins with context, but has no foundation in the text, i.e., the Word of God.

In his article about the dangers of new directions in contextualization, Parshall advises that we need to bring the issues of the C1-C6 model "before our theologians, missiologists, and administrators...before we suddenly find that we have arrived at a point that is indisputably sub-Christian."[13] Travis echoes his agreement in the same *EMQ* issue: "I agree with Dr. Parshall; it is time for missiologists, theologians, and others . . . to seriously seek God's will over this C5 issue."[14] Unfortunately both of them reached this conclusion about ten years too late. The theological base should have been laid before the concept was released. The text should always precede the context, but there has been little progress. In 2005 Travis outlined ten premises that form the structure to understand the C5 phenomenon. The last of these premises relates to the contextual theology

---

[10] Dean S. Gilliland, "Context is Critical in 'Islampur' Case" *EMQ* 34(2): 415; cf. Joshua Massey, "Misunderstanding C5: His Ways Are Not Our Orthodoxy" *EMQ* 40(3): 297.
[11] Ray Wheeler, "The Legacy of Shoki Coe" *IB* 26(2): 9.
[12] Douglas J. Elwood (1980). "Asian Christian Theology in the Making: An Introduction." In Douglas J. Elwood (Ed.). *Asian Christian Theology: Emerging Themes* (28). Philadelphia: Westminster Press.
[13] Parshall, "Danger!" 405.
[14] Parshall, "Danger!" 411.

Travis believes must be developed. He sets up the conditions from which this contextual theology should evolve, though he has not yet developed a theology supporting the C1-C6 model.[15] He bases some of these premises on Christian theology while others are based on secular observations. My point here is simple: mission premises are futile without a comprehensive biblical base.

Attempting to create a text for a contextual concept (C5) without a text for the entire framework (C1-C6 Spectrum), these practitioners become more and more conflicted. In a recent article in *IFJM*, Kevin Higgins supports typical C1-C6 thinking. He employs C5-type exegesis of both the story of Naaman and Paul's Athenian argument.[16] Naaman's story supports his contention the Bible supports worship of God the Father while still in one's prior religion, whereas Naaman clearly said, "Behold, I know that there is no God in all the earth, but in Israel" (2 Kgs 5:15 NASB). When Naaman asks permission to escort the king to his worship (v. 18), he could not mean that he himself would participate in that heathen worship. If a convert in Indonesia were to ask if he could take an elderly parent to the mosque, I am sure all the evangelists would give assent; one needs to take care of one's parents. Even though this would necessitate showing respect for the mosque by wearing a hat and other appropriate clothes, taking off one's shoes, and other customary actions, it does not mean one would join in the prayers.

Old Testament history condemns the worship of foreign gods. The first commandment declares: "Thou shall have no other gods before me." Can it be faithful to Old Testament exegesis to propose the prophet would give Naaman permission to return to foreign worship? Higgins exacerbates this mistake by contending Paul's message on Mars Hill promotes the same notion by saying that in Paul's sermon, Jesus is unnamed: "this Person is unnamed in this sermon, though Paul may be assuming his hearers will connect the reference to Jesus."[17] The story's context (Acts 17:16-34) shows that Paul **was** preaching Jesus and the resurrection (v. 18). The name of Jesus is precisely what brought Paul to the explanation (vv. 22-31). Unfortunately many of the arguments constructed by C1-C6 proponents are not based on a careful reading of the text. In a decisive article, Scott Woods tactfully demolishes the interpretation of many of the Bible proof texts used by C1-C6 practitioners.[18] It does not seem necessary to repeat all his points here, though I do not see evidence C1-C6 advocates are interacting with his arguments and correcting their own eisegesis.

It seems to me the rationale of C1-C6 practitioners is inconsistent and unsupportable. For instance, Massey argues the C5 concept can only be

---

[15] Travis, "Contextualization" 13.
[16] Kevin Higgins, "The Key to Insider Movements: The "Devoted's" of Acts" *IJFM* 21(4): 158, 161.
[17] Higgins, "The Key" 161.
[18] Scott Woods, "A Biblical Look at C5 Muslim Evangelism" *EMQ* 39(2): 188-195.

understood if one has the right perspective.[19] D.A. Carson, Research Professor of New Testament at Trinity Evangelical Divinity School, writes about the Massey article:

> The language and argumentation are perpetually manipulative. On almost any disputed subject, one can find authorities behind every option. But genuine scholarship thinks through opposing views very carefully, and cites opposing arguments, and does not simply opt for what one wants. [Massey] is guilty in this respect again and again. For example, on Rom 9:5, there is a very substantial literature, and quite frankly most scholars, from every theological tradition, now support the view that this is an affirmation of the deity of Christ. Again, [Massey] quotes Dunn on Phil. 2, but on this passage N. T. Wright, whom [Massey] happily quotes in another connection, has written masterfully refuting Dunn.[20]

Among other things, Massey argues that Muslims do not necessarily need to understand and experience the Trinity because "not one biblical writer felt it necessary to extrapolate that God *is* Father, Son and Holy Spirit."[21] Although the doctrine is not promulgated (if that is what Massey means) there are scores of references in the New Testament to the unity of Jesus with the Father and with the Holy Spirit. This is an emphasis in John's Gospel. Massey also states, "the Qur'an itself is proving to be a powerful apologetic in the hands of Muslim believers for restoring Muslim confidence in the inerrancy of Scripture."[22] This occurs, he believes, when they understand what the Qur'an really says about the Bible. Massey seems to have a typically postmodernist viewpoint so that terms such as inerrancy of Scripture take on new meaning. His position seems to make the Qur'an the determining factor for Muslims in seeking the truth of God. These examples show that without a theological basis the C1-C6 practitioners are moving farther afield.

Moving on further from the C1-C6 Spectrum

While the C1-C6 Spectrum seeks to describe perceived categories of Christian ministry among Muslims, the C5 emphasis supports the reality of Muslim followers of Jesus who do not give up their Muslim identities. Travis wants us to believe the outside evangelists are not the ones determining the beliefs or actions of Muslim converts. He writes, "How they view Islam is not prescribed by us, but left to them as they are guided by the Word and the indwelling Spirit."[23] These kinds of statements are

---

[19] Massey, "God's Amazing Diversity" 5-14.
[20] D.A. Carson, personal letter (1 February 2005). Quoted with permission.
[21] Massey, "Misunderstanding" 298.
[22] Massey, "Misunderstanding" 302.
[23] Travis,"Messianic" 53.

misleading. Anyone who understands Islam knows that practitioners who are regarded as the experts in religion lead adherents. To insinuate that new believers are making their own theological conclusions without outside help reveals Travis' lack of experience in evangelism and pastoral ministry.

The unique language and rudimentary theology of C5 have been developed by non-Muslims. It is a far reach to assume that Muslims would describe themselves as *Messianic Muslims*. Their theology teaches that Jesus is the Messiah for the Jews, not for Muslims. The biblical concept of Messiah is not the same in Islam. I have not seen any articles about C1-C6 theology or method written by non-Westerners, but since so much of this material is anonymous, it is hard to tell.

Joshua Massey is much more creative than Travis in describing what so-called C5 groups are doing. He states, "C5 advocates encourage Muslim believers to view the Jesus act from their seat in the human auditorium."[24] Massey means the Muslim comes to know Jesus within his own religious framework, remaining a Muslim who follows Jesus. According to Massey, this means "C5 Muslim believers are, of course, rethinking and redefining Islam according to the authority of the Bible."[25] His proposition seems to be that a supernatural transformation of Islam will occur, allowing a place for the person and work of Jesus Christ, the Son of God.

As I understand the reasoning of these practitioners, the process of implementing C5 methodology will change the definition of both *Christian* and *Muslim*. C5 philosophy proposes the possibility that Scripture can be reconciled with Islamic teachings. Thus, Muslim believers will be both Christian in their core beliefs and Muslim in their basic tenets. This is an impossible proposition. It seeks to integrate two opposing worldviews, harmonizing conflicting theological bases. This defies all logic. The Christian evangelist errs by justifying a non-biblical worldview. I urge every missiologist to examine these C5 claims before buying into this immature conception of reality with its grandiose claims of success. The delusion of this approach has led some Western missionaries to pray the *shahada*, thus becoming Muslims. This is a tragedy. Where is the accountability?

One key to C5 theology and methodology

One critical key facilitating C5 is new Bible translations. In 1987 an alleged harmony of the Gospels was produced for Muslim readers. This book is a diglot with opposing pages printed in Arabic and English. It is a very important example of a C5 effort to retheologize the Son of God for the Muslim reader.[26] Some C5 Bible translators have felt the need to shade the meaning of certain Greek terms such as *Lord* and *Son of God* so those of other faiths will be more open to the claims of Christ.

---

[24] Massey, "Misunderstanding" 301.
[25] Massey, "Misunderstanding" 301.
[26] See Roger Dixon, "Identity Theft: Retheologizing the Son of God." *EMQ* 43(2): 220-6.

Perhaps this unusual and unexpected divide in Bible translation has come about because of the philosophy that spawned dynamic equivalency. Whatever the original intent of this translation model, it has been used as a vehicle allowing the insertion of the translator's interpretation into the translation. Translators can also manipulate the word-for-word correspondence model, but this is more difficult. The thought-for-thought translation (dynamic equivalency) allows the translator to nuance the text according to the culture.

It is customary for evangelists to use the biblical record selectively and to introduce theological truths at various stages in evangelism and Christian nurture, but there is no justification for changing God's Word. This removes the foundation upon which the Christian life is built. If God's record no longer exists as he revealed it, what is the framework of truth for a new believer?

The Scriptures, as recorded in the original languages, are the only source we have for a biblical worldview. When we integrate the message of the Bible with that of other religions, we lose the foundation of our worldview and move into syncretism. While we acknowledge that there is some truth in other religions, we also recognize the ways in which that truth has been integrated into a non-biblical worldview. Changing Bible translations to agree with the qur'anic worldview or the any other faith system moves us from our touchstone.

Redefining traditional methodology

The final issue may seem less critical than the previous, nevertheless it is important: C5 advocates often misrepresent mission history and methodology. This involves the camouflaging of traditional mission methodology, perhaps due to a lack of knowledge or an anxious plea for affirmation of their approaches. C5 practitioners seem to thrive on new missiological philosophies and avant-garde approaches. While the only new idea these practitioners propose is Massey's hopeless concept of unifying Christianity with Islam, there are many other ideas they present as original.

An example is the insider movements (IM). The Travises seek to link the C5 movement with IM.[27] The term is used in the title of his article and is the subject of this entire book; however, what is described as IM is really not any different from what has happened over and over throughout the history of Christian missions. Phil Parshall notes the example of Kiai Sadrach, a convert in Java in the 19th Century.[28] I presented Sadrach's case study in an article on the Javanese church in which I described that church's struggle to produce a contextualized Javanese Christianity.[29] Sadrach was one of the spiritual fathers of a movement that has brought millions of

---

[27] Travises, "Contextualization" 12-13.
[28] Parshall, "Lifting the Fatwa" 289.
[29] See Roger L. Dixon, "The Major Model of Muslim Ministry" *Missiology* 30(4): 443-454.

Muslims into the kingdom of God. It would be wise of us to first study what has actually happened before creating new buzzwords in missiology.

C5 advocates dubiously link their approaches with some of the giants of missiology. Travis speaks of Samuel Zwemer's model of respect for Muhammad, but doesn't mention Zwemer's transparent criticism of Islam.[30] The *Kitab Suci Injil* (Holy Gospel and so-called culturally appropriate Bible translation in Indonesia) is claimed to be in the tradition of W.G. Shellabear. What is not mentioned is Shellabear shared Zwemer's criticism of Islam. In his Malay translation he "eliminated words he regarded as foreign to Malay, such as the Arabic *fasik* and *Bait*."[31]

Another example is Massey's use of "Christ-centered" as opposed to "Church-centered."[32] He writes as though Christ-centered people are not the Church, rather some group outside the Church yet inside their own cultural traditions. Mixing vocabulary and skewing the meaning of words does not promote incisive thinking about critical issues. If one's theology allows the separation of believer and Church, one must clearly delineate this. The invisible church exists alongside institutional churches; Church-centered people by definition should also be Christ-centered.

Travis changed some of his original C1-C6 descriptions from Church to Christ-centered. These designations are not helpful. They give the impression one can bring souls to Christ without having them received into his Church. Such views result from the influence of parachurch organization theology; however, new mission workers are not going to be able to discern these nuances. This language creates confusion among new believers about their status in the worldwide fellowship of Christians.

Finally, the C5 proponents must stop using proof texts. There are simply no Bible texts that describe or support their methodology. Their use of 1 Corinthians 7:24 is a good example. Paul advises remaining in the condition in which one was called. C5 people interpret this to mean one can continue in a religious tradition where the Lordship of Jesus Christ as the Son of God is not recognized. It is not possible that the apostle who suffered all of his life for the Gospel could have meant that. If a C5 missionary really believed it could mean that, he himself could not participate in the non-Christian religious practices of other faith groups because he himself would then no longer be in the condition in which he was called.

Conclusion

In this chapter, I have analyzed briefly some of the ways the C5 methodology is viewed erroneously as a contextual model and the illusion it gives that a believer can experience the contradictory existence of being

---

[30] Travis, "Messianic" 56.
[31] Robert Hunt (1996). *William Shellabear: A Biography 1862-1848* (164). Kuala Lumpur: University of Malayu Press.
[32] Massey, "Misunderstanding" 300.

both a follower of Christ and active in the faith tradition of another religion. I discussed the lack of a theological base for the C1-C6 Spectrum and the lack of a biblical base for all C5 teaching. Bible translations have been promoted in order to create a theological base and biblical worldview more in line with Islamic teaching (or other religions). These new translations reinterpret the person and work of Jesus in various ways so that members of other religions do not need to assent to the full meaning of the person and work of Jesus. The Trinitarian theology of Jesus as Son of God and Lord of life is minimized so that it does not become a stumbling block to people of other faiths. Finally, I described the way new buzzwords are used to give one the impression that traditional mission approaches are, in fact, innovative models for our generation.

In closing, let me reaffirm that my critique does not imply a rejection of innovative approaches to other religions or a condemnation of those who try them. It is simply a call to prepare oneself theologically and culturally to understand what is happening in mission models. Let us bring them all to the Church. I do not believe the advocates of C1-C6 have done that. Let us move on from the C1-C6 Spectrum. May the Holy Spirit lead us to be established in him so that "we are to grow up in all aspects into him who is the head, even Christ" (Eph 4:15b NASB).

3.2 Pagan Religious Practices and Heretical Teaching: What Is to Be Our Attitude? Gleanings from the Old and New Testaments

David Talley

David graduated from Grace Seminary (MA, biblical counseling, MDiv and ThM, OT), and Trinity Evangelical Divinity School (PhD). He not only teaches, but pastors, and is involved in educational and short-term mission trips (the latter twice per year). As one involved in training missionaries going to the 10/40 window, his desire is to train up men and women who are rightly dividing the Word of God.

Introduction

The way in which God deals with his people throughout time has some distinctions. In the Old Testament, the Lord sought to create a **physical** *sacred space* in which his people were to dwell so that he could create a sanctified space in the tabernacle where the Lord's presence could dwell in their midst. Consequently, the land had to be cleansed for this to happen, and the people had to live separately from the nations. They were to be a *light* to the Gentiles as they lived in light of the Lord's commands and as a result would be recipients of the outpouring of his blessings (cf. Deut 26:16-19). As the nation was blessed over and above any surrounding nation, the nations of the world would be drawn to know their "god" (cf. the days of Solomon). This is the way I understand the thrust of "evangelism" in the Old Testament.

However, in the New Testament, the Lord is seeking to create a **spiritual** *sacred space* in the body of Christ, in whose individual members the presence of the Lord dwells, with the intent that this body is to be *salt* and *light* (Mt 5:13-16) as it lives in the midst of all the nations of the world. Hence, the commands to go *into* the uttermost part of the world and to preach the Gospel (Mt 28:18-20).

In this chapter, some important implications will be gleaned from both testaments, concerning God's perspective on teaching or practices that are considered outside of his revelation. This will be accomplished by drawing implications from the Old Testament teaching on the *ban*, which demonstrates God's attitude toward the pagan religions and religious practices of those who occupied the Promised Land before Israel occupied it. Then, further in the Old Testament, specifically in the book of Judges, we will draw implications from the account of what happens when pagan religions and religious practices are allowed to infiltrate the community of God's people. Finally, in the New Testament, we will draw implications from 2 John's teaching on how to deal with those who teach falsely, but still maintain that they are in the body of Christ. Each of these topics provides us with important considerations as we wrestle with missiological practices to reach our world, which is filled with pagan religions.

Part One - The teaching in the Old Testament concerning the ban: what is God's attitude toward pagan religions and religious practices?

The Old Testament practice of the ban may seem somewhat foreign to New Testament believers, but there are implications of this practice that are important for us as we consider the pagan religious practices that still abound in our world today. Therefore, it is important for us to draw out those implications and apply them to our contemporary situation of living as the people of God.

Definition of the ban

The *Theological Dictionary of the Old Testament* defines ban as to "consecrate something or someone as a permanent and definitive offering for the sanctuary; in war, consecrate a city and its inhabitants to destruction; carry out this destruction; totally annihilate a population in war; kill."[1] The point in war is to annihilate it all. This practice was found in other Ancient Near Eastern dynasties, so it was a common practice for these other nations.

Old Testament teaching concerning this practice

The legislation for the ban is first provided in Deuteronomy 7:1-11 (regulations for warfare when the nation is still out of the land) and Deuteronomy 20:10-18, especially verses 16-18 (regulations for warfare once the nation has occupied the land). In Deuteronomy 7:2, it states, "you must destroy them totally. Make no treaty with them, and show them no mercy." This command is directed toward the seven nations of Deuteronomy 7:1 (cf. Deut 20:17; Ex 23:23; 34:11), generically referred to as the Canaanites in that they are the people who inhabit the land of Canaan.

This legislation is clearly followed in the book of Joshua (6:17-19, 21; 8:1-29; 10:28, 30, 32-5, 37, 39-41; 11:8, 11-12, 20-3; Judg 1:17; cf. Deut 2-3, Sihon-Og). However, it is important to note two particular passages, Joshua 13:13 and 16:10, which hint at the fact that Israel is not complete in her obedience to the Lord's command. These *veiled* statements are developed in the book of Judges, which clearly demonstrates the consequences for not following the command of the Lord concerning the ban (See Part Two of this chapter).

---

[1] N. Lohfink, (1981). "Haram" (188). *Theological Dictionary of the Old Testament* (vol. v). G. Johannes Botterwerk, Helmer Ringgen, and Heinz-Josef Fabry (Eds.). Grand Rapids, MI: Eerdmans.

In studying this apparent atrocity of God's people being commanded to destroy all the people of the land, it is important to note that God is the One who is behind all of this warfare (cf. Josh 11:18-20). God is the ultimate Judge and Executor of judgment, but he is doing so through the instrumentality of Israel's warfare.

Old Testament teaching concerning the purpose

It is important not just to underscore the teaching of this practice, but also to highlight the reasons behind it. In order to accomplish this, it is necessary to back up and see the big picture of the broader story. Although there are probably other significant factors, at least the following can be set forth as a rationale for the practice.

First, it is a form of judgment directed toward the wickedness of the people who occupied the land. God has patiently endured their abominations, but now he chooses to act out of his holy wrath (cf. Gen 15:16; Lev 18:24-25, 27; Num 35:34). Genesis 15:16 is one of the foundational passages for the promise that Israel will occupy the land. The Lord's promise to Abraham is that in the "fourth generation" the nation will return to the land to occupy it as an inheritance. The reason provided in this passage is that the "sin of the Amorites has not yet reached its full measure" (NASB). The point is that God is not yet filled to the full with the sinfulness of these pagan people. Their sin must be judged because God is just, but God is still being merciful in the time of Abraham and even throughout the four generations after him. However, over time, his mercy (i.e., patiently waiting for them to turn from their sin) is continually despised through the multiplication of abominations and, as a result, his wrath will be enacted.

Leviticus 18:24-25 (NASB) provides the explanation for the destruction of the Canaanites:

> Do not defile yourselves by any of these things, for by all these the nations which I am casting out before you have become defiled. For the land has become defiled, therefore I have visited its punishment upon it, so the land has spewed out its inhabitants.

God uses Israel's taking over the land, which was promised to them, as a means of providing judgment to the abominable inhabitants, who have not responded to his mercy.[2]

Second, a major concern of Yahweh for his covenant people was that they would not be negatively impacted by the wicked practices of the pagan nations with regard to idolatry (cf. Deut 7:3-4; 20:16-18). In other words,

---

[2] It is important to note that Israel is warned that they too will be expelled from the land if they commit the same abominations (cf. Lev 18:26-30). Note the "but as for you." The Lord is making it clear that there is no room for compromise in following him. He must be honored above all and obeyed completely.

the Lord is creating a context where Israel would not become followers of these false gods like the Canaanites living in the land. The Lord was seeking to protect his people from the temptations that the gods of the land presented to them.[3] The nation had a natural tendency toward idolatry because of the polytheistic culture in which they lived. So the Lord's plan is to destroy, i.e., completely annihilate, the people and their gods. The logic of the passage is as follows: a) if the people remain, then b) the Israelites will intermarry with them; then c) the Canaanites will turn Israel's heart away from the Lord; then d) the Israelites will serve the false gods; and finally e) this will incur the Lord's wrath. We must note that this is the Lord's understanding and appraisal of the natural inclination of his people, even for all of humanity. Humanity naturally gravitates toward the idolatry of the culture if it is allowed to flourish. As a consequence, the Lord goes to the first step in the logic of the passage and destroys the people, their gods, and their ideology.[4] The point is that the purity of God's people is to be preserved and protected. Exposure to pagan systems can lead to the embracing of these systems, which can lead to the adoption of these systems and the subsequent rejection of Yahweh.

This same concept is found in the New Testament. Even though we live in the world and are to be salt and light to the world (cf. Mt 5:13ff), we are clearly commanded, "Do not love not the world, or anything in the world" (1 John 2:15). In reference to our new self where "Christ is all in all," we are to put to death or lay aside anything that is not consistent with the command to "set your hearts on things above" (Col 3:1). With regard to false teaching: "Preach the word; be prepared in season and out of season; correct, rebuke, and encouraged with great patience and careful instruction" (2 Tim 4:2). Even though some may desire to have their itching ears tickled, we are to stay the course with the inspired Word of God and proclaim him. Similarities abound in the new covenant. The consistency throughout is summarized in two points: one, the need for truth (light) to be embraced and perpetuated without compromise (darkness); and two, the danger, even tendency, for darkness to overtake light.

Third, the Lord was seeking to protect the holiness of his people. The nation was to be set apart, clearly identified as his people (cf. Deut 7:6; 20:18). God is holy or *other than* anything or anyone in this world. His people are also to be holy or other than the people of this world. His followers should be clearly marked as his followers. This marking is not

---

[3] The Ancient Near Eastern understanding of the pantheon of gods was very much a part of Israel's worldview. The temptation to shift allegiance and worship from god to god was a normal pattern in the culture of the day. The Lord is seeking to combat this worldview by destroying the gods that may tempt them.

[4] Even after being in the land, idolatry was not to be tolerated, but rather obliterated (cf. Deut 13:12-18). This is a consistence practice throughout the teaching of the Old Testament and the failure to obey it is the cause of the constant failures of the nation.

simply internal (as marked by loving the Lord with all of one's heart, soul, might, and strength), rather was to have a definite external sense (even beyond circumcision). The people were to be *in* the world but not *of* the world. They were markedly distinct as the people of the Lord. At issue here is that the people were never to give their love to or even have the appearance of acknowledging the pagan gods of the land. Looking like a pagan through tolerance of false gods and religion or worse the practice of false gods and religion was not an option. With the Lord as their sovereign *god*, there was no room for the embracing of anything less than the other than of his person. Everything was to be defined by his person and work, and everything was to reflect him.

Fourth, this command was to confirm the Lord's oath given many generations before to Abram (cf. Gen 15:16; Ex 34:11). God was continuing his movement toward reconciliation with humanity by creating a people for himself to worship him exclusively (cf. Deut 9:5; 7:8-9). They were chosen by him to be his people in his land with the sole focus of worshipping him and carrying out his purposes in this world. There would be no room for paganism and idolatry. God is doing a work in this world, drawing people to himself. He accomplishes this even through the most bizarre circumstances. In this instance he makes a people from those who are not a people, he takes a people from a nation to make them a nation, he sets his affection on those he chooses, etc.

All of this teaching is set in the Mosaic or old covenant context. The Lord does not call his followers today to occupy a territory, such as Hollywood, and make it sacred space by obliterating the Canaanites of that city and destroying the idolatry of that industry. However, it does point to certain implications about the Lord, his work in this world, his view of pagan religion, and his concern for his people.

Implications from the Old Testament teaching on the ban

1. The Lord is holy. R. C. Sproul states that this is defined as the Lord being other than anything or anyone in this world. No theology book can contain him. No human word is adequate to reference him. No human mind can fully grasp him. There is nothing in physical reality, which can compare to him. He is simply other than. As such, he is to be presented in all his glory with no reducing of his majesty. If presenting the Lord in this light is offensive to people, then that is between them and the Lord. The Lord's people are not in any way to compromise the Lord's character, words, purposes, or actions in this world. Any openness to or toleration of pagan religions or practices is an abomination that profanes his name. Pagan thoughts, practices, and teaching are to be crushed, obliterated. He redeems people *out of* this and intends that they remain out of this as a people who are distinctly his. We are to steadfastly and unashamedly proclaim him (cf. Col 1:28). People need to see his glory.

2. The Lord seeks to maintain the holiness of his people. The

holiness of his people, the other than of their lives, matters to him. In no way are his people to *give way* to anything that compromises their own holiness. In other words, it is imperative that they look like the one they are following. They are to be distinct from the world around them in belief and worship and living. This is the Lord's primary concern here. If other nations have a problem with those the Lord has recreated as his followers, then that is between them and the Lord. The Lord's people are to live as the people of the Lord, committed to his purposes and glory in all things, loving the nations, but being radically different from them.

3. Pagan religions and pagan religious practices are not to be tolerated in any way. The posture of one who follows the Lord is to destroy these practices. They are not allowed to live because they bring death because they defy the holiness of the Lord. In a contemporary context, it would mean that the Lord's people do not embrace any aspect of these religions or religious practices or encourage any of their teaching or practices as to legitimacy, but rather expose them as contrary to the Lord. Idols, whether false worship, teachings, or practices,[5] are not to be preserved or given a new name, painted with a new face, given an alternate meaning or justified as good. They are to be exposed and denounced. There is very little that is seeker friendly or culturally sensitive about this. This approach does not disregard wisdom or "speaking the truth in love," but it is bold and clear. **The focus is to honor the person of Christ rather than being sensitive to cultures.**

4. The Old and New Testaments are simply two different ways of living out the clear teaching that light has nothing to do with darkness except to be shined in a manner that overtakes or removes the darkness. In no way is darkness to have any place in light. There is to be no covenant or marriage between the two. "God is light; in him there is no darkness at all" (1 John 1:5). In the Old Testament the light overwhelmed the darkness, and in the New Testament the light penetrates the darkness. In both cases, darkness is to be obliterated. In neither case is any aspect of darkness embraced. When light shines, darkness ceases to exist. When darkness is pursued, the light is left behind.

Part Two - A test case from the book of Judges: what happens when pagan religion and religious practices infiltrate God's people?

When we get to the book of Judges, we must ask how could Israel have strayed so far from what Yahweh intended? How can they be his chosen people in his chosen land for his chosen purposes and be living so contrary to his calling? What happened? The answer to this question is

---

[5] It is interesting that in a book focused on the three tests of Christianity (the person of Jesus having come in the flesh, obedience to the Lord's commands, and loving the brethren) John closes with "Guard yourselves from idols" (cf. 1 John 5:21). Idolatry is ultimately anything or anyone—or even any doctrine—not consistent with the revelation of God.

extremely important as an implication to the application of this Old Testament teaching, especially in light of certain insider movements' practices.

The problem, 1:1-2:9
This is where the veiled references in the book of Joshua (chs. 13 and 16, "but they did not drive out") are now brought to the light and made clear. In chapter 1, there is the failure to completely conquer Canaan (vv. 20-1, 28-30, 32-3). Chapter 2 shows the failure to destroy Canaanite religion.

The result, 2:10-23
The result is basically a presentation of the cycle that repeats itself throughout the book of Judges. The process is a) the people walk with the Lord for a while; b) they fall away and follow the gods of the land; c) the Lord in his mercy raises up an enemy nation to oppress them (in order to turn them back to him); d) the people cry out to the Lord in their pain; and e) God raises up a deliverer to deliver his people. Because neither the people nor the gods of the land are completely destroyed, they repeatedly tempt the people away from covenant faithfulness. However, the Lord's loving kindness is indeed everlasting, and he relentlessly pursues his people, constantly making a way for them to come back into relationship with him.

Judges is a sad book because Israel's experience in the Promised Land is not what it was supposed to be. Instead of experiencing the Lord's blessing, they are continually punished for their rebellion; consequently, they miss out on the blessings the Lord intended for them. The final chapters in Judges (17-21) give a rather crass picture of how bad it became.

The explanation: why was this area such a struggle for them?
First, monotheism was not normative for them. At Mt. Sinai they were taught about the one true God. This was a shift in their thinking about gods (cf. Amos 5:25-6; Jer 7:25). It was not simply the number of gods that provided them difficulty, rather the concept of the gods (cf. Ps 16:4). They were steeped in their pagan understanding that gods influenced the different realms of nature and needed to be satisfied in order to bring blessing. This was their worldview. With the proliferation of gods in the lands because they were not destroyed as God commanded, Israel was easily led astray. Slowly any recognition of the Lord began to pale in her everyday life.

Second, Israel forgot her history. We see the evidence of some remembrance (cf. Judg 6:13), but overall Israel drifted quickly. This is why we find the challenge to *remember* throughout the book of Deuteronomy (4:9-10; 5:15; 6:12, 20; 7:17-18; 8:2, 11-20; 9:7; et al.). So a major purpose in writing the book is to show that Israel's spiritual condition determined its political and material situation. As long as she called out to and lived for

Yahweh, she knew the deliverance that only God could bring. However, if she disregarded Yahweh, she experienced the judgment of oppression (cf. Ps 107). Ultimately Israel became so engrossed in the culture, which remained because she refused to be completely obedient, that she became less conversant in her own history. Pagan ideals began to dominate her thinking and actions. When considering the entirety of Israel's history, the nation never recovered. This is to be a sobering thought for anyone who lives in proximity to the world's religions.

Implications from the study of the infiltration of pagan religions and religious practices

1. The Lord's concern that the failure to destroy pagan religions and religious practices would result in Israel's own apostasy comes true. The boundaries the Lord sets up for his people are for their good. It seems to be a tendency of humanity to become dark when darkness comes close, is embraced, or even tolerated. Any hint of darkness eventually overtakes the light, slowly consuming it when the Lord is not followed closely. The Lord seeks to radically shift people from their worldview—there is to be no playing with it. When one's hands are on the plow, there is no looking back. *Repent* is to turn away from; leave behind the old worldview.

2. Humanity has a tendency toward idolatry, and people become like that which they worship (cf. Ps 115, especially v. 8; Jer 2:5). Idols change as worldviews change, so they vary from culture to culture, even from person to person. What people allow to prosper in the deepest recesses of the heart, that is, an idolatrous worldview, must be exposed and turned away from. If not, the tendency is to drift back to it.

3. The more engrossed a person becomes in a pagan way of thinking and living, the more the Lord begins to pale in comparison (cf. Jer 2:19). When the toleration of worldviews becomes the focus (the method), then the focus will shift from the magnification of the Lord (the message). Worldviews have a powerful pull on the Lord's people (cf. the NT exhortation to "set one's mind on" in Rom 8:5-8; Col 3:1-4).

4. To be salt and light (cf. Mt 5:13-16) has less to do with sensitivity to culture (the method) and more to do with sensitivity to Christ (the message). The *salt* can become tasteless (cf. Mt 5:13) and the *light* can be hidden (cf. Mt 5:14-15). We proclaim him (cf. Col 1:28-29) with no hesitation, no limitation (except in our finite abilities to proclaim him who is *other than*), no denigration, nothing hidden and nothing added. To be *salt* or *light* means we are to be unashamed of the Gospel.

Part Three – a test case from the Church: what is our response to false teaching in the body of Christ?

I recently saw a tattoo that read, "Only God Can Judge Us." As a whole, this is good theology, but the message behind it is often, "You cannot say anything about any aspect of my life because it is none of your business; I am only responsible to God, so butt out!" God is indeed the only judge, but God calls us to honor him by perpetuating and guarding the truth he has revealed to us. He expects us to be jealous for his truth.

Introducing two letters about false teaching

The twin towers for John are truth (defending the truth about Jesus), and love (we love one another as an act of obedience to Christ). So the letters of 2 and 3 John are occasioned by the same theme: **living the truth**. There are two dimensions to this theme: first, loving those who abide in the family of God; and second, exposing or chastising those who want to dismantle that family. Note that there is a similar structure for each letter:
   a. Personal Greetings
   b. An Exhortation to Love
   c. Dealing with a Particular Issue
   d. Closing

John is warning against community destroyers. At issue is the question: are we to love—or better, to tolerate—those who disagree with us concerning truth?

Understanding 2 John, vv. 1-3, 12-13

About 2 John, Yarborough writes,

> As to the number of words, one can ask, why the author bothered to write at all. But as to the weight of the words, one wishes the author had lingered longer over, expanded upon, and fleshed out virtually every clause."[6]

The letter

The letter begins with some introductory comments. The author is identified as "the elder" (v. 1). Much discussion could be offered about the identification of this person, but suffice it to say that John pens the letter, especially since 1-3 John engage the same issues. The Church has been established and leadership is in place, so *elder* rather than *apostle* would be normative (cf. 1 Pet 5:1, "fellow elder").

I intend to keep the concerns about the identification of the author and the addressee simple because it does not ultimately affect the interpretation of the contents of the letter. The letter is first addressed "to the elect lady" (v. 1). Again much discussion surrounds the identity of this addressee, but I will conclude that the letter is addressed to a congregation or group of believers. Often in the Bible, the Church and Israel are referenced in the feminine, as a woman, bride, etc. In addition, the author uses the second person plural throughout (that is, a group). Peter uses a

---

[6] Robert W. Yarborough (2008). *1-3 John* (2331). BECNT Grand Rapids, MI: Baker Academic.

similar title for his audience in 1 Peter 1:1, "To God's elect, strangers in the world."

The letter is also addressed to "her children" (v. 1). I conclude this to be the members of this local body of believers. So John is writing to a congregation and all who fellowship there.

In addition, the letter ends with a request to greet "the children of your chosen sister" (v. 13). Based on the brief arguments above, I would conclude similarly here about the identification these people. This letter is referencing a sister church and all who attend that fellowship. So we have a fellowship of churches, which have strong connections.

Initial comments

John has an obvious affection for this group of believers (vv. 1b-2, 12). He was a pastor-evangelist, who established several churches in western Asia Minor. He was an important leader in these churches. Pastors throughout the area traveled to Ephesus to learn from John and hear his stories about Jesus. The seven churches of Revelation 2-3 may have been in his territory, meaning John must have also traveled to them from time to time (v. 12). So John is watching over this group, guarding, shepherding, and encouraging them to abide and stay the course. He needs to visit them, but, first, it is imperative that he quickly sends the contents of this letter to these believers.

John begins with the point that it is truth that binds (vv. 1-2). The Gospel is powerful to save, to transform, and to unify. Knowing this truth, guarding this truth, and abiding in this truth is extremely important in the Christian life. It cannot be reduced to simply going to Church and talking about Jesus. The Church must be getting into the very heart of God and getting his heart into us–that is abiding!

It is increasingly popular to state, "I can worship anywhere." This is not true, unless worship simply involves a moment of God-focus. For John, worship is all of life, and he cannot imagine worship that does not include a central focus on Jesus, knowing and obeying the commands, or actively and intentionally being in the lives of others and loving them (cf. the three tests of 1 John). John states, "This binds us."

Great rejoicing with a call to excel still more, vv. 4-6
    Great rejoicing, v. 4

Initially John says he "rejoiced greatly." He must have had some recent contact, probably with a group who came to him to seek his advice or to report concerns, which led to this positive response. Again the reference to "children" implies those members of the congregation. Why the rejoicing? Some, and probably the whole of this group, which met with John, were "walking in truth" or walking in an exemplary manner (cf. 1 John 1:6-7; 2:6). It is the doing of our knowing, and it is the ordering of daily life in truth. They are abiding. John notes that this is "just as the

Father commanded us." This is the second of the three tests of 1 John (cf. 1 John 2:3). The group is passing that test.

Call to excel still more: love, vv. 5-6

Then John calls for further faithfulness: "I ask that we love one another." Note that this is a request, not a command. The basis for everything that John is about to write is love. He is about to make some difficult comments and he wants love to be the foundation. His focus is the whole group as he uses the singular *you* for the singular *lady*, which represents this body of believers. He is emphasizing oneness (many members, yet one), and the group, including himself, *we*. As in 1 John, John states this is not a new commandment (1 John 2:7-8; John 13:34).

John either saw or heard evidence of some deficiency in love, possibly the result of the theological battles working themselves out in this fellowship of churches. To be clear, he continues, "And this is love." Love is defined as walking in the commandments (cf. 1 John 5:2-3). Once again, it comes back to the three tests of 1 John: one, belief in Jesus as he is revealed; two, obedience of God's commands; and three, loving the body of Christ. These are the true tests of a believer.

This seems to be a request to "excel still more" (cf. 1 Thess). John is stating, "Some of you are walking in the truth, may you excel still more!" The unity of the body was being threatened. The integrity of truth was being challenged. The body was being hit from all sides, and they needed to walk in truth and excel in love in these difficult days. This is the necessary foundation.

A reminder of false teaching, v. 7

The core of the epistle is found in vv. 7-8. The word *for* follows vv. 4-6. They must evidence this love *for*. Then, in what follows, John identifies his main concern. We must note that similarly in 1 John, the use of *deceivers* and *liars*, as John had a similar concern in that book. The threat continues to be the Incarnation (cf. 1 John 4:2-3). This is not a marginal truth as it is absolutely central to the Gospel. The doctrine of these false teachers violated what God already revealed and established (cf. 1 John 1:1-3).

The many issues of the seven churches of Revelation 2-3 may represent additional theological disagreements John battled.
- 2:2, some are making false claims to apostleship
- 2:6, works of the Nicolaitans
- 2:9-10, the synagogue of Satan (false claims to be Jews)
- 2:14, teaching of Balaam, eating food sacrificed to idols and committing idolatry
- 2:15, teaching of the Nicolaitans
- 2:20, tolerating the prophetess, Jezebel, who teaches the practice of sexual immorality and eating food sacrificed to idols
- 2:24, the deep things of Satan

- 3:1, the synagogue of Satan

These threats mattered to John, and as Revelation 2-3 makes clear, they matter to God. In each of his letters, John is seeking to maintain that "which was from the beginning." He strives to stay the course, maintaining the purity of doctrine. God has spoken, and he intends to honor God by honoring his word, especially as he received it from Jesus.

Necessary pastoral instruction, vv. 8-11
Warning, vv. 8-9

There are two commands in the letter, the first of which John gives now: "Watch out." This has the idea of know it, get it in your heart, live it, abide in it! They must continue to be mindful of the truths of God's word. John longs for his flock to stay the course. So John's first concern is his flock. He wants to secure the standing of his flock. How would they lose a full reward? Much could be debated about this idea of future reward or lack thereof. John is not focused on this as much as the reasons behind it. He is concerned that they might lose out by compromising their belief and behavior. So John is urging them to stay the course, to not lose their perspective or way, to not be pulled away and to keep paying attention! Eugene Peterson's book, *A Long Obedience in the Same Direction*, is a title that captures what John is encouraging. Believers must constantly be mindful of the Lord, of eternity and what we live for (cf. 2 Tim 4:6-8).

John's reference to "anyone who runs ahead" carries the idea of representing Christ in ways that are inconsistent and irreconcilable with established apostolic recollections (cf. 1 John 1:1-3) that have been crystallized in Christian congregations. John's call is to abide in truth! The Apostles' Creed captures what the early church held firmly:

> I believe in God the Father Almighty; Maker of heaven and earth.
> And in Jesus Christ his only Son our Lord;
> who was conceived by the Holy Spirit, born of the virgin Mary;
> suffered under Pontius Pilate, was crucified, dead and buried;
> the third day he rose from the dead;
> he ascended into heaven;
> and sits at the right hand of God the Father Almighty;
> from there he shall come to judge the quick and the dead.
> I believe in the Holy Spirit; the holy catholic Church;
> the communion of saints; the forgiveness of sins;
> the resurrection of the body; and the life everlasting. Amen.

It has always been a concern of the Church to preserve truth. There are always those who seek their own agenda. A new focus in the Church today is believers being encouraged to create their own theology. So theology changes as cultures and communities change? No! God creates theology. We must abide in his revealed truth.

Implication, vv. 10-11

John drives home his point, "If anyone comes to you and does not bring this teaching"—the body of truth historically embraced by the body of Christ—"do not take him into your house or welcome him." This is the second command and John's second concern, which is how to deal with these false teachers. The point here is not focused on hospitality to non-Christians, rather he has in mind aiding people who are undercutting the doctrines found in God's word, taught by Christ, and perpetuated by the apostles. It seems these false teachers were making the rounds and spreading their new teachings with the goal of gaining a following.

Context is extremely important for this book. Missionaries from the enemy are trying to make inroads into the Church. The very existence of the Church is at stake. Three basic elements from the context of this letter must be underscored. First, the Church's opponents are attacking a theological issue at the center of the Church's faith; namely, Christology. Second, John is warning against teacher-leaders who are out to sabotage the local church. In other words, this is not innocent contact between Christians and unbelievers or heretics. These are aggressive teachers trying to gain access to a congregation in order to win an audience and gain a following. Third, John's instructions to repel these teachers and to refuse them access into homes involve their survival as people who are committed to the three tests of 1 John. Serious action is needed.

To receive them is to grant to them and their doctrine the honor and respect that are due only to true Christian faith and practice. It is to embrace them and their teaching. It is providing an endorsement, and allowing entrance into the Church. The phrase, "do not . . . welcome him," makes it clear that they were not to offer these teachers the strong affection on the basis of shared conviction regarding a commitment to the apostolic Christ, often accompanied with a kiss, that was granted to believers.

So what does it mean to us?

First, we must be willing to expose those opposing core doctrinal beliefs. John is not denying the need to love (cf. Mt 5:43-7), rather he is focused on the need and responsibility to protect the body (cf. Acts 20:24-32). There is no place for darkness. Despite the strong push of culture, tolerance is not the supreme virtue. Strong action is appropriate when individuals jeopardize the very integrity of the Church. Consider the teaching of Matthew 18:17 concerning a member sinning seriously and unwilling to turn. Also, consider 1 Corinthians 5:1-5 for similar teaching. Tolerance must have its clear limits if the Church is to maintain integrity.

How do we decide the importance of issues? How do we determine essential doctrine vs. disputable matters? It is obvious that some matters are more central than others. The evangelical church holds to core beliefs,

and as one moves out from these core beliefs, a particular teaching is open to more debate. Guidelines must be established to determine the degree of importance of specific matters. One proposal is that where issues fall can be determined by the degree of the following criteria:[7]
1. Biblical clarity
2. Relevance to the character of God
3. Relevance to the essence of the Gospel
4. Biblical frequency (how often in Scripture it is taught)
5. Effect on other doctrines
6. Consensus among Christians (past and present)
7. Effect on personal and Church life
8. Pressures from contemporary culture to compromise

The elders of the church I serve have engaged difficult theological issues from time-to-time. They are not simply committed to positions. They are committed to coming to proper understanding of issues and jealously standing for God and his truth. It matters to the leaders, and they want it to matter to congregation. Church leadership must be committed to protecting the body and boldly walking into false teaching that arises and seeks to lead astray those for whom Christ died.

Second, truth must matter to God's people. John's concern is that which was heard from the beginning. There is clearly a standard, and that truth must be known. The issue of verse 9, "Anyone who runs on ahead and does not continue," is to be avoided. To do so, one must know what the Bible teaches. We not only abide in Christ, we also abide in the teachings of Christ. We have much to learn from those who have gone before us and fought theological battles. The historical creeds are the evidence of those battles for truth.

Implications for our response to false teaching in the body of Christ

1. The Lord intends that we guard, protect, and be jealous for his truth *from the inside.* False teaching is not to penetrate into the body. Shepherds are to guard the flock "which He (God) bought with his own blood" (Acts 20:28). This teaching is clear: if a particular teaching is from the inside, we need to boldly deal with it.

2. It follows, then, that the Lord intends that we guard, protect, and be jealous for his truth as the body penetrates into the worldviews we encounter. This means that, as we represent Christ as his ambassadors, we do so without compromise in any way. Truth matters to us. We should not feel the least bit apologetic for the truth that God has given to us. We jealously guard it and offer it to others unapologetically.

3. 2 John is built on the foundation of 1 John, which offers the three tests of being a true disciple of Christ: one, belief that Jesus is the Son of

---

[7] These criteria were taken from a paper delivered by Wayne Grudem at the National ETS conference.

God who came in the flesh; two, obedience to the Lord's commands; and three, love for other disciples. The first test is to be guarded. It is absolutely crucial to our faith. It is the grace of God in the face of Christ that sets Christianity apart from the religions of the world. We proclaim him (cf. Col 1:28) that "so that in everything he might have the supremacy" (Col 1:18). Christ needs to be known. We are not passing on a religion, we are passing on Christ who saves by his atoning sacrificial blood through grace to be received by faith.

4. John writes to the Church: we are *called out* ones. We are to be set apart as we also strive to be salt and light. We are not insiders. Coming to Christ has always been a *calling out* to come and follow with one's whole heart. Our ministries should reflect this.

At issue is when does cultural sensitivity lead to or result from doctrinal impurity? What is the difference between living **in** the world but not **of** it and living **in** the world and **of** it? What are the absolutes of doctrine that must be embraced in order to maintain purity while still remaining sensitive to the culture?

So, what is to be our attitude? God's word is clear. Light is to overtake the darkness as we boldly take the Gospel to a world that needs to hear, letting our light shine brightly.

Specific thoughts on the insider movements

It seems to me that no one at the table of this debate is longing for heresy or pushing an agenda to destroy Christianity. It seems that no one is attempting to knowingly denigrate Christ or refuse his exaltation. From what I understand, this debate is made up of Christians, and there seems to be a legitimate desire to take the Gospel to the nations who have never heard.

At issue seems to be at what point the practical concerns of ecclesiology become doctrinally heretical when the Bible does or does not (I leave this open) explicitly provide parameters? At what point does sensitivity to culture (**method**) become the focus to the extent that the exaltation of Christ (**message**) is no longer the focus or even denigrated? One of the main difficulties seems to be the different means of evangelism in the culture of each testament, operating under different covenants. However, in neither testament is darkness—that which is contrary to the Lord—legitimized as having anything to offer to that which is of the Lord. In neither testament is darkness given any value to be preserved for or integrated into the sacred.

The Old Testament's teaching on the ban may, on the one hand, simply serve as a normative warning when it comes to taking the Gospel to a culture dominated by a pagan religion. It serves as a "Watch out!" On the other hand, it may serve as foundational teaching and normative directive to what it means to take the Gospel to another culture. As such, the intent of its teaching must be transferred to our new covenant context and serve as part of our paradigm for evangelizing, especially as it pertains to the discussion of the IM. Or, as a final possibility, it may serve as a both-and to these first two possibilities.

What I think is clear is that the Lord's people tend to drift, regardless which covenant one is in. The book of Judges shows us the dangers resulting from not fully following the Lord and 2 John shows us that we are to be uncompromising in maintaining the core of truth. The question, then, becomes at what point is adapting to a culture (method) a compromise that denigrates the Lord (message) and leads to this inevitable drift? The history of the Jewish people in the Old Testament clearly points to any compromise as the open door that unavoidably leads to drift. The history of Christianity as found in the New Testament and beyond points to the same. My own life points to the same, as I am certain your life does. The New Testament calls believers to be yoked with Christ (Mt 11:29-30) and to not be "bound together with unbelievers" (2 Cor 6:14-18 NASB). So, at what point is the IM binding itself to unbelievers (method) to the exclusion of Christ (message)?

One more point that needs to be explored is our understanding of the Gospel. What is the power of the Gospel? How does one finally get to a point of yielding to Christ? Is it the movement of the Spirit of God in a person (cf. 1 Cor 1:26-31, especially verse 30, "by his doing") or well thought out apologetics that win the mind or blurring the distinctions between pagan religions and our own so as to make them comfortable and open to discussion (along the lines of the very popular seeker friendly church movement)? It seems that everyone brings something different to the table that must be taken seriously and must be presented humbly. Where does each person need to be refined? And more importantly, how do we stay the course and bring glory to the Lord in everything?

3.3 Theology of Religions: Would Jesus Be Caught Dead Working in Islam?

Jeff Morton

Introduction

The focus of this chapter is to develop a theology of religions (TR) vis-à-vis Islam. That it is a theology of religions and not of **religion** is important. A theology of religion is a psychological and anthropological approach to how one understands religion as a human expression,[1] but TR is a Christian activity (though not solely) that asks these questions:

- What does the Bible say about non-Christian religions?
- What should our attitude be towards the practitioners of those religions?
- What does it mean that Jesus is savior to those who have never heard?
- How do we maintain the tension of Jesus' exclusive claim with the truth that God is universal in his love?

In order to develop my understanding of a biblical TR, I want to begin with the common definition of exclusivism, inclusivism and pluralism. Kevin Higgins, a major advocate of IM, acts as my foil for this topic. Following these definitions comes the heart of my discussion: how does a proper TR reflect the concepts of divergence and continuity? My purpose is to clarify that many IM proponents have veered off course in their theology of religions.[2]

Three categories of TR

In light of these questions, a tripartite typology has developed historically. It is not my purpose to speak to this typology, but for the sake of clarity, let me list them, give IM advocate Kevin Higgins's definitions,[3] and follow up with a brief comment or two.

Higgins writes that an exclusivist "tends to see all non-Christian religions as either mankind's rebellious attempt to find their own way or as the result of demonic activity"[4]

---

[1] The two phrases are often used interchangeably, for example: "The theology of religion asks what religion is and seeks, in the light of Christian faith, to interpret the universal religious experience of humankind; it further studies the relationship between revelation and faith, faith and religion, and faith and salvation" (Jacques Dupuis (1997). *Toward a Christian Theology of Religious Pluralism* (49). Maryknoll, NY: Orbis.).

[2] What about the title of the chapter? It is a bit strange, I admit, but I trust it becomes clearer as the chapter develops.

[3] Kevin Higgins, "Inside What? Church, Culture, Religion, and Insider Movements in Biblical Perspective" *SFM* 5(4): 74-91.

[4] Higgins, "Inside What?" 84.

Higgins's definition misses the real point about exclusivism: Jesus is unique and this uniqueness is expressed exclusively in global Christianity. A much more thorough understanding of exclusivists includes the centrality of Jesus—his uniqueness—and the understanding of other religions. Therefore, exclusivists understand that Jesus is uniquely the savior of all mankind and other religions are insufficient (read *a rebellious attempt*) for salvation.

I am an exclusivist. I believe Jesus is uniquely the God-man, Messiah, savior, and soon coming king. Every knee will bow to him, either in this life or the next. There is salvation in Jesus alone and so it is my privilege to be part of the body of Christ that gives witnesses to him. In all fairness, it is my belief that advocates of IM also share this perspective—I think. My attitude toward other religions is one of tension: that is, tolerance and evangelism. I accept their right to exist and propagate, but I will share with the adherents of any religion the good news of the uniqueness of Christ. Again, I believe this is a typical IM view despite what I see as shortcomings in Higgins's definition of exclusivism.

Higgins continues by saying an inclusivist "tends to assume that since Christ is Lord of all and is the light that gives light to all, He is at work in other religions and cultures even when people do not know it is Jesus. Christianity is sometimes seen as *fulfilling* the best insights of other religions."[5]

Inclusivism presents a subtle shift of emphasis in its movement away from exclusivism. Inclusivists insist that Jesus is unique—salvation comes only through him—yet Jesus is working in other religions to bring people to salvation. The practical outcome of this assumption is that Jesus is working in Islam (or any religion) to bring men and women to himself. Again, I do not necessarily disagree with this. God does work in the lives of men and women who are Muslims, Hindus and Buddhists. There are many biblical examples of this; however, the question is, what does that work look like?

Here I want to be very clear: the subtle difference between exclusivism and inclusivism is the added value inclusivism gives to religion. The inclusivist insists on the uniqueness of Jesus, but also attaches an implied inherent worth to every religion because Jesus is working in the religion. Is this biblical? I will come back to this, but first I need to speak about the examples Higgins uses to promote this view.

Many of the illustrations Higgins and other proponents of IM use, come from the Old Testament showing the "ways in which God is at work in other religions, and suggests in at least some cases that members of other religions are in relationship with God Himself."[6] Higgins cites Abraham, Melchizedek, the non-Jews of Amos' day, Balaam and so forth. So what is the problem?

---

[5] Higgins, "Inside What?" 84.
[6] Higgins, "Inside What?" 85.

Each example is about people, not their religion. Not one of the examples shows a person's religion helping him discover the reality of Yahweh. For instance, it seems fair to ask how Naaman's worship of Rimmon helped him discover he had an incipient relationship with the God of Israel (2 Kgs 5:1-14). There is no indication in the story that Naaman's religious experience with Rimmon bridged him to Yahweh. If there is a bridge at all, it is the slave girl of Naaman's wife, a young Israelite. She expressed her wish that her master's husband might be healed (v. 3). What is the relevance of Naaman's religious experience with Rimmon in all of this? The story does not make it clear there is any.

What does this story—and all the others Higgins cites—tell us about how God works in the lives of people? It seems better to say that God does work in the lives of individuals **in spite** of their religions, **not because** of them. This is not too fine a point to make for this is, arguably, the core of the argument between IMers and Historicals. Is God working in other religions, implying there is a value in each religion, or is he working, wooing and calling people out of those religions? Is God using other religions to call people to himself? Inclusivism makes this unwarranted leap. From Yahweh's perspective there is no value in the religions of the world, but there is great value in the people of those religions. It seems to me Higgins's conclusion overreaches his examples.

Finally, on the third category, Higgins writes the pluralist "sees all religions as equally legitimate pathways to God. For some pluralists, Christianity can be said to be the unique path, but only *for me*."[7] I do not believe there are any IMers that are pluralists.

Methodology

Having laid some groundwork, we can now ask: What is the degree of continuity and divergence between Islam and Christianity? I am not attempting to create a new category to add the aforementioned three. My hope is to bring clarity to the inclusivistically-oriented question: How closely related is Islam to Christianity? Or perhaps more sarcastically (and pardon my American idiom): would Jesus be caught dead working in Islam? Why or why not?

As to my approach, I first want to speak about the meanings of continuity and divergence. Following a working definition, I apply these concepts to the question of the relationship of Islam to Christianity. Finally, I will end with some observations and implications for our understanding of the IM and work with Muslims.

Continuity and divergence

The ideas of continuity and divergence are illustrated in the relationship of Christianity and Judaism. Without Judaism, there would be

---

[7] Higgins, "Inside What?" 84.

no Christianity; without the Torah there would be no Acts; without Isaiah, there is no Messiah. God's plan to redeem mankind was germinated in the garden, birthed in Abraham and the twelve tribes, then developed through the Exodus, the Promised Land, the Davidic and Solomonic kingdoms, the Babylonian exile and the return. Yet God's plan did not come to maturity until his son came to earth and said from the cross, "It is finished."

This is true Judaism. Christianity is the fulfillment of Judaism as Jesus is the fulfillment of the Torah, the Writings, and the Prophets. This is continuity. What God began, he finished. The themes, motifs and patterns begun in the Old Testament, he wove into the completed tapestry found in the New Testament.

Continuity, then, is the degree to which one ideology relies upon another; its connection to and link with another religion, philosophy or worldview. For the purposes of this chapter, continuity does not refer to the phenomena (rituals, observances, rites, holidays, terms, etc.) of two ideologies or religions, only to the deeper, worldview assumptions. For instance, at a surface level Mormons and Protestants are very similar. Both have similar types of Sunday worship services, engage in foreign missionary work, share similar religious vocabulary, and in fact are categorized as Christian by demographers. These shared phenomena are only similar at the surface level. Continuity requires that we dig deeper to the worldview level, the stratum of assumptions, perceptions, and beliefs about reality.

Continuity should be thought of as a continuum rather than a true or false statement (Figure 6). How much do the ideologies, the worldviews, and the religions overlap? I believe the greater the overlap, the greater the continuity; the less overlap, the less continuity. For instance, without materialism (M), communism (C) would probably never have come into existence. There is a strong connection and reliance of the latter upon the former. What about the continuity between evolution (E) and communism? Could we have had the birth of communism without the theory of evolution? Absolutely. There is much less—if any—continuity between evolution and communism. So, evolution maintains a high degree of continuity with materialism, but a low degree of continuity with communism (or as the figure illustrates, no continuity).

Figure 6. Continuity illustrated as overlap of materialism, communism and evolution.

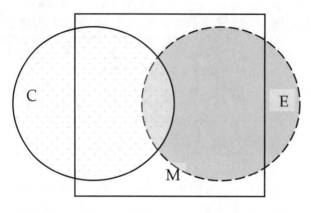

In the world of religions, Hinduism has high continuity with Buddhism (see Figure 7 where H/B is the Hindu view of Buddhism). One the one hand, most Hindus believe Buddha was one of the ten avatars of Vishnu. Hinduism's big tent philosophy embraces Buddhism as just another of the many paths to freedom from *maya* and ignorance about a person's true nature. There is a large overlap between Hinduism and Buddhism at the worldview level. On the other hand, the link of continuity is much less between Hinduism and Sikhism since the latter is strictly monotheistic and was in fact a revolt against the Hindu scripturally based caste system.

Figure 7. Continuity of Hinduism and Buddhism.

+ continuity-----------H/B--divergence+

What then is divergence? It is discontinuity, a disruption, or a break between the two ideologies. Just as continuity is measured on a continuum, so is divergence. Hinduism and Buddhism are high on the scale of continuity. On the one hand, this means a Hindu can practice Buddhism and remain an honest Hindu. One the other hand, can a Buddhist be a Hindu?

Continuity and divergence are reciprocal: that is, there are two sides to the perspective. What is the Buddhist perspective of Hinduism? Unlike Hindus who believe the continuity between the two religions is very high, Buddhists see divergence between themselves and Hindus. Hinduism teaches every person has *atman* (soul). To the Hindu humans are an *atman* looking for release from this body. This stands in direct opposition to the Buddha's teaching that there is neither an individual nor an individual soul (*annata*). This is just one difference, but for Buddhists, it is a deal breaker. Therefore, I would graph (see Figure 8) Buddhism's view of Hinduism as much more divergent than continuous.

Figure 8. Divergence of Buddhism and Hinduism from a Buddhist perspective.

+ continuity----------H/B------------------------------B/H----------divergence+

Islam and Christianity: continuity or divergence?

Where do Islam and Christianity fit on the continuity and divergence scale? Just as with Hinduism and Buddhism, there are two perspectives. First, let me address the Islamic view. I have heard many Muslim converts from Christianity speak about the two religions in this way: Christianity was the skeleton of my religion and Islam put the meat on the bones.[8] Many reverts to Islam see the continuity of the two religions without using the term.

Historically and theologically Islam is quite dependent upon Christianity. Christianity supplied Islam a Messiah, the *Injil,* and prophets.[9] Muhammad believed he was the final prophet in the line of the biblical prophets. He believed he brought a message that both Jew and Christian would accept. Without belaboring the point with countless references to the Qur'an and hadith to prove the point, I believe the Islamic view of Christianity is one of high continuity (Figure 9).

Figure 9. Islam's perspective of continuity between it and Christianity.

+ continuity--------------I/C--divergence+

Lest I be accused of dereliction in my assessment of Islam, I am not overlooking the great proclamations by the Islamic prophet against the Peoples of the Book. The list of qur'anic accusations is numerous:
- They forgot the covenant Allah made with them (5:14).
- They are punished for their sins (5:18).
- They will be judged on the final day (2:113).
- They are constantly attempting to lead Muslims away from Islam (2:120).
- The religion of Abraham was neither Judaism nor Christianity (2:135, et al).

My point, however, remains: while there are differences of opinion between the Islamic and Christian worldview, ultimately the Islamic view of Christianity is one of greater continuity rather than divergence. Islam believes it worships the God of the People of the Book; the Qur'an confirmed and preserved what was accurate of the previous revelations of the Jews and Christians; and Muhammad was the last of the biblical

---

[8] I note this in my DMiss dissertation, *Embracing Islam: Conversion Narratives of American Muslims Living in Southern California.* Biola University, 2003.

[9] I am not suggesting the *Isa* or Allah of the Qur'an is the same as their counterpart in the Bible; they are not. I am only offering the Islamic perspective of Christianity.

prophets.

We know the Islamic view of Christianity, but what is the biblical view of Islam? This is easily answered by asking a few key questions. But before I ask these questions, let us first look at IM's view of Allah. This will clarify and intensify the difference between the IM and Historical perspectives, as well as between Christianity and Islam.

The *Common Ground Workbook* (*CGW*, see Figure 10) illustrates an IM-TR in a trio of telling slides (I am only showing one slide). They write, "the Qur'an has a shortened list of God's names," meaning that Muslims "don't know all that has been revealed about God, from the Bible," but "what they know of Allah is true of God." It is this last statement that is especially troubling.

Figure 10. *CGW*, p. 16, slide 1.[10]

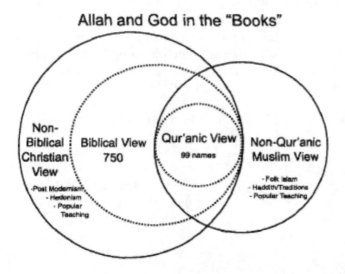

The IM view is that the biblical revelation of God encompasses the qur'anic view. Everything about Allah, his character, his names and titles, his manner of interaction with his creation, his self-disclosure and revelation are biblical—as far as it goes. In other words, the entire corpus of qur'anic revelation that touches upon the Creator shows great continuity with the biblical revelation. Besides being a tacit admission that the Qur'an is the revealed word of Yahweh, the problem with this view is the additional value of religion. Remember, this was the problem I pointed out with the inclusivist TR. Jesus is at work in Islam; here it is in graphic form.

Is this IM understanding of Islam correct? For the sake of clarity, here are a few questions for IM about Allah and the God of the Bible:

---

[10] I received permission to use the slide on the condition I send this chapter to *Common Ground* (www.comgro.org). In asking for permission, I also suggested the chapter might open doors for further conversation. No response was offered.

- Is Allah as revealed in the Qur'an, the God of the Bible?
  - Does he relate to mankind in intimacy and covenant?[11]
  - Does he enter time and space?[12]
  - Is his character such that he can be described as a God of love?[13]
  - Is he a God of self-disclosure?[14]
  - Has he revealed himself as Father, Son and Holy Spirit?[15]

If these questions can be answered affirmatively from the Qur'an, the God of the Bible **is** Allah. If these questions are answered negatively from the Qur'an, the God of the Bible cannot be the God of Islam regardless how nice the previous circle diagram looks.

Here are a few more questions to help clarify a mistaken IM-TR:
- Is *Isa* bin al-Maryam al-Masih the Jesus of the Bible?
  - Did he die on the cross?[16]
  - Did he rise from the dead?
  - Will he return to establish his kingdom as an inheritance for the nations?[17]
  - Is he Immanuel? The Son of God? The Lamb of God? The Prince of Peace?[18]

---

[11] No. While Allah may be closer to us than our jugular vein (Q50:16), this aya has never been understood by Muslim exegetes as referring to the immanence of Allah. It simply means Allah knows our plans, schemes and wiles because he knows us. What about covenant—does Allah relate to mankind through a covenant relationship? Here I would give a qualified no. The Qur'an speaks of covenant, but it is actually a contract, closer to the OT concept rather than the new covenant Yahweh makes with his people (see Q13:20-5). Allah promises to reward those who keep the covenant. Allah curses those who fail. The new covenant offered in Jeremiah 31:31ff is one that cannot be broken because God puts his law in the minds and hearts of his people. In other words, whereas the previous covenant was indeed broken by the Jews, the new covenant cannot be broken because of the power of God in Christ.

[12] No. Unlike the God of the Bible who walked in the garden, Allah is not in the Garden in any of the similar qur'anic scenes (Q2:29ff; 7:11ff; 15:26ff; 20:115ff). Allah is known for his transcendence—and is ironically, unknown—not for his immanence.

[13] None of the ninety-nine names of Allah communicate this biblical concept, but more importantly the Qur'an is full of such explicit statements as "Allah guides whom he wills" (Q22:16). He also does not love those who do evil (Q28:77).

[14] No. Orthodox Islam teaches the one who submits to Allah knows nothing of Allah's essence; even his names are merely projections of what he wants us to think about him rather than accurate descriptions of his essential character: "Is he who creates like him who does not create?" (Q16:17).

[15] No. For example, Q4:171b states, "So believe in Allah and His Apostles. Say not 'Trinity': desist: it will be better for you: for Allah is One Allah: glory be to him: (for Exalted is He) above having a son."

[16] No. Q4:157 denies Jesus died on the cross, therefore the resurrection did not take place.

[17] No. The Qur'an does not speak to this matter although the hadith literature is ripe with this information. Jesus will return, but only as mediator for his followers. He will also correct the misguided notion that he is to be worshipped as the Son of God. His second coming is not associated with the kingdom of God, rather the Day of Judgment (al Bukhari has many details).

[18] None of these are Jesus' titles in Islam.

- Is the Holy Spirit of the Qur'an the same person we meet in the Bible?[19]
- Are the Hebrew and Greek Scriptures, specifically the *Injil*, as revealed to the biblical prophets and writers still authentic and relevant for today?[20]

I do not know a single Muslim who could answer a single one of these questions in the affirmative. If a Muslim did answer positively, he not only places himself outside the boundaries of orthodox Islam, but is a deceiver. While the Islamic view of Christianity is continuity, the Christian understanding of Islam is of great divergence (Figure 11), exactly the opposite of the Islamic view. This is, I believe, the heart of the IM problem: **they have the wrong worldview**: an Islamic theology of religions.

Figure 11. Divergence between Christianity and Islam.

+ continuity----------I/C--------------------------------C/I----------divergence+

Implications

The last thing this chapter was meant to do was impugn the motives of the advocates for the IM. We will leave motives to God; only behaviors can be observed and judged. With that caveat, what are the implications of these thoughts on continuity and diversity vis-à-vis the IM and ministry among Muslims?

1. With the clear understanding that Islam and Christianity are much less continuous than Islam teaches, what can we expect of Christians from a Muslim background?

When repentance is real, the believer **turns from** sin and his or her religious experiences of the past and **turns to** the reality of a new heart and experience with the living God of the universe. Inherent in the act of repentance is the acknowledgment that one's previous religion, whatever it might be, no matter how much truth it contains, is a false religion. The divergence between the new convert's old religion and his new reality with Christ is too great, too real, and too refreshingly intimate with the Creator to be maintained within the confines of Islam. Islam does not permit the intimacy Yahweh desires. This means the believer must ultimately come out of Islam. He must come out; his relationship with Yahweh demands it. The question of when is not the subject for this chapter, but I believe the matter of divergence establishes the necessity that the new believer must turn from Islam. There are two religions, two books, two Messiahs, two Spirits, and two Creators. Who can serve two masters?

---

[19] No. The Holy Spirit is the angel Gabriel (cf. A. Yusuf Ali (1989). *The Meaning of the Glorious Qur'an* (fn. on Q16:102). Beltsville, MD: Amana).
[20] No. The Qur'an corrects the previous revelations where they are corrupted.

2. I believe the devastating categorical error of IM is its poorly developed worldview and theology of religions. The IM is guilty of adopting the **Islamic view** of Christianity rather than understanding, appreciating and operating within the **Christian view** toward Islam. As illustrated in the figures above, Islam's own perspective is based on the assumption it is the fulfillment and continuation of Christianity. The IM has adopted the wrong worldview.

As I understand heresy (a denial of essential Christian doctrine, e.g., the Triune God, the divinity of Christ, his sacrificial atonement, etc.), this is not it. I am firmly convinced the proponents of IM desire to see Muslims come to Christ, to see Muslims discipled in Christ-likeness, and to see churches established among the various unreached Muslim people groups. While the IM is not heretical on this point—I do believe much of their stated strategies are based on error. As the qur'anic Adama and Hawa erred in paradise rather than sinned,[21] so our IM brothers and sisters have erred. They've succumbed to the whispers of a seductive temptress: compassion and sloppy theology. The IM has the wrong worldview because it has not developed a biblically based TR, but one founded on the error of pitting compassion against truth.

Let me return to the question I sarcastically ask at the beginning. Would the Jesus of the Bible be caught dead working in Islam? How could he? The *Isa* of Islam is not the Jesus of the Bible. *Isa* would not be caught dead because he never died and rose from the dead. How can *Isa*, a man that took part in the deception of the cross, call men and women to embrace the truths of the Bible when his very existence is evidence for the falsity of the Bible?[22]

3. Finally, there is an implication here for those of us who take issue with the IM. Have we examined our own motives and methods in all that we are doing vis-à-vis the IM? Are we on a witch-hunt or are we truly attempting to correct a brother who has erred? Our approach to a brother in error ought to be quite different than with a brother in sin. Therefore, we must endeavor to keep the bar of the discussion at a very high level—as one among brothers and sisters in the Lord who only desire the best for believers—a developing, loving, maturing relationship with the God of the universe in churches that are growing in grace.

---

[21] Cf. Q7:20-4.

[22] According to Q5:156-9, *Isa* did not die on the cross although the witnesses were convinced it was him on the cross. Allah's deception stood as the truth of Christianity until the ruse was revealed in the Qur'an 600 years too late.

3.4 Dhimmitude, Muslim Replacement Theology, the Stockholm Syndrome and the Insider Movements

Roger Dixon

Introduction

This chapter examines three concepts of power relationships that relate to the insider movements (IM). They are dhimmitude, Muslim replacement theology, and the Stockholm Syndrome. The Islamic practice of dhimmitude and Muslim replacement theology has been brought to the attention of the world and clarified by Bat Ye'or, a Jewish writer raised in Egypt. Psychologists hypothesized the Stockholm Syndrome after the famous robbery of *Kreditbanken* in Stockholm. I believe these three concepts of power give us some understanding of the spiritual influences that are happening in the insider movements. As we look at these influences, John's warning comes to mind. "Beloved, do not believe every spirit, but test the spirits to see whether they are from God, for many false prophets have gone out into the world" (1 John 4:1).

Background

While many are discussing the "what, where, when, and who" of IM, few seem to be asking about the **why**? Rebecca Lewis defines IM as a movement in which believers in Jesus stay in their native religious system.[1] Many of the proponents (mostly Western missionaries) are creating new Bible translations in which filial language such as Father and Son, the *Son of God*, and the designation of Jesus as Lord of life, is eliminated or minimized to accommodate the religious prejudices of other world religions.

Since 1990 when some American tentmakers in my field of endeavor insisted on imitating a new approach that was being used in other countries, this basic question has plagued me. Why were they changing the traditional orthodox or evangelical understanding of the biblical meaning of repentance, baptism, discipleship, and other teachings that are the foundation of Christianity? Most of the workers in my area were from evangelical churches and many of them had been trained in evangelical Bible schools and seminaries. What was it that made some shift to a Gospel that would allow a person to continue in their traditional religion,

---

[1] Rebecca Lewis' definition of IM: "a) the Gospel flows through pre-existing communities and social networks, and where b) believing families, as valid expressions of the body of Christ, remain inside their socio-religious communities, retaining their identity as members of that community while living under the Lordship of Jesus Christ and the authority of the Bible" ("Promoting Movements to Christ within Natural Communities" *IJFM* 24(2): 75).

confessing belief in Jesus as a prophet while claiming also to be *followers of Jesus* (whatever that might mean)?

Is the IM the result of the influence of the emergent church movement, or some other aspect of postmodernism? Is it an element of relativism or multiculturalism? Have slogans such as "Muslims, it's their time" created a euphoria of doctrinal dissonance? Are they victims of spiritual deception? Is it a satanic delusion that is slowly spreading because of the overwhelming challenge of the Muslim, Hindu, and Buddhist worlds? Is Satan creating a distraction because Muslims and Hindus have begun to come to Christ in significant numbers? The questions abound and we must address the why as we look at IM.

During recent years, some Western church-raised missionaries have been imitating Muslim faith practices; some have even made the Muslim confession of faith: "There is no god but Allah and Muhammad is his prophet." What began as a way to contextualize the ethnic culture of the Muslim converts metamorphosized by absorbing certain aspects of the Islam. What made these men and women capitulate to the Muslim culture rather than just contextualizing the ethnic culture of the Muslim people? The answer to these questions is not easy, but some insight is found with those who have struggled to understand power relationships in Islamic dominated areas.

Bat Ye'or's hypothesis of dhimmitude

Bat Ye'or has written extensively about the power of the Muslim faith to control peoples' loyalty and subvert the religious allegiance of non-Muslim people. One of the primary ways this is done is through the process of dhimmitude. She writes,

> The civilization of dhimmitude does not develop all at once. It is a long process that involves many elements and a specific mental conditioning. It happens when peoples replace history by myths, when they fight to uphold these destructive myths, more than their own values because they are **confused** by having transformed lies into truth. They hold to those myths as if they were the only guarantee for their survival, when, in fact, they are the path to destruction. Terrorized by the evidence and teaching of history, those peoples prefer to destroy it rather than to face it. They replace history with childish tales, thus living in amnesia, inventing moral justification for their own self-destruction.[2] (emphasis added)

Dhimmitude is the first concept of power relationships that I relate to

---

[2] Bat Ye'or, "Myths and Politics: Origin of the Myth of a Tolerant Pluralistic Islamic Society:" Address on 31 August, 1995. http://www.dhimmi.org/LectureE1.html (accessed 9/14/10).

IM. The seeds of IM are easily seen in Bat Ye'or's exposition of dhimmitude. It seems to be nothing less than the tragedy of saved peoples whose freedom is in Christ Jesus submitting once again to a structure controlled by Islamic values. Although most Muslim peoples may have indigenous ethnic structures that are not Islamic, it is clear that the Islamic religious structures dominate. The development of a Church model that is under the power of the Islamic socio-religious community is to ensure its ultimate failure to develop a biblical Church.

In this respect, IM is promoting a dhimmi mentality among new converts before they are even formed as a fellowship of faith. It seems that the fear of the Church planters in the face of the authoritarian Islamic structures has led them to keep enquirers within those structures with the false notion they will be able to thrive.

Muslim replacement theology

The second concept of power relationships that affects IM is Muslim replacement theology. We can see how far IM has gone astray by examining some of its theological expressions. Muslim replacement theology is another term used in Bat Ye'or's writings to describe how Muslims appropriate the biblical history. It is common knowledge to all who have studied Islam that the early proponents of that religion sought a history by placing the locus of their faith in the Old Testament patriarchs such as Adam, Noah, Abraham and Moses. What is not so commonly understood is that by doing so, they attempted to artificially absorb the entire story of God's dealings with the Jews as their own personal history. In addition to this, they also claimed Jesus to be the prophet *Isa*, and in doing so emptied him of his true identity as the Son of God, the Lord of Life, and the Savior of the world. This contextualization process has continued up to the present day.

In an interview with World Magazine, Bat Ye'or said,

> There are many processes of Islamization. One of them is through theology and the adoption of the Muslim replacement theology, whereby the biblical figures from Adam—Abraham, Moses, down to Mary and Jesus—are all considered as "Muslim prophets." Hence, Israel's history is transferred to the Muslim Palestinians, and it is easy to see from there the final transition to Islam where the Jewish Jesus becomes an Arab-Palestinian-Muslim prophet.[3]

Many in the insider movements have also caved-in to this power relationship by following many of the Islamic terms and teachings that contradict biblical theology. Among the most telling is acknowledging Islam as an Old Testament faith, ascribing divine inspiration to the Qur'an, and

---

[3] *World Magazine*, November 18, 2005 20(45): 18.

referring to Jesus as a prophet who has a biblical place in Islamic faith.

Power relationships

Bat Ye'or's insight led me to investigate power relationships. Note her word *confused* above. If IM proponents mix Islamic and Christian theology, they are certainly confused or deceived. Could it be that the overwhelming power of the Islamic, Hindu, or Buddhist structures and socio-religious systems are so mighty that they force some people to defer to them, thus surrendering their own characteristic faith and practices?

Biblical examples

In Deuteronomy we find a number of references about the power of the Canaanite tribes. Moses talks about God's power to drive out "nations greater and stronger than you" (Deut 4:38; cf. 7:1 and 11:23).

Most interesting about these predictions is that Moses connects them to a condition for their fulfillment. The people must "carefully observe all these commands I am giving you to follow—to love the LORD your God, to walk in obedience to him and to hold fast to him" (Deut 11:22; cf. 12:29-30).

In Exodus 23:30 we read, "Little by little I will drive them out before you, until you have increased enough to take possession of the land." Then God warns them: "Do not make a covenant with them or with their gods. Do not let them live in your land or they will cause you to sin against me, because the worship of their gods will certainly be a snare to you" (23:32-3; cf. 34:11-12).

Psychological studies

It is eminently clear that God is not talking just about nations with greater military might, but also people who have socio-religious power to influence the people and divert them from true worship of the LORD God.

Richard Newbold Adams describes power in two different kinds of relations. One is control over environment and the other is power over an individual. Control is exercised over things, which can include people. Power is exercised in social relationships. "Power rests in the conjunction of what the individual perceives of his own internal being, what he perceives in the world about him, and how he relates these perceptions to establish his relations with other human beings."[4]

Jeff VanVonderan explains how the weaker party feels the pressure to conform: "The treatment we have all received in past relationships is the source of a powerful current—our sense of emotional and spiritual well being."[5]

---

[4] Richard Newbold Adams (1975). *Energy & Structure: A Theory of Social Power* (21-2). Austin, TX: University of Texas.

[5] Jeff VanVonderan (1989). *Tired of Trying to Measure Up* (29). Minneapolis, MN: Bethany House.

The Stockholm Syndrome

A modern example of this power relationship is what psychologists call the Stockholm Syndrome.

> The term takes its name from a bank robbery in Stockholm, Sweden, in August 1973. The robber took four employees of the bank (three women and one man) into the vault with him and kept them hostage for one hundred thirty-one hours. After the employees were finally released, they appeared to have formed a paradoxical emotional bond with their captor; they told reporters that they saw the police as their enemy rather than the bank robber, and that they had positive feelings toward the criminal.[6]

> As a basic concept, Stockholm Syndrome is the duality of a power relationship over someone. A person captured becomes deeply involved with the captor due to the typical confine of the circumstances, and because even through the abuse and threats, they still must accept them as the only source of contact and nurturing that focuses on them.[7]

It seems likely the Stockholm Syndrome describes the situation in which the insider movements' people feel they exist. All or much of their sense of power has been removed. They are at the mercy of the majority religion and must accommodate themselves to it. Praising the religion as having intrinsic value for all people and needing only minor changes so that it can be fully biblical in its tenets and practices restores power. This capitulation to the majority religion has, in turn, led to the feeling that one can find one's place in the majority religion if it is altered in some respects. Thus they are deceived into thinking it is consistent with biblical theology to create *so-called churches* that "**retain their identity** as members of their socio-religious community while living under the Lordship of Jesus Christ and the authority of the Bible"[8]

The final outcome is the development of a submissive attitude to the non-biblical religion and the leadership of the religion. The *so-called churches* are marginal and in some cases, may exist as sects of the majority religion. There are examples where this approach has culminated in missionaries following the religious practices of the majority faith and, in the case of Islam, joining the mosque and participating in the daily prayers, the fast month, and in other ceremonies reserved for the faithful.

Marguerite Schuster describes a socio-religious structure in this way.

---

[6] http://medical-dictionary.thefreedictionary.com/Stockholm+syndrome (accessed 9/12/10).
[7] http://serendip.brynmawr.edu/exchange/node/1896 (accessed 9/12/10).
[8] Rebecca Lewis, "Insider Movements: Honoring God-Given Identity and Community" *IJFM* 26(1): 33.

"When we put structure and will together, the result is power."[9] She goes on to describe our options when we find ourselves at a disadvantage in a power relationship. We have to make a choice to oppose it, flee from it, or find a way to accommodate ourselves to it. It appears to many observers that the IM proponents have chosen to accommodate themselves to the overpowering influence of Islam, Hinduism, and Buddhism.

William and Candace Backus write that giving in is not as infrequent as people might think. Even in serious issues we can be controlled. In all relationships there are controllers and the powerful party is usually the controller. "It is not as hard as you think to be controlled by someone. Many of us **let** ourselves be controlled."[10] This seems to be the condition of IM. Its advocates have become victims of the Stockholm Syndrome and caved-in to the pressures of powerful non-biblical worldviews.

Standing on the word of God

The surest way we can avoid being controlled by those who are more powerful socially, politically, and culturally is to maintain a firm commitment to our own spiritual and psychological moorings. Deuteronomy 12 exhorts us to not follow the ways of worship of other peoples. "For you are a people holy to the LORD your God. The LORD your God has chosen you out of all the peoples on the face of the earth to be his people, his treasured possession" (Deut 7:6). The covenant given to Israel is ours as well because we, too, are the sons of Abraham through the Messiah, Jesus Christ, the Son of God, Lord of all.

---

[9] Marguerite Shuster (1987). *Power, Pathology, Paradox* (99). Grand Rapids, MI: Zondervan.
[10] William and Candace Backus (1988). *Untwisting Twisted Relationships* (136). Minneapolis, MN: Bethany House.

3.5 IM: Inappropriate Missiology?

Jeff Morton

Introduction

Charles Kraft's important volume dedicated to Dean Gilliland, *Appropriate Christianity*, is the backdrop to this chapter. Kraft's fingerprints can be found on the missiological model proposed by the IM; in fact, I argue that many pro-IMers have devleoped an **inappropriate** missiology, rather than an appropriate one.

When I use the word missiology, I mean the critical study of missions, and a missiologist is one who, armed with biblical theology informed by the social sciences, attempts to make sense of what has happened, what is now occurring and what may yet take place in light of the Gospel. By calling this missiology inappropriate, I argue less in the direction of heresy (a theological concept) and more in the direction of a reexamination of foundational IM premises (missiological methodology).

In order to best address inappropriate missiology, this chapter explores just two of the assumptions or premises upon which the movement is based. John and Anna Travis presume that

1. Jesus did not come to begin a new religion, but to establish the kingdom of God. Therefore those who pledge their allegiance to Jesus do not need to change religions.
2. There are some Islamic practices and beliefs that align with Scripture.[1]

The first premise

I completely agree that Jesus did not come to start a new religion, but there is more to the premise than meets the eye. Jesus did not come to establish a new religion because he came as one who was a Jew, as one who preached biblical Judaism, but I deal with this later. For now, there are at least three areas of discussion.

a) What does it mean that Jesus came to establish the kingdom of God?

Each of the Gospels mentions Jesus' consistent preaching of this message (Mt 4:16-17; Mark 1:14; Luke 1:32; John 3:3). The irony is that his view of the kingdom was not that of the typical first century Jew. Jesus did not come to establish an earthly reign (John 18:36), but a new covenant between the Father and his people (John 3:1ff; Jer 31:33ff). This kingdom

---

[1] John Travis and Anna Travis (2005). "Appropriate Approaches in Muslim Contexts" (397-414). In Charles H. Kraft (Ed.). *Appropriate Christianity*. Pasadena, CA: William Carey Library.

is one of relationship, of renewed hearts, and worship in spirit and truth (John 4:23). The kingdom of God was indeed the focus of Jesus' preaching, but what are we to think of the kingdom vis-à-vis religion?

Jesus spoke harshly to the religious people of his day although we should not see this as Jesus being anti-religion. We are familiar with his tongue-lashing of the Pharisees (Mt 23) and his cleansings of the temple (Mt 21:12ff; John 2:13ff). While these events are ostensibly anti-religion, Jesus' behavior shows his love for the Jewish religion, so much so that he critically corrects its errors. True, Jesus did not come to establish a new religion, but neither did he come to abolish it (Mt 5:17). He came with zeal for the house of God, the temple. He knew and loved the Scriptures, an essential component of the Jewish religion (Mt 5:18-19). He encouraged the proper practice of certain religious rites and rituals: presenting offerings (Mt 5:23-4), keeping one's righteous deeds private (Mt 6:1ff), prayer (Mt 6:5ff), and fasting (Mt 6:16-18). Each of these outward forms or manifestations of religion held great meaning to Jesus; otherwise he would not have spoken about them.

Again, I agree that Jesus did not come to establish a new religion; rather he corrected the established religion. Jesus was not anti-religion; rather he was against the abuse of religious forms evidenced by his correction of the various rituals and teachings of Judaism perverted by ill-motivated individuals. This included his view of the kingdom.

b) The premise does not include something Jesus said

Not only did Jesus preach the kingdom, additionally he said, "I will build my Church" (Mt 16:18). In light of this we must not confuse the kingdom with the Church. The Church is the servant of the kingdom. The Church is the community of the kingdom; the "kingdom of God becomes visible in any community whenever a cluster of people gather in Jesus' name."[2] There is an organic link between the Church and the kingdom that we must recognize. On one hand, overemphasis upon the kingdom can lead to neglect of the Church – as if the Church has no place in God's dealings with Muslims. On the other hand, an overemphasis upon the Church may cause one to ignore the kingdom. What is needed is a balanced appreciation of the relation of the Church to the kingdom.[3]

It appears some proponents of IM place the kingdom opposite or **against** the Church. This first premise associates the Church and

---

[2] David W. Shenk and Ervin R. Stutzman (1988). *Creating Communities of the Kingdom* (23). Scottdale, PA: Herald Press.

[3] The Travises' chapter contains ten premises; only one even mentions the church: "Due to the lack of Church structure and organization, C5 movements must have an exceptionally high reliance on the Spirit and the Word as their primary source of instruction" (409). It is not my wish to impugn IM as seeing the church as irrelevant. It does not. The problem is that so little is said of the church in light of insiders, that one is hard pressed to know what is meant exactly is by *Church* beyond "simple home-based C5 fellowships" (409).

Christianity with religion rather than with the kingdom. Jesus, pro-IMers argue, was concerned with the kingdom as opposed to religion. This premise diminishes the importance of the Church. It makes the Church an obstacle to the work of God rather than the means by which he expands the kingdom. Let me illustrate the subtlety of this premise.

Some time ago speaker came to Biola University, captivating the students with accounts of drinking tea with the Taliban and telling imams and sheikhs stories about Jesus. He related a story of how he answered the question, "Are you a Christian?" He said that he was a follower of Jesus. Another time he was asked if he would share about Christianity, but he claimed he knew little of Christianity, saying that while he could not speak about Christianity, he could speak about Jesus. And more importantly, he said, "Jesus didn't come to establish a religion called Christianity."

The speaker, without intending to, and with the best of motives, belittled the Church. By refusing to speak about Christianity, by neglecting the importance of the bride of Christ, the body of Christ, and the holy priesthood, revealed a veiled contempt for the most important means God has for actually promoting the kingdom: the Church. He allows Muslims to define Christianity and the Church for him. Do Muslims permit Christians to define the *ummah* (the global Islamic community) or *tawhid* (oneness of Allah) for them? No. Yet we permit Islamic perceptions of *Christianity*, a *Christian* and *Church* to remain unchallenged. This bait-and-switch tactic ("I'm not a Christian, but I follow Jesus") borders on Christian *taqiyya*.[4]

Some proponents of IM struggle to appreciate the Church, believing it is a stumbling block for Muslims. Therefore they allow Muslims to believe a lie by speaking only of Jesus as if he had no connection with the Church.[5] This is naïve at best and deceptive at worst. We need a renewed interest in and appreciation for the bride of Christ as it relates to the kingdom, not a dismissal of the Church because it carries the baggage of being a religious artifact of Christianity. After all, Jesus is coming back for his bride not her luggage.

---

[4] *Taqiyya* is dissimulation under certain conditions. "Muhammad said: 'Lying is wrong, except in three things: the lie of a man to his wife to make her content with him; a lie to an enemy, for war is deception; or a lie to settle trouble between people'" (Ahmad, 6.459).

[5] There are several lies we Christians let Muslims believe: one, a Christian is one who swills alcohol to excess, eats pork (as if it were manna), makes crusade against Islam, attends church on Sunday then lives for the devil the rest of the week; two, the Church coerces Muslims to convert to Christianity through bribery or the offer of jobs; and three, Christianity is just another religion like any other religion—what really matters is Christ. The latter is a lie because it makes the individual the center of conversion, not God, Christ, his Scriptures or his Church. This is but another flaw of pro-IM missiology: an incorporation of the North American value of individualism. Salvation is really about *God and me*. Is it? Church seems unnecessary for believers (at least in C6, and for C5 it is certainly an entity to avoid if it already exists). Is it? Apparently all the individual needs is the kingdom of God, not the fellowship of the God's people, the Church.

c) What is conversion and is there a need to change religions?

What are the biblical injunctions for new believers? Do new believers come away from their old religion or do they stay in it? Many pro-IMers argue there is no need to leave one religion for another since Jesus never called his followers to join a religion. It is not necessary for a Muslim who wishes to follow Jesus to become a Christian—or to leave Islam. Again, there are some suppositions at work that I want to tease out from the premise.

The premise supposes all religions are the same

Most pro-IMers argue it is foolish to swap one religion for another. Religion is a man-made contraption that Jesus eschewed.[6] Becoming a follower of Jesus is a matter of heart allegiance, not joining a local congregation. Who thinks that simply sitting in the Church makes one a Christian any more than sitting under an apple tree makes one Sir Isaac Newton? But are all religions the same?

Jesus spoke with the Samaritan woman, an adherent of another religion. When he said to her that "salvation is from the Jews" (John 4:22), was he telling her that Judaism was no different, no truer, no better than her own religion? In fact, Jesus made a bold declaration about Judaism, true Judaism: it was the only religion in which one finds salvation.

I need to be careful here. I do not believe Jesus called the woman to Judaism, at least not first century Judaism; however, I am convinced Jesus invited her to biblical Judaism. It is a Judaism in which "true worshipers will worship the Father in spirit and truth" (4:23). Jesus is neither denigrating her religion nor his; rather he is helping her understand **there is a true religion** and that the practice of her religion falls short of what he offers.

Jesus did not have a pluralistic view of religions; he was an exclusivist. He inaugurated the kingdom of God through his practice of Judaism—yes, through religion—the Judaism that was experienced by Abraham who was reckoned righteous by faith (Gen 15:6). It was the Judaism of Isaiah, the missionary religion of light for the nations (Gen 42:6). Jesus lived Jeremiah's Judaism, the religion of a new heart and covenant (Jer 31:31-3). It was the Judaism of Joel in which God called for a holy fast, a ritual of religion (1:13f). Not all religions are the same. There is a true religion: the religion of Jesus. There is false religion: every other religion. Most pro-IMers have the wrong understanding of religion. They do not seem to understand that every religion, except Jesus', is a stumbling block. Jesus did not stumble over authentic Judaism; he lived it. I humbly suggest IMers do

---

[6] For a nuanced view from the pro-IM perspective, see Kevin Higgins's "Inside What? Church, Culture, Religion, and Insider Movements in Biblical Perspective" *SFM* 5(4). He offers his understanding of the biblical perspective of religion: it is "the rejection of the truth of God" (84), it incorporates the demonic; yet (ironically) God is at work in all religions.

not have Jesus' understanding of religion.[7]

The premise is based on an over reliance on social science

We can argue until the cows come home about whether or not Islam is a religion, a culture or some combination, but it is indisputable that followers of Jesus are said to have their eyes opened from the effects of darkness to the blessings of the light (Acts 26:18; 2 Cor 6:14; Eph 5:8; 1 Thess 5:5; 1 Pet 2:9). If Islam does not have Jesus, the kingdom, the Gospel, or the Church, then it must have spiritual darkness as its primal substance. Therefore, it is a system that must be **turned from** as part of one's **turning to** the light.[8]

If it is necessary to turn from one's previous position of darkness, unregeneration, and spiritual blindness to Christ and thus becoming incorporated into the body of Christ, how is that some pro-IMers assume it is not necessary to leave Islam when following Jesus? Some pro-IMers seem to think Islam is merely cultural: a way of life. This type of missiology assumes a Durkheimian view of religion in which religion is the cement of society.[9] Therefore a Muslim who leaves Islam is not simply leaving a religion, but his culture, his family, his society, and every bit of his identity. This understanding of Islam allows new believers to maintain their Islamic culture as they explore what it means to be a follower of Jesus. I speak to this notion in the following section.

The second premise

At first blush this seems reasonable. Muslims pray; Christians pray. Muslims have a creed; Christians have a creed. Both have their own Scriptures, but it is illogical to think similarities mean equality. First, do the beliefs and practices of Islam genuinely align with the Bible? Second, if they do align, what specifically are those practices? Consider the following examples offered by the Travises in their essay:[10]

- They [Muslims] recognize as Scripture the Torah (*Taurat*), the Psalms (*Zabur*) and the New Testament (*Injil*);

---

[7] See my "3.3 Theology of Religions: would Jesus be caught dead working in Islam?" in this volume (pp. 123-33).

[8] It is not my argument that one who turns from Islam must immediately exhibit complete understanding of Islam, Christianity, the new birth, and sanctification. More often than not, the turning from and turning to is a gradual process, but there will come that point when repentance is decisive. It is then the Christian from a Muslim context will have his or her eyes and heart opened fully to see the error of the old religion, the darkness of Islam, and the seduction of remaining in Islam as something that is sinister, and not pleasing to Jesus.

[9] Emile Durkheim believed in a scientific study of society, so much so, he developed laws to explain the whys of societal functions. He believed religion was necessary for society to exist; religion is not simply rituals and rites, but it provides the framework or structure upon which society rests. I do not necessarily disagree with Durkheim (and IM) and have probably overstated the case vis-à-vis Durkheim, but I do so to make the point that their theology of religions is less biblical than it must be.

[10] Travises, "Appropriate" 406.

- They believe in the divine birth and ministry of Jesus;
- They acknowledge as prophets most of the major Biblical figures;
- Jesus...the Word of God (*kalimat Allah*), the Spirit of God (*ruh Allah*), and the Messiah (*al-Masih*).

What is the Islamic view of the Bible?

The Qur'an was revealed to confirm and guard previous revelations such as the Torah, Psalms and Gospel. It was also given to provide a more complete and profound understanding of Allah's previous message (Q10:37, "it is a confirmation of [revelations] that went before it, and a fuller explanation"). So, the Bible is viewed in Islam as the corrupted and altered word of Allah. It is corrupted to such a degree that it is difficult to distinguish the words of Allah from those of men. Therefore it was necessary for the Qur'an to come down from Allah to straighten out the confusion.

Does Islam recognize the Torah, Psalms and Gospel as Scripture? Yes and no. A. Yusuf `Ali writes, "The correct translation of the *Tawrah* is therefore 'The Law.' In its original form it was promulgated by Moses, and is recognized in Islam as having been an inspired Book. But it was lost before Islam was preached."[11]

Does Islam consider Christian Scripture as Scripture? Only as much as we still have the original words of Moses, which are lost. Abul A'la Maududi believes the "earlier codes were abrogated by the advent of Muhammad . . . who gave the world a complete code of life."[12]

Does Islam consider the Christian Scriptures as Scripture? No, they have been replaced. Consider this statement from Ibn Kathir:

> "As for Allah's Books, they are still preserved and cannot be changed." Ibn Abi Hatim recorded this statement. However, if Wahb meant the books that are currently in the hands of the People of the Book, then we should state that **there is no doubt that they altered, distorted, added to and deleted from them**. For instance, the Arabic versions of these books contain tremendous error, many additions and deletions and enormous misinterpretation. Those who rendered these translations have incorrect comprehension in most, rather, all of these translations.[13]

Does Islam consider the Scriptures of the People of the Book to be Scripture? No. They have been altered, distorted and completely changed. The Islamic view of the Scriptures of Jews and Christians is that they are

---

[11] A. Yusuf Ali (1989). *The Meaning of the Glorious Qur'an* (290). Beltsville, MD: Amana.
[12] Khurshid Ahmad (Ed. and trans). (1977). *Towards Understanding Islam*. Lahore: Idar Tarjuman-ul-Qur'an.
[13] From the abridged tafsir of ibn Kathir found at www.tafsir.com. The comment is made about Q3:78. (emphasis added)

from Allah in their original condition, but they have since been altered and changed. They are therefore unreliable and not to be trusted. Is this the teaching of the Church throughout history? I believe the Travises' statement is misleading.

Birth and ministry of Jesus in the Qur'an and hadith

The Qur'an tells us the angel Gabriel appeared to the Virgin Mary. He informed her she would bear a son over her exclamations of being chaste: "So [it will be]: thy Lord said, 'that is easy for Me: and [We wish] to appoint him as a sign unto men and a mercy from us': it is a matter [so] decreed" (Q19:21).

But what do the Travises mean by *divine birth*? As Christians they believe the Spirit of God overshadowed Mary and caused her to become pregnant. Is this the Islamic understanding? Ibn Kathir writes,

> Many scholars of the predecessors *(Salaf)* have mentioned that at this point the angel [who was Jibril] blew into the opening of the garment that she was wearing. Then the breath descended until it entered into her vagina and she conceived the child by the leave of Allah.[14]

The Islamic understanding of the divine birth is that the Holy Spirit (Gabriel) huffed and puffed until Mary became pregnant. Is this the biblical account of the son who "is conceived in her from the Holy Spirit" (Mt 1:21)? I agree the birth of Jesus in Islam is viewed as *divine*, but it is a qualified divine: it is not the Holy Spirit of God, but Gabriel, a mere angel, who impregnates Mary.

Does Islam acknowledge biblical prophets?

Yes and no. Again, we have a problem of perspectives and definitions. The Qur'an speaks of twenty-five prophets, most of whom are biblical. One question will clarify the matter: which of the prophets of Islam called upon God in the Qur'an using his covenant name, Yahweh? In fact, none of them did. Even the final prophet, the seal of the prophets, never uttered the name Yahweh. How is it possible for a prophet not to know the name of the deity for whom he speaks?

Islam acknowledges the biblical prophets, but these prophets are not the prophets of the Bible. The Qur'an presents cardboard-like, two-dimensional caricatures of the biblical personalities. Roberto Tottoli speaks to this very issue:

> The Qur'an . . . does not contain an unequivocal definition of the stories of the biblical prophets . . . apart from its function for the mission of Muhammad, the Qur'an does not consider these narrative

---

[14] www.tafsir.com.

parts as a precise genre that can be distinguished from the rest of the revelations.[15]

The sole purpose for including the stories of the biblical prophets is that they introduce, predict, parallel, and explain the prophethood of Muhammad. The biblical prophets have nothing to do with calling the nation of Israel back to Yahweh (except to show how evil the Jews are). The biblical prophets have nothing to do with condemning the sin of the nations who surround the Jews. The biblical prophets have nothing to do with the promise of Messiah. They may be biblical prophets from the Islamic perspective, but they are simple cutout paper figures with no depth, meant only to provide background for the one real prophet of lasting significance: Muhammad.

Are the titles of Jesus in the Qur'an biblical?

Consider the three major titles given to Jesus in the Qur'an. Are they equivalent to the biblical titles?

Jesus is the Word of God (*kalimat Allah*)
- In Christianity, this refers to Jesus the second person of the Trinity (John 1:1 et al).
- In Islam, it means Jesus is a created being, an apostle (Q4:171; 3:59).

Jesus is the Spirit of God (*ruh Allah*)
- This is a title neither attributed to Jesus nor taken by him in the Bible, though some Christians insist it is some type of biblical reference to Jesus in the Qur'an.
- For the Muslim, this means Jesus is a spirit proceeding from Allah (Q4:171), that is, a human being created by Allah.

Jesus is Messiah (*al masih*)
- In Christianity, Messiah is the anointed suffering servant who brings forgiveness of sin through his atoning death and resurrection.
- In Islam, *al masih* is simply a title or a name given to Jesus with no understanding or explanation of Messiah's purpose.[16]

Of the world's religions, only Islam is explicitly anti-Christian in its beliefs. *Isa* of the Qur'an is not the same Jesus that Christians see in the Gospels. Yes, there are similarities beyond the name, but surely there must be a point at which the similarities pale in light of the differences? It seems that some proponents of IM willingly overlook the dramatic disparities for the sake of building bridges. I am certainly interested in building bridges with Muslims for the sake of evangelism, but not at *any* cost, and surely not

---

[15] Roberto Tottoli (2002). *Biblical Prophets in the Qur'an and Muslim Literature* (11). Richmond, UK: Curzon Press.

[16] For a narrative exploration of why Jesus the Messiah cannot be *Isa al-Masih*, see Jeff Morton (2011). *Two Messiahs*. Colorado Springs, CO: Biblica.

at the cost of equivocating over key theological issues. A bridge can be an effective tool of communication, but a bridge leading nowhere promises only a long drop.

What are the Islamic forms that align with the Scriptures?

At the root of IM's premise about Islam is a missiology heavily influenced by Charles Kraft. Kraft's writings are appreciated by most of us for he articulates a meaningful and helpful assessment on such matters as worldview, communication of the Gospel, contextualization, and form and meaning. It is the latter concept, form and meaning, especially as it relates to Kraft's understanding of the neutrality of culture, I wish to address as the underlying assumption of IM's methodology.

Kraft traces his own understanding of form and meaning to anthropologist Homer Barnett.[17] Every religion has both form and meaning. Form is the outward phenomenon we see in a religion (e.g., *salah*, the Islamic form of worship). Meaning is the deep level significance ascribed to the form (e.g., *salah* symbolizes the submission of the slave to the master, the believer to Allah). Clifford Geertz speaks to this matter when he says, "Whatever the ultimate sources of the faith of a man or group of men may or may not be, it is indisputable that it is sustained in this world by symbolic forms and social arrangements."[18] These forms are the practice of religion; the meanings are the stories behind the forms. Guided by the principle of form and meaning, Kraft theorized the possibility of contextualizing Christianity into Muslim cultural forms.[19] The utilization of these cultural forms that align with Scripture lies at the heart of IM. There are at least three questions in light of this premise.

Islam: culture, religion, or mixture of both?

The Travises write, "For Muslims, culture, politics and religion are nearly inseparable, making changing religions a total break with society."[20] The authors believe Islam is a religio-cultural phenomenon. Indeed, Muslims often tell me Islam is a complete way of life. Even Muslims seem to believe Islam is more than a religion; Islam is their culture. How then do we handle this notion of Islam being a culture?

Missionaries often removed new believers from Islamic culture, turning them into bad impersonations of the missionary. The new convert left his culture, adopting the missionary culture. This is extraction; it may

---

[17] Homer Barnett (1953). *Innovation, the Basis for Culture Change.* New York, NY: McGraw Hill.
[18] Clifford Geertz (1968). *Islam Observed: Religious Development in Morocco and Indonesia* (2). Chicago, IL: University of Chicago Press.
[19] Not all missiologists agree with the form and meaning distinction as proposed by Kraft; the most notable is Paul Hiebert (see Paul Hiebert (1989). "Form and Meaning in the Contextualization of the Gospel." In Dean S. Gilliland (Ed.). *The Word Among Us* (101-20). Dallas, TX: Word.). Hiebert theorizes that form is the meaning in many cases.
[20] Travises, "Appropriate" 403.

not be the best method of discipleship, but it was what missionaries practiced. It did create new disciples; however, the problem was the distance the extractive process created between the convert and his culture. It meant the end of contextualized sharing of the Gospel by the new convert.

Not extracting the new convert—the pro-IM proposal—keeps the new convert within his Islamic culture, allowing the Christian to be cloaked with Islam, thus allowing for a contextualized preaching, sharing, and ministering of the Gospel by the convert.

Just upon the basis of the last two paragraphs, who could deny the efficacy of the non-extractive approach? Why would anyone practice extraction if remaining in one's culture might produce new believers? The problem is not so simple.

This brings us back to the question of Islam as culture or religion. We must determine whether Islam is too interwoven with culture to untangle. Most of us who know Islam agree: the religion has cultural elements knit into it. Islam does provide every Muslim, regardless of his or her own secular culture, a new culture. This culture is called the *sunna* of the prophet, and is situated in the hadith.

Sunna means "way of acting."[21] It has come to mean the way the prophet of Islam behaved. The *hadith* contains his behaviors, his disapprovals of various items, and even the actions of some of the earliest Muslims. These traditions are the manner in which Muslims today, 1400 years after the death of their prophet, live their lives. The culture of Islam is found in the *sunna* of the prophet.

The traditions contain reports of how Muhammad slept, ate, washed, prayed, fought, blew his nose, laughed, interacted with his wives and behaved in the toilet. If all these behaviors are the appropriate way to live one's life as a Muslim, how can the new believer sift through the forms to decide what part of his *culture* he should keep and which he should discard? The Travises are right: the culture and religion of Islam are virtually inseparable.

Islamic understanding of Islamic forms

Have you ever seen a Muslim father instruct his son about the proper form of *salah*? It occurs every day because there is a right and wrong way to perform *salah*. If it is performed correctly, the worship is valid; if not, the worshipper's efforts are voided.

What is the proper way for Christian worship to take place? Do we raise our hands or clap them? Do we stand or sit, kneel or jump? Do we dance and sway or simply stand still? Is it possible for Christian worship to be nullified by performing worship in the wrong manner? While a Muslim's

---

[21] G.H.A. Juynboll (2006). "Sunna"(163). In Jane Dammen McAuliffe (Ed.). *Encyclopaedia of the Qur'ân* (v. 5). Leiden: Brill.

worship may be voided if not performed according to the *sunna*, there is no one Christian form that carries the entire meaning of worship. The God of the Bible allows every culture to shape worship; however, this is not the case in Islam. **In Islam the form is the meaning; the meaning is the form.** The two are inseparable. In the case of Islam, Kraft's general principle mentioned earlier, cannot be applied indiscriminately as if slathering butter on a piece of bread. That is, the missionary cannot simply take an Islamic form, determine its meaning, then perform surgery to remove the Islamic meaning, replacing it with a new Christianized meaning. Islam's forms do not allow the replacement of its DNA to create something new. This creates something that is not Islam!

Muslims themselves say this. Shahzad Bashir states, "The body is the fundamental ground on and through which a person constructs one's identity as a Muslim."[22] The implication here is that *salah*, a ritual that fully engages bodily movement, is involved in defining Muslim self-perception. Even more to the point is the thought of Indonesian Muslim scholar Nurcholish Madjid: "When performed with devotion and attention and accompanied by the tranquility of every member of the body, [*salah*] is a perfect declaration of faith."[23]

What I am arguing is that Islam's forms and meanings are so innately linked, that to perform *salah* is to be Muslim; therefore to change one or the other is to change the whole. If the missionary (or new Christian) attempts to keep the Islamic form while changing its meaning, the hybrid, like the mule, is sterile.[24] But should the missionary or new convert insist upon creating a hybrid, what does Islam say about it?

The form of *salah* is the manner in which Muhammad prayed. If Muhammad did it, it is *sunna* and therefore incumbent upon all Muslims to pray in the same manner. No one may add to or subtract from *salah* lest he be charged with the sin of *bid`a* (innovation or heresy).[25] Muslims perform

---

[22] Shahzad Bashir (2010). "Body" (80). In Jamal J. Elias (Ed.). *Key Themes for the Study of Islam*. Oxford: Oneworld.
[23] Nurcholish Madjid (1998). "Worship as an Institution of Faith" (72-3). In John Renard (Ed.). *Windows on the House of Islam*. Berkeley: University of California Press.
[24] On a similar though ironic note, Rick Brown states the biblical phrase *son of God* cannot be understood rightly by Muslims. He advocates against an idiomatic translation because its "biological meaning . . . and its blasphemous connotations are so deeply entrenched in the minds of most Muslims that it is impossible simply to erase it from their minds and hearts." Although I disagree with his conclusion, the irony is that an IM proponent is agreeing that this form cannot take on a new meaning to the Muslim, the true meaning—just the opposite of the general pro-IM approach to Islamic forms (cf. Rick Brown, "Explaining the Biblical Terms 'Son(s) of God' in Muslim Contexts" *IJFM* 22(3) and 22(4): 92.).
[25] The following hadith shows the form of *salah* comes from the prophet of Islam: "Ibn `Umar said, 'While the Prophet was on the pulpit, a man asked him how to offer the night prayers. He replied, 'Pray two *Rakat* at a time and then two and then two and so on, and if you are afraid of the dawn (the approach of the time of the *Fajr* prayer) pray one *Rak'a* and that will be the *witr* for all the *Rakat* which you have offered.' Ibn 'Umar said, 'The last

the obligatory prayers because Muhammad said so. *Salah* has a divinely revealed form and meaning. How can this form be filled with Christian meaning when Islam itself determines the meaning? Should a Muslim see a Christian performing *salah* he will think that person is Muslim—not a Christian giving new meaning to *salah*.

Is another perspective on culture possible?

Kraft utilizes the principle of form and meaning in light of his understanding of culture; namely, that culture is neutral.[26] Cultural behavior is neutral when it does not contradict a scriptural standard. Female infanticide must not be incorporated into Christian worship because it violates a scriptural standard. Prayer, while placing a chicken on one's head, is a neutral act as there is no biblical injunction against it (although one would certainly want to know why the chicken is on the practitioner's head). Is Kraft's view of neutrals in culture the only or the best view? If it is, the premises of IM are right and those of us who disagree are being petulant at best and heresy-hunters at worst.

Sherwood Lingenfelter does suggest an opposing, and more appropriate view of culture. According to Lingenfelter, culture is not about neutrality, rather culture is a prison from which we need to escape.[27] Since man is sinful, he creates sinful structures; these sinful structures are our cultures. There is not much neutrality in culture if it is sinful. It is therefore the goal of discipleship to lead a person out of the bondage of culture into the freedom of knowing Christ. Every follower of Jesus, every Christian, is on a pilgrimage away from his culture, his prison of bondage, and into full obedience to Jesus.

The problem with Kraft's neutral forms is that Islam does not distinguish between form and meaning, therefore his assumptions about culture lead to real problems. Accepting Lingenfelter's premise—sinful man creates sinful structures—mitigates these problems. This view of culture permits new converts to see Islam for what it is: a pit, a prison, a noose, and a snare of the devil. Islam is a religion of death, chains, blindness and pride. It is a religion of death because should one leave it, death is prescribed for the apostate. It is a religion of chains binding its practitioners to a creed that keeps them from experiencing intimacy with

---

Rakat of the night prayer should be odd for the Prophet ordered it to be so.'" Narrated by Nafi from *Sahih al-Bukhari* 1.461 (cited from `Alim, ISL Software).

[26] Culture, for Kraft, is "like a road . . . with boundaries on which people may walk or drive. People may choose to walk or drive off the road" (*Anthropology for Christian Witness* 31). Therefore, culture itself is not that which constrains behavior, but is "a vehicle or milieu, neutral in essence, though warped by the pervasive influence of human sinfulness" (Charles H. Kraft (1979). *Christianity in Culture* (113). Maryknoll, NY: Orbis.). Neutral cultural phenomena are open for critical contextualization for Gospel presentation and utilization by the church as valid, relevant cultural expressions of worship and Christian life.

[27] Cf. Sherwood Lingenfelter (1998). *Transforming Culture* (2nd ed.). Grand Rapids, MI: Baker.

our heavenly Father. Instead, it chains them to a human being, an alleged prophet, whose very lifestyle should make even the most sympathetic of observers wince. Islam is a religion of blindness because it advocates unquestioning allegiance to a god one cannot know. It is a religion of pride because it encourages its adherents to do the very best they can in order to be accepted by Allah on the Day of Judgment.

Is this a religion we want new converts to remain in and borrow from? Or is this the type of religion from which the new convert must make his pilgrimage? Using Kraft's view of culture, many pro-IMers propose the former. I believe, Sherwood Lingenfelter has given us a better understanding of culture: it is a prison of disobedience. Let us help every convert begin the pilgrimage away from the darkness of his prison cell to the light of the kingdom of God.

Conclusions

I have examined two important premises of the IM. The first suggested a nearly total dismissal of the Church. If the premise is allowed to play out to its logical conclusion, the Church plays little role in the life of the new follower of Jesus. It seems to me the IM is proposing a very individualistic type of Christianity: *God and me* rather than *God and we*. Why would we want to impose an essentially North American value on the rest of the world? Is this not a type of colonialism at which we all grimace? Why would we allow a Western ideal to replace the biblical understanding of community, congregation, fellowship, and worship? For some IM proponents, the Church's role is minimized in the believer's life since he is not coming into the Church, but the kingdom of God.

The second premise concerns the nature of Islamic forms and why these forms cannot be brought into the believer's walk with Christ. I posed Charles Kraft's view of culture against Sherwood Lingenfelter's view to show the latter's greater applicability to missionary work among Muslims. Ideas matter; they form behaviors and behaviors have consequences. The consequences of IM are not a clearer understanding of the believer's identity in Christ, but an amalgam of Church and mosque, Jesus and *Isa*, Moses and Muhammad. Such a methodology cannot continue if we expect the Church to be built and the kingdom to expand—appropriately.

3.6 Insider Movements' Equivalent of Limbo: The CAMEL Method

Emir Caner

> Emir is the son of a Turkish Muslim leader, but gave his life to Christ and was disowned by his father. He attended Southeastern Baptist Theological Seminary (MDiv), and earned his PhD in History from the University of Texas, Arlington. He has served the Church as pastor and educator; he was the founding dean of the College at Southwestern and now serves as the eighth president of Truett-McConnell College. A prolific author, including the best seller *Unveiling Islam*, Emir's works and ministry emphasize evangelism and missions, religious liberty, and apologetics.

At the beginning of the fourteenth century, the Italian poet, Dante Alighieri (AD c.1265 – 1321), penned his *Divine Comedy*, a vivid and provocative vision of Heaven, Hell, and Purgatory narrated by the Roman poet, Virgil and, later, Beatrice, a woman with whom Dante was obsessed his entire life even though both parties were married to another. In his section *Inferno*, Dante imagines the Roman Catholic doctrine of Limbo, the state where there is neither suffering nor joy. In Limbo, which translates as *edge* or *boundary*, unbaptized yet virtuous souls—souls including Moses, Noah, and Muslim warrior Saladin[1]—exist, awaiting their exit from this first ring of hell into the splendors of heaven.

Limbo was, in a very real way, the mediation that would draw those most fortunate to enter it the opportunity to earn a better place. Dante lays bare his heart and hope that those he admired most, Greek poets like Homer and Greek philosophers like Socrates, would be given the privileged chance of entering the promise of Paradise. Limbo developed as a tradition in order to remediate the problem of those who were born before Christ's sacrifice or those whose original sins were not removed by infant baptism. It was the **bridge** between the Church and its doctrine and sinners and their fate.

So, too, is the creation of the CAMEL method, a missiological model

---

[1] How ironic that a Medieval Catholic writer and contemporary of Catholic Crusaders would honor a Muslim who conquered the holy city of Jerusalem. Dante justifies putting Saladin (AD 1138-1193), whose actual name was Sultan Yusuf ibn Ayyub, in Limbo by setting him apart from other Muslims in terms of his virtue (*Inferno* 4.129). Saladin, according to *The Dante Encyclopedia*, was seen as overly generous. Nonetheless, commentators, as discussed in the encyclopedia, are unsure why a man with such close contact with Christians would be included in a destination for those who were "'born too early or too far away' to be included in the redemption of Christ" (cf. Richard Lansing (Ed.). (2000). *The Dante Encyclopedia* (521). New York, NY: Garland Publishing).

put together by International Mission Board (SBC) missionary Kevin Greeson that attempts to prove the Qur'an declares a biblical Jesus through a closer look at Q3:42-55. The title of the book is actually an acronym that spells CAMEL[2] and is a methodology that fancies itself as a pre-evangelistic bridge enabling open-minded Muslims called "persons of peace" to cross a bridge they would not normally cross due to their fear or disdain for the Bible. Those who use this method maintain that it is necessary—or at the very least more pragmatic—to use this method since Muslims would not otherwise receive the words of Scripture. Intentionally or unintentionally, the Scripture is declared insufficient in its power to draw men to Christ (John 20:31).

This method also serves as a bridge between the insider movements (IM) and traditional Evangelical methodologies. For example, one missiological model commonly known as the C1-C6 Spectrum developed by John Travis, attempts to give a scale for various missiological models based upon linguistic, cultural, and religious contextualization. The more contextualized a missionary is the higher the number on the spectrum. The CAMEL method, recognized as C4, is placed squarely between the IM (commonly equated as C5 or C6), and traditional methodologies categorized as C1–C3.[3] When reading the second edition of *The CAMEL*, Greeson sounds orthodox on one page and dangerously close to heterodox on another. His work literally tests the limits on denominations such as Southern Baptists who openly deny IM, and yet are flirting with this seductive mistress. Examples of Greeson's perilous statements include the following:

> I agree with what the Qur'an says about Muhammad. . . .
>
> It is important for you to understand that this is not a simple question, because the word "Muslim" has two meanings. On the surface, it simply means "one who has submitted to God's will." At this superficial level, no Christian would want to respond with "No! I have not submitted to God's will."[4]

The first sentence above demonstrates either a pure ignorance of what the Quran asserts of Muhammad or disregards truth so not to offend the Muslim. The second sentence is a typical example of the deceptiveness

---

[2] *C* – Chosen, *A* – Angels announced the good news, *M* – miracles, *EL* – eternal life.

[3] John Travis (1999). "The C1 to C6 Spectrum"(658-9). In Ralph D. Winter and Steven C. Hawthorne (Eds.). *Perspectives on The World Christian Movement: A Reader* (3rd ed.). Pasadena, CA: William Carey Library (cf. Rick Love (2000). *Muslims, Magic and the Kingdom of God* (188). Pasadena, CA: William Carey Library).

[4] Kevin Greeson (2007). *The Camel: How Muslims Are Coming to Faith in Christ!* (144 and 99). Arkadelphia, AR: WIGTake Resources. If Greeson still holds to this statement, then he believes in the following beliefs about Muhammad found in the Qur'an: brings Message as revealed (10:15-16), delivers revelation directly (11:12-14), the excellent exemplar (33:21), inspired (18:110), and foretold by Jesus (61:6).

within the book. Rare is the Muslim who would differentiate the term *Muslim* into the two meanings given by Greeson. In fact, if a Christian missionary maintains the word *Muslim* is not a direct reference to an adherent of the Islamic faith, the Christian should also not be offended if a Muslim apologist calls himself a *Christian* since he respects Christ. It seems that the deconstruction of truth by secularists—postmodernism—has enveloped our own ranks.

Furthermore, examples of the CAMEL as an embryonic IM can be found in his statements of the end results of his evangelistic efforts. Statements from *CAMEL* converts demonstrate an Islamization of Christianity and include the following:

> They referred to their pastor as an imam. . . .
> When asked for converts to identify themselves, most MBBs replied, "I am an Isahi Muslim.". . .
> Unlike the traditional Churches with their long wooden pews, these worshipers sat on the floor and held their open hands in front of them as they prayed. . . .
> The full truth of this wonderful gift from Allah is fully revealed in the earlier Scriptures (i.e., the Bible).[5]

Incredibly, Mr. Greeson even recognizes that these outcomes were not merely cultural, but Qur'anic and Islamic. He concludes, "As we discovered more of how they lived and spread their faith, we knew we would need to learn more about the Qur'an which defined so many things in their culture."[6] How shocking that missionaries would not reject a methodology that seems more founded upon the Qur'an than the Bible itself.

Using Dante's analogy of *circles* or *rings*, this chapter will deal with two decisive issues about The CAMEL: one, interpretation of the Quran; and two, assumptions that must be made from usage of the technique.

Limbo's first circle: hermeneutical gymnastics

The doctrine of special revelation is the paramount issue that is most troubling about The CAMEL. Its premise: a high regard for the Qur'an. Greeson describes Islam's holy book as an "amazing truth that gives hope of eternal life in heaven."[7] Dr. Keith Eitel, Dean of the Roy Fish School of

---

[5] Greeson, *The Camel* 34, 35, 40, 118. I reject the label MBB as it would define my identity by who I was and not who I am. We do not refer to a former prostitute as a FBB (Fornicating Background Believer) so what benefit do we have at this label. Those using MBB argue that the term "Christian" is held in disdain their countries. But the three times the word Christian is used in the New Testament (Acts 11:26; 26:28; 1 Pet 4:16) is also used with derision and yet the disciples see the tag as a badge of honor.
[6] Greeson, *The Camel* 34.
[7] Greeson, *The Camel* 106.

Evangelism and Missions at Southwestern Baptist Theological Seminary, and perhaps the premiere missiologist among Southern Baptists, maintains this approach elevates the Qur'an to equal or greater importance than God's sufficient revelation:

> In the contextualization dance sequence between Koranic truth claims and the Bible, Islam is allowed to begin the process. It then controls the rhythm and pace of thought. A subtle but dialectical truth structure emerges that sets the Koran on equal footing with the Bible, even if it is intended to be temporary. The net effect is a filtering of the Bible through the grid of Koranic truth claims, hence making the context dominant. This often causes syncretistic outcomes that blend biblical truth with cultural error. To take the truth claims of the Bible and Christ, place them into an Islamic theological frame of reference, and utilize Koranic theological syntax to communicate the biblical Gospel yields too much.[8]

The book goes on to assert that "walking through these verses [of the Qur'an] together, it [is] easy to show [Muslims] that Jesus was much more than a prophet."[9] Greeson states in another section, "Sura al-Imran 3:42-55 attests to divine attributes of *Isa* that no Muslim can deny."[10] Greeson claims that the Qur'an makes audacious statements of Christ, including:
- Jesus came directly from Allah and that He did not have a father;
- Jesus, called the *Word*, is part of Allah himself;
- Jesus is the only prophet who was given power over death;
- Jesus knows the way to heaven;
- It was Allah's plan to cause Jesus to die.[11]

The problem with the method is not merely that a Christian is implying the Qur'an asserts the Gospel; the problem expands because we turn to deceptive exegetical techniques in order to find an interpretation of the Qur'an that fits the Bible. We need to be clear here: **we have no more right in abusing and reinterpreting the Qur'an than someone has to blatantly misinterpret our Scriptures in order to prove a presupposition.** Greeson's ignorance of the Qur'an is no excuse to patently misrepresent what the Qur'an is actually saying. So for the statements above, consider the following: "Jesus came directly from Allah and did not have a father."

This is a deliberate misrepresentation of the Qur'an (3:45-7). This verse does not say that Jesus came from heaven, but that Allah said, "'Be,'

---

[8] Email exchange with Keith Eitel, 9 December 2010.
[9] Greeson, *The Camel* 42. This statement seems contradictory to another statement he makes in the book: "We knew we would never have their broad knowledge of the Muslim Scriptures, and we really did not want to know it that well" (41).
[10] Greeson, *The Camel* 103.
[11] Cf. Greeson *The Camel* 107, 131, 108, 135ff, and 138 for each of these respective points.

and it is!" (Q3:47). Greeson conveniently skips over aya 47 in his analysis. Of course, the highest sin in Islam is to partner anything or anyone with Allah (*shirk*). The Qur'an attempts to further illustrate Jesus' mere humanity by stating in the same chapter, "The similitude of Jesus before Allah is as that of Adam" (Q3:59).

Greeson also states Jesus, called the *Word*, is part of Allah himself. Quoting part of Q4:171 that Jesus is a "Spirit proceeding from [Allah]," Greeson argues that the divinity of Christ "shines through" this verse. However, he does not quote the entire verse:

> In your religion: nor say of Allah aught but the truth. Christ Jesus the son of Mary was (no more than) a Messenger of Allah, and His Word, which he bestowed on Mary, and a Spirit proceeding from Him; so believe in Allah and His Messengers. **Say not 'Three:' desist:** It will be better for you: For Allah is One God: Glory be to Him: (Far exalted is He) above having a son. To Him belong all things in the heavens and on earth. And enough is Allah as a Disposer of affairs. (Q4:171; emphasis added)

How astounding that *The CAMEL* would use a verse that explicitly rejects Christ as God and demands Christians desist from allegedly believing in the three gods. It is key to note that this methodology will only be useful to Muslims who are ignorant of their own Scriptures due to illiteracy or neglect of study. Far be it from Christians to use their ignorance for our advantage.[12]

Finally, if the Spirit breathing into someone is evidence of deity, then according to the Qur'an, Adam is a god (Q15:29) and so is Muhammad (Q42:52).[13]

Next Greeson posits Jesus is the only prophet who was given power over death. Once again this statement, based on Q3:49, assumes the ignorance of the listener. Greeson skips over the meaning of the text. The reason why *Isa*, the Islamic Jesus, has power over death "is a Sign for you" (Q3:49). Unbelievers must "fear Allah" and "worship Him" just as Jesus worships Allah (Q3:51).

Additionally, do not our Scriptures illustrate that Elijah has the power over death? Did not the Apostles, having been given the authority by Christ Himself, have power over death?

Then there is the idea that Jesus knows the way to heaven. The way to

---

[12] It should be noted that the Arabic word for three used in Q4:171 relates to a polytheistic attitude. The Qur'an does not use the Arabic word for Trinity.

[13] Traditional and orthodox Islamic exegesis asserts that the spirit mentioned in these two verses is none other than the angel of revelation, Gabriel. Therefore, the reason why Adam, Jesus, and Muhammad are singled out with this characteristic is because they are prophets who received a message from Allah (cf. Yusuf Ali (1989). *The Holy Qur'an* (1494, fn 4601). Beltsville, MD: Amana).

heaven is stipulated to those who "believe and work righteousness" (Q3:57) and hell is assigned to those who are not Muslims, who "reject faith" (Q3:56). This passage, therefore, advocates an Islamic worldview of salvation based on faith and works.

Finally *The CAMEL* tells us it was Allah's plan to cause Jesus to die. The Qur'an is absolutely clear on this point: Jesus did not die on the cross (cf. Q4:157-8). The verse states, "But they killed him not, nor crucified him. Only a likeness of that was shown to them." However, Greeson argues the passage only denies that Jews did not kill him. His statement is wrong on two levels. First in Acts 4:10, Peter addresses the Sanhedrin and says, "Let it be known to you all, and to all the people of Israel, that by the name of Jesus Christ of Nazareth, whom you crucified." Second the Qur'an asserts in the very next verse that "Allah raised [Jesus] up to Himself;" Jesus did not die on the cross.[14]

In the end, one cannot "discover an amazing truth" but only a repudiation of the crucial doctrines of Christianity. If Greeson has misinterpreted the Qur'an, the missionary is back to square one and cannot use such an erroneous technique.

Limbo's second circle: dangerous assumptions

Imagine approaching a Muslim with the CAMEL method and what you must presume upon the encounter. First, your presentation of the CAMEL is a method sprung from a Muslim proverb that only a camel knows the one-hundredth name of Allah. Thus the presentation itself is based upon the theory that the first ninety-nine names of Allah lead to his one-hundredth name, a definite danger of syncretizing our Lord with Muhammad's imaginary monotheistic invention. That presumption is fortified when you will open the Qur'an with the Muslim and speak about the Allah of the Qur'an as if he was the same as the God of the Bible.[15]

Second, after you have established rapport with a Muslim and have determined him to be open to discussion,[16] you have to believe that

---

[14] Cf. David Brown (1969). *The Cross of the Messiah*. London: SPCK. Brown argues that the phrase, *take you* in this passage, "could mean that Jesus died a natural death, but it can also mean that he was taken to heaven without undergoing the experience of physical death" (29-30). Regardless, the Qur'an is clear that Jesus was not crucified. Medieval Islamic apologist, Ibn Taymiyya (AD 1263-1328), offered a traditional understanding: "Not a single one of the Christians was a witness with them (the Jews). Rather the apostles kept a distance through fear, and not one of them witnessed the crucifixion" (Norman Geisler and Abdul Saleeb (2002). *Answering Islam* (280) (2nd ed.). Grand Rapids, MI: Baker). This, of course, is in direct contradiction to biblical accounts that illustrate the Apostle John's presence at the cross (John 19:25-7).

[15] The words of this sentence are carefully chosen so that one realizes this is not an argument of linguistics. Whether one chooses to use Allah to speak of the Christian God is a wholly different discussion than the discussion presented here. To say that the God of the Quran and the God of the Bible are the same is a grave inaccuracy.

[16] Using Luke 10, Greeson and other missiologists maintain that missionaries should spend the bulk of their time with those open to the Gospel. While there is wisdom in this Luke 10

Muslims can find salvific hope within the Qur'an and assume that the Islamic holy book actually teaches the Good News of Jesus Christ. You must believe that Muhammad was close to the truth or even worse, that he received divine revelation about the essential truths of the Gospels and sadly, those truths have been hidden for centuries under the heavy cloak of false teachers.

Third, you have to believe the terms and doctrines stated in the Qur'an are synonymous to the terms and doctrines delineated in the Bible. But the Qur'an redefines them. For example although Jesus is considered the *Word* (Q3:45), the very same verse defines that term as "nearest to Allah" and rejects His deity in favor of Christ as a messenger who "shall speak to the people" (Q3:46). The passage used by the CAMEL also purportedly supports the virgin birth of Christ. Yet a closer look reveals the virgin birth is fully rejected and replaced with a created Jesus (Q3:47) who is just another Adam (Q3:59). The Qur'an only states Jesus was "strengthened by the Holy Spirit" (Q2:87). Those using the CAMEL method must admit they are actually using a passage more in line with Arian heresy than Christological orthodoxy.[17]

Fourth if one presumes the passage speaks truth, the Christian must wrestle with stories founded in apocryphal writings. Q3:49 maintains that Jesus made birds out of clay, which is first found in *The Infancy Gospel of Thomas* (chapter 2:1-7). In addition to the Qur'an having partial revelation, now we must recognize Gospels long since rejected by the early church. It is also interesting to note the same Gospel that chronicles Christ's miracle of turning clay into birds also portrays Jesus as a ruthless youngster who called another child a "godless, brainless moron" and then put a child to death (3:1-4).[18]

Finally, and perhaps most disturbingly, you must hope for the pure, unadulterated ignorance of the person to whom you are witnessing. If the person has even a superficial knowledge of the Qur'an, he will know your exegesis is perverted and will prove your ignorance. You must feel comfortable with Christianizing the Qur'an, skipping verses and putting forth interpretation that has rarely, if ever, been seen in Islamic history. Imagine if the Muslim points out to you that according to Q3:42-55, Jesus was only close to Allah, created by Allah and worshiped Allah. Imagine if a Muslim points out that Jesus was a Muslim and that the disciples were Muslims (Q3:52). Imagine if the Muslim demonstrates the passage shows a

---

does not support that argument and the book of Acts is filled with illustrations of apostles preaching to those who seemingly mock the Gospel (Acts 26).

[17] Bishop Arius (AD c.256-336), a North African bishop, was most famous for believing Jesus was created, different in essence from God the Father. His most famous purported statement was "there was a time when [Jesus] was not" (Earle Cairns, (1996). *Christianity Through the Centuries* (127) (3rd ed.). Grand Rapids, MI: Zondervan).

[18] For various translations of the *Infancy Gospel of Thomas*, see http://www.earlychristianwritings.com/infancythomas.html (accessed 12/9/10).

works-based salvation (Q3:57) and a god that hates sinners (Q3:57: "Allah loves not those who do wrong"). Imagine.

A call to sufficiency of Scripture: Luke 24:24-52

During conferences on Islam that I lead I am often asked the question, "What do you use to share Christ with a Muslim?" The question, understandable as it is, illustrates three tragic deficiencies in Western Christian culture. First, it grossly assumes a program is the save-all of evangelism. It argues, secondly, that a Muslim can only be reached through unique means of sharing the Gospel, as if Muslims are a different species than the rest of the world. Third, it demonstrates that Western Christians, the vast majority of whom are religiously ignorant and biblically illiterate, have a poor understanding of the power and sufficiency of the Word of God.

However, many evangelists and missionaries to Muslims argue that it is nearly impossible to gain a hearing from a Muslim, especially a devout Muslim, unless one has a culturally savvy and innovative technique, which finds commonality between two people.[19] Proponents point to anecdotal proof; they do not give the examples that argue against this superfluous statement. This view is insulting to a Muslim's intelligence and worldview. Islam is a cradle-to-the-grave religion that encompasses all of life. Many Muslims desire to speak of their faith openly; they do not mind disagreements, but they do despise deception. They are aware of the differences between the two faiths and if confronted forthrightly and compassionately, many times love to begin a conversation on faith and its consequences.[20] Regardless of an experiential argument, the supremacy of the Bible demands we follow its precepts and commands.

The best technique is, therefore, already in place in Scripture. Randy Newman, in his critically acclaimed book, *Questioning Evangelism*, persuasively demonstrates the biblical technique is an open and honest conversation of questions and statements as seen in the Old Testament and in the life of Christ Himself. This form of confrontational conversation makes room for the Christian to discover the spiritual condition of the other person. It does not require forced statements or leading questions; rather it encourages both Muslim and Christian to speak openly. The Christian witness, which assumes the Muslim is a traditional adherent until otherwise noted, can begin recognizing the barriers to faith in Christ. There is ample opportunity

---

[19] My argument is not against the use of techniques such as Evangelism Explosion; rather, we are to use them secondarily and begin training Christians primarily to use their Scripture, memorize their Scripture, and honor their Scripture. Other techniques are supplemental at best.

[20] When approaching a Muslim man or woman, I usually begin an open conversation with the following statement: "I want to let you know up front that you are welcome to speak freely and I will not be offended regardless of what you say. I also hope you will allow me to be as open with you as you are with me."

to follow the leading of the Holy Spirit through the Word to share passages that speak to the Muslim. As seen in Luke 24:27, the Christian must recognize that the sufficiency of Scripture is articulated through the Savior who "beginning at Moses and all the Prophets, he explained to them what was said in all the Scriptures concerning himself." The Word of God, which convinced the disciples 2000 years ago, remains as powerful today and will clearly point to the risen Lord who saves.

When the disciples heard Christ's message they were empowered and proclaimed, "It is true! The Lord has risen" (Luke 24:34). The disciples knew that a suffering Savior called them to suffer; to die daily was an appeal to their evangelism as well. When speaking with those who wish to share Christ with Muslims, we must remember we are not called to be a twenty-first century Church, but a first century Church in a twenty-first century world. We must stand **beside** the persecuted Church, not behind it. We must endure hardships along with those who suffer due to denouncing Islam and standing for Christ. A unified message only comes through a unified stand.

Finally evangelism does not end at the point of conversion. The Great Commission commands us to baptize and teach. Any technique that diminishes the importance of following all of the Great Commission must be eliminated for one that clearly delineates a biblical view of discipleship. The Muslim, like everyone else who comes to Christ, must take a public stand for his or her faith and be immediately connected to a local body of baptized believers who can disciple him in the faith. He must realize that he is part of a "holy nation" (1 Pet 1:9) who "live a life worthy of the calling" he received (Eph 4:1). As a new creation in Christ (2 Cor 5:17) we must help him remove the theological baggage that ensnared him for so many years. The heavy baggage of ritualism, such as the Islamic prayers, is replaced for a relationship with Christ that has no such requirements. He is free and his freedom is a godly witness to others still in bondage. In the end, any truly effective evangelism will be accomplished through the demonstration of transformed lives. Truth is immortal.

4

IM and Translation Problems

4.1 Islamizing the Bible: Insider Movements and Scripture Translations

Joshua Lingel

It is often said that having the Bible available in the vernacular language is critical to the success of other ministries such as Church planting and discipleship. Testimonies abound about how the translation of Scripture in the heart language has transformed individuals, churches, tribal groups, and societies, arresting and reversing cultural and moral decline, stimulating growth in the Christian faith for individuals and the number of believers. It is well known the translation of the Bible into the English and German languages had a marked effect not only on spiritual growth and general morality of these peoples, but on the development of literacy and the creation of a common literary form for those languages. The ministry of Bible translation into minority languages of the world is recognized for the key role it plays in reaching and discipling the nations with the message of Christ; in bringing a variety of beneficial changes to individuals, clans, tribes, and societies.

Any threat to the integrity of translation is a threat to the indigenous church for she depends upon a reliable and trustworthy translation of the word of God. As the psalmist lamented (Ps 11:3), "When the foundations are being destroyed, what can the righteous do?" Applying this verse to translation, should a Bible translation be subjected to any compromising influence, the very foundation for believers of that language is threatened. I believe one of those compromising influences is the insider movements' (IM) advocacy of accommodation of Muslim prejudices toward the teaching of Scripture on the part of some. The key issue is the Islamic rejection of God as Father, Jesus as the *Son of God*, and the Holy Spirit as the third person of the Trinity. Some IM proponents are translating the biblical concept of *Son of God* in a manner that does not reflect eternal sonship. Those who view this as acceptable refer to such translations as Muslim-idiom translations; those of us who oppose the idea call them (much more negatively) Muslim-compliant translations. Whatever it might be called it is clear that this shift in translation is but one component of IM.

Postmodern bias

Various trends and factors could be identified as having led to the current crisis in contemporary Bible translation. The one phenomenon I want to mention is the influence of postmodern literary hermeneutical biases. In the last half century a subtle but significant shift has occurred among postmodern literary theorists and critics about the methodology of establishing the meaning of a written text. Despite the obvious etymological relation of *authority* and *author*, there seems to be a distinct trend toward shifting the authority for determining the meaning of a text from the author to the *reader*. Is this trend affecting Bible translation? While it may be difficult to establish, it seems this is exactly the premise underlying some of the apologetic offer by IM advocates. In other words, the sensitivities of Muslim readers of Scripture are considered a major factor for the removal of *Son of God*, replacing it with terms much more acceptable to Muslims. We are seeing *Messiah* or *Word of God* (Qur'anic-equivalent terms acceptable to Muslims) replace *Son of God* in Muslim-compliant translations.

Rick Brown is perhaps the best-known advocate for such a change. His many articles are published in *IJFM* and *EMQ*. A search of his published writings shows no less than ten uses of the term *evoke* to describe the feelings and understandings arising in the mind of Muslims when a particular term is used. Knowing that *Son of God* offends and disturbs Muslims, he makes the argument that this is a problem for translators. It is true enough that the concept of the *Son of God* evokes misconceptions, misunderstandings and wrong ideas in Muslim minds. Albeit the truth of the statement, it appears Brown is suggesting there is a fixed inventory of possible cognitive and emotional understandings and responses to this term. In other words, a Muslim reader is limited to those **and only those** already existing possibilities.

Brown is advocating that whatever the reader brings to the text, his own thoughts and emotions, determines the absolute limit on what the text can ever communicate. Such an assumption precludes the possibility of any change over time. The belief system of the reader is set in concrete; he may read these altered Scriptures, but his way of thinking does not change.

Jesus' bias

Jesus never shied away from demanding drastic change of his hearers. Both John the Baptist and Jesus Christ began their public ministries with a call for repentance. This was a cry for radical change; we may suppose it was certainly offensive to many. The word group *metanoeo* (verb) and *metanoia* (noun), commonly translated "repent, repentance," means a change of thinking. A new way of thinking brings consequent changes in behavior, attitudes, and actions. This in turn requires alterations in affiliations, allegiances, and loyalties. While using the available inventory of words in the language of the day, Jesus introduced ideas that were dramatically counter-cultural, and in some cases completely outside the range of acceptability. It is what led to his crucifixion, and as we all know, his definition of discipleship included the acceptance of one's own possible crucifixion (Luke 9:23; 14:27).

Frankly, **we need to be willing to allow the word of God to offend.** While we should do our best to avoid gratuitous offense, it is unwise and unrealistic to expect that no offense should ever occur. Ultimately, the Gospel must offend us if we are to be changed by it. If it does not offend at some point, it is probably not the Gospel. It must expose us as the sinners and rebels we are, challenging us to admit that we need to repent, to change, and to acknowledge we are wrong, both in our behavior and thinking. Otherwise conversion is not really conversion, but merely adding new idea on top of an existing one. This is syncretism.

The power of God's Word

To assume the term *Son of God* should not be used in translations for predominantly Muslim audiences raises several serious issues. The first concerns the question of the power of the Word of God. Christians believe that the Word of God has dynamic and transforming power that does not depend on an existing cultural inventory of understandings, beliefs, prejudices, and commitments. But Brown has stated, "The biological meaning of this phrase (*Son of God*) and its blasphemous connotations are so deeply entrenched in the minds of most Muslims that it is impossible simply to erase it from their minds and hearts."[1] He then goes on to assert a literal translation of the term removes any possibility of Muslims understanding the message of salvation before they have the opportunity to hear it.[2] In other words, what the Qur'an says about Jesus Christ as the Son of God has pre-empted and overcome what the Bible says about his sonship. Do we therefore concede defeat, abandoning the biblical doctrine inherent in the term itself, even to the point of leaving it out of the Bible? Do we take seriously what God has said through the prophet Isaiah that his word will accomplish the purpose for which he sends it (Is 55:10-11)? Do we take seriously Paul's statement that he did not come with cleverness of speech, but in the power of God (1 Cor 1:17-18)? Is God's word living and active, able to operate independently within its hearers to judge the thoughts and intents of the heart (Heb 4:12)?

God is able to bring a dramatic change to hearts that have previously rejected very fundamental premises. Consider the repentance worked by the Holy Spirit in Peter's proclamation of the message on the Day of Pentecost. The harvest of souls that came about on that day did not depend on Peter's carefully working within the existing prejudices of those people. It was quite the contrary; the conviction that came depended on the power of the Holy Spirit applying truth to their hearts that had previously been rejected or ignored. Then, as now, truth is the antidote to falsehood.

Son of God was acceptable to Paul, a Jew and former Pharisee, and to the other disciples. All of them were Jews with high a view of monotheism, rejecting anything suggesting polytheism as the notion of sonship might. How is that different from the Muslim sensitivity to Allah's oneness? Yet, these first century Jews all used *Son of God* in their texts, despite its

---

[1] Rick Brown, "Explaining the Biblical term "Son(s) of God" in Muslim Contexts" *IJFM* 22(3): 92.
[2] Brown, "Explaining" 92.

biological connotations.

Muslims know that sonship is not just biological, but can be used metaphorically. Q2:177 uses the term *ibn ul sabeeli*, *son of the road*, and is translated as traveler. I have never met a Muslim who objected to this translation, knowing full well that a son of the road has no biological relationship with the road itself.

I believe the reason behind their rejection of sonship has more to do with what that term truly denotes. Muslims know that if Jesus claims to be the Son of God, he is claiming something much greater than simply being his biological child, something they know the text is not saying. No, he is claiming equality with God the Father. He shares in the same nature and essence with his father, who is God Himself. They know that with this term he is claiming to be God Himself, and so they vociferously reject the title. Ironically this is the same reason the Jews rejected Jesus when he used the title before the Sanhedrin (Mt 26:62-6). They called for his death because of it. If the Muslims really do understand the true significance of this title, then all the more reason we should not change it.

If certain translators desire to change the title, they must retain the meaning we find in Scripture. If both the Jews and the early Christians knew that in this title Jesus equated himself with God, the alternative should have just as strong a claim to divinity as Son of God. What the Muslim-compliant translations have done is replace this divine claim with terms such as prince, Messiah (Islam has the same title, of course, but they do not know its significance), mercy seat, and messenger. All of these titles are understood by Muslims as honorifics, but certainly not as a reference to deity. They are titles any of the prophets might have. In a desire for clarity the translators have demoted Jesus from deity to prophet; in fact, they make him equal to *Isa* of the Qur'an. Is it any wonder Muslims are so ready to read these translations rather than the more traditional and theologically sound classical translations?

Once translators realize their mistake will they be able to go back and fix the translation? Muslims already condemn Christians for changing the Scriptures. How will these changes be justified?

A strategy for evangelism?

A second area of inquiry is the assumption that *Son of God* should not appear in translations for Muslim audiences as a strategy for evangelism. While the translated Scripture is an effective tool for evangelism among unreached groups, it should be pointed out that Scripture is covenantal literature. Almost all of the literature of the Bible was written for people who were in a covenantal relationship with God.[3] This is obvious with the New Testament epistles, almost all of which were written to churches. But

---

[3] See Vern Poythress, "Bible Translation and Contextualization: Theory And Practice in http://www.frame-poythress.org/poythress_articles/2005Bible.htm (accessed 1/23/11).

even the Gospels seem to have been written with an audience of believers in mind. No doubt the intent included sharing the stories with non-Christians, but if a translation is oriented entirely toward non-Christians, it seems inevitable that translators will be tempted to accommodate to the prejudices and biases of the readers. In the case of Muslim readers who have beliefs that sharply conflict with biblical teachings, the temptation is greater still. Several problems emerge from this scenario.

The clear biblical call to change one's thinking is muted. If a believing community does eventually arise, they will have no basis for understanding who the triune God truly is because the translator has obscured the language of Father, Son and Holy Spirit. A new translation is then needed, one that uses biblical terminology to accurately express biblical concepts and doctrines, as opposed to those acceptable to Muslims.

Translation governed by pragmatism

A third area of concern is that the basis for translation seems to be the reaction from non-Christians. Muslims react negatively to the biblical language of sonship; therefore, it is reasoned, the terms must be changed. A planted seed may lie fallow for years before it bears fruit. There are many testimonies about how a completely unanticipated response to the initially rejected Gospel came about long after the translation was available. God does not always work immediately, and we must not assume a lack of evident initial response automatically means there will never be a genuine response. It appears the Scripture-use programs of Bible translation agencies today do no allow for that possibility. They seem to reason that in order to ensure the use of the Scripture, it may be necessary for translators to change the offensive *Son of God* to something acceptable—even if it means changing the meaning of the passage.

When assessing the seriousness of the problem of removing references to Jesus as the *Son of God* or to God as Father, one wonders how the larger mission community and Church can be assured the Bible is being faithfully translated. How can we know that the text is not impoverished by adaptation to the religious understandings and sensibilities of peoples who not only do not hold Christian belief, but specifically reject core Christian beliefs? For the first half-century of the modern Bible translation movement, nearly all work was done among tribal peoples holding an animistic worldview. While that worldview is markedly different from the Christian worldview, it does not have the level of systemic animosity to essential elements of the Christian worldview as found in some of the major world religions such as Hinduism and Islam. Although translators working among animists took great pains to correctly translate concepts such as spirit, prayer, and God in order to avoid communicating wrong meanings based on pre-existing religious and cultural understandings, the temptation to modify the message itself to avoid strong prejudices against the Bible was not there. There was no first-century controversy equal to the call for changing of *Son of God* to something that does not communicate Christ's relationship as son to the Father.[4]

But another factor may have been at work in those days that has diminished now: the degree of commitment to core elements of biblical faith. We live in an age when we are influenced both consciously and unconsciously by the postmodern presuppositions of our day. These include not only the hermeneutical practices mentioned above, but also influences from the emergent church. Contemporary Christians often mistrust doctrine. Influenced in part by the political and social trends of our day, many prefer inclusiveness over doctrine, avoiding boundaries and divisions based on doctrinal consideration. Non-negotiable elements of Christian faith and morality are fewer; conversation has replaced conversion as the evangelical goal of the day. Unfortunately, when such trends lead to hiding or compromising fundamental biblical truths or even the integrity of the biblical text itself, we are seeing the foundations of our faith being destroyed before our very eyes.[5] What is the solution? Is there any system of checks and balances in place that will ensure quality in the finished product?

Importance of accuracy

Bible translators have long said there are three guiding principles in translation that must be kept in tension: accuracy, clarity and naturalness. Naturalness means the language of the text does not sound foreign, even if concepts foreign to the culture are introduced. Clarity means the text is understandable, regardless of whether or not its message is acceptable. Bible translators have asserted for decades that every human language is capable of conveying any and all biblical truth, even if the ideas being introduced are foreign to the cultural and theological presuppositions of the language. But who finally determines if the text is actually communicating in a way

---

[4] It must be kept in mind that unlike animism, Islam arose within a context in which Christianity already existed. Islam specifically opposed Christianity, and in many cases, persecuted and displaced it.

[5] The decision whether to replace offensive terms such as *Son of God*, involves more than a rough equivalent translation. A community of seekers or believers depends on a translation, for they have no direct contact with the original languages to help them develop an indigenous theology. Removing the original phrasing alters the original context from which they theologize. This is crucial, since as insiders, they have no contact with the visible church and her understanding. Therefore insiders develop theology and doctrine based a translation team's notions of what the biblical authors intended. Brown's initiative will have a deep, long-term impact on the theological development of the entire community and of its relations to other believers, visible or otherwise. It is worthy of consideration, since the early church's theological trajectory depended on her own interpretation of the relationships between key terms such as *Father*, *Son*, and *Son of God*. We must consider how words were used harmonically in order to arrive at doctrinal norms, not just how they can each be individually paraphrased. Is Brown's practice of finding and replacing the offensive terms locally appropriate or does it compromise the intra- and inter-textual coherence of the text and hence, its meaning?

that is both clear and natural? The speakers of the language are the final judges of those qualities. They are the experts; as Scripture portions are tested among them, they become the part of the system of checks and balances – a type of accountability – that will ensure a quality product in that regard.

But who is the final judge of accuracy? Again, the answer has already been in place for many years. The methodology for checking accuracy of meaning has always been accomplished by a translation consultant external to the immediate translation team. This worked well until now, but it appears some translators and consultants—even some translation agencies—have adopted the practice of avoiding the biblical terms *Son, Son of God* and *Father*. Could it be they do not understand the theology themselves, since they are linguists first and theologians second? As a result we find ourselves doubting the reliability and objectivity of the consultant checks. As the ancient Romans put it, *quis custodiet ipsos custodes?* (Who will guard the guards themselves?) Who will verify that consultants are assuring fidelity to the meaning of the original text? If this process fails the same scenario is played out as in the Enron scandal. Enron's accounting firm failed to give the objective evaluation of Enron's financial practices, which they were morally and legally required to provide. Is this the way of Bible translation?

A call for accountability

In conclusion, it may be that translation agencies will be eventually called upon to provide better public evidence for the validity of their translations. The broader missions and evangelical communities could provide this through requiring copies of back-translations from the vernacular into the national language. Consultants use this methodology for ensuring accuracy. Perhaps these back-translations should be filed with the Bible translation agency and publisher, available for inspection to the public, including theologians that understand the theology behind the text. For example there are four references to *sons* or *son* and two references to *Father* in Galatians 4:4-6. How are they translated? What of Matthew 3:17 and 17:5 where God himself speaks from heaven to identify Jesus as his Son? In Revelation 2:18 the *Son of God* is described as having eyes like blazing fire? How is *Son of God* translated here? Do we need methods of accountability in place to insure the message of sonship is not tampered with in order to keep with the warning in Revelation 22:18-19?

Although mission agencies and parachurch organizations routinely provide open access to financial records, we hope we do not come to the point of requiring similar open access to back-translations to keep translation agencies accountable for the accuracy of translation. If that is what is required to maintain integrity in the finished product, perhaps it is time to begin to implement procedures to ensure it.

Are there examples that support my claims of distortion? In the charts that follow I provide examples of the changes taking place. Mazhar Mallouhi produced *The Correct Meaning of the Gospel of Christ* (Dar al-Farabi, Beirut, Lebanon 2008), an Arabic translation of the Gospels and Acts. The examples show Mallouhi, a firm advocate of IM, replacing Father (Chart 2)[6] and Son (Chart 3) with non-familial language. The next chart compares Arabic *The Lives of the Prophets* with the Bengali Bible translation showing the removal of the language of Father and Son (Chart 4). Chart 5 reproduces the same problems with the Malay Bible translation. Let the reader decide if these Muslim-compliant translations hurt or help the understanding of the triune God.

Chart 2. Examples of substitution of "Father" in Mallouhi's, *The Correct Meaning of the Gospel of Christ*.[7]

Ref.	KJV	Arabic Text	Muslim-compliant translation
Mt 5:16	your Father which is in heaven	الله وليّكم الاعلى	God, your supreme guardian
Mt 5:45	the children of your Father which is in heaven	اولياء الله	guardians of God
Mt 5:48	your Father which is in heaven	الله تعالى	God, Most High

Chart 3. Examples of "Son of God" removed in *The Lives of the Prophets*[8]

Ref.	NIV	*Lives of the Prophets*
Luke 1:32, 35	32 He will be great and will be called the Son of the Most High. The Lord God will give him the throne of his father David, 33 and he will reign over the house of Jacob forever; his kingdom will never end. . . .	The Spirit of God will come down upon you and this thing is the proof that this child is the awaited Christ who will rule forever.

---

[6] Charts 2 and 3 are only partial. See the same charts in Adam Simnowitz's chapter, "How the Insider Movements Affects Ministry: Personal Reflections" (pp. 212-42).

[7] Translation from the Arabic by Adam Simnowitz.

[8] Back translation from Arabic by Wycliffe International personnel. The file was offered to Adam Simnowitz and received upon request from Rick Brown of SIL through a local missionary with Wycliffe Bible Translators. Simnowitz created the chart and added the NIV and Verses columns.

Ref.	NIV	Lives of the Prophets
	35 The angel answered, "The Holy Spirit will come upon you, and the power of the Most High will overshadow you. So the holy one to be born will be called the Son of God."	
Luke 4:3	The devil said to him, "If you are the Son of God, tell this stone to become bread."	If you are truly the Messiah of the Most High God, command these stones to become bread.
Luke 4:9	The devil led him to Jerusalem and had him stand on the highest point of the temple. "If you are the Son of God," he said, "throw yourself down from here."	Afterward, the Devil took Him to Jerusalem and stood Him on the edge of the House of God. If you are truly the Messiah of God, throw yourself down from up here

Chart 4. *Son of God, Father God* and *Son of Man* removed in the Bengali compared with the Arabic Translation.

Ref.	NIV	Lives of the Prophets	Bengali translation
Luke 1:32, 35	32 He will be great and will be called the Son of the Most High. The Lord God will give him the throne of his father David, 33 and he will reign over the house of Jacob forever; his kingdom will never end.... 35 The angel answered, "The Holy Spirit will come upon you, and the power of	The Spirit of God will come down upon you and this thing is the proof that this child is the awaited Christ who will rule forever.	He will be great. He will be called the Messiah of the Almighty and the God of the world would give him the throne of his ancestor David. He will reign upon the descendants of Jacob. His kingdom would never end.... The angel told her, "The Holy Spirit would come upon you and the power of the Almighty

Ref.	NIV	*Lives of the Prophets*	Bengali translation
	the Most High will overshadow you. So the holy one to be born will be called the Son of God."		would fall upon you. For this reason the Son to be born would be holy, and he would be called Messiah."
Luke 4:3	The devil said to him, "If you are the Son of God, tell this stone to become bread."	If you are truly the Messiah of the Most High God, command these stones to become bread.	The devil told him, "If you the Messiah of God, then tell this stone to become bread."
Luke 4:9	The devil led him to Jerusalem and had him stand on the highest point of the temple. "If you are the Son of God," he said, "throw yourself down from here."	Afterward, the Devil took Him to Jerusalem and stood Him on the edge of the House of God. If you are truly the Messiah of God, throw yourself down from up here.	Then the devil led him to Jerusalem and had him stand on the peak of the Holy Temple and said, "If you the Messiah, then fall down by jumping from here."
Luke 8:28	When he saw Jesus, he cried out and fell at his feet, shouting at the top of his voice, "What do you want with me, Jesus, Son of the Most High God? I beg you, don't torture me!"	Oh . . . oh . . . Jesus . . . oh Messiah of the most high God . . . what do you want from me? I beg of You, don't torture me.	Seeing Jesus he fell at his feet and crying loudly he said, "Jesus, the Messiah of the Almighty God, what is your relationship with me? I beg, please do not torture me."
Luke 9:35	A voice came from the cloud, saying, "This is my Son, whom I have chosen; listen to him."	They heard a voice from heaven saying: "This is the beloved Messiah whom I have sent, so listen to Him and obey Him."	Then a voice told from that cloud, "This is my Messiah, my chosen one; listen to him."
Luke 22:70	They all asked, "Are you then the	Then You are the Messiah of God?	They all asked, "Then are you the

165

Ref.	NIV	*Lives of the Prophets*	Bengali translation
	Son of God?"		Messiah?"
Luke 6:36	Be merciful, just as your Father is merciful.	Just as God is merciful, be merciful to people.	Be merciful, as your Guardian is merciful.
Luke 9:26	If anyone is ashamed of me and my words, the Son of Man will be ashamed of him when he comes in his glory and in the glory of the Father and of the holy angels.	Whoever is ashamed of Me and My teachings, the Son of Man will be ashamed of him on the day on judgment when He comes in His glory and in the glory of God and of the pure angels.	Those who are shameful with me and my word, he too would be shameful with them, when the Son of Man would come with the glory of his own and God and his holy angels.
Luke 11:2	He said to them, "When you pray, say: 'Father, hallowed be your name, your kingdom come.'"	When you pray, say: Our loving, heavenly Lord	He said to them, "When you pray, then say – 'O our Guardian God, hallowed be your name, your kingdom come.'"
Luke 11:13	If you then, though you are evil, know how to give good gifts to your children, how much more will your Father in heaven give the Holy Spirit to those who ask him!"	If you being evil, know how to give your children good gifts, then how much more is it true of the Lord of the world who gives His Holy Spirit to the people who ask Him?	Then if even being evil you know how to give good things to your children, then those who ask to God, how sure is this that he would give them the Holy Spirit?
Luke 22:28-30	28 You are those who have stood by me in my trials. 29 And I confer on you a kingdom, just as my Father conferred one on me, 30 so that you may eat and drink	You who were patient with Me in My trials, I will give you the right to sit and eat and drink at the table in the kingdom that God the praised and most high has bestowed upon Me.	You only are with me during my trials. I give the kingdom to you in the same way my guardian has given me a kingdom, so that you eat with me in my kingdom and

Ref.	NIV	*Lives of the Prophets*	Bengali translation
	at my table in my kingdom and sit on thrones, judging the twelve tribes of Israel.		judge the twelve tribes of Israel by sitting in the throne.
Luke 22:42	"Father, if you are willing, take this cup from me; yet not my will, but yours be done."	Oh Lord . . . If it's Your will, take this effort or suffering away from Me. But oh Lord, by Your will and not My will.	"O Guardian, if you are willing, then remove this glass from me. Yet not my will but your will be fulfilled."
Luke 23:34	Jesus said, "Father, forgive them, for they do not know what they are doing."	Oh Lord, forgive them. They don't know what they are doing.	Then Jesus said, "Ye God, forgive them, because they do not know what they are doing."
Luke 23:46	Jesus called out with a loud voice, "Father, into your hands I commit my spirit." When he had said this, he breathed his last.	Oh Lord . . . oh Lord, I surrender My Spirit into Your hands.	Jesus called out loudly and said, "O Guardian, I commit my spirit into your hands."
Luke 24:49	I am going to send you what my Father has promised; but stay in the city until you have been clothed with power from on high.	And I will send the Holy Spirit to you, so remain here until this strength from heaven comes to you according to God's promise.	And I am going to send what my Guardian promised you to give. Stay in this city until you receive the power from above.
Mt 28:18-20	18 Then Jesus came to them and said, "All authority in heaven and on earth has been given to me. 19 Therefore go and	God has given Me all authority in heaven and on earth, so go and tell the people from all the nations about the message of salvation so that	Jesus talked to them by coming near. He said, "I have been given all power and rights of the heaven and earth. So, you go and

Ref.	NIV	Lives of the Prophets	Bengali translation
	make disciples of all nations, baptizing them in the name of the Father and of the Son and of the Holy Spirit, 20 and teaching them to obey everything I have commanded you. And surely I am with you always, to the very end of the age."	they may be My followers . . . and baptize them with water in the name of God and His Messiah and the Holy Spirit. And teach them to do all that I commanded you to do. And be sure that I am with you all the days until the end time.	make all nations my disciples. Baptize them in the name of Allah, Messiah and the Holy Spirit. And teach them to obey the commands I have given to you. And remember, I am with you every day until the last days."
Luke 9:23-4	Then he said to them all: "If anyone would come after me, he must deny himself and take up his cross daily and follow me."	Anyone who comes with Me must deny himself and bear persecution for My sake.	If anyone wants to be my follower, let him deny himself. And follow after me by bearing own cross daily.

Chart 5. *Son of God* removed in the Malaysian translation.[9]

Ref.	NIV	Shellabear Revision
Luke 1:32, 35	He will be great and will be called the Son of the Most High. The Lord God will give him the throne of his father David, and he will reign over the house of Jacob forever; his kingdom will never end. The angel answered, "The Holy Spirit will come upon you, and the power of the Most	32 Dia akan menjadi mulia dan Dia akan digelar Putera Allah Yang Maha Tinggi. Allah, Tuhan kita akan mengurniakan takhat Daud, nenek moyang-Nya itu kepada-Nya. 35 Malaikat itu menjawab, "Roh Suci akan turun ke atasmu, dan kuasa Allah Yang Maha Tinggi akan menaungimu. Oleh itu, anak suci yang akan dilahirkan akan digelar Putera Allah.

---

[9] Translation from Malay by Ricky Zachariah.

Ref.	NIV	Shellabear Revision
	High will overshadow you. So the holy one to be born will be called the Son of God."	He will become majestic and known as the prince of God the Most High. God our God/Lord will bestow the throne of David, his ancestor to him. The angel answered, "The Holy Spirit will descend over you, and the power of God most high will shelter/cover/protect you. Because of that, holy child that will be born and known as the prince of God."
Luke 4:3	The devil said to him, "If you are the Son of God, tell this stone to become bread."	3 Iblis dating kepada-Nya lalu berkata, 'Jika Engkau Putera Allah, perintahkanlah batu-batu ini menjadi roti.' The Devil came to him and said, "If you are the prince of God, order these stones to become bread."
Luke 8:28	When he saw Jesus, he cried out and fell at his feet, shouting at the top of his voice, "What do you want with me, Jesus, Son of the Most High God? I beg you, don't torture me!"	28 Ketika dia melihat *Isa*, dia berteriak lalu sujud di hadapan-Nya dan berkata dengan suara yang lantang, 'Mengapakah Engkau mengganggu aku, ya *Isa*, Putera Allah Yang Maha Tinggi? Aku minta janganlah seksa aku.' When he saw Jesus, he knelt before him and said with a loud clear voice, "Why do you bother me, Jesus, prince of God Most high? I ask you don't torture me."
Luke 4:9	The devil led him to Jerusalem and had him stand on the highest point of the temple. "If you are the Son of God," he said, "throw yourself down from here."	Kemudian, Iblis membawa *Isa* ke Baitulmaqid lalu menempatkan-Nya di atas mercu rumah ibadat dan berkata kepada-Nya 'Jikalau Engkau Putera Allah, terjunlah ke bawah The devil brought Jesus to Jerusalem and placed him on top of the highest place of the temple and said to him, "If you are the prince of God jump down."

Ref.	NIV	Shellabear Revision
Luke 9:35	A voice came from the cloud, saying, "This is my Son, whom I have chosen; listen to him."	Lalu kedengaran suara dari dalam awan itu mangatakan, 'Inilah Putera-Ku yang Aku pilih. Dengarlah kata-kata-Nya!' Then a voice was heard from the cloud saying, "This is my prince who I've chosen. Listen to his words."
Luke 22:70	They all asked, "Are you then the Son of God?"	Mereka semua bertanya, 'Kalau begitu, Engkaulah Putera Allah?' They all asked, "is it so you are the prince of God?"
Luke 6:36	Be merciful, just as your Father is merciful.	Kamu hendaklah berbelas kasihan seperti Bapamu yang berbelas kashihan. You should feel sympathy & pity like your Father feels sympathy & pity. *[Note: I think their use of father is good; I'm translating "berbelas kasihan" – feel sympathy/pity as Malays would hear it. I can't think of a single word or phrase to describe God's mercy as the concept is not really in their culture.]*
Matt 28:18-20	Then Jesus came to them and said, "All authority in heaven and on earth has been given to me. Therefore go and make disciples of all nations, baptizing them in the name of the Father and of the Son and of the Holy Spirit, and teaching them to obey everything I have commanded you. And surely I am with you always, to the very end of the age."	18 *Isa* berkata kepada merkea, 'Segala kekuasaan telah diserhkan kepada-Ku, bai di syurga mahupun di bumi. 19 Oleh itu pergilah, jadikan semua bangsa pengikut-Ku. Imadan mereka dengan nama Bapa, Putera dan Roh Suci. Jesus said to them, "All power has been handed over to me in heaven and earth. Because of this, go make all races my followers. *Imadkan* them with the name of Father, prince and Holy Spirit."

Ref.	NIV	Shellabear Revision
John 12:23	And Jesus answered them, "The hour has come for the Son of Man to be glorified."	23 *Isa* al-Masih adalah Junjungan Yang Esa, untuk mendatangkan kemuliaan kepada Allah Bapa. *Isa* berkata kepada mereka, 'Sudah sampai masanya Putera Insan dimuliakan. Jesus said to them, "the time has already come for the *Prince of Flesh* to be glorified."

4.2 A World of Riches[1]

David B. Garner

David B. Garner is associate professor of systematic theology at Westminster Theological Seminary in Philadelphia and a former missionary to Bulgaria.

Introduction

In some biblical translations selected vocabulary has been removed to eliminate cultural stumbling blocks. For example, missionaries in the 1980's replaced familial language for ostensibly less offensive terms in a Bangladeshi translation of Scripture: *Messiah* for *Son of God*, *Guardian* for *Father*. Naturally, Muslims take offense to the sonship of Christ and the Fatherhood of God as the familial language threatens their view of the unity and transcendence of Allah.[2] The Qur'an speaks without qualification: "It is not befitting to (the majesty of) Allah that He should beget a son. Glory be to Him! When He determines a matter He only says to it 'Be,' and it is" (Q19:35). Moreover, believing Jesus' divine sonship as blasphemous, followers of Allah could never dare consider themselves God's sons.

The offense is universally recognized. What missiologists do not share is *how* to address it. In the wake of modern biblical and sociological studies, discerning the theological boundaries of contextualization has created an entirely new context for debate. If bread were religiously offensive (or even simply unfamiliar) to a culture, would we possess the right to exchange Bread of Life for Rice of Life? If shame-based cultures do not readily grasp legal culpability, are we free to substitute the doctrine of objective guilt with the teaching of restored honor? Is proclaiming a human Messiah as the rice of life who died to remove my shame *the Gospel*? What are the appropriate limits for contextualization?[2]

Our particular purposes here are not to answer these vast, complex missiological questions. Such investigations are vital, but they are beyond our purview. It is our task, rather, to discern whether or not the familial language in Scripture specifically that of *adoption*—possesses essential, irreplaceable, and transcendent theological significance.

---

[1] This chapter was originally published on reformation21.org (http://reformation21.org) by the Alliance of Confessing Evangelicals. The Alliance calls the twenty-first century church to a modern reformation by broadcasting, events and publishing. This chapter and additional biblical resources can be found at AllianceNet.org. Copyright 2011, Alliance of Confessing Evangelicals, Inc., 1716 Spruce Street, Philadelphia, PA 19103 USA. Used by permission.

[2] This latter question, as popular as it has become, should itself be carefully scrutinized. Should addressing contextualization questions derive from pressing the limits of propriety? How should the unique authority of Scripture functionally shape the contours of contextualization?

The Gospel and familial language

Even a surface reading of the New Testament evidences how speaking of Jesus apart from his sonship at the very least obscures Scripture's descriptions of his eternal and incarnate identity. He is the Messianic and resurrected Son of God because He was first the eternal Son of God (Heb 1:1-4). For our purposes here we simply point out that sonship does not serve peripherally concerning the identity and work of Jesus Christ (see, e.g., Rom 1:1-7); rather Christ's eternal sonship provides the very structures for who he is and what he does in history as prophet, priest and king.

Grounded in his eternal sonship, Christ's Incarnation bursts with meaning, culminating in his unprecedented sonship status attained at the resurrection (Rom 1:3-4). As Herman Bavinck puts it, though Son of God bears kingly significance in its fuller biblico-theological contours, "the name *Son of God* when ascribed to Christ has far deeper meaning than the theocratic. . . . He is Son of God in a metaphysical sense: by nature from eternity."[3]

In addressing biblical translation, Vern Poythress usefully clarifies the distinction between referent and content: "*Messiah* is not an adequate substitute for *Son of God*. Both have the same **referent,** namely Jesus the Messiah, the Son of God. But they do not have the same **meaning**."[4] Yet as represented by the Bangladeshi insider translation, a contextualizing train continues to barrel down the tracks in many countries and contexts, its cars empty of the familial language, which dominates the New Testament in its presentation of Christ, the Trinity and the Church. Besides the revelational, interpretive, and epistemological questions raised by such translation substitutions, **whether or not we can even speak the Gospel properly apart from sonship language is an all-important question.** More specifically, does Paul's presentation of the Gospel of God require the familial terms he employs? Is adoption in the Son of God at the heart of the Gospel?

Challenges to the familial cast to the Gospel are not new and they are not only missiological. At various points since the Reformation, the familial thrust of the Gospel has found itself virtually **orphaned**. In part, ironically, this neglect stems from the Reformation's rediscovery of the Gospel. With the need to articulate and defend the exclusively forensic character of justification against Roman synergy and infusion, the Reformers rightly trumpeted alien imputed righteousness. As forensic justification gained its proper prominence among Protestants, law-Gospel paradigms centered soteriology in legal language: "The Gospel is, strictly speaking, the promise of forgiveness of sins and justification because of Christ."[5] Justification

---

[3] Herman Bavinck cited in William Hendriksen (Ed. and trans.) (1977) *The Doctrine of God* (270). Edinburgh: Banner of Truth.

[4] http://www.frame-poythress.org/poythress_articles/2005Bible.htm (accessed 3/8/11).

[5] Melanchthon, "Apology of the Augusburg Confession" (113). In Theodore G. Tappert (Ed. and trans.). (1959). *The Book of Concord: The Confessions of the Evangelical Lutheran Church*. Philadelphia, PA: Fortress.

truly is a most stunning Gospel privilege that centuries of reflection have yet to exhaust.

To be fair we must note how Luther also appreciated Gospel sonship: "It is not enough to say that we are friends. No, John says we are called **children of God**."[6] For many Reformers (Calvin particularly excepted), however, familial Gospel dimensions did not permeate their understanding in a manner commensurate with the legal blessings. Yet though some might lay surly charges, the first generation of reformers is hardly to blame for understating the filial, because their context of **infusion confusion** necessitated the unrelenting articulation of the thoroughly forensic character of justification.

A reorientation to the familial

Thankfully in recent years, "the impact of biblical theology on systematic theology has demanded a reorientation of soteriology towards the concept of sonship."[7] But this fresh focus on sonship has birthed a mixed blessing, as along with many valuable insights concerning biblical sonship has come a host of distortions. From the Federal Vision (FV) revisionism of covenant theology according to social and familial Trinitarianism,[8] to the birth of the Jack Miller sonship model, in which an exclusively *ordo salutis* model of adoption diminishes not only other redemptive benefits but sonship itself, the full-orbed biblico-theological riches of adoption have suffered reductionism both by neglect and misrepresenting exposure. Even since the grand and unprecedented attention given adoption in the *Westminster Confession of Faith*, this doctrine "has been more often in the dark than in the light."[9]

To be sure, the pressures of current biblical scholarship simply do not help. I remain convinced that a driving component popularizing the New Perspective on Paul (NPP) is a sense of dissatisfaction with the preponderant forensic articulation of the Gospel. Though coupled to most post-Reformation dogmatic forensic emphases (justification) are transformative components (sanctification), oft squeezed from prominence are the relational and ecclesiological: the familial (adoption). And while FV

---

[6] Martin Luther, "Lectures on the First Epistle of St. John" (265). In Jaroslav Pelikan and Walter A. Hansen (Eds.) (1967). "Luther's Works" (v. 30). In *The Catholic Epistles, American Edition* Walter A. Hansen (trans.). St. Louis, MO: Concordia. (emphasis added)

[7] Sinclair B. Ferguson (1986). "The Reformed Doctrine of Sonship." In Nigel M. De S. Cameron and Sinclair B. Ferguson (Eds.). *Pulpit and People: Essays in Honour of William Still* (84). Edinburgh: Rutherford House.

[8] Cf. Peter Leithart (2004). "Trinitarian Anthropology: Toward a Trinitarian Re-casting of Reformed Theology" (58-71). In Calvin Beisner (Ed.). *The Auburn Avenue Theology*. Fort Lauderdale, FL: Knox Theological Seminary.

[9] Nigel Westhead (1995). "Adoption in the Thought of John Calvin." *Scottish Bulletin of Evangelical Theology* 13 (1995): 102. Some contend that the isolating locus treatment of adoption in the Westminster Confession has served to obscure the concept from its broader contours.

and NPP have improperly turned the epiphenomenon of the Church into the Gospel phenomenon,[10] squashing the soteriological beneath the ecclesiological, these movements' concerns for the communal and familial ought not go neglected. This is not because N. T. Wright is right, but because N. T. (New Testament) Paul is. Let us turn briefly to the apostle.

Adoption and familial language

Although the Apostle Paul alone uses the term *adoption* (Greek, *huiothesia*) only five times, its sparse use belies its significance. Tempting would be to weigh adoption's significance on the scales of its textual appearances. It is wiser to consider the way in which the term is used and the way in which its usage and the related familial themes of sonship, inheritance and family permeate Paul's understanding of the Gospel of the Son of God.

Huiothesia for Paul engages the Gospel's Christological, Pneumatological, eschatological, relational, covenantal, forensic and transformational themes. The believer as adopted child of God is united to the risen **Son of God**, and by this union enjoys the fullness of that resurrection dynamic in all of its familial and relational glory. The nature of its five uses exposes a significance that explodes beyond *ordo salutis* categories into *historia salutis* ones, in which the believer as a fallen son of Adam is united to the eschatological Son of God by the Father's adoptive grace. I can here only render a brief summary of the treasure trove that adoption tenders in its expansively rich biblico-theological contours, but even a brief survey discloses a splendid filial tapestry.

Let us first look at adoption in its pre-creation context. In Ephesians 1:3-6, the Pauline doxology sets *huiothesia* in the purposes of the Father from before the world's very foundations. Adoption is the goal of his predestinating love through his own Son, Jesus Christ. In other words, as Paul extols God's elective love in Christ, he describes this pre-temporal determination attaining an exalted (and exalting!) end for the believers. This end is adoption. The parallel structures of verses four and five underscore how realized holiness and blamelessness will occur by the believer's union with the Son (1:6). As determined by the Father before time, eschatological holiness is filial holiness in his beloved Son. According to the wisdom of God before all worlds, redemptive transformation of the elect sons of Adam was to occur in the Son of God by adoptive grace.[11] Adoption here entails the culminating redemptive blessing determined in the mind of the Father.

---

[10] Cf. N. T. Wright (1997). *What Saint Paul Really Said: Was Paul of Tarsus the Real Founder of Christianity?* (see especially 151ff). Grand Rapids, MI: Eerdmans.

[11] Adoption for Paul refuses a forensic straightjacket. While justification is exclusively legal and sanctification/glorification are transformational, huiothesia establishes the familial solidarity of the believer with the Son of God, identifying the justified and sanctified one as a son placed in the fullness of Christ's resurrected sonship.

Out of God's eternal wisdom flows an unfolding of revelation in history. In Romans 9:4-5, Paul lists the uniquely enjoyed privileges of old covenant Israel, typological blessings which come to their eschatological realization in the risen Christ. Paul's anguish over his unbelieving kinsmen is intensified by his awareness that the very redemptive privileges historically enjoyed and owned by Israel actually find their raison d'être and come to fruition in Jesus Christ. Paul strikingly infers the question, "What extraordinary advantage had God not given to this people?"[12] At the top of Paul's list of Israelite privilege is **adoption** (cf. Ex 4:22-3). This typological and corporate adoption evidences God's faithful paternal care to his ancient people, but also demonstrates the familial strands of loving grace which attain their consummate realization in "the Christ who is God over all, blessed forever. Amen" (Rom 9:5b). In considering his own adoption in the Son of God, Paul sees himself as "never more truly a Jew than when he had become a Christian."[13] Or more to the point here, Paul's Israelite adoption in **type** found its comprehensive realization in his union with the true Israel, Jesus Christ the Son of God. It is this Son, sent by the Father, from whom he will never be separated (Rom 8:31-9:3). Typological adoption is historically and eschatologically secured in the Son of God par excellence. At the coming of Christ then, typological adoption culminates in eschatological cursing for those who reject the substance of its blessing, the Son of God incarnate (Rom 9:1-2, 22-4), and in eschatological blessing for those predestined for conformity into this Son's resurrected image (Rom 8:29). Truly, the *wow* of the Gospel for Paul centers in adoption realized: in his dynamic personal union with Jesus Christ, the Son of the living God.

Paul sustains this biblico-theological outlook in his presentation of *huiothesia* in Galatians 4. Having shown that both Jews and Gentiles under the pre-Christ era find themselves imprisoned in sin (3:22) and enslaved under the law and its inadequacy to provide redemption, Paul rejoices in the fullness of the time (4:4a) wherein those conjoined to Christ are "justified by faith" (3:24). Prominent in chapters three and four of Galatians is realized sonship for those who are the spiritual heirs of Abraham by faith (3:7-9, 26, 29). The eschatological realization of sonship centers in the divinely sent, incarnate Son of God (4:4). *Huiothesia* serves here to encapsulate the entire scope of Christ's redeeming work, as it describes the eschatological, Spiritual, existential and familial blessing that Christ's work renders on behalf of his people (4:4-7). Even the grammatical structure of Galatians 4:5 points us to recognizing the teleologically comprehensive status of adoption. In other words the two purpose clauses in this verse draw us to recognize adoption as the ultimate purpose of Christ's

---

[12] Anders Nygren (1949). *Romans* (356). Carl C. Rasmussen (trans). Philadelphia, PA: Muhlenberg.

[13] R. Alan Cole (1989). *The Letter of Paul to the Galatians* (148) TNTC (2nd ed.). Leicester: InterVarsity.

humiliation and, by clear inference, his exaltation. The Spirit's cry in the adopted sons' hearts, which mimics that of the Messianic Son (Mark 14:36), reinforces their filial solidarity with the Son. The Spirit's cry is "because you are sons" (4:6a), a marker of the eschatologically privileged relationship enjoyed by those in this age of mature redemptive revelation. The fullness of time brought the Son of God so that we might attain the divinely bestowed familial inheritance in Him; this in Christ, in the Son, apprehended inheritance is for Paul captured in *huiothesia*.

Paul's remaining treatment of *huiothesia* occurs in two places in Romans 8 where he centers his thoughts upon the Spirit of God. Having mentioned the Spirit only four times in Romans 1-7, Paul now employs the term *pneuma* (spirit) twenty-two times in this chapter alone.[14] Of course, this Spirit-focus here "represents before anything else the stage of salvation which the Church of Christ had reached by the coming of the Son."[15] The eschatological tension of already but not yet realities converges in *huiothesia* as Paul speaks lucidly about adoption present and future—spiritually linked in the believer's filial solidarity with the resurrected Son of God. Present living involves joining in the suffering of the Son (8:12-15); future living involves joining in the glorious bodily resurrection of the Son (8:23). Adoption displays that filial and eschatological solidarity of the believer with the life, death, and resurrection of the Son (8:1-3, 10-11), which consummates on the last day in his fully glorified transformation in the Son of God (8:29-30). The utterance here (8:15) once again of the exact words of the humiliated Son in his Garden of Gethsemane crisis (this time by the child of God himself *in the Spirit* of adoption) discloses how adoptive grace involves full participation in Christ's suffering. As we await the Son's return our adoption **requires** that we suffer like him, for our filial union with him now prepares us for our fully realized filial union with him in glory (8:17). Paul then confirms, by his equating our consummate bodily redemption with final adoption, that adoption involves more than just a forensic declaration, but a constitutive transformation (8:23). It is in our resurrection on the last day that we come to the full enjoyment of our adoptive solidarity in the Son.

It ought not surprise us that Paul *adopts* this familial term. In what better way could he maintain the incomparable uniqueness of Christ's sonship and yet preserve the believer's comprehensive participation in the Son's humiliation and exaltation? Bringing together the familially rich themes of *imago Dei* (cf. Rom 8:29), inheritance (cf. Eph 1:13-14), and Christological union, Paul employs the term *huiothesia* to speak of resplendent Gospel reality. The compound term derives from two other

---

[14] In one additional use of *pneuma* in Romans 1-7, he speaks of his own human spirit. Of the twenty-two times *pneuma* appears in Romans 8, only one of these times he necessarily means human spirit (the second *pneuma* in Rom 8:16).

[15] Herman Ridderbos (1957). *When the Time Had Fully Come: Studies in New Testament Theology* (52) Grand Rapids, MI: Eerdmans.

words, *huios* (son) and *tithemi* (to place or put). It is in Christ as resurrected Son (Rom 1:3-4) that we are placed, becoming blessed participants in his unprecedented glorified filial status. We are sons of God in Christ the Son of God.

By the grace of the Father "believers are . . . put in the same position as Christ, who is the firstborn among many brothers (Rom 8:29). He was the Son of God by nature (8:32) and was so designated at his resurrection (1:3); believers become the 'children of God' by adoption."[16] While he has attained his sonly throne by right, we join with Him in his filial and kingly glory by grace through faith. His resurrected sonship is our resurrected sonship. For Paul the entirety of our redemption—from the mind of God before creation itself until its eschatological completion in our bodily resurrection—is expressed by **filial** reality, **filial** identity, **filial** union, by **adoption**.

Implications

What does this brief survey of adoption reveal to us about our opening questions? Can presenting an incognito, sonless[17] Messiah adequately commend the Gospel? Not hardly.

No matter our motivation, there is no pure Gospel apart from the ontological and incarnational sonship of Jesus Christ. Some will protest: sonship and Messiahship are functionally interchangeable. To be sure, the redemptive-historical theme of Scripture interweaves Christ's kingly and Messianic functions with his sonship status. But the Christological fabric becomes unraveled when we rip the Messianic warp from the filial woof. We cannot speak of Christ as Messiah apart from understanding that regal and redemptive functioning **in light of him being the Son of God**. We also cannot speak of his exalted Sonship apart from his reign as King. Sonship and regal redemptive reign are mutually informative and indivisible; but though the ideas share referentiality, their meanings are not identical. So when the biblical authors employ language laden with such distinct qualities, we have no interpretive right to regard that language as negotiable.

And it is because Jesus is Son of God that we must speak of Christians as adopted sons and daughters of God. We must express Gospel truth in a way that honors the true familial expressions of Scripture, and avoids compromise by unintentional truncation or even well intended yet obstructive contextualization. We cannot speak of the true Gospel apart from the filial character of our union with Christ, for we are united to the Son of God and no one else. The filial and familial language of the Gospel

---

[16] Herman Bavinck (227). John Bolt (Ed.). (2008). *Reformed Dogmatics* (John Vriend, trans.). Grand Rapids, MI: Baker.

[17] Of course, by sonless we mean not being a son.

then is not contextually optional; it is transcendently central.

Paul's warnings in Galatians 1 ought give us terrifying pause. Removing familial language eclipses the **Christ of the Gospel** and it distorts the **Gospel of Christ**. Ultimately an incognito Christ is a misrepresented Christ. A misrepresented Christ is a false Gospel. A false Gospel is the turf of the sons of darkness. Tragically strands of the insider movements and their sonless Messiah will leave people outside the kingdom of the Beloved Son. This tragedy is no arcane matter, as many in places like Bangladesh have followed a false christ, an image put inside their minds in part by insider translations, persuading them of a Messiah that is *not* the Son of God. Some may be mercifully rescued; others will die in their sins.

While many post-Reformation formulations of the Gospel are not guilty of the overt and corrupting compromises of these missiological methods, too many continue to betray the thoroughly filial cast to the Gospel. This is no call to bury the forensic beneath the filial or to conflate justification and sanctification in cloaked Romanizing argumentation. Rather it is to remember that, as Paul points out unequivocally, Christ as Son and believers as sons of God by adoption are the content of the Gospel. These rich realities set the divinely revealed, trans-cultural context.

Accordingly, we must revel in and broadcast boldly the Gospel of Jesus Christ, the Son of God. We must relish and declare the grace of our familial union with the Messiah. Capturing the prominence of adoptive grace in the Gospel, Richard Sibbes puts it so well, "**All things** are ours by virtue of adoption, because we are Christ's and Christ is God's. There is a world of riches in this, to be sons of God."[18] As adopted sons of the Father, we possess this world of riches; we must proclaim these riches to the world.

---

[18] Richard Sibbes (iv.502). In Alexander B. Grosart (Ed.). (1983). *Works of Richard Sibbes* (7 vols). Edinburgh: Banner of Truth Trust. (emphasis added)

4.3 Jesus the Eternal Son of God

David Abernathy

David Abernathy has an MA in Biblical Studies from Reformed Theological Seminary in Charlotte, NC. He taught Greek, Hebrew, biblical exegesis and sociolinguistics in Kenya, assisted in translation workshops in Nigeria, and has also lived and worked in Mexico. He currently lives in the U.S. and does exegetical research.

Introduction

In recent decades there has been a trend among missionary Bible translators working among Muslim people groups to avoid a literal translation of the phrase *Son of God* because of the negative Muslim reaction. However, the term has tremendous theological significance, both for understanding God's Trinitarian nature, and understanding the nature of the relationship believers in Christ share as God's children. This theological significance may be missed if the translation of the *Son of God* does not clearly indicate that Jesus was truly the Son of God in a real sense; that is, in a sense that is essential to his eternal nature and being. The purpose of this chapter is to describe the significance of the term *Son of God* in light of historical creeds and biblical theology.

Understanding the problem

The Qur'an anathematizes anyone daring to say that Jesus is the Son of God; guaranteeing that they will go to hell, possibly even causing the earth and heavens to shake (Q4:165; 5:18; 6:101; 9:30; 17:111; 19:35, 88-92; 23:91). Muslims have traditionally taught that the phrase *Son of God* can only mean that Christians believe that God produced offspring by a sexual union with a woman. In some parts of the world, it seems nearly impossible to convince devout Muslims that any other meaning is even possible. The presence of the offending term could prevent the translated text from ever getting a hearing, much less transform the thinking of the readers, unless a significant change in understanding is made through a deep move of the Holy Spirit.

Missionary Bible translators have long operated under the premise that if the reading audience gets little meaning, no meaning, or the wrong meaning from a passage, then the wording of the passage must be altered in order to solve the problem. Consequently, some translators have opted to use different wording for *Son of God* in order to avoid the wrong meaning Muslims attach to the phrase. Translators reason that since *Son of God* is a metaphor, a suitable non-metaphorical equivalent can be substituted. Because the Qur'an uses the terms *Messiah (al masih)* and *Word* to refer to Jesus, some translators, wanting to avoid the reaction that the prohibited term *Son of God* causes, choose to use *Messiah*, *Word* or *God's beloved* in place of *Son of God*. However, most Christians have understood the phrase *Son of God* to mean that Jesus actually is God's eternal, preexistent Son. Changing the phrase to *Messiah* or *Word*—or anything else—fails to communicate the reality of this eternal Father-Son relationship.

The meaning of the term *Son of God*
Metaphorical or metaphysical?

One of the arguments translators use for substituting *Son of God* is that the term is considered a metaphor, and as such, can be altered to communicate the same intended non-metaphorical meaning, whatever the metaphor's meaning is determined to be for the context. The rationale is that since Jesus does not have a divine mother, he cannot literally be the Son of God; so it is assumed that the only other option is that he is *Son* in some metaphorical sense. That is, if the sonship is not physical, it can only be metaphorical. No other alternatives are recognized.

But when talking about the persons of the Trinity, there is a third category in addition to the physical and the metaphorical: the metaphysical. Christ's sonship is a metaphysical and essential sonship that is eternal and real; it is the essence of who he is eternally. As St. Hilary of Poitiers put it, "He is the only-begotten, perfect, eternal Son of the unbegotten, perfect, eternal Father."[1] The statement that "God sent his own Son" means that Jesus was already the Son of God when he was sent; that is, Jesus is the eternal, preexistent Son of God.

The church has always understood Christ's sonship in this way, going far beyond metaphor. If *Son of God* simply were a metaphor, it would originate in human relationships—with divine relationships described in terms of the human. This implies that God is at a loss for ways to describe his being, and can only draw from human experiences to do so. This is not the case. Just as a computer hard drive must be formatted before data can be written to it, so the human experience and personality is stamped with certain eternal patterns enabling us to understand something of the essential nature of the God who created us in his image. The Father-Son relation is an eternal pattern, inherent in the very nature of the persons of the Trinity. It is a pattern God has built into human experience in order to teach us something about himself.

Paul says, "I kneel before the Father, from whom his whole family in heaven and on earth derives its name" (Eph 3:14-15). Paul is saying earthly fatherhood has its origin in God himself. Most Reformation confessions of faith assert the Son is eternally begotten of the Father, as do many of the ancient creeds. Most of the doctrinal statements of mission organizations, Christian academic institutions, or denominational church bodies that are conservative enough to have a doctrinal statement, will assert, in one form

---

[1] Hilary, *De Trinitate* 3.3.

or another, that God exists eternally as Father, Son, and Holy Spirit. If God exists eternally as Father, Son, and Holy Spirit, then fatherhood and sonship are an eternal aspect of their relationship: God is Father eternally and Jesus is the eternal Son.

Metaphor, archetype, and inherent sonship

Dutch theologian Herman Bavinck argued that when we refer to God as Father, we are not using a metaphor, as though fatherhood is primarily an attribute of humanity, and so referring to God only in a secondary or derived sense.[2] Bavinck said the relation is reversed: "God is Father in the real and complete sense of the term."[3] His fatherhood pertains to his eternal essence, and fatherhood on earth is but a dim reflection or shadow of God's eternal fatherhood. The eternal character of God's fatherhood implies the eternal character of Christ's divine sonship.[4] Fatherhood and sonship are archetypes: eternal patterns that correspond to realities encountered within the temporal and natural realm. Human fatherhood and sonship are, by comparison, faint copies of the eternal Father-Son relation.[5] The nouns *Father* and *Son* have their proper biblical meaning only in relation to each other; that is, the Father is called the Father of the Son, and the Son is the Son of the Father.[6] Richard Bauckham comments in regard to Jesus' revelation of himself as being one with the Father (John 10:30):

> The terms *Father* and *Son* entail each other. The Father is called Father only because Jesus is his Son, and Jesus is called Son only because he is the Son of his divine Father. Each is essential to the identity of the other. So to say that Jesus and the Father are one is to say that the unique divine identity comprises the relationship in which the Father is who he is only in relation to the Son and vice versa.[7]

Only God is Father in the fullest sense for he was the first father. Bavinck went on to conclude that whoever refuses to honor God as Father shows more disrespect toward the Father than the one who does not

---

[2] Herman Bavinck 1977 (1977). *The Doctrine of God*. (307) Carlisle, PA: Banner of Truth Trust.

[3] Athanasius, commenting on Eph 3:15, said, "God does not make man his pattern, but rather, since God alone is properly and truly Father, we men are called fathers of our own children, for of him every fatherhood in heaven and earth is named" (*Contra Arianos* 1.7.23).

[4] Herman Bavinck. In John Murray (1982). *Collected Writings of John Murray: Studies in Theology* (v. 4, 66). Carlisle, PA: Banner of Truth Trust.

[5] Merrill C. Tenney (1981). *The Gospel of John*. (196). EBC Grand Rapids, MI: Zondervan.

[6] Robert Jensen. "The Trinity in the Bible." *Concordia Theological Quarterly*. 68(3–4): 204.; cf. Murray, *Collected writings* 66. Calvin, citing Augustine, says that Christ is called *God* with respect to himself, but *Son* with respect to the Father; the Father is called *God* with respect to himself, but *Father* with respect to the Son (*Institutes* I, xiii, 19).

[7] Richard Bauckham (2008). *God Crucified and Other Studies on the New Testament's Christology of divine identity* (106). Grand Rapids, MI: Eerdmans.

acknowledge him as creator. Douglas Kelly believes it is significant that both the Apostle's Creed and the Nicene Creed mention the fatherhood of God before speaking of him as creator; that is, he was always Father, but he was not always creator.[8] This understanding of God's eternal fatherhood is common; Athanasius elaborated the point in the fourth century.[9]

The epistle to the Hebrews illustrates the concept of archetypes. The earthly tabernacle was a copy that corresponded to a heavenly reality (Heb 9:11, 23). Likewise, Melchizedek, as a priest and king, is *like* the Son of God. The writer is not using the Jewish tabernacle as a pattern for heavenly realities, nor is he taking Melchizedek as a pattern for Jesus' ministry. He does exactly the reverse. The earthly tabernacle and the earthly priest-king, Melchizedek, display certain similarities to the preexistent heavenly realities.

Note also that the Father-Son-Son of God conceptual cluster, which occurs several hundred times in the New Testament, occurs far more frequently and is distributed far more widely than normal biblical metaphors. The biblical authors do not indicate that Christ's sonship is metaphorical. They viewed it as substantive and real in the fullest sense. This is also true of the sonship of believers. 1 John 3:1 says, "How great is the love the Father has lavished on us, that we should be called children of God! And that is what we are!" We do not need to assume the term *Son of God* must be metaphorical. It does not have to be understood in a literal-physical sense. There is an eternal and metaphysical sense in which Jesus is the divine Son, the Son of God.

Divine sonship as prototype for humans becoming God's sons and daughters

Many scholars state it is Christ's natural and eternal sonship that leads to our adoption as sons and daughters of God. The mission of God's Son was to bring others into a relationship with God as his children.[10] It is Jesus' uncreated, natural, eternal sonship that makes all the other sons of God possible.[11] Larry Hurtado notes that in Paul's view, God's purpose in sending his Son was that we might become sons by adoption.[12] In Romans

---

[8] Douglas F. Kelly (2008). *Systematic Theology: Grounded in Holy Scripture and Understood in the Light of the Church* (449). Fearn, Ross-shire, Scotland: Mentor.

[9] Athanasius said, "It belongs to the Godhead alone that the Father is properly father, and the Son properly Son, and in them, and them only, does it hold that the Father is ever Father and the Son ever Son." *Against the Arians: Discourse Four, Ch. VI, section 21.* http://www.ccel.org/ccel/schaff/npnf204.xxi.ii.iv.html (accessed 2/3/11).

[10] George Eldon Ladd (1974). In Donald A. Hagner (Ed.). *A Theology of the New Testament.* (458) (Rev. ed.). Grand Rapids, MI: Eerdmans.

[11] Donald G. Bloesch (1978). *Essentials of Evangelical Theology: God, Authority, and Salvation* (126). San Francisco, CA: Harper and Row. Calvin notes that although God was never Father to either angels or men, but only with regard to his only begotten son, he nevertheless enables sinful men to become God's sons by free adoption through Christ, who is the Son of God by nature, and who always possessed sonship (*Institutes* II, xiv, 5).

[12] Larry W. Hurtado (1993). "Son of God" (905–906). In Gerald F. Hawthorne and Ralph P. Martin (Eds.). *Dictionary of Paul and His Letters.* Downers Grove, IL: InterVarsity; cf.

8:29 and Galatians 4:4-6, Paul shows that it is through the work of the preexistent Son whom God sent to die for us that we are adopted as God's sons.[13] The Son leads other sons to salvation as well as to the inheritance associated with sonship; this inheritance is both his and theirs.[14] This means that Jesus, as the divine Son, whose sonship is not derived from another, is the prototype and agent granting others the right to be God's sons. The sonship of Christians is derived from Jesus' own sonship and patterned after it,[15] and the pattern of that sonship is obedience.[16] Jesus mediates for believers a new relationship with God, bringing them into the same intimate relationship with God that they may call him *Abba*.[17] Through the Son of God, believers are accepted as children of God, calling his Father, their Father.[18] Dumitru Staniloae says,

> The revelation of the Trinity, occasioned by the incarnation and earthly activity of the Son, has no other purpose than to draw us after grace, to draw us through the Holy Spirit into the filial relationship the Son has with the Father.[19]

Further, Staniloae characterizes this relationship as one of eternal love and communion.[20]

According to J. N. D. Kelly, it is through the incarnation that the Son of God revealed the heart of God to the human race. On their behalf and in their place, he gave the perfect filial responses required by God so they could know the Father as the Son knows him.[21] F. F. Bruce characterizes the process this way:

> The Son and the Father exist together in an eternal relationship of reciprocal love, and all those who are united to the Son through

---

Gerald O'Collins (1999). *The Tripersonal God: Understanding and Interpreting the Trinity* (62). New York, NY: Paulist Press.

[13] I. Howard Marshall (1980). "Titles of Jesus Christ" (778). In J. D. Douglas (Ed.). *The Illustrated Bible Dictionary*, part 2. Downers Grove: InterVarsity; cf. Millard Erickson (1991). *The Word Became Flesh* (35). Grand Rapids: Baker Books.

[14] Kenneth Schenk (1997). "Keeping His Appointment: Creation and Enthronement in Hebrews." *Journal for the Study of the New Testament* 66: 98, 102.

[15] Hurtado, "Son of God" 905 906; Schenk, "Keeping" 99.

[16] D. R. Bauer (1992). "Son of God" (774). In Joel B. Green and Scot McKnight (Eds.). *Dictionary of Jesus and the Gospels*. Downers Grove, IL: InterVarsity.

[17] I. Howard Marshall (1967). "The Divine Sonship of Jesus." *Interpretation* 21: 90; cf. Craig L. Blomberg (1997). *Jesus and the Gospels* (405). Nashville, TN: B & H.

[18] Norval Geldenhuys (1977). *Commentary on the Gospel of Luke: The English Text with Introduction, Exposition, and Notes* (130). Grand Rapids, MI: Eerdmans.

[19] Dumitru Staniloae (1994). *Orthodox Dogmatic Theology: The Experience of God* (249). Ioan Ionita and Robert Barringer (trans.). Brookline, MA: Holy Cross Orthodox Press. Cited in D. F. Kelley, *Systematic Theology* 261.

[20] Staniloae, *Orthodox* 249.

[21] J. N. D. Kelly (1972). *Early Christian Creeds*. Essex, England: Longman/Pearson Education Ltd.

believing in him are welcomed into this relationship: the Father of Jesus becomes their Father too.[22]

In other words, our own union with God "depends upon the intimate union of the Father and the Son."[23] The salvation granted to believers as part of God's eternal plan—making us his own sons and daughters—was accomplished through the perfect Son, our model.

The historical development of Christological and Trinitarian doctrine
The creeds, the Trinity, and the Son

At the conclusion of Matthew's Gospel, Jesus gives his apostles their marching orders using an aorist imperative: make disciples of all nations. Then using two present participles in an imperatival sense, he describes the activities that accompany discipling: baptizing and teaching them everything he taught them. Baptism was to be in the name (singular) of the Father, the Son, and the Holy Spirit. This is the only place in Scripture in which a member of the Trinity speaks objectively to name the persons of the Trinity. This is why it has become the normative Trinitarian formula. The book of Acts has seeming variations in the baptismal formula, but it is unknown whether these are a matter of abbreviation on Luke's part for literary reasons, or—and this seems more likely—the formula had not yet been standardized.

The Didache is a church manual of instruction written toward the end of the first century or beginning of the second century. The Didache's baptismal formula is the same as Matthew 28:19: "In the name of the Father, the Son, and the Holy Spirit." The formula is used today in the west (Roman Catholic and Protestant) and in the east (Orthodox, Coptic, Maronite, Roman Catholic and other communions). In other words, the use of the Trinitarian formula is nearly universal.

In Latin tradition the baptismal formula of Matthew 28:19 culminated in the Apostles' Creed. The same formula resulted in the Nicene-Constantinopolitan creed.[24] It is natural that creeds would develop from earlier baptismal confessions. Baptismal candidates were catechized to profess the faith into which they were baptized.[25] In the early third century, Hippolytus records a baptismal interrogation that included a three-fold profession of faith, corresponding to the three persons of the Trinity.[26] J.

---

[22] F. F. Bruce (1986). *Jesus: Lord and Savior* (167). Downers Grove, IL: InterVarsity.

[23] William Sanday and Arthur C. Headlam (1971). *A Critical and Exegetical Commentary on the Epistle to the Romans* (389). ICC Edinburgh: T. & T Clark; cf. Geerhardus Vos (1953). *The Self-disclosure of Jesus* (200-1) (Rev. ed.). Phillipsburg, NJ: Presbyterian and Reformed Publishing House.

[24] J. N. D. Kelly, *Early Christian Creeds* 89–91, 96, 121.

[25] J. N. D. Kelly, *Early Christian Creeds* 206; Schaff http://www.ccel.org/ccel/schaff/creeds2.iii.i.x.html (2/3/11).

[26] Ralph Martin. (1964). *Worship in the early church* (61). Grand Rapids, MI: Eerdmans.

N. D. Kelly notes that the Trinitarian baptismal command of Matthew 28:19 was "the creative model on which the baptismal questions, and so baptismal creeds, were constructed."[27]

The creeds not only tell us how the early church understood the Trinity, they reveal how Christ was understood. The old Roman creed, the predecessor of the Apostles' Creed, clearly implies that Christ was the Son of God, and as the only begotten, he was the preexistent Son.[28] The creed's nucleus is the command given by Christ to the apostles in Matthew 28:19. In the phrase, *Father, Son, and Holy Spirit*, we have the heart of the Christian Gospel: God, who is a Father, revealed himself in history through one who was at the same time both God and man—and who continues to operate in the lives of his followers by his Spirit. This is "the uniqueness of Christianity."[29]

The Word, the Son, and Marcellus

During the first three centuries of the post-apostolic era, many Church fathers made considerable use of the term *logos*. This was natural given their ties to Greek philosophical traditions, but they also continued to use *Son of God* or *Son*. This is evident in Justin Martyr's *Apology*, Clement of Rome (*Epistle to Diognetus*, chapter 9), Athenagorus (*Plea*, chapters 10, 24), Ignatius (*Letter to the Ephesians*, chapter 20), *The Martyrdom of Polycarp* (chapter 14), Irenaeas (*Against Heresies*, chapter 3), and others. While they could speak freely of Christ as the *logos*, they did not lose sight of his eternal sonship. However, when eternal sonship is removed, as happened in the case of Marcellus of Ancyra, problems ensue.

Marcellus lived during the theologically turbulent fourth century as the debates with the Arians were raging. As a signer of the Nicene canons, Marcellus was a respected and influential theologian of his day, but had never promoted the Nicene Creed. Marcellus's legacy is his teaching that prior to the incarnation, Jesus existed as *logos* not as Son. Many interpreted his view as a new variation of the old modalist[30] heresy. Although it was not his intention, his teaching added fuel to the speculations of the Arians. His error was rejected in the twenty-six anathemas of the First Sirmian Creed in 351. Marcellus was condemned as a heretic at the council of Constantinople in 381, and a year later in a council called by Pope Damasus. One of the twenty-four anathemas from Constantinople stated, "If anyone denies that the Father is eternal, that the Son is eternal, and that the Holy Spirit is

---

[27] J. N. D. Kelly, *Early Christian Creeds* 203–204.
[28] J. N. D. Kelly, *Early Christian Creeds* 148.
[29] Kenneth Scott Latourette (1997). *A History of Christianity: to A.D. 1500* (135). Peabody, MA: Prince Press.
[30] Modalism denies the Trinity, claiming that God is not three persons but one person who reveals himself at different times in three different modes, Father, Son, and Holy Spirit.

eternal, he is a heretic."³¹

Marcellus's error was his belief that the eternal *logos* did not become the Son of God until the incarnation; therefore, Christ was not the personal, pre-incarnate Son.³² God's self-sacrifice of his own son means much less if sonship begins at the incarnation.³³ Marcellus reasoned the *logos* existed as Word, but not as a hypostasis (understood then as a personal entity). In fairness to Marcellus, it must be noted that he was not fully a modalist or an adoptionist³⁴ in the original sense of those terms, but the conclusion of Constantinople that a sonless Trinity is conceptually and theologically unworkable was correct.

The council of Chalcedon (AD 451) addressed the two natures of Christ in one person. This was the last major council to deal with Trinitarian and Christological issues. The doctrine was defined and though many of the same heresies continued to recur, the Chalcedonian creed affirmed Christ as God the Word. As did its predecessors, the council described Christ as Son. It affirmed the Son as only begotten (or unique, *monogenes*); begotten by the Father before all ages, thus agreeing with the Nicene Creed and most Eastern creeds. Chalcedon did not change the Church's understanding of eternal sonship; it affirmed it.

Son of God in biblical theology
Four senses of Christ's divine sonship

Geerhardus Vos outlined four different senses in which the designation *Son of God* is applied to Jesus in the New Testament. These four aspects are not mutually exclusive, but are integrally related to one another. One sense is moral and religious: Jesus lived as an obedient *Son of God* in terms of his perfect faith and character.³⁵ When Jesus says the peacemakers will be called *sons of God*, he is speaking of this moral and religious sense of sonship. In a greater way Jesus proves himself to be God's Son by the way he lived, showing God's character and nature through obedience to the Father as a faithful son. Commentary on this aspect of sonship is found throughout exegetical literature, especially with regard to Jesus' temptation in the wilderness, where the real issue was not whether Jesus was actually the Son of God, rather what kind of Son he would be.

The second sense of Jesus' divine sonship is the nativistic: the basis for Jesus' occupancy of throne of his father David is not human paternity, but divine action (Lk 1:32, 35). This nativistic aspect of Jesus' divine sonship is

---

³¹ John Calvin, dealing with a similar error taught by Servetus and others, says that Jesus did not become Son of God at the incarnation, but is so by virtue of his deity and eternal essence (*Institutes* II, xiv, 6).

³² Harold O. J. Brown (1984). *Heresies: Heresy and orthodoxy in the history of the Church* (121). Peabody, MA: Hendrickson.

³³ Vos, Self-disclosure 221.

³⁴ Adoptionism believes Jesus became the Son of God at his baptism, part of a testing required to prove his worthiness.

³⁵ Vos, *Self-disclosure* 141-142.

linked to his genealogy reaching back to Adam. Adam is called a son of God in the sense that his existence was directly due to the action of God, not human parents.

The third sense of sonship is Messianic. A few, largely critical scholars, view this as the primary meaning—some, the only meaning—of the term *Son of God* in the Gospels, especially the Synoptics. They interpret it as an adoptive sonship, keeping with Psalm 2, Isaiah 42:1, and 2 Samuel 14:7.

The eternal sonship, the fourth sense is the view held traditionally by most interpreters. Vos argued that because the Messiah must act as an absolute representative of God and is promised dominion over the ends of the earth (both in Psalm 2 and in Revelation), only a Son in the highest sense is able to adequately fulfill the Messianic office. A world ruler in such a comprehensive sense as the Old Testament prophecies describe him, needs to be super-human.[36]

Eternal sonship: the basis of Messianic ministry

As Vos stated, it is this eternal sonship that qualifies the Son for the Messianic sonship, which is simply the eternal sonship expressed in history. Only a Son could fulfill such an office because it involves inheriting God's rule over the world; such a world ruler must of necessity be superhuman.[37] It is crucial here **not** to make the mistake of assuming that divine sonship is equivalent to being the Messiah; far more is involved. Eternal sonship is the basis for the Messianic sonship.[38] That is, Jesus is the Christ by virtue of being the Son of God; he is not the Son of God because he is the Christ. Being the Son of God means more than being the Messiah; the two are not the same.[39]

Son of God in the New Testament
The Gospels

The Church did not slowly evolve an understanding of Christ's deity over the first few centuries of Christianity. His deity is made obvious by the New Testament, and especially by the four evangelists. The titles *Son* and

---

[36] Vos, *Self-disclosure* 190, 192.

[37] Vos, *Self-disclosure* 190–192.

[38] Vos, *Self-disclosure* 190; cf. Donald J. Verseput (1987). "The Role and Meaning of the *Son of God* Title in Matthew's Gospel." *New Testament Studies* 33: 538, 548; cf. Murray, *Collected Writings* 68; Ladd, *Theology* 163-166; Marshall, "The Divine Sonship" 99; Richard N. Longenecker (1994). "The foundational conviction of New Testament Christology: The obedience/faithfulness/sonship of Christ" (95-6). In Joel B. Green and Max Turner (Eds.). *Jesus of Nazareth: Lord and Christ: Essays on the Historical Jesus and New Testament Christology.* Grand Rapids, MI: Eerdmans.

[39] Douglas J. Moo (1996). *The Epistle to the Romans* (45 fn 27). NICNT Grand Rapids, MI: Eerdmans; cf. John Nolland. (2005). *The Gospel of Matthew.* (163-4). NIGTC Grand Rapids, MI: Eerdmans; Darrell L. Bock (1994). "A Theology of Luke-Acts" (108). In Roy B. Zuck (Ed.). *A Biblical Theology of the New Testament.* Chicago, IL: Moody Press; Rudolph Schnackenburg (1995). *Jesus in the Gospels: A Biblical Christology* (310, 312). O. C. Dean Jr. (trans.). Louisville KY: Westminster John Knox Press.

Son of God—and Jesus' self-revelation connected with the titles—are at the heart of the evangelists' understanding of his deity and the Trinity. William Lane believes the Church developed her understanding of the Trinity through God's salvific activity as Father, Son, and Holy Spirit.[40] The Church came to know the second person of the Trinity as Son because of the relation Jesus, the man, enjoyed as Son to the Father. Since God's self revelation in history is true to his real being, the church was able to draw conclusions about God's eternal, triune being. The New Testament writers believed in the deity of Christ, Lane says, and as they made reasonable conclusions about him as the preexistent, divine Son, were able to think in terms of the Trinity. The starting point for Christology was the historic Christ: Christians worked from Christology to Trinity, not the other way around.[41] T. F. Torrance agrees with this, saying, "The incarnational and saving self-revelation of God as Father, Son and Holy Spirit was traced back to what God is enhypostatically and coinherently in himself, in his own eternal being as Father, Son and Holy Spirit."[42]

Even from the beginning the Church did not hesitate to use the title *Son of God* to indicate the supreme place occupied by Jesus.[43] Turner states that it was the resurrection that helped develop the early church's belief in Christ's deity. He says that although Jesus clearly revealed himself to be the unique Son to God, it was not so clear that he was God the Son—at least not at first. The primary stimulus that changed the disciples' understanding was the resurrection, which enabled them even in the forty day period between the resurrect and ascension, to recognize his divinity—as Thomas did when he confessed Jesus as Lord and God (John 20:31), or the disciples when they worshipped him on the mountain in Galilee (Mt. 28:17).[44] In commenting on Matthew 28:19, Blomberg also cites the resurrection as being the event that brought clarity to the eternal aspect of Jesus' sonship. He notices that after the resurrection, the term *Son of God* is used in a manner that would be employed in later Trinitarian formulas; namely, Jesus is deity and the Son of God is "God's ontological equal and one part of the Godhead itself."[45]

---

[40] Cf. William L. Lane (1974). *The Gospel According to Mark*. NICNT. Grand Rapids, MI: Eerdmans.

[41] A. N. S. Lane (1982). Christology beyond Chalcedon (275-6). In Harold H. Rowdon (Ed.). *Christ the Lord: Studies in Christology presented to Donald Guthrie*. Downer's Grove, IL: InterVarsity.

[42] T. F. Torrance (1991). *The Trinitarian faith* (199). London: T & T Clark. Cited in D. F. Kelly, *Systematic Theology* 450.

[43] Ladd, *Theology* 168.

[44] M. M. B. Turner (1982). "The Spirit of Christ and Christology" (173, 190). In Harold H. Rowdon (Ed.). *Christ the Lord*.

[45] Blomberg, *Jesus* 408. All the major Christian doctrines are interdependent. An adequate doctrine of salvation requires an adequate Christology, which in turn presses for a satisfactory special theology of the Trinity (Brown, *Heresies* 150-2). Murray agrees, saying a faith and confession that is not "conditioned by the faith of God as Trinity, and by the intra-divine and intrinsic relations involved in Jesus' identity as the eternal Son, does not provide

We should not underestimate the significance of Jesus' divine sonship in the Gospel accounts; it is of paramount importance. I. H. Marshall calls it "the supreme category of interpretation of the person of Jesus in the Gospels."[46] He says it is a category that subordinates even his Messiahship. Bauer suggested that the title, *Son of God*, is not only the "foremost category" in each of the Gospels, but possibly the most significant Christological title in the entire New Testament.[47] Similarly Longenecker comments that just as Jesus' filial consciousness undergirded all he did, so also the evangelists had a keen awareness of Jesus' unique sonship, a consciousness that served as the foundational conviction for all they wrote. The synoptic evangelists, he notes, edited and arranged their material, each in his own way, to communicate to their readers the importance of Jesus' sonship. It was as though they said, "To understand Jesus, one must see his divine sonship as basic to all that he did!"[48]

Schnackenburg points out that as the *Son of God* stands at the center of Paul's Christological statements,[49] it also pervades the Gospels. For example, Mark's picture of Jesus is suffused with the divine sonship and John's theme of the *Son of God* is woven through his story. Schnackenburg concludes that the early church found an enduring way to express Jesus' deepest essence and significance: the title, *Son of God*.[50]

Interpreting the Gospel authors' intended meaning of *Son of God*

Interpreting the term *Son of God* in the Gospels involves multiple levels of meaning. Not every person in the Gospels who called Jesus the Son of God necessarily expressed the author's intended meaning of the title. A variety of players in the drama use the title: soldiers, disciples, the high priest, God, Satan, demons, angels, and even Jesus himself. The title *Son of God* is used to express a variety of thoughts: worship (Mt 14:33); fear and awe (Mt 27:54); even mockery (Mt 27:40). It takes on new dimensions when spoken by supernatural beings: God the Father's deep affection for the Son (Mt. 3:17; 17:5); demonic terror (Mark 3:11); and for Satan, it becomes leverage for evil at the temptation (Mt 4:3ff).

Our interpretive task is to determine the author's intention. Although we may know little of the reading audience, by the process of evaluation and drawing conclusions from the literary clues, the authorial intention is established. The authors of the four Gospels did not write their story as one

---

the Christology biblical revelation demands. The true Christology is one that has its starting point and finds its basis in Christ's intrinsic sonship and therefore in its Trinitarian correlatives" (Murray, *Collected Writings* 80).

[46] Marshall, "The Divine Sonship" 99.
[47] Bauer, "Son of God" 769.
[48] Longenecker, "Foundational Conviction" 476, 484-5.
[49] Cf. Gal 1:16; 2:20; 4:4; Rom 1:3-4; 8:2, 32.
[50] Schnackenburg, *Jesus* 310, 312.

would write fiction; rather they functioned as gatekeepers, each choosing the material for his account, arranging and shaping its final form. The Gospels convey real events and dialogues, but each author crafted his own story with an individual literary purpose. Therefore to determine the meaning of the terms *Son of God* and *the Son* in the Gospels, we primarily focus on what each evangelist intends to communicate to his audience.

At the time the Gospels were being written, the evangelists and their audiences knew more about Jesus than those in the events being recorded. Jesus' life, his teachings, his miracles, and especially the resurrection and the coming of the Holy Spirit at Pentecost—followed by serious theological reflection in the light of these events over three or more decades—brought about dramatic changes to the Church's understanding of Jesus and his titles. Consequently we cannot limit our understanding of *Son of God* and *the Son* to the first century Jewish understanding of Messiah prior to the incarnation. One of the themes throughout the Gospels is that even Jesus' closest friends did not understand him. It was not until after the resurrection—and more importantly, because of it—that everything changed.

Son of God and *the Son* in Matthew's Gospel

Matthew has three episodes in which the Father is mentioned and Jesus refers to himself as the Son (11:27; 24:36; 28:19). Two of the episodes help us understand Jesus' self-awareness of his divine sonship (11:27; 28:19). According to Verseput, the title *Son of God* is the key motif for understanding Matthew's literary and theological purpose.[51] Matthew and his audience share a common understanding that Jesus is the Son of God; therefore his readers easily follow the direction of Matthew's storyline.[52] Carson concurs that as Matthew's readers move through the text of the Gospel, they know things that people of Jesus' day did not know, since many Christological truths were only understood after the resurrection and exaltation. The reader can understand the deeper truths about the Son of God, things not understood by those involved in the actual Gospel accounts. Carson notes that those who confessed Jesus as Son of God may have meant no more than Christ—even that understanding was probably lacking recognition of Christ as Suffering Servant, or an ontological connection with deity. Matthew's readers, on the other hand, are able to appreciate the significance of Jesus, the Son of God, far beyond the understanding of the actors in the drama itself.[53]

Matthew introduces the theme of Jesus' divine sonship with key questions scattered throughout his Gospel. In 13:56 the people of his own hometown, after hearing his parables and about his miracles ask, "Where

---

[51] Verseput, "The Role" 532.
[52] D. A. Carson (1982). "Christological ambiguities in Matthew" (97–114). In Harold H. Rowdon (Ed.). *Christ the Lord*.
[53] Carson, "Christological" 113.

did this man get all these things?" The crowds ask, "Could this be the Son of David?" (12:23), and later, "Who is this?" (21:10). In 11:2-3 John the Baptist questions whether Jesus is the one they are waiting for, or is another coming—i.e., is a greater One coming, or are you the One? Jesus himself asked the question, "What do you think about the Christ? Whose son is he?" (22:42).

The disciples had a significant question following the calming of the storm: What sort of man is this? (8:27). Matthew words these questions to guide the reader to the correct answer.[54] According to Nolland, the answer to all these questions comes at the calming of the second storm (14:33): the disciples worship him. Jesus has acted as only God can; they know they are in the presence of God, saying, "Truly you are the Son of God."[55] Garland observes that the disciples' confession, Jesus is the Son of God, answers the question raised during the first storm. They had asked, "What kind of a man is this? Even the winds and waves obey him!" (8:27). At the second storm they have their answer—the answer to all the questions raised by others in Matthew's Gospel account, whether by John the Baptist, the crowds, or the people in his hometown.[56] Peter's confession of Jesus as the Christ and Son of the living God (16:16) is a Christological high point of the Gospel. At the end of Matthew's story, the centurion and the soldiers assigned to execute Jesus, acknowledge that he is the Son of God. Regardless of what they actually meant, this profession seems to be Matthew's desired climax to the Gospel. As Gundry notes, Matthew, as well as Mark, intended their readers to understand that Jesus is the Son of God.[57]

Son of God and the Son in Mark's Gospel

Mark introduces his Gospel with, "The beginning of the good news of Jesus Christ, the Son of God"; that is, his Gospel is about the Son of God. Later there are similar statements: the heavenly voice at Jesus' baptism; the terrified imploring of demons (3:11; 5:7); God's announcement at the transfiguration (9:4); and Jesus' own executioner, the centurion (15:39). Regardless the centurion's meaning of *Son of God*, Mark's readers knew the meaning—Jesus' divine sonship is at the heart of the Mark.

Schnackenburg observes that in Mark *Son of God* is mentioned in passages particularly crucial for Christology. This is especially true of the centurion's confession, a point of crystallization for the proper understanding of Jesus. According to Schnackenburg, the Gospel is framed at the beginning and the end by the profession of Jesus as the Son of

---

[54] John Nolland (1989). *Luke 1–9:20* (372). WBC Dallas, TX: Word.
[55] Nolland, *Luke* 603.
[56] David Garland (2001). *Reading Matthew: A Literary and Theological Commentary* (160). Macon, GA: Smyth and Helwys.
[57] Robert H. Gundry (1982). *Matthew: A commentary on his literary art* (578). Grand Rapids: Eerdmans.

God.[58] Although *Son of God* may mean no more than *Christ* to some—such as the high priest (14:61)—when augmented by the accounts of healing, miracles, exorcisms, powerful teaching, forgiving sins, the supernatural events that accompanied his death, and of course by the resurrection, Mark uses the phrase to prompt thoughts of Jesus' divinity in his Roman readers.[59]

Son of God and *the Son* in Luke's Gospel

Luke employs *Son of God* differently than Matthew and Mark; of those who acknowledge Jesus' divine sonship, the only human is Jesus himself. Luke reports Peter's more abbreviated confession. He also records the centurion saying only that Jesus is a righteous man; however, this does not mean *Son of God* is unimportant in Luke, or that it only has the connotation of Messiah. On the contrary, Jesus' sonship is quite important in Luke. Even at the temptation, which focuses on God's statement at Jesus' baptism, two of the three trials are directed at his sonship. Luke intends to have only supernatural agents testify to Jesus' divine sonship: the angel at the annunciation (1:32, 35), the voice of God at Jesus' baptism (3:22), Satan in the wilderness temptation (4:3, 9), demons being exorcised (8:28), and the voice of God again at the transfiguration (9:35). Luke's purpose may be to show that these supernatural beings understand Jesus' sonship in a manner qualitatively different from the incomplete and partially skewed understanding of humans.

Son of God and *the Son* in John's Gospel

In the Gospel of John, Jesus calls God *Father* over one hundred times, and refers to himself or is referred to as *Son* about thirty times. As Ladd said, Jesus' sonship is the central Christological idea in John's Gospel. John's account is written so that people may believe that Jesus is the Messiah, but more than Messiah: he is the Son of God, partaking of deity. The Father-Son relation woven throughout the fabric of John's story, is a relationship characterized by the object of divine love, Jesus, having an exclusive knowledge of the Father, and being given the power to mediate not only life, but to bring humanity to God himself.[60] Tenney describes sonship in John's Gospel as expressing close fellowship and intimacy between the Father and Son, as well as a unity of nature. Since he shares the Father's nature, he is able to reveal God.[61] On this unity and intimacy between the Father and the Son, Bruce wrote,

> The relationship which the Father and the Son eternally bear to each

---

[58] Schnackenburg, *Jesus* 45, 49.
[59] Robert H. Gundry (1993). *Mark: A commentary on his apology for the cross* (34). Grand Rapids, MI: Eerdmans
[60] Ladd, *Theology* 283-5.
[61] Tenney, *The Gospel of John* 196 and 38.

other is declared to be a coinherence or mutual indwelling of love. Jesus is in the Father; the Father is in him. And the purpose of Jesus' coming to reveal the Father is that men and women may . . . be drawn into this divine fellowship of love, dwelling in God as God dwells in them.[62]

Thomas's confession (20:31) necessarily involved a belief in Jesus' deity. The Son possesses the divine nature and is God by nature. This intimate and eternal knowledge of God qualifies the Son to reveal God's nature and character. Whereas the sonship of believers is an adoptive sonship, Christ's sonship is essential. He was in complete intimate fellowship with the Father before and after the incarnation.[63] D. Kelly says that in Christ's high priestly prayer (John 17), his saving work for humanity is expressed in terms of the "eternal love and glory between Father and Son that are conveyed from the very heart of the Father to them."[64] The high priestly prayer is indisputably a transaction between Father and Son born of mutual interests, culminating in mutual glory, and drawing new sons and daughters into the oneness and glory of the eternal Trinity.

Christology of the *Son of God* in the epistles of Paul

Paul does not often refer to Jesus Christ as God's Son; however, it is definitely a concept of central importance for him, as he often uses the title in key places in his letters.[65] For instance if we judge only from a statistical standpoint, we would have to say the phrase, "the righteousness of God," was unimportant to him. It occurs only about ten times, all but two of them in Romans, but it is significant in Romans because those passages state the central theme of the letter. Paul does not often mention the kingdom of God or Jesus' role as Messiah, but this does not mean they are unimportant to him.[66] Jesus as the Word (*logos*), occurs in only two verses of John's Gospel, once in 1 John and Revelation, though never in any clear reference by other New Testament authors. The importance of *logos* hardly needs to be mentioned, as it has gripped the imagination of Christian theologians, scholars, and preachers throughout the centuries.

We may conclude from this that a term occurring infrequently may still have theological importance. Marshall observes that, statistically speaking, the fifteen occurrences of the *Son of God* theme in Paul make it relatively unimportant (only one tenth the number of times he calls Jesus *Lord*). He goes on to say that Paul uses this title for Jesus when summing up the content of the Gospel or for other generally important statements (e.g., in

---

[62] F. F. Bruce (1983). *The Gospel of John* (14). Grand Rapids, MI: Eerdmans.
[63] Murray J. Harris (1992). *Jesus as God: The New Testament use of Theos in reference to Jesus* (87). Grand Rapids, MI: Baker.
[64] D. Kelly, *Systematic Theology* 273.
[65] O'Collins, *The Tripersonal God* 59.
[66] Ladd, *Theology* 449-450.

contexts about Christ's relationship with God and in traditional statements about "God sending his preexistent Son into the world"). Marshall also notes that Paul uses *Son* to emphasize that through his work as Son, believers are adopted as God's sons.[67] When Paul discusses divine sonship he is usually focusing on soteriology, the Son's role as savior.[68]

Barclay commented that Paul's use of Jesus as the Son of God at the beginning of his letters, indicates that sonship was "the keynote of the Christian Gospel."[69] Schnackenburg says the theme of Jesus as the Son of God stands at the center of Paul's Christological statements.[70] Ridderbos goes even further: "Christ's being the Son of God is none other than being God himself."[71]

When Paul writes, "God sent his Son," obviously Jesus was already Son; conservative scholars are in consensus on this point. For Paul then, God gave his Son as a sacrifice, the ultimate proof of his love.

> For if, when we were enemies, we were reconciled to God through the death of his Son, much more surely, having been reconciled, will we be saved by his life. (Rom 5:10 KJV)
> He who did not spare his own Son, but gave him up for us all—how will he not also, along with him, graciously give us all things? (Rom 8:32)

Paul teaches that believers are adopted as sons through the eternal son, their predetermined destiny is conformity to the image of God's Son (Rom 8:29).[72]

Finally, we can see Paul's exalted Christology in Colossians 1:15-20. The passage begins with *hos estin* (*Greek*, who is), referring to the phrase "his dear son" (1:13). This makes it clear that Christ's sonship is as Lord over all created things. God's son is the image of the invisible God (v. 15), in whom all the fullness of God was pleased to dwell (v. 19). He is the firstborn of all creation (v. 15) for whom all things have been created (v. 16), and he is before all things (v. 17). So despite the relatively infrequent occurrence of the title *Son of God* in Paul's letters, Jesus as God's Son is at the heart of Paul's theology, just as it is at the heart of his Gospel.

Some final reflections on Jesus' divine sonship

The author of Hebrews tells us that God's enduring plan is to bring

---

[67] Marshall, "Titles" 778.
[68] Marshall in Michel, O. (1986). "Son of God." In Colin Brown (Ed.). *The New International Dictionary of New Testament Theology* (634-644). Grand Rapids, MI: Zondervan; cf. Marshall, "Titles" 778.
[69] William Barclay (1958). *The Mind of St. Paul* (56). New York, NY: Harper and Row.
[70] Schnackenburg, *Jesus* 312. See Gal 1:16; 2:20; 4:4; Rom 1:3-4; 8:3, 32.
[71] Herman Ridderbos (1975). *Paul: An Outline of His Theology* (77). John Richard de Witt (trans.). Grand Rapids, MI: Eerdmans.
[72] Hurtado, "Son of God" 905-906.

many sons to glory (Heb 2:10). Jesus is not ashamed to call believers his brothers because they are from the same "one," whether that means from the same Father (NRSV) or family (NIV) (Heb 2:11). There is an organic, familial relation with God that goes to the heart and core understanding biblical truth. Our hope of glory is to have Christ in us (Col 1:27), and it is Jesus' sonship that is our access to glory (John 17:5, 22). Our destiny is to be conformed to the image of God's Son (Rom 8:29). We are made in God's image. The reason we are conformed to the image of his Son is found within the archetypal Father-Son pattern inherent to God himself. As C. S. Lewis said in his sermon, "The weight of glory," we are on a journey toward home. I believe that if we delight ourselves in the Lord, he will give us the deepest desires of our heart. Our deepest desire on this journey toward home is to live in close, loving relationships. Relationships are most deeply experienced within families. God is the eternal Father, and we who believe in his Son are his sons and daughters, moving toward the glory of eternal oneness with him in conformity to the character of his Son.

In summary, what are the theological and practical values of Christ's eternal, divine sonship for the believer? These treasures include:

- Jesus' sonship, a union as Son with the Father, is the avenue for humans to be one with God (see John 17, especially vv. 1-2, 21-2). Jesus grants human beings access to relationship with God similar to what he himself has, a relationship that is unequivocally expressed by his use of the term *Abba, Father,* in prayer. Because Jesus is the Son of God, his followers may become sons and daughters of God who can likewise address God as Father (Rom 8:14-17; Gal 4:4-5).
- Jesus' sonship is the basis of God's sending the Spirit to his children, the Spirit of sonship (Rom 8:15; cf. Gal 4:6).
- Jesus' sonship is the basis of his high priestly ministry, providing us access and giving us acceptability with God (Heb 4:14). It is also the basis of his eternal priesthood, in which he intercedes for his people (Heb 7:25-8).
- As the Son Jesus has full authority to reveal God (Mt 11:27). His sonship also completes God's revelation, which comes through him (Heb 1:1-2).
- God's willingness to sacrifice his Son is the basis for our assurance of the depth of God's love and permanence of God's acceptance of us (Rom 8:32; 1 John 4:9-10).
- Jesus' sonship is the basis for granting believers true freedom (John 8:36).
- We are transferred from the kingdom of darkness into the kingdom of God's dear Son. In the Son we have redemption (Col 1:13-14).
- Our eternal destiny is conformity with the Son (Rom 8:29).
- The Son gives eternal life to whomever he chooses (John 5:21;

6:40).
- The Son's authority to judge terrified the demons, guaranteeing their doom. Satan attacked Jesus' sonship in the wilderness, attempting to corrupt his Sonship into a self-serving distortion (Mt 4:3-6).

In short, Christ's eternal identity as Son of God is the heart of our faith; it is fundamental to our existence as believers. As Murray puts it, John 3:16 implies that the faith by which believers are saved is faith directed to him in his character as the Son, just as it is faith in the Son of God that gives us life (Gal 2:20). I will let Murray's cogent statement summarize the centrality of the term, *Son of God*:

> The rudiment of faith in Jesus as Lord and Savior is that he is the Son of God. His sonship belongs to his identity, and a faith or confession or proclamation that is not conditioned by what he is in this specific character falls short at its center and thereby robs the Savior of the honor that is intrinsically his.[73]

---

[73] Murray, *Collected Writings* 62-3.

4.4 How Insider Movements Affect Ministry: Personal Reflections

Adam Simnowitz

Adam Simnowitz is a minister with the Assemblies of God. He has a BA in Biblical Studies from Central Bible College (Springfield, MO) and studied Arabic in the Middle East. He lives and ministers in Dearborn, MI, both within his fellowship and across denominational and organizational lines.

An impassioned plea to the body of Christ

The insider movements (IM, also known as C5)[1] among missions to Muslims have been aided and abetted by many who are opposed to them. Lack of discernment, silence, and inaction, governed by misguided notions of love, have helped to not only provide space for the growth of this spiritually noxious plant, but have had a *greenhouse effect* by offering cover and a conducive environment for its extensive growth. From the internet and printed pulpit of *IJFM*[2] to the open and behind-the-scenes encouragement and production of Muslim-Idiom Bible translations in audio and in print by Wycliffe Bible Translators and SIL to the personal contact with Muslims by Jamie Winship,[3] Kim Gustafson[4] and others, it may not be an exaggeration to say that **every** professing evangelical missions organization in witness to Muslims has been affected by the syncretistic beliefs and practices of the

---

[1] IM/C5 is defined in this chapter as any approach in which Muslims are told that they can retain their Muslim identity and have saving faith in Jesus Christ. See H. L. Richard, moderator, "Unpacking the Insider Paradigm: An Open Discussion on Points of Diversity" *IJFM* 26(4): 176. One follows Jesus as a Hindu, as a Muslim, as a Buddhist, or in the socio-religious community one lives. According to John Travis, "*Insider* pertains to the local Muslim population; *outsider* pertains to the local non-Muslim population" ("The C1 to C6 Spectrum" *EMQ* 34(4): 408). Beyond this definition there are variations of belief and practice such as acceptance-denial of the prophethood of Muhammad, the inspiration-lack of inspiration of the Qur'an, etc.

[2] *IJFM* is the official journal of the International Society for Frontier Missiology (ISFM) and is a publication of William Carey International University, founded by Ralph Winter in 1977. http://ijfm.org.

[3] Jamie Winship is the founder and director of the *Jesus in the Qur'an* (*JIQ*) seminars, http://www.jesusinthequran.org. Winship is listed in the Southern Baptist Convention (SBC) 2008 Annual as an associate pastor in Wilson, NC.

[4] "Mr. Kim Gustafson is involved in training and equipping people to reach their Muslim friends, both here and overseas. Common Ground is a residential training community that is also reaching out to Muslims in the Twin Cities area. Kim oversees, and trains during, the two national *Insider Consultations* (Yearly in the U.S., January and June) and several *Insider Consultations* internationally each year. Kim was a Navigator Area Representative from 1973-2008 and Founder and President of Common Ground Consultants, Inc., 1996 to present." http://www.themastersinstitute.org/seminary/faculty/38-kim-gustafson (accessed 8/6/10).

IM. Such a state of affairs has come about, in part, because of *silent hatred*.[5]

"Do not hate your brother in your heart" (Lev 19:17a) is one of over twenty specific commands given to help us understand, "love your neighbor as yourself," the Second Greatest Commandment (cf. Lev 19:1-18; Mt 22:34-40; Mk 12:28-31). It is equally applicable under the New Covenant as it was under the Old.[6] Immediately following this command not to hate one's brother is the following: "Rebuke your neighbor frankly so you will not share in his guilt" (Lev. 19:17b). Keeping silent about a matter that is worthy of rebuke, therefore, is not only a form of hating your brother in your heart, but makes the one remaining silent an accomplice to the erring brother's guilt.[7]

Where is the Church's opposition to the errors espoused in the pages of *IJFM*? Where is the leadership of SIL and Wycliffe International to address the questionable scholarship and biblically-erroneous claims by Rick Brown[8] that are used as the justification for the removal-by-substitution and-or reinterpretation of *Son of God, Son of Man, Father,* and other key terms in the Bible? Why does the Southern Baptist Convention tolerate Jamie Winship's teachings? Why has Navigators adopted the insider movements approach without being called to public repentance? Why are churches hosting *Common Ground* and *Jesus in the Qur'an* seminars and speaking well of them even after Muhammad is presented as a prophet-messenger of God and the Qur'an, at the very least, partially-inspired Scripture? Where is the protest of the believers and churches that pray for and financially support these individuals and organizations? The silence of the body of Christ is

---

[5] Some may wonder why I am mentioning names in some instances, but not in others. I have limited the naming individuals and organizations in this chapter to those that have named themselves through published writings whether in print, electronically, the conducting of seminars, and teaching in institutions. For those who feel that this is unloving and unwise, consider that Paul, by inspiration of God the Holy Spirit, specifically mentioned the following individuals when contending for the faith: Peter, Barnabas, Demas, Hymenaeus, Alexander (Gal 2:11-13; 1 Tim 1:20; 2 Tim 4:10, 14); John mentioned Diotrephes (3 John 9). Thankfully Peter and Barnabas did not remain in their error. It is my hope and prayer that every individual and organization mentioned in this article would follow their examples.

[6] In its original context in Leviticus, the second greatest commandment is the summarization and governing principle of how a person should treat others, in light of God's command to be holy. That this truth is applicable under the New Covenant and not part of any temporal ceremonial law that is no longer binding on believers in the Lord Jesus Christ is seen clearly from Jesus' teaching and New Testament passages (cf. Rom 13:9; Gal 5:14; James 2:8).

[7] An excellent example of this is seen in the details given to Ezekiel about being a watchman to his fellow brethren. God would consider any failure on Ezekiel's part to rebuke them as sinful, guilty behavior (Ez 3:17-21). For a New Testament warning against guilt by association, consider Paul's command to Timothy about not being too quick to *commission* people into the ministry (1 Tim 5:22).

[8] Rick Brown is with SIL-Eurasia and holds the following three positions: Associate Area Director, International Translation Consultant, and Consultant for Special Audiences. http://www.sil.org/sil/roster/brown_richard.htm (accessed 8/6/10).

not only deafening in this matter, but also deadly. The Church is wounding itself, guilty of taking away the key of knowledge (Lk 11:52) from many Muslims and hindering their entrance into the kingdom by its tacit acceptance of a corrupted Gospel.

As a minister of the Gospel of Jesus Christ among Muslims, I now invite you to read of some personal encounters with the insider movements. While I have often strongly expressed myself, this chapter is **not** about personality clashes and permissible ministry styles, but the authority of the Bible and the integrity of the Gospel. It is my desire that you are not swept up in the IM and that you challenge and confront its advocates. It is for you this chapter is written.

Father of the IM for Muslims

My first encounter with the IM came in 1998 when I read Fouad Elias Accad.[9] Accad is considered by many to be the father of the IM for Muslims. The Navigators, owners of NavPress, adopted this strategy as its own. What I best remember from this book was an undue reliance upon the Qur'an through a Christian reinterpretation of its message.

Rick Brown, Wycliffe Bible Translators/SIL, and *Son of God*

While studying Arabic in Jordan during the spring of 2000, I attended a presentation by Peter Twele on behalf of SIL/Wycliffe Bible Translators. He was promoting *The Lives of the Prophets* and *The Lives of the Apostles*. Billed as *An Audio Panoramic Bible for the 10/40 Window*,[10] the first set covered the lives of people from the Old Testament with whom Muslims are familiar such as Adam, Noah, Abraham, etc., ending with Jesus. The second set covered the Apostles. The series was produced in the Baghdadi dialect of Arabic. While I did not give the series too much thought, Twele's reliance on the writings and research of Rick Brown on the titles *Son of God* and *Son of Man* proved distressing.[11] He told us that *Son of God* and *Son of Man* mean the opposite of their traditional understanding. *Son of God* designates Jesus' humanity and *Son of Man* his deity. Unconvinced, I thought this would not go very far. I did not realize it would reach across the Atlantic to impact our ministry and ministerial relationships upon our return to the United States.

My wife and I returned to America in May 2000 to a growing community of evangelicals committed to evangelizing Muslims. That same

---

[9] Fouad Elias Accad (1997). *Building Bridges: Christianity and Islam.* Colorado Springs, CO: NavPress.

[10] Rick Brown, PowerPoint, 11 Feb. 2004, slide one. Although this documentation was produced after the event under discussion it is nonetheless a primary source and an accurate description of the product. For those who can read and understand Arabic these two series can be heard online at http://www.alanbiya.net (accessed 8/14/10).

[11] See Rick Brown, "The 'Son of God:' Understanding the Messianic Titles of Jesus" *IJFM* 17(1): 33-9.

month a local missionary obtained several sets of *The Lives of the Prophets* and *The Lives of the Apostles* on cassette. In spite of my misgivings I took several sets from him, although I did not listen to them at that time. I kept a set for myself and gave one or two sets away over a span of several years.

In 2003 the following email exchange between a missionary in the Middle East and a leader from SIL was forwarded to me regarding this audio series:

> **Missionary**: Wycliffe Bible Translators (WBT) is still moving forward with the production of materials in the Middle East that has removed the term *Son of God* (replaced by simply the *Messiah* . . . all references to God as *Father* (replaced by simply Allah) and all references to the *Son of Man* (if I am not mistaken by "he who became flesh") . . . as reflected in the *Life of the Prophets* tape series in Baghdadi Iraqi dialect, and an *unauthorized* dubbing of the Jesus film into Iraqi dialect . . .
>
> As most of you are aware it was Dr. Rick Brown's paper on the issue of the terms *Son of God/Son of Man* that has been used as an *irrefutable* justification for these changes. The overall response by Wycliffe people so far has been to dismiss the concerns of people like us as a few lone voices of dissent that don't reflect the majority.
>
> **SIL Leader** (2/18/03): Thank you for your concern . . . Translators have been debating for many years the question of how to translate terms like *Son of God/Son of Man* and other key terms in ways that communicate the original meaning. . . But in response to your criticisms, I would like to send copies of the paper to some of the leading conservative Bible scholars for their evaluation. But before I can do that I need you to provide specific criticisms on two areas: flaws in the exegesis, and flaws in the proposed translations or explanations . . .
>
> **Missionary** (2/27/03): I provided you with most of that correspondence, which I believe articulates all of my concerns. Tragically the course that Rick Brown has sought to give justification to—namely the removal of key revelatory terms (which were equally if not more offensive to the Jewish ears that first heard them) will hurt the cause of Christ in the Middle East amongst Muslims. As I wrote in my first response to Rick, "We have been assuring our Muslim friends for centuries that the Bible has never been changed or tampered with, and now finally we will be giving them the evidence that has never before existed." However, I am convinced that the most serious consequence will be amongst those who come out of Islam using these *new* materials but whose Christology never moves from heterodoxy to orthodoxy—leading them to water but never enabling them to drink from it.

This missionary in the Middle East stated his concerns about the liberties taken in the *Audio Panoramic Bible* regarding the removal of the terms *Father, Son of God,* and *Son of Man*. Remembering Twele's presentation, I emailed Rick Brown. We exchanged several emails in which I challenged his contentions, especially concerning *Son of God*, arguing that a plain reading of the Gospel of John clearly shows that the Jews of Jesus' day understood his use of *Son* (in reference to Himself), *Father* (in reference to God), and *Son of God* as a claim to deity (cf. John 5:16-18; 10:25-33). Neither Rick nor I convinced the other, but I recall him writing that I was "too emotionally attached to the Westminster Catechism." With all due respect to creeds and catechisms, my commitment to the terms *Father, Son, Son of God, Son of Man, Holy Spirit,* etc., is based on the language and teaching of the Bible. More than shaming me it reveals Brown's thinking on this matter.

My next encounter with *The Lives of the Prophets* came in November 2006. A local worker with WBT sent out an email about a campaign for a mass distribution of this audio series to occur February-March 2007. Attached to this email was a PowerPoint file created by Rick Brown. The following is part of my response to this email:

> Although I have occasionally given out this series on cassette, I have to admit that at first I was unaware (and then have forgotten) that Rick Brown was a major part of this series. Without wanting to rekindle a long email exchange that we had together, suffice it to say that his substitution for *Son of Man* when the NT texts clearly read *Son of God* is not justifiable. I know that God can still work through this (and I am sure that He has) but as Temple Gairdner brought up in his, "God as Triune, Creator, Incarnate, Atoner," we have no right to play fast and loose with terms that the Holy Spirit inspired. It is a slippery slope that leads to an abandonment of God's Word as being inspired.

Rick Brown's response was forwarded to me:

> Obviously Adam has his facts wrong, but binary thinkers will never be convinced that there is more than one way to translate something. I suggest that in general, when people question this issue, that you refer them to my two-part article on the subject, as follows: "Explaining the Biblical Term 'Son(s) of God' in Muslim Contexts." International Journal of Frontier Missions, 2005, 22(3): 91-96.
> URL: http://www.ijfm.org/PDFs_IJFM/22_3_PDFs/91-96Brown_SOG.pdf.
> "Translating the Biblical Term 'Son(s) of God' in Muslim Contexts." International Journal of Frontier Missions, 2005, 22(4): 135-145.
> URL: http://www.ijfm.org/PDFs_IJFM/22_4_PDFs/135-145%20Brown_SOG.pdf.

Having read both of these articles (as well as others by him), I

highlight five points of disagreement with Brown's claims:
1. A disregard for the plain reading and interpretation of the Bible, especially the Gospels;
2. Dependence on extra-biblical writings (i.e., non-inspired);
3. Use of flawed premises;
4. Incorrect assertions about Scripture; and
5. Accommodation to Muslim sentiment.

First, Brown's conclusions ignore the plain reading of John 5:17-23 and 10:30-9. When Jesus calls God, *Father* and himself, *Son [of God]*, he is **correctly** understood to claim deity. Second, Brown relies heavily on questionable interpretations of intertestamental writings to support his claims whereas the Old Testament is the primary document for understanding the meanings of words, phrases, and imagery used in the New Testament. For a sound understanding of *Son of God*, consider these comments by S. Herbert Bess:

> We are being consistent with a well established usage of an Old Testament idiom when we maintain that the expression *Son of God*, when applied to Jesus Christ, means possessing the nature of, displaying the qualities of, God. By comparison with Old Testament usage, the term need not refer to his origin. . . .
>
> The terms *son, firstborn, only begotten,* and *begotten*, as defined by the Bible's own use of them, all declare that Jesus is the uncreated, ungenerated, co-eternal, co-equal Son of God the Father.[12]

Third, Brown writes, "In most of the occurrences in which *Son of God* is used for Jesus, the usage is Messianic, meaning the focus is on Jesus' role as Lord and Savior."[13] Brown repeatedly makes the mistake of substituting reference for meaning.[14] As I am a son, father, husband, brother, uncle, clergyman, teacher etc., all of these terms have the author as the referent; but to say that all of these terms have the same meaning is mistaken. If *Son of God* is merely a synonym for *Messiah*, why did God the Holy Spirit inspire the writers of the Old and New Testaments to use both terms? Jesus' self revelation by differing names and titles is consistent with God's self-disclosure in the Old Testament. Brown's last comment to me is quite revealing: "No cardinal doctrines are at stake, only traditions about wording, and the wordings are just temporary, a bridge to the Bible."[15]

---

[12] Herbert Bess, "The Term 'Son Of God' In The Light Of Old Testament Idiom" *Grace Journal* 6(2): 18, 23. http://faculty.gordon.edu/hu/bi/Ted_Hildebrandt/OTeSources/23a-Prophets/Text/Articles/Bess-SonOfGod-GTJ.pdf (accessed 2/16/11).

[13] Rick Brown, "Part I: Explaining the Biblical Term 'Son(s) of God' in Muslim Contexts" *IJFM* 22(3): 93.

[14] I am indebted to one of my OT professors at Bible College for his help in so clearly identifying this issue.

[15] Dec. 13, 2006.

Fourth, Brown makes incorrect assertions about the Bible. For example: "Palestinian Jews understood the various senses of the phrase *Son of God*, but Greeks did not use this phrase in the same ways, so Luke and Paul use the term very little in their writings to Gentiles."[16]

In light of at least forty examples of filial language (see Chart 6), i.e., *Father*, *Son*, or *Son of God*, as used by Luke and Paul, one wonders how many more references it would take for Brown to consider their use of such language sufficient to exceed his designation of "very little."

Chart 6. NT examples of filial language.

Lk 1:32	Rom 1:4	1 Cor 1:9	Gal 4:6-7
Lk 1:35	Rom 1:9	1 Cor 15:28	Eph 1:3
Lk 3:22	Rom 5:10	2 Cor 1:3	Eph 4:6
Lk 3:38	Rom 8:3	2 Cor 1:19	Eph 4:13
Lk 4:3	Rom 8:14	2 Cor 11:31	Phil 4:20
Lk 4:9	Rom 8:19	Gal 1:4	Col 1:13
Lk 4:41	Rom 8:29	Gal 1:16	1 Thess 1:3
Lk 8:28	Rom 8:31	Gal 2:20	1 Thess 1:10
Lk 22:70	Rom 9:26	Gal 3:26	1 Thess 3:11
Acts 9:20	Rom 15:6	Gal 4:4	1 Thess 3:13

Lastly, Brown clearly states he is accommodating Muslim sentiment:

> Not surprisingly, seekers and believers from Muslim backgrounds regularly single out the term *Son of God* as the biggest obstacle to reading the Gospel. Some will not even touch a Bible because they fear this blasphemous term is in it. So obviously it is important to explain what the phrase means and what it does not mean. Unfortunately, explanations do not remove the nasty connotations of the phrase; they just mitigate them. Even Muslim background believers (MBBs) are reluctant to say the phrase because of its repulsive connotations.[17]

Brown admits his approach is pragmatic. He wants Muslims to read the Bible without the hindrance of *Son* and *Son of God* because he is convinced that this poses the biggest stumbling block for Muslims in reading the Bible. This is an unjustified assertion. I have been involved in witness to Muslims since 1987 and have personally distributed hundreds of Bibles, New Testaments, and Scripture portions and do not recall ever having a Muslim reject any Scripture portion because of the presence of *Son [of God]* in the text. Even if Brown's experience has differed from mine, it

---

[16] Rick Brown, "Part II: Explaining the Biblical Term 'Son(s) of God' in Muslim Contexts" *IJFM* 22(4): 140.
[17] Brown, "Part I: Explaining" 92.

is unbiblical to espouse the principle that the end justifies the means. We have no authority to change the message entrusted to us by God.

In the fall of 2006 I finally listened to the complete series of *The Lives of the Prophets*. Although I had the information in the earlier email from 2003, it was not until I heard the account of Jesus' life that shock really set in. Not only was *Son [of God]* absent from this recording, so was *Father* in reference to God.[18] This latter point makes me suspicious of Brown's true motivations. Even if one were to admit his arguments about *Son [of God]*, he shows no linguistic justification for not rendering Father as such. Why the Trojan horse? This really has nothing to do with translation as much as it has to do with pushing an agenda. Chart 7 shows how and where *Son [of God]* and *Father* are removed and their substitutions.

Chart 7. Removal of familial language from *The Lives of the Prophets*.[19]

Ref.	*Lives of the Prophets*	NIV
Luke 1:32, 35	The Spirit of God will come down upon you and this thing is the proof that this child is the awaited Christ who will rule forever.	32 He will . . . be called the Son of the Most High . . . 35 The Holy Spirit will come upon you, and the power of the Most High will overshadow you. So the holy one to be born will be called the Son of God.
Luke 4:3	If you are truly the Messiah of the Most High God	If you are the Son of God
Luke 4:9	If you are truly the Messiah of God	If you are the Son of God
Luke 8:28	Oh . . . oh . . . Jesus . . . oh Messiah of the most high God . . . what do you want from me?	What do you want with me, Jesus, Son of the Most High God?
Luke 9:35	This is the beloved Messiah whom I have sent, so listen to Him and obey Him.	This is my Son, whom I have chosen; listen to him.
Luke 22:70	Then You are the Messiah of God?	Are you then the Son of God?
Luke 6:36	Just as God is merciful, be merciful to people.	Be merciful, just as your Father is merciful.

---

[18] It is interesting to note that the transcript of the *Jesus Film* by Campus Crusade was modified without Campus Crusade's permission. The additional absence of the Prodigal Son parable is striking in light of this discussion, especially considering that the first two parables in Luke 15 are retained. [At least one representative of Campus Crusade has assured us that any such modification is without official consent or endorsement - eds.]

[19] The text from the column, *The Lives of the Prophets*, is taken from a *back translation* produced by WBT.

Ref.	Lives of the Prophets	NIV
Luke 9:26	in the glory of God and of the pure angels.	in the glory of the Father and of the holy angels.
Luke 11:2	When you pray, say: Our loving, heavenly Lord	When you pray, say: "Father"
Luke 11:13	how much more is it true of the Lord of the world	how much more will your Father in heaven
Luke 22:29	that God the praised and most high has bestowed upon Me.	just as my Father conferred one on me
Luke 22:42	Oh Lord . . . If it's Your will, take this effort or sufferance away from Me. But oh Lord, by Your will and not My will.	Father, if you are willing, take this cup from me; yet not my will, but yours be done.
Luke 23:34	Oh Lord, forgive them. They don't know what they are doing.	Jesus said, "Father, forgive them, for they do not know what they are doing."
Luke 23:46	Oh Lord . . . oh Lord, I surrender My Spirit into Your hands.	Jesus called out with a loud voice, "Father, into your hands I commit my spirit."
Luke 24:49	and I will send the Holy Spirit to you, so remain here until this strength from heaven comes to you according to God's promise.	I am going to send you what my Father has promised; but stay in the city until you have been clothed with power from on high.
Mt 28:19	and baptize them with water in the name of God and His Messiah and the Holy Spirit.	baptizing them in the name of the Father and of the Son and of the Holy Spirit,
Luke 9:23	Anyone who comes with Me must deny himself and bear persecution for My sake.	If anyone would come after me, he must deny himself and take up his cross daily and follow me.

Trying to be sincerely gracious in spite of my misgivings, I wrote the following to my WBT friend on Nov. 21, 2006:

> It was not my intention to create controversy or provoke an argument. As I said to you on the phone, in spite of my misgivings of Rick's beliefs on these issues, because of Rick's commitment to the deity of Jesus, I have not refused to hand out the Lives of the Prophets—this is why I offered some suggestions on distribution. Ultimately, Muslims who are committed to finding out what the Bible says after listening to these tapes are still going to have to come to terms with *Son of God*.

I changed my stance soon after writing this. I cannot in good conscience partake in the distribution of this series.[20] In January of 2007, my WBT friend wrote in an email that there was no intention to incorporate this removal-by-substitution in printed texts.[21] Another local WBT missionary confirmed this. I will come back to this point.

I conclude this encounter with two quotes; the first from W. H. T. Gairdner and the second from Bruce Waltke; both are significant voices:

> Still undoubtedly this doctrine of Fatherhood and Sonship is an enormous stumbling block to Muslims. Their repugnance is so instinctive, so engrained in their very constitution, that it may be really questioned whether Christians do well to give such prominence to terms which are so capable of being misunderstood, and which, were perhaps only used at the first to shadow forth the ineffable substance of eternal truth. If they only succeed in doing the exact reverse of this—namely, suggest error—why not drop terms of so dubious utility and seek fresh ones to shadow forth in a more fruitful way the truth (if so be) which lies beyond? If the whole point of terminology is to facilitate explanation, what is the use of terminology which itself needs so much explanation? Why not drop it?
>
> The answer to this is: Because we have no right to play fast and loose with expressions that God has sanctioned with such tremendous emphasis; because their continued existence in Holy Writ and use by His Church are like the preservation and employment of a standard which we cannot afford to lose. Depend upon it, if this terminology were banished from religious usage today, a great deal more would go too. Sooner or later the reality, to which these expressions are a continual witness, would be utterly lost sight of. And, if the idea of the Fatherhood of God were lost to us, many of us would lose interest in all religion.[22]

---

[20] *The Lives of the Prophets* has been translated into other Arabic dialects and languages. Missionaries and others need to be aware of the content of the materials they are distributing. A local pastor, even though he disagrees with this removal-by-substitution has told me that he has no problems distributing them because of God's sovereignty. I wonder if he would feel the same way if one were to distribute the *New World Translation* of the Jehovah's Witnesses that willfully mistranslate Bible verses to support their anti-biblical doctrines.

[21] Excerpt from this email: "One final point that we will bring out tomorrow, I think you are feeling that the *Lives of the Prophets* is a Bible Translation. It is NOT and never claimed to be. They are Dramatized Bible Stories and are made up of selections of Scripture and are based on Scripture but in no way do we intend it to be word for word or to replace a printed text."

[22] W. H. T. Gairdner (1916). *God As Triune, Creator, Incarnate, Atoner* (4-5). Madras: The Christian Literature Society for India.
http://muhammadanism.org/Gairdner/Triune/triune.pdf (accessed 8/1/10).

[God] identifies himself as Father, Son, and Spirit . . . Jesus taught his Church to address God as Father (Luke 11:2) and to baptize disciples "in the name of the Father and of the Son and of the Holy Spirit" (Matthew 28:19). . . . It is inexcusable hubris and idolatry on the part of mortals to change the images by which the eternal God chooses to represent himself. We cannot change God's name, titles, or metaphors without committing idolatry, for we will have reimaged him in a way other than the metaphors and the incarnation by which he revealed himself. His representations and incarnation are inseparable from his being.[23]

Navigators and IM

Some of my experiences with the IM involve Navigators personnel. A short but telling encounter of IM's affects on ministry to individuals came through a Navigators encounter with a Muslim man from the Middle East. Both of us had contact with the same man independently from one another. In 1995 our family was introduced to Daoud[24] through some of our colleagues. The following year, Daoud, who had been attending some of our Sunday afternoon services, took offense to a message that I had preached. He felt that I was trying to convert him and told me that I was not showing him the same respect that he was showing me (since he, as a Muslim, was not trying to convert me to Islam). The family cut off contact with us at that time.

A few months after this, Daoud and his family met and began what would become a very close relationship with the Navigators missionary family. The husband faithfully exposed Daoud to the Bible. After a while Daoud began to confess certain beliefs about Jesus that seemed biblical as opposed to the Qur'anic witness of Jesus Christ. This missionary was convinced that Daoud had become a believer in Jesus Christ; however, a missionary from another organization expressed doubts about Daoud's faith after speaking to him in Arabic (the Navigators missionary spoke limited Arabic).

In 2008 another local minister and I were visiting Daoud (we reestablished relations after my return from Jordan in 2000). As we were discussing the Bible, Daoud told us quite animatedly the Qur'an and Muhammad were *number one* regarding holy books and prophets. He told us the Arabic language in the Bible could not compare to Qur'anic Arabic, and that Jesus was special but not on the same level as Muhammad. All of this was said in Arabic (except *number one* was in English), causing me to observe:
- The necessity of learning the native language: it is too easy to misinterpret a Muslim's spiritual standing without gaining a certain

---

[23] Bruce Waltke (2002). *Old Testament Theology* (244). Grand Rapids, MI: Zondervan.
[24] A pseudonym.

fluency in his/her native tongue.
- What criterion do Navigators rely on when declaring a Muslim to be a believer in Jesus Christ?
- How many such believers are being treated as disciples when they need to be evangelized?

Unfortunately, this attempt to harmonize Islam and Christianity is not an isolated case with the Navigators.[25] Consider the following excerpt of an email I received from a missionary to Muslims about the role of a former leader of Navigators in support of such syncretism:

> Attached is a file with recent article from *World Magazine*.[26] While most of it investigates the political/financial aspects of "The Fellowship," it is worth noting that Doug Coe has been a key figure among the *Common Ground* movement, particularly in Minneapolis. A close friend of ours recalls hearing him address a large group of Somali refugees [intellectuals, ex-government officials, etc.] there in 1999. He stressed the need for them to "unite in the Spirit of Jesus"; when queried as to which Jesus, the one of the Bible or the one of the Quran, he said it didn't make a difference. Our friend also commented that Coe is revered with almost prophet-like status by the *Common Ground* proponents. Given Coe's background in the Navigators, and the fact *Common Ground* is an off-shoot of that organization, any scholarly research into origins of *Common Ground* theology need to take his role into account. It appears a key element in Coe's thought is the

---

[25] This line of reasoning is extremely popular among proponents of IM/C5. If a way can be found to harmonize the Bible with the prophethood of Muhammad and the inspiration of the Qur'an, it logically follows that Muslim as a self-identity, the repetition of the *shahada*, the performance of *salat*, etc. are not unbiblical practices, merely a participation in the types and shadows of Christ, as with the first-century Jewish believers in Jesus who continued to participate in the various Old Testament ceremonial laws.
In January 2008 I attended Nabeel Jabbour's class on "Islam and the Twenty-First Century" at Columbia International University. I am certain Dr. Jabbour likened Muhammad to a prophet of the Old Testament. According to my class notes, he taught us Muhammad had five major teachings: God is one; God is the Judge; God is merciful and compassionate; God is the Provider; and we need to care for widows and orphans. In class I asked, "Even if Muhammad taught the five things that you said was his only message, including none of the blatantly anti-Christian parts, I cannot conscientiously accept his *prophethood* and accord him respect because he does not [openly] point to Jesus. In all fairness to Dr. Jabbour, he insists he did not liken Muhammad to an Old Testament prophet. In subsequent conversation he flatly denies believing it. His own position reflects a more nuanced treatment that depends on literary criticism that, while it is still highly problematic in its own right, does not attribute any sort of prophethood to Muhammad
In my opinion the best analysis of Muhammad and Islam from a Christian standpoint is found in S. W. Koelle's, *Mohammed and Mohammedanism*. http://muhammadanism.org/Koelle/mohammedanism/Default.htm (accessed 9/3/10).
Other troubling courses include *Perspectives* and *Encountering the World of Islam*.
[26] Cf. *World Magazine*'s article, "The ABCs of C Street" August 29, 2009. http://www.worldmag.com/articles/15778 (accessed 7/3/11).

dichotomy between "its all about Jesus" vs. Christianity/the Church.

How could a movement that is based on the reading and memorization of the Bible accept syncretistic practices? I believe it is not only due to Fouad Accad's role in Navigators—who I previously mentioned—but also because of Waldron Scott. Scott pioneered the Navigators' work in the Middle East. His battle with lust, flirtation and extra-marital sexual activities are discussed frankly throughout his autobiography, *Double Helix*.[27] Reflecting in part on his time in the Middle East, Scott wrote:

> What was going on at this point in my life created great confusion in my soul. At every turn, and in spite of the recent opposition just noted, I had ample evidence of God blessing others through me. The same was true with Joan [i.e., his first wife] as well. In spite of what she herself thought of as weakness or spiritual failure or sin, God was clearly using her in the lives of others. **In short, there seemed to be no true cause-effect in ministry. It appeared one could walk with God and be blessed in ministry in spite of moral failure.**
>
> Did this mean that what I had always believed was in fact untrue? That the covenantal relationship laid out in Scripture was not what we Navigators thought it was? I don't know if Joan ever thought along these lines, but I did, and more so as time passed. My worldview was beginning to disintegrate. Meanwhile, the God-given drive for intimacy was gradually shading into a drive for sexual gratification.[28] (emphasis added)

Scott writes, "There seemed to be no true cause-effect in ministry. It appeared one could walk with God and be blessed in ministry in spite of moral failure." What frightful words! Whenever our devotional life or ministry consists of outward compliance, with no corresponding inner purity, we need to remember Jesus' teachings on the guilt of merely thinking evil thoughts (e.g., Mt 5:21-32). If the pioneer of the Navigators in the Middle East was excusing his own lack of inner purity, it only follows that he would not and could not be a vehicle God used to call others to keep their thought-lives in check. Scott's leadership thus greatly contributed to an atmosphere in which winning disciples and creating reproducing discipleship groups is the ultimate criteria for success. If the Bible's demands for holiness can be ignored in order to make "disciples," then compromising the truths of the Bible with Islam in order to "win" Muslims

---

[27] http://www.waldronscott.net/id103.html (accessed 7/3/11); cf. *Waldron Scott: The Visionary Leader*, by Paul Hensley, p. 15:
http://www.navigators.org/us/staff/paul_hensley/asia-legacy-project/scott_visionary_leader_0.pdf (accessed 7/3/11).
[28] Hensley, *Waldron Scott* 552.

into the kingdom follows the same principle—the Bible can be disregarded if it is perceived to hinder one's "success in ministry."

Mazhar Mallouhi and *Pilgrims of Christ on the Muslim Road*

In the summer of 2008 I came across two publications: a book by Paul-Gordon Chandler,[29] and *Seedbed*.[30] The first is a book about Mazhar Mallouhi, "a self-identified *Sufi Muslim follower of Christ*."[31] The following are a few of Mallouhi's anti-biblical statements:

> When I hear the Psalms read, for example in church, and when it says "The God of Israel," I find this a stumbling block for me, because this presents a tribal God. . . .
>
> I cannot reconcile God ordering massacres in the Old Testament.
>
> . . . We are part of several groups of Muslim mystics, Sufis; sometimes we meet in our home, other times in theirs. But we walk together this spiritual journey toward God. . . .
>
> I have met many Muslims who I believe are farther spiritually than me, and a million miles closer to God, loving God and devoted to God with complete sincerity. . . .
>
> If people do not have the revelation of God in Christ, this of course does not mean that they do not know God. . . .
>
> I fully expect to see Gandhi when we are privileged to enter God's presence in eternity. . . .
>
> It is very hard for me to picture God, whom I love, and whom I know loves humanity; his creation, sending anyone to an eternal hell. God is just. And if he treats evil with evil then what difference is there between him and us.[32]

Had I seen only this book, I would have prayed for Mallouhi and considered my responsibility towards him complete. However, what motivated me to write a book review was the second publication. *Seedbed* contained articles by three people I know and with whom I ministered— and they are also Mallouhi's friends. It was because of my commitment to my brothers in Christ I felt compelled to thoroughly read the book, write a review and then speak to them frankly about how they excused some of Mallouhi's heresies. It would have been easier simply to shrug this off as

---

[29] Paul-Gordon Chandler (2007). *Pilgrims of Christ on the Muslim Road: Exploring a New Path Between Two Faiths*. Lanham, MD: Cowley.

[30] Don Little, (Ed.). "The Identity of Christ's Pilgrims in the Muslim World" *Seedbed* Volume XXI (First Trimester-No.1, 2008). *Seedbed* is a publication of Arab World Ministries (AWM). It states that it "is a forum for the exchange of ideas. Opinions expressed are those of the authors and do not necessarily represent the views of the editor or of Arab World Ministries."

[31] My review of the book is found at http://answering-islam.org/Reviews/chandler_mallouhi.html.

[32] Cf. Chandler, *Pilgrims* 181, 193, 193, 91, 123, 198.

their problem or as "not a part of my calling." I could not in good conscience remain silent.[33]

It is unthinkable that professing believers in Jesus Christ would defend Mallouhi's heretical statements and consider themselves his friends and faithful brothers in the Lord. Greg Livingstone, the founder of Frontiers says this about Mallouhi:[34]

> I fear that [the author] is describing Mazhar more in the way that he wants Mazhar to be. Not with a bad motive, but maybe, in places, Paul-Gordon is really saying more about his own hopes and perspective than he is accurately describing Mazhar. Christine Mallouhi disagrees, but I still feel like he *led the witness* (i.e., he interprets Mazhar to say what he himself wants to say), particularly in the doctrinal area. . . . He's an evangelist, not a theologian.[35]

Since most of Mallouhi's quotes are from an interview in the last chapter of the Chandler's book, it is virtually impossible to say that the author has misrepresented him, especially when Livingstone writes that Mallouhi's wife confirms that they accurately represent her husband's views.

Another reviewer, who ministered with Mallouhi in the past, advised me to take these statements with a grain of salt.[36] My response to him was that no evangelical organization would accept a person who held to these beliefs. I would certainly lose my ministerial papers if I were to hold to such beliefs. His silence was deafening.

One of the contributors, after reading my book review, wrote to me:

> I cannot disagree with your review . . . **Though my *head* agrees with you,** my emotions often go with the guys who are so exercised by the horrible fact that a billion Muslims go to bed nightly with no access to the claims of Christ in their own language and milieu. Mazhar is among those who simply cannot live with the insipid, ineffective, often mindless approaches to the Muslim who is imprisoned by fourteen hundred years of conflict and hatred between people called *Christians* and people called *Muslims*. Thus, he, like many others, unthinkingly *goes*

---

[33] It is worthwhile to do a word search on *conscience* in the New Testament (cf. 2 Cor. 1:12; 2 Cor 4:1-2; 1 Tim 1:5, 18-19; 3:9; Heb 13:18; 1 Pet 3:16, 21).

[34] Frontiers is a missions organization founded in 1982. Their current motto is "With love and respect, inviting all Muslim peoples to follow Jesus." Although they do not officially embrace IM, they tolerate it among their workers. A number of current and former Frontiers' personnel are outspoken advocates of insider movements including Jay (also John) Travis (pseudonym), Rick Love, and Carl Medearis.
http://www.frontiersusa.org/site/PageNavigator/about/about_faqs (accessed 7/3/11).

[35] Greg Livingstone, "My Primary Mentor in the Arab World: an Interview with Greg Livingstone" *Seedbed* Volume XXI (First Trimester-No. 1, 2008) 7.

[36] In all fairness, this person was unconvinced that Mallouhi really meant what was written; however, I disagree with his position.

too far in trying to get rapport with those he is trying to rescue.[37]

In light of the issues under discussion, is there any room for a conditional response? Is Mallouhi's message of universalism anything less than a mindless approach to witness? It is exactly through accommodating responses like these that IM has flourished.

On August 31, 2008, I spoke to Mallouhi in person. He chided me, saying that I should have come to him privately with my concerns, alluding to Matthew 18:15-20. I responded by saying that he forfeited this privilege by going public through the printing of the book. He replied that he was neither the author nor publisher of the book. I replied that the book could not have been produced without him and he was responsible for his statements. The following day we spoke by telephone. He reiterated that he was neither the author nor publisher of *Pilgrims of Christ on the Muslim Road*. I told him several times that regardless of how he feels, some of his statements in the book are anti-biblical. He has a responsibility to Jesus to do whatever he can to let people know what he believes, if indeed his beliefs differ from what he states in the book.

Some of Mallouhi's statements were to be clarified in a subsequent interview with a well-known missions organization with which he has a "quiet" agreement. It was initially announced that it would be made available to the public, so I offered to post it with my book review, wanting to give him an opportunity to "set the record straight." Unfortunately, the organization decided to not to publish the interview. Regardless of motives, Mallouhi has yet to "produce fruit in keeping with repentance" (Mt 3:8; cf. Acts 26:20) evidenced by the fact that he continues to sell copies of this book through his website.[38]

Why is Mallouhi allowed to continue with this professing evangelical missions organization? This inaction and tacit approval of universalism is an abdication of the leadership's responsibility towards God, the body of Christ, Mallouhi, and unbelievers, including Muslims who are hearing another Gospel.

In light of what I wrote about silent hatred at the beginning of this article, I still have questions. Why would any believer in Jesus write a defense or a praise of a professing brother in the Lord who espouses the errors that Mallouhi does? Why would *Seedbed*, notwithstanding its policy of being a forum that allows dissent, not have a strong editorial in the same issue disavowing the heresies within *Pilgrims of Christ on the Muslim Road*?

I strongly believe the presentation of this issue was a serious error in judgment. If a professing believer is questioning or denying such cardinal doctrines as the inspiration of the Old Testament, the necessity of confessing and knowing Jesus as Lord, and the everlasting punishment of

---

[37] I am maintaining the privacy of the author of this email sent to me August 11, 2008.
[38] www.al-kalima.com.

the unsaved, the last thing that needs to be done is to write in defense or praise of him. The loving thing is to confront and rebuke him.[39] I contend that my willingness to confront Mallouhi shows true love and concern for his spiritual well being. It is unfortunate that some of his closest friends and spiritual authorities feel otherwise.

Mistranslating the Gospels and Acts

At the end of *Pilgrims of Christ on the Muslim Road*, Mallouhi speaks of undertaking a "new translation for Muslims"[40] of the Gospels and Acts into Arabic that has since been published.[41] This now brings us to the issue of Muslim-friendly translations of the Bible. Charts 8 and 9 show how *Father* is translated by substitution.

Chart 8. Substitution of *Father* in Mallouhi's *The Correct Meaning of the Gospel of Christ*.

Ref.	KJV	Arabic Text	Arabic to English
Mt 5:16	your Father which is in heaven	الله وليكم الاعلى	God, your supreme guardian
Mt 5:45	the children of your Father which is in heaven	اولياء الله	guardians of God
Mt. 5:48	your Father which is in heaven	الله تعالى	God, Most High
Mt. 6:1	Your Father which is in heaven	ربكم	your Lord
Mt 6:9	our Father	ولينّا	our guardian
Mt 6:14	heavenly Father	الله وليكم الاعلى	God, your supreme guardian
Mt 6:18	thy Father	ربكم	your Lord
M. 6:18	thy Father	--	not translated
Mt 6:26	heavenly Father	الله	God
Mt 6:32	heavenly Father	ربكم	your Lord

---

[39] Cf. Lev 19:17; 1 Cor 13:6; Rev 3:19; Pr 27:5-6; 2 Tim 4:2-4.
[40] Chandler, *Pilgrims* 204.
[41] Mazhar Mallouhi (Ed.). *The Correct Meaning of the Gospel and Acts in Arabic* (2nd ed.). Beirut: Dar-Alfarabi.

Ref.	KJV	Arabic Text	Arabic to English
Mt 7:11	Your Father	ربّكم الرحيم	your merciful Lord
Mt 7:21	my Father	الله	God
Mt 10:32,33	my Father	ربّي	my Lord
Mt 11:25, 26	O Father, Father	يا، يا ربّي اللهي	O, my Lord, O my God
Mt 28:19	baptizing them in the name of the Father, and of the Son, and of the Holy Ghost	و طهّروهم بالماء باسم الله و مسيحه و روحه القدوس	and cleanse them with water in the name of God and His Messiah and His spirit
John 17:11	Holy Father	وليّي القدوس	my holy guardian

Chart 9. John 3:13-18 from Mallouhi's *The Correct Meaning of the Gospel of Christ*.

NIV	Arabic to English	Arabic Text
13 No one has ever gone into heaven except the one who came from heaven-the Son of Man.	13 For no one has ascended to heaven to tell about it, but the master of humanity came from heaven, and he is the one who is able to speak to us about it.	فما صعد احد الى ها، السماء فيُخبر عن و لكنّ سيد البشر اتى من السماء، و هو الذي يستطيع ان يحدّثكم عنها.

NIV	Arabic to English	Arabic Text
14 Just as Moses lifted up the snake in the desert, so the Son of Man must be lifted up,	14 For as the Prophet Moses lifted the serpent in the desert on a pole, so must the master of humanity be lifted on a pole,	فكما رفع النبي موسى الحيّة في الصحراء على خشبة، كذلك لا بدّ ان يُرفع سيّد البشر على خشبة،
15 that everyone who believes in him may have eternal life.	15 that everyone who believes in him receives his portion in the eternal garden [of Paradise].	حتّى ينال كل من يؤمن به نصيبه في جنة الخُلد.
16 For God so loved the world that he gave his one and only Son, that whoever believes in him shall not perish but have eternal life.	16 God so loved all of humanity that he sacrificed his unique Son (i.e., his only-beloved) [as] a ransom for them, so there is no fear upon those who believe in him, because the garden [of Paradise] is their destiny.	لقد احب الله كل البشر حتّى انّه ضحّى بابنه الوحيد (بحبيبه الوحيد) فداءً لهم، فلا خوف على المؤمنين به، لانّ مصيرهم الجنة.
17 For God did not send his Son into the world to condemn the world, but to save the world through him.	17 God most high did not send his only-beloved to people except for deliverance–nor did he send him as a watchman to punish [them], therefore whoever believes in him is rescued from God's punishment,	و لم يرسل الله تعالى حبيبه الوحيد الى اذًا و لم الناس إلّا منق يرسله رقيبًا معاقبًا، فمن يؤمن به له النجاة من عقاب الله،

NIV	Arabic to English	Arabic Text
18 Whoever believes in him is not condemned, but whoever does not believe stands condemned already because he has not believed in the name of God's one and only Son.	18 but God has decreed punishment for whoever rejects him because he has refused the Son of the indivisible God (i.e., the beloved of the indivisible God).	امّا مَن يحجد به فـقد قضى امر الله بعقابه، لانه رفض له الاوحد ابن ال (حبيب الله الاوحد).

Concerning IM translations principles, Bill Nikides writes:

> Insiders rely on *new* translations that, in their attempt to eliminate conceptual barriers with Muslims, significantly alter the language of the Bible. *Son* and *Son of God, Father* and other terms are substituted for more *Muslim-friendly* language. The most strained reasons are given in order to justify the changes, reflecting a reliance on far less than orthodox scholarship. All of this is kept from national believers and supporters back home who fund the projects. At times, nationals say they do the work, but often they serve as fronts for the real force behind the work—expatriates.[42]

Mallouhi's translation committee included at least one prominent Arabist from Wycliffe International who strongly objected to translating *Son of God* directly into Arabic.[43] During my encounter with *The Lives of the*

---

[42] Bill Nikides, "A Response to Kevin Higgins' 'Inside What? Church, Culture, Religion and Insider Movements in Biblical Perspective'" *SFM* 5(4): 113. http://www.stfrancismagazine.info/ja/content/view/316/38/ (accessed 9/30/10).

[43] I received an email from a local WBT missionary, dated January 8, 2010, confirming Wycliffe's opposition to retaining *Son of God* in the text of this translation: "Also, another side note, the translation [Lighthouse] Mazhar is working on is not a one man show, it is happening on a committee and the committee decided to use *ibn Allah* [i.e., *Son of God*] against our [i.e., Wycliffe International] recommendations, but then decided to add in a qualifying/explanation statement in the text, not a footnote!"

I also have a CD from a Common Ground conference that took place in Arizona, January 2008. It contains files from the Wycliffe International person serving on Mallouhi's translation committee, along with numerous files from another Arabist with Navigators. There is a Word document file in Arabic, *MarkMazharv2*, that bears the initials of the said Wycliffe person, dated 4/24/2005. In place of Son of God is the same phrase, *khalifat Allah*. The use of *khalifat Allah*, (God's vice-regent) in place of Son of God will cause Muslims to think Jesus came as the one favored by Allah to represent Islam and spread it by force when

Prophets, I was told that WBT/SIL has no intention of putting removal-by-substitution methods into print. This really seems to contradict reality. Is Mallouhi merely a convenient front for this Arabic translation so that Wycliffe International and other Western mission organizations can absolve themselves of the gross liberties taken in these so-called translations? Brown's articles on the topic are used as justification for putting such translations into print.[44] WBT/SIL are very much involved in the print-production of Muslim-friendly translations. Whether it is done behind the scenes through committees or serving as consultants; whether any such translation is justified because of the writings of their personnel—Wycliffe International people should cease from making claims contrary to the truth. A simple comparison of Charts 8 and 9 with these charts and from *The Lives of the Prophets* (Chart 7) will show the similarities of key terms between print production and Wycliffe's "Audio Panoramic Bible."[45]

Let me recapitulate the problems with this Arabic translation. First, it is not directly translated from the Greek. Second, the verses are not individually numbered. Third, God as *Father*, as in *The Lives of the Prophets*, is not translated. Finally, although it retains *Son [of God]* in many places, parenthetical explanations are placed in the text that alters the meaning of this phrase.

The problems are similar, if not more, with regard to John 3:13-18. First, eliminating *Son of Man* removes the most common phrase with which to compare *Son of God*, helping us understand its proper meaning. Second,

---

necessary. *Khalifa(t)* is the same term used of the religio-political rulers of Muslims after Muhammad's death, starting with Abu-Bakr, and lasting until the end of the Ottoman Empire in the early twentieth century.

I have a copy of an email dated Oct. 9, 2009, in which a close friend of Mallouhi writes to John Piper that "Mazhar Mallouhi [worked] with Wycliffe in a Muslim sensitive translation of Gospels and Acts, did NOT substitute anything for *Son of God*, although I've seen allegations that they did."

Finally, I have an email from the Wycliffe Arabist in question, dated Dec. 14, 2009, in which he writes: "You may be interested in a recent translation we have worked on with cousin colleagues (followers and pre-followers) [i.e., *Muslims* and, in their understanding, *Muslim followers of Christ*]. It is called *The Correct Meaning of the Gospel of Christ*." You can read about it at these sites:
http://en.wikipedia.org/wiki/Bible_translations_%28Arabic%29 (accessed 7/3/11).
http://www.al-kalima.com/translation_project.html (accessed 7/3/11).
An audio recording of the text of this by two well-known cousin broadcasters has just been done, and is in the process of editing. We can send along some samples if you would like."

[44] On p. 241 from Mallouhi's translation, the following explanatory footnote appears for *Son of God* for Mark 1:1: "This expression will often appear. It is literally *Son of God*. It does not point at all to biological sonship. God forbid! This was certainly a metaphorical title pointing to the chosen king which had to be from the descendants of the Prophet David." Rick Brown, in his article, "The 'Son of God'" (see fn 9, pp. 44-45) gives the same explanation for *Son of God*, including the term *vice regent*. This is hardly coincidental.

[45] In files from the CD mentioned above, the same substitutions for such key terms as *Son of Man, Son of God, Lord, Father*, and *eternal life* are found. It appears both of the Arabists referred to in the text were part of the translation committee in light of the fact that it contains an early draft of the Gospel of Mark for Mallouhi's translation.

rendering *eternal life* as the "eternal Garden [of Paradise]" is not translation but interpretation, and a poor one at that. It reinforces the Islamic concept of a carnal afterlife. It also misses the point that eternal life is given **now** to those who believe, not merely as a reward in the hereafter. Third, explaining *Son of God* as *God's only-beloved* gives the wrong message: Jesus is special to God but not necessarily one with God in nature; and perhaps God loves only Jesus. Fourth, adding Islamic titles and names, such as the insertion of *Prophet* before Moses in v. 14, *most high* after God in v. 17, and *indivisible* before God in v. 18, reveals the translators are looking to please and perhaps placate their intended audience. The latter is especially problematic by implying a distinction between the Son and the indivisible God, thus reinforcing the Islamic concept of God as monad.

The Correct Meaning of the Gospel of Christ, is a modern targum, i.e., a paraphrased commentary of Scripture. In light of the articles on Muslim-friendly translations, it is obvious a philosophical agenda has trumped true translation work. Considering these examples of condescension to Islamic thought, one wonders if the talk of meaning-based translations is really doublespeak—evangelical readers and prayer and financial supporters assuming fidelity to the Greek manuscripts—while the translators are free to Islamize the Bible. This latter point fits well with the common idea among many IM proponents: both Muhammad and the Qur'an were in some way inspired by God.

Let us not deceive ourselves; Bible translation is the foundation to all ministry. If these cracked foundations of Muslim-friendly translations are allowed to continue we should not be surprised at the coming collapse for everything built upon them:

> One such tragedy is the proliferation of insider thinking among Bible translators. A translation of the Gospels in the Bengali language eliminates all reference to *Son of God* and all other filial language within the Godhead. I was told by Lebu in Dhaka in September, 2007, that all the older converts from Islam under his care recognize that Jesus is the Son of God. The younger generation, which is being fed Insider ideology and reads the Insider translation of the Gospels, is no longer clear on the identity of Jesus.[46]

This is the exact sentiment quoted earlier from the concerned missionary serving in the Middle East over his objections to Wycliffe Bible Translators' removal of *Father* and *Son [of God]* in their audio recreation of Jesus' life in *The Lives of the Prophets* audio series: **I am convinced that the most serious consequence will be among those who come out of Islam using these new materials but whose Christology never moves**

---

[46] Phil, "A Response To Kevin Higgins' 'Inside What? Church, Culture, Religion And Insider Movements In Biblical Perspective'" *SFM* 5(4): 118.

from heterodoxy to orthodoxy—leading them to water but never enabling them to drink from it.

Jamie Winship and *Jesus in the Qur'an (JIQ)*[47]

I never imagined I would hear in a professing evangelical church the kinds of things I heard during a *JIQ* seminar, May 1-2, 2009, at Kensington Community Church, in Troy, Michigan. Throughout the seminar taught by Jamie Winship, John Stallsmith, and Matt Reynolds, we were thoroughly immersed in the beliefs and practices of the insider movements. We were exposed to semantic fallacies, straw man arguments, leaps in logic, unorthodox interpretations of the Bible and the Qur'an in order to harmonize them.

I have recreated in Chart 10 a *JIQ* document from pages 6-7 from the *JIQ* workbook (the text in bold follows the original):

Chart 10. Ground Rules: Definitions of key Terms for *JIQ*.

Term	Literal Meaning	Common Western Understanding	Common Eastern Understanding	Meaning as used in *JIQ*
Christian	"Christ One," a follower of Christ.	1. One who trusts Jesus for salvation. 2. One who goes to Church.	Immoral, polytheistic, wine-drinking, pig-eating, loose-dressing, Western, materialistic, imperialistic, Zionist infidel.	One who is **culturally a Christian**, regardless of his faith in Christ (when we want to talk about true followers of Christ, we will say "believers," "disciples," etc.).

---

[47] http://www.jesusinthequran.org. Jamie Winship, a minister with the Southern Baptist Convention, is the founder and director of the *JIQ* seminars. Two staff members of Grace Fellowship Church, Snellville, GA assisted him: Jon Stallsmith, Creative Projects, Twenty-Somethings, Grace360; and Matt Reynolds, Midtown Campus Pastor. http://www.gracefellowshipchurch.com/about%20grace/staff2.aspx (accessed 7/3/11).

JIQ seems to be a mini version of the *Common Ground* conferences. A perusal of both workbooks will show much shared material, with slight modification. Jamie Winship is also the author of the *Seven Signs in the Qur'an*, which reinterprets seven Qur'anic to allegedly bring people to "the greatest of all the Qur'an signs—*Isa* [i.e., Jesus]."

Winship is also listed as a lead instructor for Global Professional Training, a professional development service for Middle Eastern businesses, governments, universities and especially, university students: http://perspectives-atlanta.org/2009_Spring_Atlanta/instructorbios.asp (accessed 7/3/11).

Term	Literal Meaning	Common Western Understanding	Common Eastern Understanding	Meaning as used in *JIQ*
Muslim	One who has submitted his life to God.	A heathen, unbelieving, perhaps jihadist infidel who worships Muhammad and is going to hell.	A follower of Muhammad who has found the truth of submission to God, is going to heaven, and possesses God's final revelation of truth.	One who is **culturally a Muslim**, regardless of his faith in Christ.
Church	"Called out ones," the body of Christ.	A building, God's house, a denomination, a meeting with singing and a sermon.	A place where Christians practice immorality.	A fellowship of **true believers** (the people of God in obedience to the word of God with dependence on the Spirit of God).
Mosque	A place of prostration and gathering.	A place where Muslims worship the false god Allah.	A place to meet socially, to do prayers, and to do what God requires.	The building Muslims go to for **worship and prayers**; also a social center.

The definition that caught my attention was the *JIQ* meaning for Muslim: "One who is culturally a Muslim, regardless of his faith in Christ." To claim this term has no reference to the religion of Islam is mistaken, betrays a serious ignorance of the Qur'an, Islamic Traditions (i.e., the Hadith), Islamic Commentaries (i.e., Tafsir), and is patently false.[48] This semantic ruse is employed to justify Muslims retaining their self-designation as Muslims, **while supposedly having saving faith in Jesus Christ.**

---

[48] See Sura 3:19 ("The true religion with God is Islam") and Sura 3:83, 85 ("What, do they desire another religion than God's…Whoso desires another religion than Islam, it shall not be accepted of him; in the next world he shall be among the losers."); *Sahih Al-Bukhari* Volume 1, Book 2, Number 8 and *Sahih Muslim* Book 1, Number 1; and various Commentators (cf. Jane I. Smith (1975). *An Historical and Semantic Study of the Term* Islam *as Seen in a Sequence of Quran Commentaries* (218-21). Missoula, MT: Scholars Press).

Whatever advantage some IM advocates might gain, playing with these terms shows a lack of integrity. Perhaps I should be less scandalized. John Stallsmith told us soon after the seminar began: "We may say things that are a bit confusing to you."

Statements made at *JIQ* both assumed and claimed Muhammad was a prophet and messenger from God.[49] The terms showed the speakers assumed Muhammad heard from God, offering no explanations. Their carefully-crafted statements rendered it impossible to realize the speakers were referring to Muhammad if one were unfamiliar with the Islamic texts.[50] The following references are taken from my notes:

> John Stallsmith: Muhammad was a spiritually curious man . . . was trying to figure out the various beliefs of Jews, Christians, Hanifs, etc. He went to a cave and began hearing from God.
>
> Jamie Winship: God still speaks . . . I used to believe God speaks until I went to seminary and replaced it with polemics and apologetics. Muslims are like that, too; they do not believe that God can speak to people in cave [inferring that God spoke to Muhammad]
>
> Jamie Winship: [sharing a testimony about a sheikh who had a dream and became a *believer*] The sheikh was on a straight path; someone was guiding him on a straight path towards a cave. What is significant about this? Caves are where God speaks.

The climax of the conference came as John Stallsmith asked, "Was Muhammad a messenger from God?" He interrupted his question by mentioning that a Moroccan had just come into the kingdom this week. Stallsmith was "thankful that the Qur'an pointed him to Jesus." It is fitting to note here that this seminar was filled with testimonies. Testimonies are a powerful thing, but when used to ignore or contradict the word of God, they are manipulative, emotional tools.

Stallsmith then concluded: "In my conviction, I believe that anyone that points people to Jesus can be considered a messenger [or, prophet] of God." The room of about two hundred people burst into hearty applause. Professing evangelicals, including some ministry colleagues, clapped after being told Muhammad was a prophet. One of them expressed to me that he was not clapping for this concluding statement but out of courtesy since

---

[49] Muslims use both terms to refer to Muhammad. It should be understood, however, that in Islamic theology, according to the Islamic definition of the word, a messenger (apostle) is greater than a prophet. However, in English, *prophet* usually connotes a greater significance than *messenger*, thus the second half of the Islamic creed (*shahada*) is often translated, "and Muhammad is His prophet."

[50] According to Islamic history, Muhammad received his first revelation while meditating in a cave (*Sahih Bukhari* Volume 1, Book 1, Number 3):

http://www.usc.edu/schools/college/crcc/engagement/resources/texts/muslim/hadith/bukhari/001.sbt.html (accessed 7/3/11).

it was the end of the conference. This is exactly what I mean by silent hatred; we do not rebuke a professing believer in Jesus when necessary. How much better for the cause of Christ would it have been had no one clapped, and demanded and explanation! Don Andersen, the host pastor for this event, thanked the three men for coming. He told us, "This is a game changer!"[51]

Although I wanted to leave the seminar as soon as possible, I remained for the question and answer time.[52] I had a responsibility before God to speak and not remain silent. To my great disappointment, all of the questions were about language, culture and Islamic beliefs. No one challenged any of the speakers' statements. I felt as if the whole group had been hypnotized. I then asked a question that would potentially make others in the audience think for themselves. I asked Winship: "How is what we have heard, that is, this Christian reinterpretation of the Qur'an's message any different than, when, say, a Jehovah's Witness or Mormon comes to our door, using our Bible, to get us to believe their message?"

He answered that he "starts with common ground and points to the kingdom." He shared another testimony of how God used him to witness to a Mormon. The audience applauded his answer. Afterwards, two local missionaries told me I must have been frustrated with Winship's response because he never answered my question. They invited several of us to eat dinner with the speakers. We discussed several topics including the *JIQ* workbook definition of a Muslim as well as the following two verses in the Qur'an:

> None of Our revelations do We abrogate or cause to be forgotten, but We substitute something better or similar: Knowest thou not that Allah Hath power over all things? (2:106 A. Yusuf Ali) And whoever desires a religion other than Islam, it shall not be accepted from him, and in the hereafter he shall be one of the losers. (Q3:85 Shakir)

Winship told me neither of these verses were in the Qur'an! It is unfortunate that I did not have a Qur'an with me; nevertheless, it is noteworthy that *JIQ* website's article, "The True Jihad," by Saleh Al-Nouri, was removed after it was critiqued as being full of errors, partial or incomplete references, baseless assumptions, and false explanations.[53] I

---

[51] For another critique of a *JIQ* seminar, see "Addressing Heresy in the Fox Valley:" http://www.shoutsofjoyministries.com/contextualization/Common_Ground_Conf_Refutation.shtml (accessed 7/2/11).

[52] This session was not included in the seminar schedule. I wonder if the announcement was purposely delayed until about an hour before the scheduled end of the seminar so as to keep the attendees from being better prepared to ask serious questions about the seminar's contents.

[53] From an email, May 4, 2009. The final paragraph of the article: "What then is true jihad? We have seen that true jihad is not killing people but struggling with our money and ourselves to please Allah. Our true enemy is Satan the Stoned, and not unbelievers or

also found it interesting that his Bible study in Jordan is in English with Arabic-speaking Muslim translators.[54]

Later in our conversation, Winship and Stallsmith asked me if I had ever met a Muslim follower of Christ. Without mentioning Mazhar Mallouhi by name I quoted some of his heretical statements from *Pilgrims of Christ on the Muslim Road*. I was hoping that they would realize I was citing from a book listed on the second page of the bibliography in the *JIQ* workbook. Stallsmith said the person I was describing seemed to be a little *off* and that I really needed to meet some of the "Muslim followers of Christ that they know." I was not given further information in order to contact any of them.

Winship tried to convince me that my thinking and practice was wrong—evidenced by a lack of fruit. He told me that I could continue to do things my way if I were satisfied with a small amount of fruit such as some missionaries in North Africa that he had addressed.[55] He also appealed to John 15 that disciples of Jesus would bear much fruit. Jesus, however, was not talking about compromised professions of faith!

Conclusion

I am convinced that insider movements are a numbers game to assuage the consciences of mostly Western missionaries to provide a sense of accomplishment[56] and a helpful tool for raising funds. I fear that the countless number of Muslims the insiders claim as believers is no different than the invisible clothes of the emperor in Hans Christian Andersen's, *The*

---

countries that follow unjust policies. Truly those who claim that jihad means killing people are among the lost and the owners of hellfire. Allah, guide us on the straight path and keep us far from the path of the lost who twist your words. Amen." When I searched for the webpage (5/13/09), I had to access it through cached. The url that I used was:
http://74.6.239.67/search/cache?ei=UTF-8&p=%22jesusinthequran.org%22+%22jihad&fr= slv8-&u=www.jesusinthequran.org/%3Fp%3D167&w=%22jesusinthequran+.org%22+jihad&d = Bhx2akxISwm0&icp=1&.intl=us.

[54] The first step in cross-cultural contextualization is learning the language of the people to whom you are trying to minister. I have little confidence that anyone can accurately gauge the true feelings and thoughts of believers and seekers in such studies. Experience has shown that the language barrier, coupled with the propensity for Muslims to hide their true feelings when they feel that to be truthful brings shame to the situation or relationship, cannot be overestimated.

[55] Winship said he spoke in Tunisia to missionaries representing various organizations; they had seen only five converts among them.

[56] See "An Extended Conversation About 'Insider Movements'" *MF* (January-February 2006) 16-23. John Piper and Gary Corwin took issue to IM/C5 proponent, John Travis' statement: "As we have seen the resistance toward changing religions and the huge gap between the Muslim and Christian communities, we feel that fighting the religion-changing battle is the wrong battle. We have little hope in our lifetime to believe for a major enough cultural, political and religious change to occur in our context such that Muslims would become open to entering Christianity on a wide scale."

Emperor's New Clothes.⁵⁷ Ministers of the Gospel should not stoop to such deceitful ways.⁵⁸ We are not charlatan tailors who peddle non-existent clothing leaving our victims in a state of nakedness, but heralds of the Lord Jesus Christ who longs to clothe Muslims in real robes of righteousness.⁵⁹

May Muslims come to know Jesus by the hundreds and thousands and millions because God is not willing that any should perish, but that all should come to repentance.⁶⁰ He takes no pleasure in the death of the wicked and has promised that the redeemed will come out of every tribe, kindred, nation, and language.⁶¹ It is because of this God-given motivation⁶² that some of us care enough to "correct, rebuke and encourage" (2 Tim 4:2). An altered Gospel is no longer the Gospel. Even if such an altered message were to be received, it will not save because it cannot.⁶³ Just like Daoud, who was declared to be a believer by the personal standard of a Navigators missionary rather than the standard of the Bible, some of us do not want the Daouds to remain in a state of partially acknowledged truths that, although they may "not be far from the Kingdom,"⁶⁴ still remain outside of it. It is time to stop hating IM proponents in our hearts through silence and rebuke them frankly: "he who rebukes a man will in the end gain more favor than he who has a flattering tongue" (Pr 28:23).

---

⁵⁷ Pr 14:15 states "a simple man believes anything." How can IM/C5 proponents expect to be taken seriously by their detractors if they are not willing to show off their trophies? It reminds me of Sammy Sosa, the former major league baseball player who boasted of being free from steroids but refused to take a urine test when asked by Rick Reilly, a sports journalist. No one was too shocked when several years after this incident Sosa tested positive for steroids.

⁵⁸ "Therefore, since through God's mercy we have this ministry, we do not lose heart. Rather, we have renounced secret and shameful ways; we do not use deception, nor do we distort the word of God. On the contrary, by setting forth the truth plainly we commend ourselves to every man's conscience in the sight of God" (2 Cor 4:1-2).

⁵⁹ Cf. Rev 3:4-5, 18; 7:9, 13-14; 19:14.

⁶⁰ 2 Pet 3:9

⁶¹ Cf. Ez 18:32; 33:11; Rev 7:9-10.

⁶² Cf. Rom 5:5; 2 Cor 5:13-21.

⁶³ Gal 1:6-9

⁶⁴ Mark 12:34

5
IM Inside Out

5.1 Interview of a Former Insider, Anwar Hossein

Bill Nikides[1]

Anwar Hossein is a convert to Christ from Islam and pastor of Prime Church, Bangladesh. Following his conversion, he was approached by a Western missionary to become part of the *insider movement* of Bangladesh, which he did, but after two years he made the decision to come *outside*.

His experiences as an insider in the country that is promoted by IM as its poster child gives him a clear picture of the deceptions and problems inherent to the IM.

N: It's a privilege, really more of a pleasure, a joy, and an answer to many of my prayers to be up here this afternoon with Pastor Anwar. We've known each other for a number of years. . . .

Pastor Anwar is among other things a pastor and a Church planter. He served two terms as the head of the Bengali Bible Society. He's a Muslim convert himself and a former member of insider movements. So he's a person with an almost unique set of backgrounds. The other thing that I should say about Anwar is that I know, in a country like his, Bangladesh, there are strong leaders, there are many leaders, but it's sometimes rare to find a leader that's so respected by so many different groups of people, from so many different Christian organizations, from so many different parachurch agencies. . . . Pastor Anwar is somebody that really stands out to me as being unique in my own experience in his country.

You know we have a unique opportunity by being up here and listening to his story and interacting with him. We've been talking about IM and sometimes when we do that it can be an intramural discussion between missionaries or missiologists that bat ideas back and forth.

So with that, let me go ahead and get started here. Can you describe what your present ministry what your present ministry is?

H: Thank you for this opportunity. I'm pastor Anwar Hossein. My ministry's name is Prime Evangelistic Church. We are working among the Muslims and I bring greetings from my ministry and also I bring greetings from IFB, Fellowship of Bangladesh. It is a platform fellowship; those who

---

[1] In the interview, Bill Nikides is designated as "N" and Anwar Hossein "H." It took place October 4, 2010 at the second *IM: a Critical Assessment* conference held at Liberty University, Lynchburg, VA. The interview and questions lasted approximately one hour. We have redacted the interview to help it read more easily. We have also amended some of Pastor Anwar's comments, since English is not his first language, but have not changed his meaning. [eds.]

came from the Muslim background. Also I bring greetings from Bangladesh to you.

N: What part of Bangladesh are you from?
H: I'm from the south part of Bangladesh; the district's name is Borguna.
N: Are the people from your district mostly Muslims or partly Muslims?
H: Mostly Muslim.
N: Sunni I assume?
H: Sunni.
N: What's your family background? Were you raised as a Muslim?
H: Yes, I was born in a Muslim family and I was raised as a Muslim in the southern part of Bangladesh.
N: Could you tell us briefly how you came to Christ?
H: When I was a student – at that time a Javanese group and some Bangladeshi young people came to my district in Borguna – they were selling Bibles, New Testaments and Christian books. There was one book, the life of Christ, but the jacket was very nice. I did not think about Christianity or Christian books, but I looked. The jacket was nice, and so I should buy one (laughter). And I bought it and I bring in my home and I keep it. After a few days I was thinking, Oh I paid for it so I can read it. Then I read it. There was no reaction to me.

After a few days I was thinking, Oh this year I bought a Christian book and I can read so I can visit on Christian beliefs. So maybe in Christmas time I will do it. So I was thinking, where I can go? Then I found one village is from my place to that Christian village is six hours journey by boat. And I took it. And I went there. It was not a good experience.

When I went there, close to the church, a few young were standing (there). When they saw me they immediately came to me and gave the boxing (they hit Anwar). And I was so nervous. What they are doing? Immediately one of the Catholic priests, he came and saved me. These people are alcoholic; they're drunk because Christmas Day.

Then I came back to my home. What happened? What is written on book and I have read in Life of Christ and Christian village I visited is not the same. And in that book was one coupon: If you want to more about Jesus Christ, please write us. It was Bible correspondence school. And immediately I filled it out and I sent it. And soon I got the paper.

And it was interesting when I was a student I never got more on any subject much more than eighteen because I was not a good student! But that course always I got 99, 100 . . . (laughter). It was encouraging me. Maybe within six months I got New Testament. When I got the NT there was a full address and after six months I went to that office. And there was one foreigner and he was speaking Bangla. He was the first foreigner for my life. He asked me, "Do you like coffee or tea?"

I never heard about coffee before because I came from the rural area.

So I was thinking, I can try. Coffee; I asked him (for) coffee. Then when I drank it looked like tea.

Then he asked me, "Why you are here?"

And I said, "I want to know about Jesus Christ."

And he sent me to a Bangladesh pastor. He was famous. His name is Dr. Simon Sarker. And I went there and Dr. Sarker was asking me, "Anwar, do you know after you are dead where you will go? Cannot you think you have sin?" I do not think about it.

Then he said, "Okay, you are to go back home and ask your Muslim priest after death where he will go or where you will go."

And I came back home and I asked my priest, "After you are dead where you will go?"

He said, "I don't know. If Hazrat Muhammad recommends me then I'll go on to heaven. If I don't have any recommendation, I cannot go."

I asked him, "There is no any assurance?"

He said, "No."

I told him, "I want to go. How too I can go?"

Then he advised me, "You can do good work. Through the good work you can go."

But I was not satisfied and again I came to Dhaka. I shared with Dr. Sarker. And he was explaining to me through the Bible about assurance of heaven, assurance of eternal life. And then I understand. I kneeled to Jesus and I called Jesus Christ to come to my heart and received him.

N: When did you first come into contact with or become aware of IM?

H: As I remember it was in 1984.

N: And you came to Christ in what year?

H: 1978

N: So six years later you became aware of IM; and what was your experience with IM?

H: In 1984 one of the American guys came to my home and asked me, "Anwar, what do you think if the foreign money is stopped? What will you do to evangelize?"

I said, "I don't know."

Then he said, "I have a good idea."

I asked him, "What type of idea you have."

He said, "I want to buy more than a hundred acre piece of land and I want to put modern agricultural technology and we can earn money. And new Muslim converts can come here. They can train here and work here; and through this income we can do this type of work."

I was so happy! I was thinking, Oh it's a big challenge for me. I immediately said, "Yes, I agree."

And then he said, "One condition."

And I asked, "What is the condition?"

He said, "You have to go to court and make affidavit and say you have become a Muslim."

I was shocked. I said, "Why?"

He said, "If you make a affidavit and become Muslim then Muslim people will not disturb you."

Then I said, "Thank you for a good proposal." Finally I denied it.

After a few years I had a contact with him. So finally he told me, "Now you don't need to become a Muslim. You don't need to declare you (have) become a Muslim. If you want to join, you can come." And I joined with them.

N: How long were you there with them?

H: Almost two years.

N: Why did you leave?

H: In the same time, I was the vice chairman of the Bangla Bible Society. They were pushing me, directly and indirectly, to leave Bible Society. This is the reason I leave them.

N: You had to choose between working with the Bible Society or the insider group.

H: Yes.

N: Why did they want you leave though?

H: In my experience, I did not find any positive side in this movement.

N: At that time?

H: Yes.

N: So you left because you were given a choice. You either go with the Bible Society or you stay with the insider people.

H: And the second thing is I did not find any positive things.

N: Can you describe that?

H: Positive: that means I came to the Lord. I declared (myself) as a Christian. But that IM, they never said they are Christian. They allow you to go to the mosque; they allow you to perform prayer five times. And your identity is Muslim. I could not accept it.

N: We've all read articles and books and journals about C5. We've also heard many stories from missionaries about the huge numbers of converts that come to Christ through the movement. We know that your experience is only your experience, but I want to ask you, how does your experience compare with all the stories of many, many people coming to Christ through IM? What have you observed personally?

H: We also heard about the same through out friends outside of country. Some friends asked me, "Please investigate it in the field." And personally I went to some places where the movement took place. And I did not find the reality. I have a good friend in the IM and non-IM. And both sides I was trying to investigate. I did not find any true picture. Secondly, if it had been true then definitely there would be newspaper reports everywhere, television and charges, but nobody knows. Because this is a very hot issue. If it were to happen somewhere, immediately come to the church or newspaper or radio or television. I think some of our brothers are giving false report to impress their supporters.

N: What role did you see missionaries play in the spread of IM in your country?

H: Just for your clarification, I would like to say clearly that this movement has not been accepted by our churches or our evangelical alliance. Therefore some missionaries misled a few catalytic leaders and bought them by dollars to buy use for this movement.

N: That's a very serious charge. Are you suggesting then that in your own personal experience there was a relationship between missionaries and the use of money in order to build a support for IM within your country? Are you saying that?

H: Yes.

N: What impact do IM have on the people and Churches of Bangladesh?

H: The people of IM of Bangladesh have no positive impact on the churches or on the people of our country.

N: Can you describe that? In what way is it not positive? In what way would it be negative for example?

H: Since a long time, more than 200 years, the Gospel came to my country by William Carey and other people; especially from the Protestant side. At that time they do not work among the Muslims. After liberation in 1971 our door was open for the missionary. And many missionaries came to my country. People were working through the churches. People were working through the individual, like IMF is working. I am, and here is my respected brother Mannan,[2] we came through the Church; through the mission people. Many people are come from the IM now, but if you go to them, they cannot tell you exactly why they came to the Lord. Most of the people can say, Oh, emotional.

N: So they can't really explain.

H: Yeah.

N: Now just to be very clear about this, because your experience was back in 1984; do you still have contact and relationships with people that are insiders?

H: Yes.

N: So you talk to them from time to time?

H: Yes.

N: So you believe the things that you're saying today are not just what was in the past, but things that you're experiencing now. Are you confident about saying that?

H: Yes.

N: Interesting question based on one of the lectures we had earlier: Did you ever experience persecution as an insider?

H: I can say I did not find it to be so.

N: So you didn't have anybody that was pressuring you or beating you or

---

[2] Anwar motioned toward Timothy Mannan, a leader of the IM in Bangladesh.

threatening you when you were an insider.

H: No.

N: Did you ever see insiders persecuted inside your country?

H: Inside? No.

N: I ask because I've heard reports from outside.

H: I did not hear.

N: Did you ever experience persecution as a Christian from a Muslim background?

H: Yes.

N: Can you describe that?

H: As I remember, three months ago in newspaper we had big news. Some people were going to be baptized and local people were so against it, the police came and arrested those people. There was a big article in the newspaper. That article makes trouble for Muslim converts in Bangladesh. One of the believer's name is Vaishno Igri, district of Tangail. And since he was twenty-one he has been living as a Christian. Fifteen or sixteen families are living in that village. And the village people, after this news that Muslim people make a meeting. "Oh, Christian people are doing much. They're doing very bad work so we have to stop it."

Then they call all the Christian people in that area. They give a rule: If you become a Muslim, then you can live here. And they make trouble. They cut their electricity and they make a rule: no body can go (to) their home. Nobody can talk with them. Those people are confused about what they can do. Immediately they leave the village.

When I got this news I was thinking someone can go there and pray with them and encourage them. This problem will not be always (present). Soon it will be solved. And I went there. Some young people first came to that house. "Why you are here?" they are charging me. "Why you are here?"

I said, "I came to visit them."

They said, "No, you cannot because we have a rule: nobody can go (to) his home; nobody can talk with him."

I said, "I don't know about the rule."

"No, you have to know about it." They are charging me. They want to beat me. They want to break my car.

Then I said, "Okay, if you don't like me here, I can go."

"No, you cannot go. You bring your paper. You are Christian; how did you become a Christian."

And also I told them I'm working also on human rights.

So almost two and a half hours I was there. Then two or three high school teachers came and they talked with me; and this teacher solved this problem. Teacher said to the village: "He came to visit. Why you are doing these things?"

And the government solved it. Government sent the police there and the police told them, "Nobody can do anything for their faith. If you have other complaint, you can come to me. For the faith you cannot do."

N: One of the things I was thinking while you said this was that it seems like persecution in your country often seems like pressure. You feel pressure from a community or sometimes…police or somebody that wants your papers. They just make it more difficult.

H: Yeah.

N: But you're still here and you're still church planting. Why didn't you just stop?

H: Oh, this my call! (laughter from audience) How can I stop it?

N: Are you the only one that thinks this way?

H: No.

N: The reason I'm asking this question is that sometimes the assertion is made that because of persecution, it makes witness impossible in this society. I can tell just from my own experience having interviewed hundreds of people and been with them, that's absolutely not true; that there are people all over that country and other countries I've visited that are faithful witnesses. And the fact that they're harassed or punished or persecuted does not stop them at all. If anything they just find better ways to do it.

H: I don't want persecution. I am never waiting for persecution, but I know if somewhere is persecution and result is good, we'll get good result from that.

N: I want to ask you about one subject that when I first started reading about IM and then I first met people in IM we talked about it, but we haven't talked about it very much about it in a few years. The subject is the Jesus mosques. My question is have you ever seen any Jesus mosques?

H: Yes, but not in practicality; in a video. In my country I can say there is no Jesus mosque in our country.

N: You know there would be people that will say there are.

H: I did not find them.

N: What do you think of the CAMEL method and the use of the Qur'an to evangelize and disciple Muslim seekers?

H: I heard about the CAMEL method but never got into it. My personal opinion is this: Qur'an, as introduction to Muslim seeker is okay, but definitely not evangelism and discipling Muslim seeker. We can use it as an introduction, but not for the evangelism. We should use the Bible, the Holy Bible.

N: We've heard about insider Bible translations. Can you describe what these contain in Bangladesh and what do you think of them?

H: Yes, I have my own copy of their translation they call, *The Messiah: the Gospel of Mark*. In this translation they completely removed verse one where it was written, "the Son of God."[3]

---

[3] Mark 1:1-2a (NASB), "In the beginning of the good news of Jesus the Messiah, the Son of God, as it is written in Isaiah the prophet."

In my country they have a rumor. When I came to my village, when I told them I've become a Christian, they asked, "What do you believe?"

I said, "Bible."

They asked, "How do you can believe Bible. Bible is not correct Bible. The Christian people they change it."

I said, "Do you have any proof?"

They said, "No, I don't have any proof."

I said, " So how you can say that?"

"Oh my father told us. We know."

But now we have another translation. If the Muslim people got this, now they can show, "Oh you changed Bible. This is the proof."

I don't know why few people think they need it – but in Bengali Bible Society, member of the United Bible Society, they published *Injil Sharif* for the Muslim people, and *Kitab al-Muqaddas*.[4] And it is well accepted by all people.

N: Is it written in Muslim Bangla?

H: Muslim Bangla. Holy Bible is just translation in Muslim (Bangla) – Muslim Bangla is not real Bangla. We have two versions: one real Bangla and Muslim Bangla.

N: On one of my former visits to your country I was told by some Muslim background Christian pastors they were having difficulty with people that were passing out insider translations of Bibles. Do you know anything about that?

H: They were distributing them. They have money; they can do it through this money. I can say, no church has accepted it. Every church has rejected it, the translation.

N: But they still make them.

H: They try to make them. The Bible Society sent a legal notice and from that time we heard maybe it stopped, but we heard they are trying to do it still. But I don't know exactly.

N: The Bengali Bible Society and other churches in Bangladesh said that they didn't want the insider translation, but people tried to distribute it anyway.

H: Yes. The IM went to the American Bible Society to push the Bangla Bible Society because they know the Bangla Bible Society is getting money from the American Bible Society. They pushed the American Bible Society to tell them to accept their IM translation.

N: As a Muslim background Christian leader, what would you like to say to American churches and American people who financially support IM in countries such as yours.

H: Money is yours. Decision is yours. But I would like to invite you, those here or not in here, please come to our country and visit IM activities and non-IM activities and you watch what is happening there. And then you

---

[4] *Injil Sharif* (the Gospel) and *Kitab al-Muqaddas* (Holy Bible).

decide what you will do.

N: We thought it would be a good idea to invite people to come into the country and not to try and control where they were going to go. We would invite them to some of the visible churches, and hear their stories, and then they're free to go to all the other locations and see what they want to see for themselves.

What's the best way you think that we Western Christians can help you deal with IM? How should we be addressing this?

H: Please stand beside IFB. IFB is the Isai Fellowship of Bangladesh, which is the main platform or fellowship of the MBB churches to accelerate the evangelistic work in Bangladesh. Again, you can send a team to visit us and make a fifty-fifty partnership with IFB.

N: So the people in the room here are free to contact you about how to do that.

H: They can contact or I can give the address to IFB.

N: What we're saying is we have nothing to hide in this. So why don't you come and see for yourselves? Nobody's going to steer you around. We'll give you some places to see and plenty of time to see whatever else you want to see.

I'd like to say that one of the most important moments in my Christian life just happened: to be able to stand next to my brother, and talk about something together. What we really needed was a forum where we would have missionaries, Church people, nationals, insiders, outsiders, everybody together discussing this sort of thing in one group. And I've always had the burden that until we had brothers who had been part of the IM were present, we were missing one of the very most important parts of this discussion. It was not satisfactory to me to have Americans all discuss it, or even just to have insiders that were nationals discussing it. But what about all those other people in the other countries that are not nationals; should they not speak? Bringing my brother here was something that changes the way we discuss this sort of thing and the way we hear it.

H: Thank you.

N: And you know it's for the journey brother but it's not just for that, it's for your faithfulness to the Gospel. To just encourage you to just to know that God is with you and your part of God's Church and God's Church is praying for you everyday.

Questions from the audience

Q1: You mentioned that someone wanted to let you buy a field and put you in charge of it with one condition that you become part of the insider movements. Was it a Muslim that had offered you that chance? Or it was a missionary?

H: Missionary.

Q3: Anwar you answered an interesting statistic this morning about the actual number of Muslim background believers in a country mostly by reports that have been reported. I wonder if you could tell the audience that, because I found that quite interesting.

H: The actual number I cannot tell you, I don't know. But I guess not more then fifty thousand, insider and outsider both, non-insider and insider both. Not more than fifty thousand (total Christians in Bangladesh).

Q4: I think I heard you say that a while back you thought of filing a notice against a group that was distributing the insider Bibles. Also can you explain why outsiders would file a legal notice against this group and also if they do publish the Bibles, do you contend to file a court case against them and why would you do that?

H: Well, actually Bible Society is a little bit liberal. The Bible Society is thinking those that are doing IM some are little bit wrong way, but they are Christian. So directly they don't go against a court, the first time they try to give this legal notice if it was stopped, then it will be solved peacefully, for this reason they did not go directly to court.

N: But now as I understand it, the reason that it was stopped in the first place was because the Bibles were being illegally printed. They were being printed without any copyright information…and that violates laws of Bangladesh.

H: We have a publication law: if you want to publish anything then you have to put your correct address. Publisher address, everything. But these (IM) books here, they put a little address, but it is false address.

Q4: So is he okay with the visible churches persecuting the insider movements? Are we kind of saying that's legitimate?

N: What makes that persecution?

Q7: What are the laws in Bangladesh on Christian converts to Christianity? Is it illegal for Muslims to convert to Christianity?

H: Yeah, our constitution allows it.

Q7: It is completely legal?

H: Yeah, Yeah.

Q7: And was it recently changed or has is it always been this way?

H: No, it (has) not changed. You can preach; you can change your religion. Yeah, but we have problem family side and from the society side, but not from the government side.

5.2 Flirting with Frankenstein: Insider Movements from the Inside

Abdu Murray

> The son of Shi'a Muslims, Abdul converted to Christianity when he began reading the Bible for its errors. Experiencing his own insider movement as one who accepted the truths of Bible while attempting to maintain his Islamic identity and practice, Abdu soon realized the problems of such a compromise.

In the popular depictions of Mary Shelley's *Frankenstein*, Dr. Victor Frankenstein obsessively works in his laboratory, driven by his desire to create life from death. Seduced by the allure of using science to make the world better, Dr. Frankenstein exhumes corpses from fresh graves to harvest their body parts to create a genuine person. Fueled by his genius and driven by his passion, the good doctor succeeds—somewhat. His creation, a grotesque hodgepodge of humanity, comes to life. And for a short time, the momentousness of the achievement is intoxicating and exhilarating. But the experiment soon takes a destructive turn. With no name or any semblance of an identity, Dr. Frankenstein's creation goes on a destructive path. Dr. Frankenstein's effort to bring life out of death, to mix the two, does not result in vibrant life; it results only in despair.

In many ways, this describes a part of my journey from Islam to Christ. I made an effort to mix two things that refused to be mixed—Islam and Christianity. That part of my journey is illustrative of the so-called insider movements (IM) in missions. It is a phenomenon in which Christian missionaries encourage Muslims to embrace Jesus as their Savior but remain *Muslims* by continuing to read the Qur'an, profess the *shahada*, and participate in mosque activities. They keep their faith in Christ a secret, only to be revealed (somewhat) if another Muslim asks them about Jesus. By maintaining their Muslim identities (and even their beliefs), yet purportedly believing the Gospel, those Muslims remain insiders in their communities, waiting for the potential to provide a witness to their fellow Muslims.

What makes my journey similar to the IM is the fact that I tried to embrace the Bible and the Qur'an, Islam and Christianity, at the same time. My goal was not necessarily to be an *insider* who could witness for Christ to other Muslims. Rather, mine was an attempt to intellectually harmonize two religious systems and avoid the pain of having to choose one or the other. The IM has a similar goal: offer the Gospel to Muslims, while sheltering those Muslims from experiencing the pain of rejection and persecution in their community. Like the IM, my goal was well intentioned.

But it was also misguided. For a time my effort at syncretism gave me the comfort I sought. But it also robbed me of something very valuable. The IM just may rob Muslims of that very same thing. To understand what that is, I will need to share with you a bit of my story.

The informal academy of the American Muslim home

From early on my parents and extended family encouraged me to be proud of being a Muslim. Informally, I studied the Qur'an and Islamic theology, listening to Islamic scholars and clerics and getting my hands on various books and articles. The pull of contemporary American teenage life was ever present, but I was determined to set a Muslim example among my non-Muslim peers. I was (I think) relatively well liked in high school and college but I made a stand not to drink alcohol, smoke, or give in to the usual peer pressures. Sure I allowed myself the occasional teenage indulgence, but for the most part, one of the things that defined me among my peers was my Muslim identity. In fact, it was not enough for me to just be a Muslim in my community (there weren't many of us in the area at the time). I loved talking about my faith and, if you spent any appreciable amount of time with me, you got an earful about Islam and how it is the best, in fact the only, way to God. Islam was the only true path and all others, Christianity, Judaism, Buddhism, and all other isms, paled by comparison.

My confidence in making such statements to my peers stemmed from the informal training I received (and gave myself) during my childhood and teen years in apologetics: the defense of a worldview or position and polemics, the dismantling of other worldviews. As an Arab-Muslim family, we were keenly aware of the allure and tensions of modern Western society. There were temptations to engage in all sorts of bad behavior, but the temptation most feared by Muslim families in America is the temptation to become Western, to become a Christian. Thus, in many Muslim homes in America, the parents, especially if they are first generation immigrants, sit their children down on a regular basis and teach them why they should believe Islam and reject any other worldview.

My home was no different. I recall many chats with my parents, and even my uncles and grandparents, about why Islam is superior to all other religions. The Qur'an is the word of God because Muhammad was illiterate and could not have come up with such profound language on his own. The Qur'an we have today is exactly the same as was delivered to Muhammad with no change whatsoever in fourteen hundred years. The Qur'an is proven to be miraculous because it contains scientific information and facts that have only recently been discovered. Islam provides the best way to live a moral and just life. And on the teachings would go. Those kinds of apologetics and the arguments in support of them are steady fare at a Muslim family's dinner table.

But I partook of additional food at the family dinner table: a steady diet of polemics. From a young age, I was told that although Christians may mean well and may even sincerely follow their faith, their faith is fatally flawed. God delivered The Torah (*Taurat* in Arabic) and the Gospel (*al-Injil*) to prophets of old, including Jesus, but Christians and Jews corrupted those ancient Scriptures. They changed their texts to suit their respective political and theological agendas. Thus, the Bible we have today cannot be trusted. Not only had Christians corrupted their Scriptures over the centuries, but they also invented logically ridiculous doctrines, like the divinity of Jesus and the Trinity. Those doctrines were inventions springing from the pagan, polytheistic cultures that had penetrated the culture in first century Palestine and shaped the thinking of the early Christians. Jesus and his original followers stood against any such blasphemies. The Qur'an was revealed to Muhammad in seventh century Arabia to undo the harm caused by the biblical corruption and blasphemous teachings of Christianity. Muhammad's mission was to restore true religion and it was my goal as a good Muslim to do the same.

The informal training in apologetics and polemics was not unique to my home. Every Muslim I knew, young or old, was conversant with the arguments for Islam and against Christianity to some degree. Our ancestors, those Muslims who came to America before us, feared that American culture, including its Western Christianity, could be a powerful, corrupting influence. To combat that influence, we Muslims were trained in a defense of our own faith. The goal was to keep us Muslims, to keep us from becoming anything else, especially Christians. But learning to defend our faith was not enough. We were trained to criticize the faith of others, to create a spiritual vacuum in another person and offer them Islam as a means to fill that vacuum. After all, Islam, like Christianity, is a missionary religion especially to Christians in the West.

Through the informal academy of the Muslim American home, it became readily apparent to me what it means to be a Muslim. It means that you affirm the prophethood of Muhammad and the divine source of the Qur'an, as a matter of doctrine. But it also means resisting the very idea of becoming anything else, especially a Christian, as a matter of doctrine.

Uneasy engagements

I took the informal training in apologetics and polemics to heart and used it to engage others in religious discussions. I prepared myself by reading books about Islam and Christianity—mostly written by Muslims. Armed with my ever-increasing arsenal, I set out to argue the faith right out of any non-Muslim who showed an interest in discussing matters of faith with me.

Sadly, more often than not I ran into little, if any, intellectual resistance from those I encountered, whether Christian, Jew, Hindu, or atheist. It was not a matter of competing intellects. People of other faiths far more intelligent than me would crumble under the weight of my arguments not because I was so brilliant, but because they were unprepared for them or they realized they had given very little thought to why they believed what they believed.

But occasionally I encountered someone who had actually given his worldview serious consideration. On those rare occasions, I would engage in a conversation with Christians who would have answers—good answers—to my arguments against their faith. They would come up with hard-hitting questions about Islam that required me to provide a careful, non-standard answer. In many ways, those conversations were a welcome change. They also served as a wake-up call, motivating me to become even better equipped for the engagements.

That need to become better equipped led me to study the Bible. I had studied the Bible before merely by reading textbooks, treatises and articles written by non-Christians (usually Muslims) attacking the Bible and Christianity. Now I decided to scrutinize the Bible myself. I had little interest in seeing if it had anything of spiritual value in it. My interest was solely to find fault with it, to find logical, factual, and philosophical holes in it with which to show Christians that they needed to turn way from silly notions like a triune God, a divine Jesus, or a substitutionary atonement. They needed to turn to the true faith of Abraham and Jesus, the faith of Muhammad, the faith of Islam.

While studying the Bible I came across a surprising passage in the Gospel of Luke. In chapter three of Luke's Gospel, John the Baptist is preaching to the Jews and religious leaders of his day. He is preaching repentance and a need to embrace truth above all else. In a fiery sermon, John the Baptist says to the crowd: "And do not begin to say to yourselves, 'We have Abraham as our father.' For I tell you, God is able from these stones to raise up children for Abraham" (Luke 3:8 ESV).

Though I had no intention of taking to heart anything the Bible had to say, I found those words strangely challenging and profound. John the Baptist was telling his audience that they gave their lineage and heritage an inordinate importance that eclipsed the truth. Being a child of Abraham is nothing, John preached. Being a child of truth is what matters.

Sitting in a chair in my college apartment, the force of those words clutched me. Looking back now I can see that the Holy Spirit was drawing me, causing me to see for the first time that I had been committed to Islam not because I had sincerely determined that it was true, but because it was my heritage. I had armed myself with arguments in favor of Islam, but I had not submitted my faith to any serious scrutiny. I was so concerned with showing others that their faiths were wrong that I had not bothered to even consider whether my own faith might be wrong.

I was suddenly opened up to the possibility of giving all worldviews a sincere chance to compete for my allegiance. I would stick with Islam as my default belief system for several reasons. I had confidence in some of the arguments in its favor and I had no intention of upsetting the stability in my life while looking at other worldviews. But through John the Baptist's words I was given a glimpse of a life changing insight. Heritage is not as important as truth. Tradition and DNA withered in importance compared to the profundity of truth.

An inconvenient discovery

I continued to study the Bible and the Qur'an; however, with my subtly changed mindset I found new understandings of once-familiar passages of the Qur'an. I was reading Qur'an, sura 5 (*Al-Maidah,* The Table Spread), when a verse I had read numerous times stopped me in my tracks. Vv. 46-7 of that sura state:

> And in their footsteps We sent Jesus the son of Mary, confirming the Law that had come before him: We sent him the Gospel: therein was guidance and light, and confirmation of the Law that had come before him: a guidance and an admonition to those who fear Allah. **Let the people of the Gospel judge by what Allah hath revealed therein. If any do fail to judge by (the light of) what Allah hath revealed, they are (no better than) those who rebel.**[1] (emphasis added)

I had read those words innumerable times and they always meant the same thing to me: Jesus had confirmed the original Torah and came with the original Gospel, but they had been corrupted. Therefore the Qur'an was revealed. It suddenly became clear to me—the words of that passage did not say what I had been taught they said. In both the Arabic and the English translations, the verb tenses undermined the interpretations I had come to believe. The Qur'an directed the "people of the Gospel" to judge, in the present tense, what God had revealed in it. If the Gospel had been corrupted before the time of Muhammad, then why would God direct the people of the Gospel to judge by that corrupt book? Why would God say in the very next sentence that those who do not judge by what God had revealed were rebellious?

Believing in a rational God who would not make logical blunders, I had to understand this verse in its plain sense. In the seventh century, God directed Christians to judge by the Gospel they had. Indeed, the immediate context of the verse further substantiated that reading. Verse 48, the very next verse of that sura, says:

> To thee We sent the Scripture in truth, confirming the scripture that **came before it**, and guarding it in safety: so judge between them by what Allah hath revealed, and follow not their vain desires, diverging from the Truth that hath come to thee. (emphasis added)

---

[1] All Qur'anic references are from the widely-used English translation by Abdullah Yusuf Ali (2004). *The Meaning of the Holy Qur'an* (11th ed.). Beltsville, MD: Amana Publications.

In studying this verse and the original Arabic, it became apparent to me that the English translations were not conveying the true meaning of the words. The Arabic phrase often translated in verse 48 as saying that the Qur'an confirmed the scripture that "came before it" is *beyna yadihi* or, literally, *between its hands*. This is an Arabic idiom that does not mean the scripture the Qur'an was confirming was *before* the Qur'an in terms of time. Rather, it means that the confirmed scripture was *before* the Qur'an in terms of being present with it. The phrase is much like when we say in a courtroom setting that a witness comes *before* the court to make himself present. In other words, the Qur'an was confirming scripture that the people of the Gospel had with them at the time. If, as a Muslim, I were to take the Qur'an at its word, then I had to believe that an uncorrupted version of the Gospel had to exist in the seventh century. Otherwise, the God who supposedly revealed the Qur'an would be giving a meaningless, impossible-to-follow command.

I tore through the pages of the Qur'an looking for other verses referencing the Gospel and the Old Testament. I had read each of them numerous times before, but now my understanding of them had changed. I simply could no longer believe those verses of the Qur'an and believe that the Bible had been corrupted before the Qur'an's advent. It simply was not feasible from the Qur'anic text.

The conclusion seemed to be clear to me as a Muslim. The Bible was God's word, but so was the Qur'an, because if it were not, then there was no such thing as a Muslim—because being a Muslim means belief in the divine origin of the Qur'an. But my study of the Bible revealed that the Bible we have today seems to affirm doctrines and historical events that the Qur'an and other Islamic texts seem to deny. The Qur'an seemed to deny Jesus' death by crucifixion as a historical fact (Q4:157ff), while large parts of each Gospel are devoted to narrating the passion of Christ. The Qur'an denied that Jesus is divine (Q3:59; 4:171; 5:116), while the Bible seemed to affirm that Jesus understood Himself to be God (John 8:58, 20:20, et al). Although Islam teaches all humanity is dependent on God's mercy for salvation, Islam also teaches that man does not need a savior to atone for his sins. But the Bible I had been studying proclaimed that the very reason Jesus came to earth was to die as a ransom for the world, to save us from the penalty our sins deserve.

Confronted with my realization that the Bible had not been corrupted before the revelation of the Qur'an and a growing awareness that the Bible contradicts the Qur'an, I was placed squarely in the middle of a quandary. How could I believe both the Qur'an and the Bible? They seemed to contradict one another? Suddenly, a way out of the problem presented itself. If I could prove that the Bible has been corrupted since the advent of the Qur'an, I could escape my dilemma. My task was clear: I would search out the evidence for the Bible's transmission throughout history in hopes of finding that it had not been preserved since the seventh century.

But the evidence dashed my hopes. I studied the works of those who claimed that the Bible we have today is not the same as was originally written. I studied those who held to the counter-position. I studied the textual critics and the experts. In reading whatever articles and books I could find on the subject, the likes of Bruce Metzger, F. F. Bruce, Craig Blomberg, Marcus Borg, and Bart Ehrman became my surrogate professors. The stunning manuscript evidence, the evidence from the Dead Sea Scrolls, and the writings of the early Church fathers from the first century led me to an inescapable conclusion: the Bible we have today is the same Bible that was extant and accepted as canon in the seventh century. In fact, it had been the same for centuries before.

It also became clear, as a matter of logic, I could not hold to the Qur'anic text affirming the inspiration of the Bible, believe in an almighty and just God, and yet believe that the Bible would ever become corrupted. If, as the Qur'an says, the Bible was once God's word but had become corrupted, then one of two conclusions follows. Either God is unable to protect his revelation from corruption or he is unwilling to protect it. If he is unable to protect it from human machinations, then he is anything but omnipotent. If he is unwilling to protect it from corruption, then he is unjust because for centuries he allowed millions of people all across the world to believe a blasphemous perversion of His authentic religion. If either conclusion were true, then the almighty and just God I was taught to believe did not exist. Thus if I were to be a Muslim who still believed in such a God, I had to accept that the Bible continues to be God's word and could not have been corrupted before or since the advent of the Qur'an. This was not the conclusion I was looking for.

The conclusion that the Bible was and is God's word led to another conundrum: if the Qur'an affirms the Bible as God's word, but contradicts it at fundamental theological and historical points, how could the Qur'an also be God's word? When I had begun my quest, I had to determine whether the Bible was faithfully transmitted and could be God's word. Having made that determination, I was now faced with another question. Is the Qur'an the divine revelation I had always believed it to be? If it is not, could I still be a Muslim?

Creating Frankenstein's monster

I desperately wanted to remain a Muslim, yet I wanted to be intellectually honest about what I was discovering. To identify myself as anything but a Muslim would mean betrayal of my culture, betrayal of my family—a suicide of sorts. I, like many Muslims, had clothed my identity with Islam. I was a Muslim; it was the defining characteristic of my existence. I had taken great pride in being a student of my religion and an advocate for it. But deciding to follow a different way, deciding to follow the Bible as God's word, would call for me to end that identity, to kill it, to kill myself. The potential losses of such a decision were too much to bear. In fact, they were too much to even contemplate. So I did not. Instead, I thought of a way to embrace the Bible and remain a Muslim. I would become something of an insider. Thus began my great experiment to piece together two faiths to bring to life a new creation.

The fifty-cent word for my experiment is syncretism. It is the idea of mixing different religions or schools of thought to form a new one. Many in the IM have stated that they wish to avoid syncretism, but it seems to be almost an inevitable result of that missiological model. With this syncretistic philosophy I set about to show that the Bible and the Qur'an were not incompatible after all. Finding support among the liberal theologians, I argued (more to myself than to others) that neither the Bible nor Jesus ever claimed that Jesus was divine or God the Son; rather, it was Christian theologians who had made up the doctrines of the Incarnation and the Trinity in an understandable effort to make sense of the biblical data suggesting that Jesus is God incarnate but still human. If we could just see that the Bible was referring only to Jesus' spiritual connection to God as a prophet, not as God incarnate, we could have harmony with the Qur'anic denial of Jesus' divinity. As for the Qur'an, while it seems to deny that Jesus was crucified at Calvary (Q4:157), that verse could be interpreted to say that Jesus was crucified, but he did not die on the cross. If he did not die, but recovered from his wounds, he would not have resurrected. But what was I to do with the resurrection narratives in the Bible? Again, I found support in the works of liberal theologians like John Dominic Crossan and others who argued that the resurrection narratives were not meant to be taken as historical, but were spiritual metaphors intended to convey to believers that God is ultimately able to deliver us from death and our circumstances in a spiritual sense, not a literal sense.

I was able to rationalize my way into a harmonization of several other theological issues that seemed to set Christianity at odds with Islam. Marveling at my own ingenuity, I thought I had uncovered a new way to look at these two influential faiths. In the laboratory of my imagination, I could claim to believe in the Bible while maintaining my identity as a Muslim. I had created my own amalgamated creature. I had created an insider.

Insider out

For a period of time, I was comfortable living as an insider of sorts. I continued to pray, observe the Bible and the Qur'an, and live as a good Muslim. But something was consistently, relentlessly, gnawing at my spirit. It was the ever-present feeling I was not being genuine, that I was not true to either Christianity or Islam. And there was the feeling that although I was trying to enjoy the comforts of two worldviews, I was robbing myself of a profound spiritual benefit that was as yet unknown to me.

C. S. Lewis, the famed Christian apologist and former atheist, gave a keen insight into the efforts to compromise truth to find comfort. He wrote: "If you look for truth, you may find comfort in the end; if you look for comfort, you will not get either comfort or truth—only soft soap and wishful thinking to begin with, and, in the end, despair."[2]

I would soon discover the truth of that insight. I resorted to syncretizing the Bible and the Qur'an, Christianity and Islam, because I did not want to face the possible consequences of what a decision to follow Jesus might mean. Instead of truth, I sought comfort. I went to great lengths to achieve that comfort. And for a time it worked. I found comfort and solace living with my creation, but like poor Victor Frankenstein, my efforts to create a piecemeal entity would lead to despair. Frankenstein's monster was made up of human parts, but it was not human. It could speak, but it had nothing of value to say. It was self aware, but it had no name and thus no identity. Such was my self-created *faith*. It was neither Christian nor Muslim. It was faithful to neither the Bible nor the Qur'an. Like Frankenstein's monster, I was eventually forced to ask myself the questions that had been there all along. What am I? Who am I? Am I still a Muslim? Am I a Christian? Am I a grotesque half-breed?

I had been sitting on the fence, and the fence was no longer comfortable, especially because it was of the metal, chain link variety. The unforgiving metal spikes that were the irreconcilable differences between Islam and Christianity mercilessly dug into my flesh. Shifting my weight, trying to find new angles of syncretism, provided only momentary relief. I could not elude the discomfort because I simply could not reconcile the irreconcilable. The Qur'an and Islamic authorities reject fundamental Christian doctrine. The concepts of God in Islam and Christianity are opposed in many respects. I chose to ignore the clear texts and focus on what I determined were ambiguous texts to show that
biblical Christianity and Qur'anic Islam could be harmonized. But as I sat on the fence, the unyielding vertical points that were the differences between the Qur'an and the Bible dug into me, demanding that I be intellectually honest and recognize them as irreconcilable. My emotional desire to remain a Muslim yet believe the Bible would have to give way to a new desire, which I now know was a Holy Spirit-driven desire, to make a choice. I could not have it both ways.

It took quite some time to embrace the truth that truth is worth embracing, no matter the cost. It has been said that we know what things cost, but we do not know what things are worth. I was well aware of what a relationship with Christ would cost me, but I had not yet come to realize what it is worth. I knew that fully embracing the person and work of Jesus Christ without compromise would cause me to experience (and even cause) pain with long time companions and endure ridicule strangers. I knew it would cost me the very identity that had been forged for me in the informal

---

[2] C. S. Lewis (1952). *Mere Christianity* (39). NY: MacMillan.

academies of the Muslim home and the Muslim community. Until I was able to see that Christ is worth the cost, I was not willing to pay it. Eventually I came to realize a truth that the famed Jim Eliot, who gave his own life in service of the Gospel, wrote and exemplified: "He is no fool who gives what he cannot keep to gain what he cannot lose."[3]

This statement is really a rephrasing of Paul's famous words that "Indeed, I count everything as loss because of the surpassing worth of knowing Christ Jesus my Lord. For his sake I have suffered the loss of all things and count them as rubbish, in order that I may gain Christ" (Phil 3:8 ESV).

In comparison to all one may lose, gaining Jesus is worth it. The Gospel message tells me that all of my deepest questions have answers. Because it can be demonstrated as a historical fact that Christ was crucified and rose from the dead, all of my most difficult philosophical questions have an answer, even though I may not learn that answer in my lifetime. The Gospel message tells me that I have intrinsic value that is of infinite worth to God. Because Jesus' death and resurrection is a historical reality, I can know that the infinite God paid an infinite price to provide me with an infinite future with Him. What better show of love can there be? If that is not worth paying the cost of losing relationships, identity, and personal safety, then what is?

Thank God I came to understand that. I did not come to understand it in an instant. Rather, I came to learn it—and am still learning—in the crucible of suffering for Christ. In fact, experiencing that crucible is an inevitable part of life for a follower of Jesus. Paul instructs Timothy:

> You, however, know all about my teaching, my way of life, my purpose, faith, patience, love, endurance, persecutions, sufferings—what kinds of things happened to me in Antioch, Iconium and Lystra, the persecutions I endured. Yet the Lord rescued me from all of them. **In fact, everyone who wants to live a godly life in Christ Jesus will be persecuted.** (2 Tim. 3:10-12, emphasis added)

I will not divulge all the details of the emotionally trying experiences following my public declaration of faith in Christ. I do recall an instance in which I had given serious consideration to lying to Muslims I love by telling them that I had returned to Islam. Could I say it with my mouth but keep Christ in my heart? I wouldn't exactly be denying Christ so much as I would be affirming Islam, but not really meaning it. As I struggled in that crisis, I prayed to God for wisdom. In the midst of that prayer, the Lord reminded me that each one of His apostles and disciples had suffered much to increase the fame and glory of Jesus' name. He reminded me that not

---

[3] Edyth Draper (1992). *Draper's Book of Quotations for the Christian World* (1533). Wheaton, IL: Tyndale House. This quote was found in Elliot's journal and could be a paraphrase of a similar quote by Philip Henry, father of the great Bible commentator, Matthew Henry.

only did they suffer, but also rejoiced to be counted among those who were worthy to so suffer. They rejoiced when they were beaten and imprisoned. In that moment I finally discovered what my syncretism had been robbing me of the joy of suffering for Christ's sake.

Simply believing in Christ is not all there is to following Christ. Paul, who suffered so much for the sake of the Gospel and was used for its explosive growth, penned these words that missionaries today need desperately to heed: "For to you it has been granted for Christ's sake, not only to believe in Him, but also to suffer for His sake, experiencing the same conflict which you saw in me, and now hear to be in me" (Phil 1:29-30 NASB). A life devoid of that suffering is a life devoid of the full Christian experience.

But suffering for the Gospel does more than just enrich the believer's personal experience with Christ, it actually encourages other believers to be bold witnesses and leads to evangelism. Again, Paul tells us:

> Now I want you to know, brethren, that my circumstances have turned out for the greater progress of the Gospel, so that my imprisonment in the cause of Christ has become well known throughout the whole praetorian guard and to everyone else, and that most of the brethren, **trusting in the Lord because of my imprisonment, have far more courage to speak the word of God without fear.** (Phil 1:12-14 NASB, emphasis added)

Does this not strike us as odd upon first reading it? Why should Paul's chains encourage anyone to preach the same Gospel that got Paul thrown in jail? But the reality is that it did in Paul's day—when the Church experienced both hostility and growth like no other time. And the Church exploded for 300 years because of the believer's chains.

Ironically, the IM seeks to create opportunities for indigenous witnessing by encouraging Muslims to maintain their *religio-cultural* identity and keep their faith a secret in some way. Jesus' words to his disciples make it quite clear that persecution from one's own community and family lead to opportunities to testify about Him.

> They will lay their hands on you and will persecute you, delivering you to the synagogues and prisons, bringing you before kings and governors for My name's sake. It will lead to an opportunity for your testimony. . . . But you will be betrayed even by parents and brothers and relatives and friends, and they will put some of you to death, and you will be hated by all because of My name. Yet not a hair of your head will perish. By your endurance you will gain your lives. (Luke 21:12-13, 16-18 NASB)

Well meaning but misguided insider experiment

In the interest of further scientific discovery and achievement, Victor Frankenstein pulled together lifeless body parts to create a living man. He tried to create life from death. In some ways the IM is an attempt by well-meaning missionaries and evangelists to create life from death. It is an attempt to give a Muslim the life that comes from knowing Christ while encouraging him to hold on to the lifeless thing that is a works-based system. It is also an effort to save new converts to Christianity from the pain of persecution so that they can be comfortable in their Muslim context and somehow be a witness for Christ to other Muslims. Such insiders can continue their Muslim relationships while subtly witnessing for Christ. Then Muslims may ask what the insider does that is different from the others in the community.

I tried living that double life. I tried to keep my Muslim identity while accepting the Bible. And in so doing, I robbed myself of the beauty of suffering from Christ. I was well intentioned. I wanted to seek harmony between two faiths, two cultures. But I created a Frankenstein's monster. For a time, I was neither a Muslim nor a Christian. Though I could appear in conversations as either, I was, in fact neither.

To be sure, there is something valuable in retaining one's culture after one converts to Christianity. There is no biblical requirement that an Arab convert become English or that a Pakistani convert name his first-born son Steven. But I realized it is impossible to be a Muslim and be a Christian, especially in America. As I stated before, a part of what it means to be a Muslim is the resistance to becoming a Christian. More important than that, however, is the fact that the believer who is encouraged to keep his faith a perpetual secret is robbed of the profound experience of eventually making a stand for Christ and suffering in the tradition of the apostles and the One they served. It was in those harshest moments when I felt the tendons that bound relationships together being ripped that I felt closest to God. I pray that in our zeal to make life more comfortable for those we are witnessing to, we do not unwittingly rob them of that closeness.

Good people are still dead without the life that Christ gives them. If in the IM we are trying to piece together an experience by taking some of this and some of that, we may find that we have not helped to birth a living believer. We may find that we have created a lifeless creature that may not even know it is still dead.

5.3 Observations and Reactions to Christians Involved in a New Approach to Mission

Edward Ayub

Rev. Ayub was raised as a Muslim, but was converted while in university. His MDiv is from Presbyterian Theological Seminary (Philippines) and he has worked with Campus Crusade. He is a speaker and author, and through his efforts has established and directs a network of Muslim background churches (Presbyterian) in Bangladesh.[1]

Introduction

I refer to this as our *observations* because we national believers have seen new approaches to mission with our own eyes and have discussed them extensively with one another other in a variety of seminars, conferences and personal conversations. This short chapter is a reflection on the views that I have heard as well as my own thoughts on the matter.

Prior to starting to write on this purportedly phenomenal approach to evangelism in light of the Holy Scripture, I want to mention that in the recent years in Bangladesh many have used various methods to preach the Gospel among the majority Muslims. I respectfully admit that I may be proved wrong in calling a method unbiblical or improper. I cannot be sure that my judgments are one hundred percent correct. But, judging itself is in fact not forbidden, because Christ has ordained power and ministry upon his Church. But since our judgment cannot be one hundred percent error-free and correct as God's is, Christ has warned us to be careful or to judge in light of the Scriptures and after much prayer so that our judgment will be governed by His will at the time of judging. If anything happens against and beyond the teachings of the Bible, being a follower of the Gospel, it is my duty to disclose it. If the Holy Scripture allows us and if crossing the limits of Bible is observed, we cannot be silent. We have to guard the Holy Book and its sound teachings. People will misinterpret the Bible, organize churches in an unbiblical way and present Christ wrongly for dishonest gain (Tit 1:11).

Seeing all this, we cannot remain silent and indifferent as if nothing is happening. We already bear the allegations and condemnation from Muslims that we are changing the Bible. Even churches in Bangladesh are often unaware of basic Christian doctrines.

---

[1] Bangladesh is the location of a highly touted, yet under documented insider movement. The reports we have read about an unnamed country were more often than not Bangladesh. Rev. Ayub and Anwar Hossein are part of the visible church of Bangladesh that has been forced to stand up against the funds from the West that keeps IM alive in their country. The IM is not necessary in Bangladesh, as Rev. Ayub testifies. [eds.]

I am writing to challenge this carelessness and call us to greater responsibility as stewards of God's Word. I firmly believe, however, that this distraction is momentary and that only God's Scriptures and their teachings will last forever (Acts 5:17-40). In bringing attention to these new approaches, I also believe that we are not creating division, but protecting true unity by keeping and promoting the true teachings of Jesus Christ. Those who have been promoting other teachings, rather than what the Word of God teaches, have already strayed from the truth and are ruining the household of God (Tit 1:11).

Some observations

We who work in what is termed *the mission field*, tend to explain success in shallow terms, on the basis of human wisdom and practices that have become an accepted part of missionary technique: **the number of followers in the Church, the wealth and prosperity of the Church, the number of developmental projects being run by the Church, connection of the Church with the rich and western world, and having big mission centers**. In reality the success and honesty of a work depend on its spiritual maturity.

Many argue that if these are not dependable measures of success, why does that church have so many followers? Why are they so rich? Why do they have so many buildings and houses? Has not God been blessing them? They might be on the right path, but those who have spiritual eyes see that the churches where the Holy Scripture is strictly followed and applied often get fewer followers. Why?

1. People are rebellious. They know that they will have to surrender to God if they follow the Holy Scripture. They recognize that the preaching and teaching of the true Church of the Word are all against them, which they cannot tolerate. The pure Word of God especially threatens carnal believers. Therefore, when they consider conversion, many new believers seek the easy way and, in fact, are shown it.

2. In a true Church, no one can escape sin, and we must be accountable for that. The court of Holy Scripture condemns us. But sinners find churches where they and their sins are ignored without question. It should not surprise us to see that many leaders of Christian churches now oppose these groups and few extend approval to them. Some argue that Christ came for sinners. But what kind of sinners are these rebels? Even some of the leaders commit infamous public sins every day, including theft and rape, and yet we the missional Church applaud them! Is there no accountability? Is there no punishment?

3. They are awarded with responsibility in the Church even after committing their sins. Nothing surprises we national church leaders anymore. Those who reward these people with positions in the churches are a hundred times more corrupt than the people they reward. Additionally, the churches in the West that originate and export these false

teachings into Asia are able to do so because it is assumed they have such high spiritual motivation. This is nothing more than the continuation of the colonialist mentality: whatever the white man does must be true.

4. When these people are disciplined in a good church, they just change churches because those churches need members. Our leaders should be more careful from now on, otherwise our Churches will be destroyed spiritually. Gaining money and material influence is not enough. Nevertheless, God wants them to change. Jesus loved his disciples; but because he did, he disciplined them.

Shallow approach to success: numbers game

Now, to the main issue: we need to consider the words that have been circulated concerning a number of followers. Large numbers of followers are not the principal sign of genuineness of a church. If we look around the globe, we will find that ill motivated individuals and groups flourish day by day, but because numbers are held to be the most important evidence of God's blessing, they produce exaggerated reports. Someone abroad asked me whether 10,000 mosques have been converted into churches in Dhaka. I had to answer that I know of none. Did he hear the number correctly? If he heard the number accurately, that would indicate that almost all the mosques in Dhaka had been converted into churches. Even if he heard 1000, that number could not possibly be true. **I do not know of even one**.

Some people collect money from abroad by producing appealing but imaginary stories. A missionary reported in my presence that in the southern part of Bangladesh, Muslims had rejected the Qur'an and thrown it into the water. They had finally converted their mosque into a church. Another missionary reported in a meeting where I was present that there was "every minute one baptism." We do not want hyperbolic reports published. There is no spiritual benefit for the Church from these false reports.

How are these reports produced? I think the leaders of churches and Christian organizations need to discuss this issue and stop these reports, otherwise they might bring undue persecution to the minority Christians. Rather than confronting these falsehoods, supporters of insider movements circulate photos purporting to show the success of their methods of evangelism. These are clever methods to deceive Westerners who want to believe that we have a foolproof method of converting Muslims. There are no statistics of how many ordinary people are being portrayed in the pictures without their knowledge as being baptized when they are taking their normal baths in the pond—since baptism is done by immersing in water, pouring or sprinkling.

Problems of identity

Are the people who do these things a sect of Islam like Wahabis or Sunnis, or are they Christians? They never clarify their position. They perform *namaz*[2] at the mosques. I certainly know that though they are standing in the *namaz* with the Muslims, they secretly use different oaths, recitations and suras. In one instance, they developed a separate book on prayer different from the ritual Islamic prayer system. After protests from Muslims and the government in Bogra district for being duplicitous, they destroyed all copies. Taking an oath in the name of Christ to worship Allah, reciting suras from the Bible, the Torah and most portions from Psalms, they muddy the water between Christianity and Islam. They fast, but their oaths and methods are different. They sacrifice, but with a purpose different from what Muslims suppose. Their religious activities make them look like Muslims, but in private they claim that they are different theologically. Very recently in 2009, a pastor from Dhaka went to a district of Jamalpur in Bangladesh and asked the local people what they thought about Christianity. Their answer was that Christianity was a sect of Islam and Christians are therefore Muslims. Now what should we do about these people: support them or correct them? What is our responsibility?

Avoidance of persecution

There are people who are called *Isai*.[3] When they become believers, they are driven out of the family and the society. So they have to worship in such a way that Muslims or their relatives will not know that they have become *Isai*. Can a new convert from Islam continue staying with his family without being driven out if he or she testifies that Jesus is Lord? Jesus says the following in Matthew 10:

> Be on your guard; you will be handed over to the local councils and be flogged in the synagogues. On my account you will be brought before governors and kings as witnesses to them and to the Gentiles. (17-18)
>
> Brother will betray brother to death, and a father his child; children will rebel against their parents and have them put to death. You will be hated by everyone because of me, but the one who stands firm to the end will be saved. (21-2)
>
> So do not be afraid of them, for there is nothing concealed that will not be disclosed, or hidden that will not be made known. What I tell you in the dark, speak in the daylight; what is whispered in your ear, proclaim from the roofs. Do not be afraid of those who kill the body but cannot kill the soul. Rather, be afraid of the One who can destroy both soul and body in hell. (26-8)
>
> Do not suppose that I have come to bring peace to the earth. I did not come to bring peace, but a sword. For I have come to turn a man against his father, a daughter against her mother, a daughter-in-law against her mother-in-law—a man's enemies will be the members of his

---

[2] This is the mandatory daily prayer, also known as *salat*.
[3] This is a new sect in Christianity, self-identified as Muslims following Jesus Christ.

own household. Anyone who loves their father or mother more than me is not worthy of me; anyone who loves their son or daughter more than me is not worthy of me. Whoever does not take up their cross and follow me is not worthy of me. Whoever finds their life will lose it, and whoever loses their life for my sake will find it. (34-9)

Recently in a meeting held in Dhaka with Christian leaders from different backgrounds, one leader mentioned that he once shared the Gospel with a Muslim and after much reading and waiting, the Muslim finally converted to the Christian faith. But when he met that convert in Dhaka city after few years, the convert told him, "I am really a Christian believer but for the fear of oppression, I go to the mosque and I perform *namaz* five times a day and I am also a member of mosque committee." At that point another pastor leader commented: "If there is a new convert, he or she would usually bear some sort of persecution for a period of time, but if she or he can endure for six months to one year, then the persecution should diminish gradually. Thus, it is better to suffer for this shorter time than to suffer for his whole life by hiding his Christian faith." I fully agreed with the comment since most of us have had such experience—bitterness in life for a period of time and then honor and respect from our persecutors.

The avoidance of persecution and repression is the principal logic driving this insider movement. In order to justify their actions, they try to find support from the Bible. We do not believe in converting someone into Christianity using some verses from the Qur'an, one of their most common practices. Converts that come this way do not last long.

What are they actually doing in any case? Are they supporting the Qur'an's teachings or criticizing them? Converting someone by criticizing one's religious Scripture or his prophet or the followers of his religion is not the right way to do things. Converting someone on the basis of criticism means building a house on sand. When storms come, as they always do, the house will be demolished easily. Many come to Christianity due to joblessness—normal in a country like ours where thirty million people are unemployed. Therefore, some preachers of this sect delight in criticizing persons of other religions because they think they will receive financial support in doing so. I consider it a bad practice to criticize the Qur'an or Islam, and the risk in doing so is higher than in sharing the Gospel. I think if someone is led by the Holy Spirit and comes to us, embracing Christ after hearing and reading the teachings of the Bible, we should praise him. He will become a true believer and will last forever.

Persecution cannot be avoided

These people want to avoid persecution by embracing non-biblical faiths and cultures. What do Jesus, Paul and Peter say about persecution?

Blessed are you when people insult you, persecute you and falsely say all kinds of evil against you because of me. Rejoice and be glad, because great is your reward in heaven, for in the same way they persecuted the prophets who were before you. (Mt 5:11-12)

The Spirit himself testifies with our spirit that we are God's children. Now if we are children, then we are heirs—heirs of God and co-heirs with Christ, if indeed we share in his sufferings in order that we may also share in his glory. (Rom 8:16-17)

Dear friends, do not be surprised at the fiery ordeal that has come on you to test you, as though something strange were happening to you. But rejoice inasmuch as you participate in the sufferings of Christ, so that you may be overjoyed when his glory is revealed. If you are insulted because of the name of Christ, you are blessed, for the Spirit of glory and of God rests on you. If you suffer, it should not be as a murderer or thief or any other kind of criminal, or even as a meddler. However, if you suffer as a Christian, do not be ashamed, but praise God that you bear that name. For it is time for judgment to begin with God's household; and if it begins with us, what will the outcome be for those who do not obey the Gospel of God? (1 Pet 4:12-17)

What sort of believers are these?

I served a Christian Trust for a few months, primarily as an advisor and at some point, when they were in crisis, as the Director. I had no intention to work full-time for the Trust, but since the Trust wanted to work among Muslims through literature, I agreed to take the responsibility. Among the staff I saw people employed for about ten years as believers, but not yet baptized. Others were baptized for the sake of their jobs, while their believing wives were not. I did not pay that much attention to the status of the wives of staff, assuming that all of them were baptized. Once I asked a member of staff who did not undergo baptism: "How can you serve a ministry working for the publication of Christian literature without being baptized?" The staff member told me that she had been willing to take baptism for many years, but nobody was willing to baptize her. She blamed the leaders for not baptizing her since she came to faith in Jesus Christ. We saw to it that she took baptism promptly. I learned later that the night she was baptized she sought forgiveness from the Allah of the Muslims for the entire event. In other words, all along she had had a deficient understanding of Christianity. She did not return to the office the next day. I was quite surprised.

In the process of baptism one should take oaths like, "I have received Jesus Christ as my Savior and Lord. I will lead my life according to the teachings of the Bible, and I will do whatever the Church instructs me to do consistent with it." How can a person dare to leave Christ after receiving instruction and taking oaths of this kind? Some of these workers continue to work with pride in that organization. They criticized me for leaving, but they still work there as staff. This has been an open secret for all staff and the Board, I think. I resigned in order to work for Christ, his Church and the greater society, with a vision for what we can do if we are faithful to him and his Word.

Can missionaries (the people that set up these offices and organizations) conquer Bangladesh with these sorts of Christian believers? They are workers who are proud to be employed by foreign NGOs, but without understanding or accepting Christianity. They would be better off following their previous religion, Islam. I know the supporting NGO of the Trust in question thinks that they are the only pioneers and the principal agent of Muslim evangelism in Bangladesh. They have spent large amounts of money over more than fifty years, but can they show even one visible church they have established? The main goal of this international organization registered as an NGO in Bangladesh appears to be publishing reports of questionable merit; however, this just one story. Many missionaries from different nations are wasting money in order to win Bangladesh for Christ.

Why do IM missionaries follow the methods they do? One of our friends asked, "Are these groups re-converting the converted Christians into Islam? Is this a hidden conspiracy of this group to work for Islam through spending church money?" Not only do some of these people counsel people to remain Muslims rather than confess Christ openly, they counsel those who have left Islam, having become Christians, to convert back and join mosques.

Deception

Some pro-insiders argue the convert does not need to become a Christian. The convert is, instead, a pure Muslim. How is this possible? These converts study both the Qur'an, following the portions that speak about Christ, as well as the Bible. They say that true Christians are true Muslims. These converts argue that Muslims following the teachings of Islam are not pure Muslims, but only those who believe that salvation comes through Christ are the only pure Muslims. They claim that true believers are described in the Qur'an as those who submit.

Is the Qur'an so insignificant that these men can change and distort the Qur'an according to their imagination while Muslims sit idly by? Muslims will eventually stand against this misuse of their name as their religious duty and stop these people. We members of the visible church want to distinguish ourselves from them. We do not wish to be seen as deceivers or liars. They are active throughout different parts of Bangladesh, trying to misguide and deceive the Muslims. A religious deceiver is liable to be brought under civil and criminal laws. They present Christ in such a way the listener does not understand a Christian has just preached Christianity to him. Christ must not be preached in such ways. Muslims respect Jesus (*Isa*) as a Prophet. We can talk about Jesus Christ honestly and openly, making him known to those who want to listen.

Muslims will eventually challenge those wearing Muslim caps and beards, those that talk about Jesus Christ (*Isa*). People can masquerade as Islamic scholars visiting mosques in order to talk about *Isa* and to subtly show the difference between the Jesus of the Bible and the Jesus of the Qur'an. This person may be introduced as a Muslim but, in reality, he is a Christian whenever he leaves Bangladesh and when he speaks to foreigners. To Muslims, he claims to be a Muslim; to Westerners he claims that he is a Christian working among Muslims. Ordinary Muslims should be wary of people taking pictures of their mosques because these people may portray the mosques to foreigners as converted churches. A missionary who worked in Bangladesh for more than thirty years says: "This [moral] slide is incremental and can be insidiously deceptive, especially when led by people of the highest motivation."

Money is a real issue

What about the wealth and the large mission centers and projects developed by the groups supporting this kind of work? I thought deeply about this. I observed that all these groups in the world are rich. Not a single group is poor. They have large mission centers, universities, well-decorated worship places, large hospitals, and many more physical attractions. Where do they get so much money? I have been asked this question many times. My answer: Satan supplies it. They collect money from their members.

While I was studying abroad, I came to know about a cult group named *Iglesia Ni Khristo* where one is not allowed to worship or loses membership if he does not pay his tithes. Yet they have members flooding in. Everyone knows that the group is a cult. Why then do the people pay them? Because Satan, "the god of this age," has made them blind. They may sacrifice their lives for the sake of that group, but the Scriptures say this about them:

> But there were also false prophets among the people, just as there will be false teachers among you. They will secretly introduce destructive heresies, even denying the sovereign Lord who bought them—bringing swift destruction on themselves. Many will follow their shameful ways and will bring the way of truth into disrepute. In their greed these teachers will exploit you with stories they have made up. Their condemnation has long been hanging over them, and their destruction has not been sleeping. (2 Pet 2:1-3)

I know a person of my village who was a dedicated follower of Christ for many years. He was an outstandingly talented person in our area and in Christian society. Later he became an object of controversy. Some missionaries who taught unbiblical practices exploited him. Feeling isolated and finding no alternative employment he adopted their ideas as his own. I do not go to the village very often, but my brothers and relatives often go there. This person went to pray during *Eid* (Muslim festival) at the village mosque to show that he had re-converted into Islam. The villagers, however, did not allow him to pray in the mosque yard. Some even warned that they themselves would not pray at the mosque if he were allowed to do so.

Later, he went to my maternal grandfather who is a renowned scholar in the locality and a founder of a *madrassa* (Islamic education institute). He gave his confession in my grandfather's presence and prayed with him. This was a fraud, however, because in fact he is a preacher of Christianity. It surprises me that he would even think of deceiving a respected person like my grandfather, but he did so very easily. I respect my grandfather very much even though he is a Muslim. After applying these sordid methods among Muslims in my country, this person made his exodus and now resides in the USA. As far as I know he is no longer involved in mission work. He lives as a re-converted Muslim. Some time ago he arranged marriages with Muslim boys for two of his daughters—a violation of Holy Scripture. Do men like this not read the Holy Scripture? They read it, but for the sake of money, they do not implement its teachings. Paul says, "Unlike so many, we do not peddle the word of God for profit. On the contrary, in Christ we speak before God with sincerity, like men sent from God" (2 Cor 2:17).

What exactly does an *Isai* say while confessing to becoming a pure Muslim again? What did the above-mentioned former Christian, later *Isai*, say to my grandfather? It is certain that these Muslims would not hear of Jesus Christ. I know a person from another area in Bangladesh who was advised by one such mission group as a condition for employment to become pure Muslim, to go to the mosque for prayer and confess by saying that he is not an *Isai* but a true Muslim. He refused and had to leave the job. Re-conversion into Islam is one of theological beliefs practiced by insider groups such as these.

Theology

It seems to me we need to bring these issues before our theologians, and administrators. Let us critique them before we suddenly find that we have arrived at a point that is indisputably sub-Christian. There are many witnesses in this country that can testify this missionary was once one of the pioneers of such controversial mission work, but failed and became disillusioned with the methodology.

Some of these insiders or Messianic Muslims gather support in the name of cooperative societies or micro-credit programs. They use pictures of bearded Muslims, showing that Islamic scholars are becoming Christians. We notice that these groups deceive many ignorant and illiterate Muslims. Muslims would be shocked to learn that these people do not read the Bible, do not even pray to Allah. They are actually nothing more than businessmen. They build their funds from zero to millions, becoming rich overnight. They are frauds, deceiving the Church in order to make money and gain power. After writing my book in Bangla, some of the foreign missionaries and nationals agreed with my comments that many people have been doing business in the name of Muslim evangelism. I have their emails. Some of them have taken action against such reports and methods.

The Bible does not support this kind of work. Regardless of the language they use, there is no difference between an *Isai* and a Christian. A follower of *Isa* (Jesus Christ) will be known as an *Isai* or a Christian, just as in Pakistan Christians are known as *Isai*s; however, the followers of this group do not introduce themselves as Christians or *Isai*s. They claim to be Muslims, even though that does not really describe what they are. A Muslim can ask these people two questions: "Do you believe that Qur'an is a revelation from Allah?" "Do you believe that *Hazrat* Muhammad is the last and greatest prophet of Allah?" According to Bible, an *Isai* Christian cannot believe in these two at the same time. Jesus Christ has also advised these types of people not to stand on two boats at the same time. He says that a man cannot obey two masters. I believe that, in the same way, Islam will not call a mixture of Christianity and Islam and its followers, Muslims.

If these people try to avoid these questions, we may ask them some more questions: "Is *Isa* only a prophet or do you believe him to be God? Do you believe *Isa* is the Son of God? Do you believe in the Trinity of God – God the Father, God the Son and God the Holy Spirit? Do you believe the sixty-six books of the Bible to be the only Holy Scriptures?" They often say that Muslims are the followers of Muhammad and they are the followers of *Isa*, but Allah is the same. Ask them, "What is the religious difference between the Muslims' Allah and the Christians' Allah? Is the Allah in the Qur'an the same as the Allah in the Bible?"

In fact, the doctrine of the Trinity shows that the concept of God is entirely different between the two religions. Some may remove any reference that "Christ is Allah's Son" from their published *Injil* (New Testament), substituting Messiah in place of Allah's Son in their *Injil*. In some cases the Son of Allah is completely omitted (see the Gospel of Mark).[4] What do they think about the claim of *Isa*, "I am the way and the truth and the life. No one comes to the Father except through me." (John 14:6)? How do they explain the verse of the Bible, "Salvation is found in no one else, for there is no other name under heaven given to mankind by which we must be saved" (Acts 4:12)?

Having a majority of adherents in a given place does not make a religion true or legitimate. Because Christians are the largest religion in the world—Islam is the second largest—Christians could say: "We are the majority. Therefore, we and our belief are the purest." On the other hand,

---

[4] Anwar Hossein makes the same reference in his interview. [eds.]

Muslims will say, "We are over one billion. So, ours is the truest religion. We are also increasing in Europe and America, the home of the Christians." The quality of a work cannot be determined solely by the quantity of its followers. Jesus Christ said that people full of darkness are abundant in this world. Some people of darkness are among Christian Churches, too. Far fewer are the people who follow God's path. There are also vast numbers of people without any religion. People from the majority religion are in great numbers and in spiritual blindness. Good believers exist, but they are fewer than the reports claim.

Who is Jesus? How to view the Qur'an?

Followers of *Isai* groups, who identify themselves as *Isai* at home and hypocritically as Muslims to others, praying at the mosque and sacrificing animals with the Muslims, are a new cult or misguided faction. Their wives and children never pray like they do, since most of their wives originate from Christian families. We understand that it is even hard for them to say *Assalamu Alaikum*. Why do our local Christian scholars and theologians keep silent? Have you lost your speech? Are you blessed by the crumbs of their money or are you seeking opportunities to go abroad? It is hampering the Christian community. As the early church had false churches and heresies, so the misguided cults in the *Isai* society grow among the Muslims of Bangladesh. They may work this way in order to capture Muslim lives and society by hook or by crook, but followers of this sect will one day find themselves standing on a platform that has no base in the Holy Scriptures.

This kind of *Isai* sect is wrong in the light of the Holy Scriptures in two ways. First they do not worship Jesus Christ as the Son of God and as our only Lord. These people believe in Christ, but they also believe in the founder of Islam. Much of the time they say more about their founder than Christ. They place more importance on their human inventions and stories than on the One who bought them by His blood. This group is dependent upon the Western promoters, not least because their money provides jobs. They seem so fervent about what they believe today, but they embraced something completely different just a few days ago. What will they believe next? It is difficult for anyone to guess. One thing can be said with certainty: these kinds of people do not remain steadfast. They change their beliefs and doctrine as often as they change their place. The Holy Scripture is also clear about them:

> The Jews replied, 'It has taken forty-six years to build this temple, and you are going to raise it in three days?' But the temple he has spoken of was his body. After he was raised from the dead, his disciples recalled what he had said. Then they believed the Scripture and the words that Jesus has spoken. Now while he was in Jerusalem at the Passover Feast, many people saw the miraculous signs he was doing and believed in his name. But Jesus would not entrust himself to them, for he knew all

men. He did not need man's testimony about man, for he knew what was in a man. (John 2:20-5)

Now Jesus learned that the Pharisees had heard that he was gaining and baptizing more disciples than John—although in fact it was not Jesus who baptized, but his disciples. So he left Judea and went back once more to Galilee. (John 4:1-3)

Secondly, the Bible is not enough for them. They believe in the Bible as well as the Qur'an. I was once with a Christian family who did not have time to read the Bible in the morning, but they made time for the Qur'an.

The Qur'an has been used as a bridge to discussion about Jesus Christ. Personally, I prefer to restrict my use of the Qur'an to times when arguments arise. In other words, I use it apologetically because it contains teaching about Jesus, the *Injil*, Torah and Psalms. But reading the Qur'an can make a person a true Muslim, never a true Christian Muslim. There is no relation between ordinary Bible-believing Christians and these Christian (*Isai*) Muslims. Muslim evangelists should preach to them because this group will easily re-convert to Islam. They think of themselves as another sect in Islam like the Shi'a and Sunni. They go to churches abroad and some of their wives go to local churches. Some wives have learned how to perform the *namaz*, and their husbands go to mosques. Most of them do not associate with the visible *Isai* Church. How can Muslims tolerate them? Do they want to build a bridge between the Mosque and the Church? This million-dollar project is being run in the country with 100 percent foreign aid, but the religious people do not even know the names of the people that run it or the names they give their projects!

Conclusion

We conclude that this group is pushing the whole Christian community into a great risk of persecution. Christians try to defend themselves by differentiating themselves from these groups. If they can go to the mosques for evangelism then why are they not boldly sharing the Gospel? Which is easier: evangelizing inside the mosque or outside the mosque?

While writing this I tried to align my thinking with the Holy Scripture instead of my own will because I believe in the Holy Scripture. The Holy Scripture describes clearly what we should preach and where, when and how we should do so. For that reason I ask those that have reacted negatively to my chapter to study deeply the relevant verses of the Holy Scripture and compare my arguments with them accordingly. If you do not think in the same way, show your arguments in the light of the Holy Bible. Please do not speak on your own authority. I believe everything we need in order to uphold Jesus Christ purely is in the Scriptures. Our Bible has not left us in incompleteness or doubt. The Bible is sufficient for our lives and actions. We should not nullify the truth of the Bible. If you have questions or disagreements, please write me.

5.4 Islamization of the Gospel

Elijah Abraham

Born into an Iraqi Muslim family, Elijah converted to Christ and graduated from Southwestern Theological Seminary with MDivBL. He began Living Oasis Ministries and is dedicated to informing and training the Church to understand the truth about Islam and to equip the Church to reach Muslims for Christ. His intimate knowledge of Islam and his love for Christ are manifested in his conversion story and "insider" critique of insider movements.

Introduction

I write to you as a Christian from a Muslim background whose aim is to awaken the American Church to the Islamic agenda and face Islam with the Gospel of Christ. I, alongside many other converts are furious with those who have taken the Scripture, the Gospel, our Lord Jesus Christ, and the Creator, making them conform to the Islamic theology and culture. That to me, a born again sinner from the darkness of Islam into the light of Christ, is absolute blasphemy and heresy.

Unlike those who advocate the insider movements (IM), I did not have the luxury of knowing about the Gospel and Christ from a young age and from my culture. So I do not take Christ and the Word of God for granted and I do not have the luxury to contextualize them into whatever is politically correct. I grew up as a Muslim who was taught to hate the Jews, Christians and any non-Muslim. My former religion and culture is all about revenge, hate, and conquest.

Neither my culture nor my former religion taught me that god is love let alone that he loves me. I was taught to fear him because he is a vengeful god. When I came to the U.S. and showed interest in Christianity, I came face to face with a loving God who decided before the foundation of the world to send his only Son to die for me. That was such a revolutionary concept I had to look into the details.

After much investigation I finally realized why Allah did not answer my prayers or needs. Allah did not reveal himself to mankind as Yahweh did through his Son Jesus Christ. I love what Jesus said to Phillip in John 14:9: "Don't you know me, Philip, even after I have been among you such a long time? Anyone who has seen me has seen the Father. How can you say, 'Show us the Father?" In Colossians 1:15, Paul writes, "The Son is the image of the invisible God, the firstborn over all creation." There are many other Scriptures revealed to us showing God humbled himself to be our personal Lord and Savior. That does not exist in Islam.

The Bible is so different from the Qur'an. It is God's Word that speaks to me, comforts me, encourages me, convicts me, challenges me, and gives me directions. The Qur'an does none of that. It is an absolute mistake—and in my opinion blasphemous—to equate the Bible with the Qur'an and Yahweh with Allah. I fear for those who do so, because they will someday give an account for what they are doing.

First encounter

The first time I came across a contextualized method was at seminary in 1998. Two things happened that made me question such methods and terminologies. First I was given a contextualized Arabic Bible. It used Qur'anic language instead of standard Arabic. Second, other Christians addressed me with a term I never heard before: *MBB*.

I am not an MBB. I am not a Muslim, a background or a believer. A believer in what? This Western acronym gives me a wrong identity. My identity is in Christ not in Islam. Continuing to call those who convert to Jesus, *Muslims* is an insult to us; it is an insult to the Holy Spirit who convicted us and transformed us into the image of Christ. In Christ we are a new creation, the former things (viz., being a Muslim) have died. Do the missionaries and their agencies use the same title for the Buddhist convert (BBB) or the Hindu (HBB) or Jehovah's Witness (JBB) or atheist (ABB)? Why only the converts from Islam? Again this must be a three o'clock epiphany[1] that some missionary came up with. This is an insult.

From 2000-2003 I trained missionaries for a well-known mission agency. In 2002 I noticed they adopted and promoted a new method called the CAMEL method. They wanted me to teach it, but I refused. Let me give just a few common characteristics between the CAMEL method and the insider movements. You will see why I refused the request to "ride the camel."

1. The assumption that *Isa* of the Qur'an is the same Jesus Christ of the Bible.
2. The Qur'an is valid and we can use it as a starting point to share the Gospel from the Qur'an.
3. Allah of the Qur'an is the same God of the Bible.
4. Allah and the CAMEL Method take away the privilege of suffering for Christ's sake.

The only time I use the Qur'an is to show the authenticity of the Bible. Once Muslims accept the Bible as the inspired Word of God, I concentrate on the Bible and let the Lord deal with the heart.

Insider movements' motivation

Advocates of such missionary methods would like to reach Muslims with the Christian faith, but without any complications. They believe their method should be **effective, cheap, painless, and above all it should never make a Muslim uneasy.** The pro-insiders use "Paul's method" as

---

[1] This is a reference to Peter's vision in the afternoon in Acts 9.

their method: "I can be all things to all people." When I read the Scripture, I see Paul contextualized himself to the culture, but he never contextualized the Gospel by changing it. Contextualizing the Gospel has brought many problems in the Muslim world. The missionary finds himself trapped with his title as a "Muslim." It leads Muslims from the darkness of Islam to a Christian heresy and it presents the Christians as deceivers who are unwilling to stand up and die for their faith. That is contrary to our Christian heritage.

A closer look

Most are aware of contextualization as found in the C1-C6 spectrum. Using this concept, what is worship? What is salvation? Salvation is of the Lord. The Bible says it is obedience. Even before you repent, it is obedience because we are told in Acts 17:30, "In the past God overlooked such ignorance, but now he commands all people everywhere to repent." It is a command. You have to repent. So if it is salvation and worship we are talking about; if it is central to the Gospel message, Christ Jesus is the center. What is salvation and worship in this contextualized format to a Muslim and how do we understand it?

Jesus said, "Salvation is of the Jews." This is a big hurdle to a Muslim. You will find the most violent, the worst, the most enemies of Allah to be the Jews (Q5:85). How would you contextualize that salvation is from the Jews?

We are told to worship in spirit and in truth. What is worship in Islam? Is it done in spirit and in truth? Spirit and truth both need definition because they have specific characteristics in Islam. How does Allah define worship? The highest form of worship is hate.[2] How does one contextualize that?

The God of the Bible is love. Contextualize this for me, please! Allah has enemies. This Allah of Islam cannot say, "Love your enemies." He, himself, has enemies. "Oh, you who have believed do not take enemies as your friends, your protectors. Show them no affection; no form of love…none whatsoever. Oh, you who have believed, you will never find those who believe in Allah in the last day who will show any love, any affection, to those who resist Allah and his apostle…be they their fathers, be they their brothers, be they their children, be they their kinsmen."[3] What is the problem? If anyone resisted Allah and his apostle, they suffered death. This is the rule of Allah. **Hate is the pinnacle of worship in Islam.** One who does not know this does not understand Islam.

What is in the ritual prayer? In the ritual prayer Mohammad is not invoked. The name of Allah is invoked; do they not pronounce a curse on the Jews and the Christians? "The way of those on whom Thou has

---

[2] Cf. Q4:145; 7:178; 13:27; 16:93; 32:13; 74:31, et al.
[3] Q5:51

bestowed Thy grace, those whose (portion) is not wrath, and those who go not astray" (Q1:7). The simplest Islamic commentary will point out that the Jews and Christians are those upon whom the wrath of Allah is directed. No Islamic prayer can be complete without pronouncing a curse on all the Jews and particularly the Christians. Can this be contextualized?

The big difference

Muslims and Christians have common terminology, but radically different meanings. Muslims do not accept the concepts and definitions we use. "Search our souls by the Father," Jesus said (cf. Rev 2:23). We are co-workers with His Son to bring men and women to the Father because he is seeking those who will worship him in spirit and in truth. But, does the Father exist in Islam? How would you contextualize that? And how does he seek us, really? Allah is not interested in anyone. He is ultra-transcendent and has nothing to do with us. To say, "God is a spirit" is absolute blasphemy. How would you contextualize "God is a spirit"? The Bible says man is created in the image of God; that is apostasy in Islam. The penalty for apostasy is death. Please explain to me how these words with very specific meanings can be contextualized into qur'anic thoughts.

Our faith and our salvation is relational and is based on trust and communication of that relationship. Islam does not understand that. It has no room for such a concept. **It is submission to a sword and the recitation of a creed**. The religion before Allah is Islam and whoever accepts any other religion apart from Islam, any other philosophy, or any other ideology is doomed and will not be received by Allah. Such a person is doomed in the life hereafter.

Islam is not a religion nor is it a faith from a Western, modern, biblical perspective. It cannot be. So, what is it? Islam is a whole system; it is a way of life. It is neither a religion nor a faith. Islam is first and foremost a socio-political system, a socio-religious, socio-economic, educational, judicial, legislative, military system all cloaked in Allah and religious terminology. This is the whole of Islam. How do you contextualize that?

As a system Islam has two components, but I am not talking about culture. There is in Islam religious duties. Fasting is a religious duty, but simultaneously the second component of Islam is the state. If Islam is a religion and a state then every living Muslim is a soldier in the state of Islam and therefore we face a great problem.

What do Christians from a Muslim background say about it?

Most of the converts with whom I associate are outraged and hostile to IM. Actually, outrage and hostility is an understatement. Why do we feel this outrage? We believe that such a method does not serve Muslims well eternally. It does not lead them to salvation in Christ Jesus; it does lead them to a false Jesus. It dismisses the work of the Holy Spirit in our lives, the one who leads us to His salvation. We converts suffered persecution for the Lord. We carry this with honor. We are worthy to suffer for the Lord. IM robs Muslims of such blessings. Ironically, we continue to be persecuted by fellow workers for not agreeing with these unbiblical methods.

My heart is aching for my people and those who develop such methods. As good as their intentions may be, they have no regard for the consequences. A good friend of mine is a former imam and now in the ministry. We both agree that such methodologies are not from the Lord; we must speak out against them. It is my opinion that those who created such methods are telling the Holy Spirit he needs their help and that He must bless what they are doing. What a disgrace to our Christian forefathers who were burned at the stake for the Gospel's sake.

Islam is not a religion. It is a system. What the Muslims live and practice is not a culture, but a socio-religious system. To penetrate that, to enter that, requires mercy, grace, and above all wisdom. The Bible says that wisdom is better than weapons of war. May the Lord make us vessels of honor and channels of his grace. May we minister life unto those who have not life. We must do so without fear of death, without any apology to those who are for death, because we are his servants. He seeks those who worship him in spirit and truth. Jesus said, "I am the truth." We give him glory!

5.5 The New Christians of North Africa and Insider Movements

Bassam Madany

Rev. Madany (BD Calvin Theological Seminary) is a prolific writer of scores of articles and author of *The Bible and Islam: Sharing God's Word with a Muslim*, and the book he co-authored with his late wife, Shirley, *An Introduction to Islam*. He was also the long-time voice of the Arabic-language "The Hour of Reformation" sponsored by "The Back to God Hour." Rev. Madany's experience in the Middle East is readily seen in his chapter as it sheds light on the self-understanding of the Christians of North Africa.

Introduction

As the readers of *St. Francis Magazine* will recall, the August 2009 issue dealt with the insider movements. The various articles approached the subject from a biblical and theological angle. As the editor, the Rev Dr John Stringer, puts it:

> The insider movements, also called C5 or Messianic Islam, has been a pervasive, outspoken presence in the world of missions for the last three decades. Missiological journals, Christian magazines and newspapers have been awash in anecdotes from the field extolling this purportedly new, biblical, approach to ministry. At times, it has seemed almost unthinkable to offer criticism of this broad movement. That is why this entire issue is dedicated to a detailed examination of the Insider Movement, its theology, methodology and tactics. Is the heart of the Christian faith a matter of making an individual choice?
>
> Is it fundamentally just a matter of having a personal love for Jesus? Or is the Church, organized and visible, at the heart of God's plan for the world? The subject sounds alarm bells. Evangelical Christians become increasingly susceptible to the siren song of poststructuralist (some might say anti-) postmodernism and liberalism, lacking a foundation in a theology that biblically respects the historic Church as the body of the Lord Jesus Christ.[1]

I would like to contribute a further perspective to the discussion of insider movements (IM), which will shed light on the way Muslims who convert to the Christian faith view themselves. Materials that have been appearing lately on reformist Arabic websites reporting on this phenomenon are quite intriguing. The European media have picked up on

---
[1] John Stringer, *From the Editor's Desk SFM* 5(4):2.

the conversion stories as well. One might ask why those promoting the IM seem so unaware of these reports about converts from Islam to Christianity. The conversion stories they document do not fit the schematics of their own paradigm. The reformist Arabic websites and the European press indicate that the converts are bold and forthright in their *marturia* (Greek, witness) and enthusiasm for their newfound faith.

Muslims in the Arab world becoming Christians

It was around three years ago I came across the use of the term *Masihiyyoo al-Maghreb* (The Christians of North Africa) in the Arab media. That indicated the presence of a considerable number of North African Muslims who have embraced the Christian faith. In March of 2007, a conference was convened in Zurich, Switzerland, by "Copts United," under the leadership of an Egyptian Christian engineer named Adli Yousef Abadir, and chaired by Dr. Shaker al-Nabulsi, a Jordanian Muslim intellectual. The general theme of the conference was "The Defense of Minorities and Women."

One of the lectures was entitled "The Christians of the Maghreb under the Rule of Islamists", where it must be noted that the Maghrebi converts to Christianity were called, *Masihiyyoo al-Maghreb*. They were not called "followers of 'Issa," the way the IM likes to refer to converts from Islam. Another term used for them is *"Al-Masihyyoon al-Judod fi Dual al-Maghreb al-'Arabi,"* (The Phenomenon of the New Christians in the Countries of the Arab Maghreb).

Here are translated excerpts from that lecture delivered in 2007 at the Zurich Conference:[2]

> The *New Christians* phenomenon throughout the Arab Maghreb has come to the attention of the media. For example, the weekly journal, *Jeune Afrique*, devoted three reports on this subject with respect to Tunisia, Morocco, and Algeria. In March 2005, the French daily *Le Monde* devoted a complete report to this topic. And *Al-'Arabiyya* TV channel telecast two reports on the subject that had been recorded in the *Kabyle* district of Algeria.
>
> *Jeune Afrique* estimated that the number of people who have embraced Christianity in Tunisia was around 500, belonging to three churches. A report on the website of *Al-Islam al-Yawm* prepared by Lidriss el-Kenbouri, and dated 23 April 2005, estimated the number of European evangelists in Morocco to be around 800 and that, quite often, their evangelistic efforts are successful. The report further added that around 1,000 Moroccans had left Islam during 2004. The magazine *Al-Majalla*, in its No. 1394 issue, claimed that the number of New

---

[2] The link to this Arabic-language report is:
www.elaph.com/ElaphWeb/ElaphWriter/2007/4/225336.htm.

Christians in Morocco was around 7,000; perhaps the exact number may be as high as 30,000.

The report that appeared in the French daily Le Monde claimed that during 1992 between 4,000 and 6,000 Algerians embraced Christianity in the *Kabyle* region of Algeria. By now, their numbers may be in the tens of thousands. However, the authorities are mum about this subject: as an Algerian government official put it, "the number of those who embraced Christianity is a state secret."

The newspaper report went on to mention several factors that led people to convert to Christianity:

> When we enquired from those who had come over to the Christian faith to learn about the factors that led to their conversion, they mentioned several. Among them was "The violence of the fundamentalist Islamist movements." A Christian evangelist working in Algeria reported: "These terrible events shocked people greatly. It proved that Islam was capable of unleashing all that terror, and those horrific massacres! Even children were not spared during the uprising of the Islamists! Women were raped!
>
> Many people began to ask: Where is Allah? Some Algerians committed suicide! Others lost their minds; others became atheists, and still others chose the Messiah! Quite often, the *New Christians* testified to the fact that what they discovered in their new faith was love; it formed another factor in their conversion. These are some of their words: "We found out that in Christianity, God is love." "God loves all people." "What attracted us to Christianity is its teaching that God is love."

It is quite evident that the testimonies of these new Maghrebi Christians are extremely important. The Christian message came to them through various means, but it struck them as a word of a loving God in search for his lost sheep. They embraced the Messiah who died on the cross, and rose again for their justification. Notwithstanding all the difficulties that they were to face in the future, they clung to the biblical *Injil* that had brought them peace with God, and the gift of eternal life.

Algerians converts do not want to be insiders

Almost two years after the Zurich Conference that dealt with the plight of Maghrebi Christians, I read the following report, posted on 22 January 2009, on the Arabic-language *Aafaq* (Horizons) website. It detailed the news of young Algerians who have converted to Christianity as they became alienated from Islam. Here are excerpts from the report, datelined Algiers:

> Some *Amazigh* websites have disclosed that many Algerian young

people have left Islam and adopted Christianity. They confessed that they did so due to the ugliness of the crimes perpetrated by the Salafist *Da'wa and Combat Movement* against civilians. They were tremendously disappointed and disenchanted with Islam, claiming that it was responsible for nurturing these Jihadists who have been terrorizing and murdering innocent people.

The website noted that the spread of Christianity in Algeria has even reached areas that were entirely under the influence of the Islamists, such as in eastern Algeria. Furthermore, the Christian expansion in the country was not due exclusively to missionary organizations, as certain Islamic groups claim. The reason is to be found in Islam itself. It has been associated in the minds of the youth with *irhab*, assassinations, and crimes against innocent people. They remember that many of the crimes were committed during the 1990s, and occurred in distant villages of Algeria when young women were abducted, taken to the mountains as "captives," gang-raped, and then killed by having their throats slit. Such horrific scenes took place in Algeria over several years and resulted in the very word "Islamic" becoming synonymous with *irhab*!

The report added that in Islam a woman is regarded as an enemy that must be fought with all means. She must be punished for the simplest mistake, while men go unpunished when they commit similar misdeeds. Thus, a woman is held responsible for the simplest act, and is liable to be put to death, since she is by nature a *shaytana* i.e., a female Satan. This seriously misguided and misogynist view of women causes young men to worry about their own sisters, and be anxious about their future daughters as well.

It went on to explain that the *irhabi*s who committed those awful crimes against women held to a view of Islam that took for granted that discrimination between the sexes is normal. They believe in the notion that the bed is the sole reason for a woman's existence. In northern Algeria alone, 5000 women were raped. This *Amazigh* source regards these radicals as *Allah's guards on earth* who refuse to act as civilized human beings.

The website ended its comments on the alienation of Algerian youth by stating "that as long as Islam is unable to get out of its closed circle, and evolve according to the requirements of a civil society that is open to love, tolerance, and coexistence with others, it will continue to alienate more young people. Ultimately, it is the actions of the *irhabi*s that have been responsible for the Christianization of more than 20,000 Algerians during the bloody and dark decade of the 1990s.

Reporting on the same topic of conversions to Christianity that are taking place in Algeria, on 24 April, 2009, the *Aafaq* website posted an article with this headline: "Religious Leaders in Algeria Are Demanding the

Punishment of the Apostates." Here is my translation of the news item:

> An Algerian policeman and his daughter have made a public confession that they have embraced Christianity. His announcement has precipitated a tremendous amount of discussions and arguments in Algeria, causing the religious authorities to demand that the police department should dismiss him from his position since he has become a *murtadd* (apostate).
>
> The policeman declared to the Algerian newspaper *al-Nahar* that his previous life as a Muslim was filled with anxieties and the absence of peace of mind. He added that the radical Islamist movements that had massacred women and children caused him to become fearful of Islam, which he held responsible for the bloodshed. His life was caught up in a deep struggle that eventually led him to embrace Christianity (*intaha b'itinaqihi al-Masihiyya*), that according to him, "**has given me peace of mind.**"
>
> As to the daughter of the policeman, she explained that the reason she embraced Christianity (*min jihatiha, qalat ibnat al-shuratiy annaha 'itanaqat al-Masihiyya*) was her feeling that Islam treated women as maids and concubines, only to be sexually exploited by men. Muslim men regard women only from a physical point of view. Now, having embraced Christianity, she began to feel as a dignified human being. Her decision is final, and she does not regret it at all.
>
> The Algerian religious authority reacted swiftly by declaring that *irtidad* (apostasy) is tantamount to becoming a *kafir* (unbeliever), and thus becomes subject of capital punishment, unless an apostate repents by returning to Islam.
>
> It is estimated that there are around 10,000 Christians: most of them live in the Kabyle district of Tizi Ouzou. Some unofficial sources claim that the number of Christians in Algeria is more than 100,000; they are to be found all over the country, especially in the west of Algeria around Oran and Mostaganem. Most of these converts are young men and women. They claim that the reason that prompted them to embrace Christianity was Islam's responsibility for murder, terror, and rape, as perpetrated by the Islamist groups who, in 1992, started their Jihad against civilians with the hope of getting closer to Allah!

It is noteworthy that both the policeman and his daughter openly confessed that they had embraced Christianity, using the Arabic word *al-Masihiyya* and not another Arabic term such as the qur'anic *Nasraniyya*. *Masihiyya* is used by Arabic speaking Christians throughout the Middle East. To embrace Christianity and publicly announce it is a courageous act of the *New Maghrebi Christians*.

Now having reported on the phenomenon of the New Maghrebi

Christians, I would add that we need to learn much more about the growth of the Church in North Africa since the Western media show little interest in the spread of the Gospel in *Daru'l Islam*.

IM missiology: a Western, hegemonic construct

The information gleaned from Arabic-language sources on the phenomenon of the *New Maghrebi Christians* is extremely important. Western Christians are being told by some missiologists that Muslims converting to the Lord Jesus Christ need not call themselves *Masihiyyoon*; nor do they need to stop their former Islamic practices such as attending the Friday services at the mosque, or fasting during *Ramadan*. This novel missionary theory is being offered as a quick fix to solve the problem of the paucity of fruits in mission to Muslims.

I risk being regarded as an extremely judgmental person when I describe the IM missiology as a **purely Western construct** that manifests a radical discontinuity with the missiology of the great missionaries of the past - from St. Francis of Assisi and Raymond Lull in the Middle Ages, down to the days of the pioneers of the 19th and 20th centuries such as Henry Jessup, Cornelius Van Dyck, Eli Smith, Samuel Zwemer, and J. W. Sweetman. As an Eastern Christian who has spent most of my life bringing the good news of Jesus Christ to the followers of Islam, I find it ironic that insider movements, while intending to be "culturally sensitive," become in the final analysis a rather imperialistic, even hegemonic effort. Yet, this attempt to sell a new genre of missionary theory is being implicitly rejected by those brave New Maghrebi Christians. *Masihiyyoon* is a term that gives testimony to the solidarity with other Arabic-speaking Christians and as full members of the "One Holy Catholic and Apostolic Church," in the words of the Nicene Creed.

It is my fervent hope that we will pay more attention to the biblical directives on missions, at the very time when the advocates of the IM are undermining them. Notwithstanding the Jewish and Gentile outright rejection of the Gospel of the cross, Paul did not hesitate to proclaim: "For the word of the cross is foolishness to those who are perishing, but for us who are being saved, it is the power of God" (1 Cor 1:18). While the basis of our salvation is the person and redemptive work of Jesus Christ, its instrumental means is the kerygma, i.e., the word of the cross, whether it is formally preached by a minister of the Gospel, or given as a *marturia* (testimony) by a Christian. Paul expanded on this basic missionary doctrine in verse 21: "For since in the wisdom of God, the world through its wisdom did not know Him, it pleased God, through the foolishness of the preached message (*kerygmatos*) to save those who believe."

Indeed, I cannot hide my joy when I hear news about the rebirth of the Christian Church in North Africa. I praise God for the boldness of these new Christians who are not ashamed of the cross of their Savior, but place its symbol in the humble meeting rooms where they worship Him.

They show in a concrete manner that they are *unashamed of the Injeel*, since it is the power of God they experienced in their own lives when he enabled them to leave Islam and join the worldwide company of the *Masihiyyoon* (Christians). He will also preserve them should the Islamist forces manage to take over the lands of the Maghreb.

5.6 Insider Movements: a Critique by an Iranian Convert

Sasan Tavassoli

Sasan, born as an Iranian Shi'a Muslim, came to Christ as a teenager. He obtained his MA (Reformed Seminary), ThM (Columbia Seminary) and PhD in Islamic Studies (Birmingham, UK). Sasan pastored for ten years, but is now concentrating his efforts on teaching, writing, and speaking. He is the author of the soon-to-be published *Christian Encounters with Iran*.

I was born and raised in a Shi'ite Muslim home in Iran, in a devout but very modern and educated Sufi family. Later as a teenager living in Europe, I attended a Christian school started by a group of American missionaries. It was there that I first heard the Gospel and the claims of the Christian faith about God, Jesus, human sin and salvation.

My first reaction to the Christian message was utter shock. How could Christians believe such blasphemy that a prophet like Jesus is God in the flesh? How could any rational person believe that a person can pay for another person's sins by a death on the cross?

Since I felt very challenged about my own faith in Islam, I asked my family in Iran to send me a Qur'an and I began to devote hours every day to the study of the Qur'an. I also began to attend church on Sundays and three different Bible studies during the week. I approached my study of the Bible and the Qur'an with the basic attitude that all genuine prophets have come from God with the same basic message. There might be minor differences among them, but in all essentials they must be in agreement since God would not contradict himself from one inspired Scripture to another.

I would tell my Christian friends that I did not want to deny their faith, but if there was any truth, I could find it in my own religious tradition. I read the Qur'an with great admiration and love and also would study the Bible with a great deal of love and sympathy for it. I did my best to find as much common ground as possible between the Bible and the Qur'an. Looking back at my approach, I guess I started with an insider movements' (IM) philosophy in my search for truth! Anything in the Bible that agreed with the Qur'an would delight me and anything that I found disagreeable in the Bible (especially the deity of Christ in the NT), I would attribute it to the corruption of the Bible or the fact that it was not Jesus who had said such a thing but Paul, etc.

After several months of reading both Scriptures, praying to God for guidance, reading books on apologetics, debating with my missionary friends and trying to seek for answers from my parents and Muslim authorities, I came to the compelling conclusion that the Bible and the Qur'an present us with a fundamentally contradictory message about who God is (the fatherhood of God and the doctrine of the Trinity), about Christ (his deity and death), about humanity (the problem of sin and the solution to human sin in the provision of salvation) and about Scriptures (the authenticity and the authority of Christian Scriptures).

In my case, what the Spirit of God used to convict me of the truth about Jesus was the Old Testament prophecies about the Messiah and the emphasis on love and grace in the New Testament (especially the Sermon on the Mount). I especially came to see that the deity of Christ was not the result of the corruption of the New Testament or a novel teaching by apostle Paul, but something deeply connected with the nature and mission of the coming Messiah, Immanuel (Is 7:14; 9:6). I accepted Christ as my God and Savior in January of 1985 and shortly thereafter, as I was reading John 14:6 in which Jesus claims to be "the way, the truth, and the life," I felt God's call on my life to mission and the taking the Gospel to my Iranian countrymen.

Since my conversion, I have earned one undergraduate degree in Bible and two graduate degrees in Christian theology (an MA from a conservative evangelical seminary and a ThM from a liberal seminary) with a PhD in Islamic Studies from the UK. I have been involved in Iranian ministry for the last 20 years, founded and pastored an Iranian Church, appear five days a week with five different programs on two Iranian Christian satellite channels that broadcast their programs into Iran, and teach regularly at Iranian Christian conferences. I am also intimately involved with teaching, leadership development and equipping the rapidly growing Church inside Iran. All of this to say, I know Christian theology, I know Islam, and I am deeply rooted in the context of ministry within a prominent Muslim people group. With this in the background, I would like to make a couple of brief observations about IM.

I simply do not believe IM is an honest and truthful way to deal with the text of the Qur'an. We Christians do not like it when other cults and religions twist our Scriptures to fit it into another theological mold. We of all people should take Jesus' command seriously: "So in everything, do to others what you would have them do to you" (Mt 7:12). If we allow the Qur'an to interpret itself and give Muslims the courtesy to tell us what their Scripture means, we realize that the Qur'an does not support the kind of Christian interpretations that IM proponents want to get out of it. After talking to some prominent IM leaders, it seems that there is a strange mixture of evangelical zeal, with American pragmatism and postmodern hermeneutics. There is little regard for 1400 years of Islamic scholarship concerning the Qur'an and almost no regard for the objectivity of meaning in the Qur'anic text. We cannot make a text to mean whatever we want it to mean, even for the sake of drawing people to Christ. We must be truthful and honest in our witness.

It seems to me that IM leaders are quite insensitive to the radically different contexts that exist in the Muslim world. Even supposing that IM methodology has proven to be an effective tool of evangelism in certain Asian Muslim countries, one cannot assume that it will have the same results in all other Muslim contexts. Hundreds of thousands of Iranians are coming to faith in Christ. From all available evidences, Iranian Muslims are some of the most open people groups to the Gospel. Why? For the most part, they are disillusioned with Islam and want to move away as much as possible from anything Islamic. Iranian Muslim intellectuals on the other hand have become proponents of pluralism and are advocating that there is no need for conversion from one religion to another since all major religions have come from God and teach the same eternal spiritual truths. In this context, the IM message would be detrimental to the spread of the Gospel among Iranians. The IM message would not be received well by the Iranian Muslim who is eager to leave Islam behind and at the same time the Muslim pluralist can find a strong ally in the IM message that all religions basically teach the same thing.

Thus, it seems to me very sad but ironic that IM followers of Jesus desire to proclaim the truth about God through dishonest means, and in the name of sensitivity to the cultural context of certain Muslim groups, have a total disregard for the contexts of other Muslim groups: Muslims who have no problem distinguishing the radical difference between the Qur'an and the Bible and desire to leave Islam behind and follow the Jesus of the Gospels and not the *Isa* of the Qur'an!

6

IM, the Past and Present

6.1 An Assessment of IM's Principle Paradigms

Jay Smith

An MK born in India, Jay is a missionary with Brethren In Christ, but is best known as perhaps the premier debater of Muslim apologists. Jay is respected for his incisive critique of Islam whether delivered from a ladder at Speaker's Corner or from a lectern at a University. Jay has traveled extensively and is invited to speak on college campuses, churches, radio and television.

Introduction

Towards the end of January 2009 my mission board, the Brethren In Christ World Mission (BICWM), asked me to attend the *Common Ground* (*CG*) conference in Atlanta, a group promoting and teaching the insider movements (IM) methodological model of evangelism to Islam. They asked me to assess its viability as a model for our mission work to Muslims living in a Middle Eastern country.

I knew something about the model based on the C5 category of the contextualization scale[1] due to my studies on contextualization at Fuller Seminary in the 1980s. Later on, in the late 1980s and early 1990s, my colleagues and I tried a nascent form of contextualization in a largely Muslim dominated West African country. We realized, however, that it caused confusion, as some of our African Muslim friends felt we were deceitful and dishonest, and trivialized what for them were time-honored Islamic identity codes of practice and belief.

Since then we have moved to London where, for the past twenty years, I have engaged in an apologetical as well as a more confrontational and polemical ministry with the more radical elements within Western Islam. The polemical methodology is probably as far removed from that of the IM as one could imagine (possibly a negative C5 on the contextual scale). Ironically, "Believers from a Muslim Background" (BMB's) tell me that the apologetical/polemical model of evangelism is actually a truer form of contextualization, since its forthright public style is closer to the paradigm of what a religious man should be: one who is as willing to publicly go toe-to-toe with the best, and is just as willing to die for what he believes as are they.

The assessment below, therefore, needs to be read with that history in mind. I make no apologies. I have worked for almost thirty years with Muslims on three continents. I have taught others to minister with Muslims in over twenty countries. My experiences are contextual, irenical,

---

[1] From the C1-C6 contextualization scale made popular by John and Anna Travis (pseudonyms), "Maximizing the Bible! Glimpses from our context" *MF* (Jan-Feb 2006) 21.

confrontational and controversial. This will help you understand why I take the positions I do.

Concerning the *CG* conference itself: I was not invited; I invited myself. They finally relented, with the *proviso* that I was not permitted to say anything about the teachers or the countries they represented. I can say, however, that they were quite an impressive group: eloquent, mostly my age (forties and fifties), white, and American.

Security was tight, with only delegates permitted to enter the sanctuary. I was not sure why they felt it necessary, since we were in Atlanta. Only those who had been invited could attend. We were all Christians.

It was a well-run operation with around three hundred in attendance. I understand that they do these conferences regularly, and that soon it would even be held in a Muslim country. The movement is not an aberration, but is increasingly popular among the young. From the adulation expressed by those around me, we should expect this movement to become increasingly mainstream within Evangelical Christianity.

As for my assessment, I wanted to make sure I was accurate, not simply giving my impression of what the IM missionaries were saying. Many have misquoted and misunderstood me as they critiqued my approach over the last twenty years, so I know how easy it is to be misrepresented. Following the conference, I wrote down what I believed were sixteen or seventeen core beliefs, or principal paradigms, and sent them to the conference leadership. They asked four or five of the primary leaders to go through the bullet points you see below, and respond to them as a group. Simultaneously, John Travis also responded by personal email with his reactions. Both the *CG*'s and John Travis' responses are summarized below in bullet points, followed by my assessment.

Upon receiving their replies I found that less than half of what I assumed were their core beliefs turned out not to be universal IM principles. There is a multiplicity of IM opinions and practices. Here then is the dilemma: how was I to assess something that not everyone agreed on? Much of what I thought I had heard at the conference in Atlanta they considered either unimportant or irrelevant to their paradigm. Were they backing away from what they said at the conference knowing that I was assessing them publicly? Did I misunderstand them? As one leading Christian intellectual stated,

> The insider proponents are just too slippery to pin down. Even when you quote them, they say that is not what they really mean! The movement is so fluid and vague in many ways that it raises many questions of credibility.[2]

---

[2] I have been asked not to give names or places by the leaders of the *Common Ground* conference. If there is a need to know whom I am quoting, feel free to email me privately for further references. See Appendix 2 for the affect of *Common Ground* in places other than the U.S.

With that in mind, here are the responses, and my assessments.

Assessment of IM terminology
Insider

We [leaders representing the *CG* and John Travis] define insider as "One who embraces Jesus, yet remains as a light in his oikos (household) so that as many as possible might be saved." (Mt 5:15)

Jay's Assessment: I wanted the leadership to define what they meant by insider, but they declined, possibly because there are so many different definitions and practices within the movement. A recent definition calls it, "a popular movement to Christ that bypasses formal and explicit expressions of the Christian religion."[3] To be more specific, an insider is someone who considers Jesus as his Lord and Savior, yet remains inside his culture (viz., Islam), inside his biological family (*oikos*), continuing to be called Muslim (cf. Q5:111).[4] There are variations of this definition depending with which Muslim group one ministers.

Let me focus on *oikos:* one's Muslim biological family. There is nothing wrong with wanting to remain inside one's *oikos*, but not to the exclusion of one's greater family in Christ. I do question the use of *oikos* as one's biological relatives. Jesus clearly redefines the family in Matthew 12:46-50. Pointing to his disciples, he said, "Here are my mother and my brothers. For whoever does the will of my Father in heaven is my brother and sister and mother." Do new believers from a Muslim background have a stronger allegiance to their biological Muslim relatives, or to the local Christian community? The local Christians are their new brothers and sisters in Christ. Ironically, it is the biological family members who persecute them. New believers need the help of their new brothers and sisters in Christ.

"As many as possible" seems to be a common motivation in IM circles. In conversation with IM promoters, the introduction of numbers suggests that one of the primary reasons the IM is attractive is their numerical success. I have heard that anywhere from 100,000 to millions have come to Christ through this methodology. The implication is the 'ends justify the means'. This is seductive and dangerous, as it leads to blindly adopting practices without examining long-term consequences, not only to the worldwide Christian community, but also to the local Christian community in which the new believer may or may not participate.

---

[3] David Garrison, "Church Planting Movements vs. Insider Movements: Missiological Realities vs. Mythiological Speculations" *IJFM* 21(4): 51.

[4] One who recites and believes the *shahada* (God is one and Muhammad is his messenger), continues to go to the mosque, prays five times daily, participates in the *Ramadhan* fast, and performing *hajj* (pilgrimage).

Extraction
New believers should not be extracted from their Muslim families (*oikos*). Mt 5:15 says to shine as a light in one's *oikos*. The dictum is actually "remain in." The Holy Spirit will tell them some things that are okay. The point is that a believer is uniquely gifted by virtue of bloodline and upbringing to reach those of his natural *oikos*. So our desire is to see this natural gifting used for the sake of the Gospel. The goal is for people to be salt and light in their *oikos*.

Assessment: For clarification, at the conference and in much of their literature, IM suggests the new believer should continue to call themselves Muslims, continue to pray the *salat*, go to the mosque regularly and participate in the yearly fast. In other words, others see them as Muslims.

This may not seem too alarming for some of us. In many C3-C4 ministries (with which I agree), we encourage new converts to remain initially within their families as secret believers, with the hope that at a more convenient time they will come out publicly as Christians, staving off immediate persecution. What is problematic here is that most IM proponents believe that remaining inside Islam, calling oneself a Muslim, is not necessarily temporary, but permanent.

I want to look at the inference of shining as a light found in Matthew 5:15: "Neither do people light a lamp and put it under a bowl. Instead they put it on its stand, and it gives light to everyone in the house." If Christ is speaking about the light of the Gospel, this is evidenced by one's good deeds (v. 16). Does not light confront darkness? Should not the darkness of Islam in the believer's family be confronted, which may cause rejection, leading to extraction and persecution by the family.

If true, I wonder how the analogies of salt and light suggest acquiescing to the existing Muslim lifestyle? This includes the ritualistic prayers, mosque attendance, and the *Ramadan* fast. Each of these Islamic pillars is a rejection of institutions modeled by Jesus. Perhaps proponents of IM believe these institutions are nothing more than benign practices, devoid of any spiritual overlay, easily accepted, adopted, and adapted within a biblical framework?

Returning to the problem of one's *oikos*: allow me to join Matthew 5:15 with 10:35-7, where we find that a disciple of Christ should expect to be a, "son against his father, and a daughter against her mother" and "a man's enemies will be the members of his own household." This assumes a clear extraction, and even an expectation that once one becomes a believer they should expect flogging, arrest, hatred, persecution, even death (Mt 10:17-23). In a Muslim context the problems for the believer begin in the *oikos*. There are many passages in the New Testament that propose extraction for the sake of Christ.[5]

---

[5] Mark 8:34-8 and 1 Cor 6:14-18 are but two of many.

The early church assumed it as well. How can IM proponents read the story of the early church in Acts, the history of the first three hundred years of Christianity, as well as the last seventeen hundred years and assume that we must avoid extraction? Extraction was not only expected by Christ in Matthew 10, but encouraged by the early church. It was the reason so many hid. Extraction resulted from the persecution of 'salt and light' Christians in their *oikos*, yet it also resulted in the great stories of courage and resolve in those who sacrificed their lives for the Lord. The Church is strongest when forced to depend totally on the Lord for her protection. Refusing to acquiesce to the demands of the *oikos* strengthened each believer and the Church.

A Believer from a Muslim Background (BMB) here in London, read the above, then asked:

> What are [IM proponents] saying to the hundreds of believers like me, who have obeyed Mt 5:15, have refused to keep our faith in Christ hidden, or under a bowl, have been salt and light to our families, have refused to compromise (i.e., claiming to be what we were not), and as a result have been persecuted for our obedience, tortured, and some of us even killed; yet have a strengthened faith because of our extraction, which led to persecution, and now are blessed by the inclusion into a worldwide family?[6]

This then leads to the question of the worldwide church. How will IM believers who remain in their Muslim families be involved with the worldwide Christian community? They will have little to no contact with even their indigenous churches, and will feel alienated by everything they do. I travel all over the world as a public speaker. In every country I go I am overwhelmed by the love and care I receive unconditionally from my Christian brothers and sisters, a love that will not be there for these insiders due to a self-imposed isolation.

Furthermore, it seems IM's primary concern is that new believers be the agents to bring others into Christ's *oikos*. But how can they, when they have no contact with them, remain in their Muslim families, and retain Islamic practices? Is this not naïve? What's more they will certainly be vulnerable to the seductions of Islam, to the spiritual forces within Islam, and especially to the strong emotional, social and physical control Muslim families have over them. With little discipling from more mature Christians—due to the constraints of an overwhelming Muslim family influence—the new believer may easily fall back into their old faith and allegiances.

I have just returned from a Western country where a number of Western Christian couples have chosen to voluntarily join their local

---

[6] Personal correspondence with author.

Muslim community as hidden Christians themselves. They have risen into positions of authority within this Muslim community but, according to a Christian acquaintance, have now lost any belief in Christ's divinity. If long-standing Christians can so easily and quickly be seduced by the power of Islam, why do we think the same will not happen to new believers?

Seven Signs

It is one effective tool, of which there are others (i.e., shame-honor illustration is another). It has been field-tested and is effective. It allows us to step into a Muslim's world dominated by the Qur'an. The Seven Signs in skeletal form are found in the Qur'an. It is used primarily by the *CG* proponents.[7]

Assessment: It is similar to the Chronological Method, another tool we used in West Africa to good effect. It begins with the stories of the prophets in the Old Testament and points to the sacrifice that is yet to come, leading to the Messiah who is Jesus.

My concern is that, unlike the Chronological Method that begins with the Bible, the Seven Signs begins with the Qur'an, and often misinterprets Qur'anic passages. This may inadvertently give authority to the Qur'an unless used only as a bridge to then lead the Muslim to the Bible. I simply ask that in our zeal to bridge with the Qur'an, we exegete it correctly, and not give it undue authority, making it harder to be critical of the Qur'an when necessary.

Holy Books

We say the *Tawrat, Zabur,* and *Injil* point to the kingdom of God, while the Qur'an teaches a) Monotheism, b) against idolatry, c) points to Jesus, and d) points to earlier books. Thus it can be used as a stepping-stone, a candle of light that shines toward Jesus and the Bible.

Assessment: Here is a case of moving the goalposts from what was stated earlier. The Atlanta conference implied that due to the areas listed above the Qur'an was one of four authoritative God-breathed books. There was a speaker whose adulation for the Qur'an bordered on incredulity. Having studied the Qur'an for thirty years she considered it almost divinely inspired, and found hundreds of biblical parallels. She said the Qur'anic equivalent of the incarnate Christ was *al-Batin*, the 'Inner One', accepting that Jesus spoke from the cradle because *al-Batin* certainly could,

---

[7] From *CG* material, these are the seven signs: "Speaking on a very general level, the message of the Qur'an is that God has reveled to mankind various 'signs' which help people to partially understand His eternal provision and mankind's lack of gratitude and submission. This fallen state is to be corrected by God, through the greatest of all the Qur'anic signs—*Isa.*" [eds.]

unknowingly crediting authority to the early apocryphal texts.[8]

According to a study of C5 believers carried out in 1998, 45 percent of the respondents said they felt close to God when hearing the Qur'an read, 96 percent said the Qur'an was a book revealed by God—along with the *Tawrah*, *Zabur* and *Injil*—while sixty-six percent said they considered the Qur'an to be the greatest of the four heavenly books.[9] Yet the *CG* leadership says the Qur'an can be used as a stepping-stone or candle – something I do not dispute. Until they come out clearly with what they believe concerning the Qur'an, it is hard to offer a fair assessment.

Should we use the Qur'an with our Muslim friends? Certainly, but only as a point of clarification. The Qur'an gives authority to the previous Scriptures (Q10:94; 21:7; 29:49; 4:136; 5:45-6, 68). Their revelation gives more authority to Jesus than to Muhammad (Q19:19-20; 3:46-9). At no time, however, should we assume the Qur'an is our authority or that we can find the Gospel within its pages. It seems many in IM believe the Qur'an may be placed alongside the Bible as one of God's inspired revelations. Let us not accommodate our Muslim friends by giving authority to the Qur'an. My doctoral studies have made clear to me the Qur'an is a fraud, written and compiled by men, with borrowed material from many apocryphal Jewish traditions and Christian sectarian documents.[10]

Muslim-compliant Arabic Bible

Mazhar Mallouhi's Muslim-compliant Arabic translation attempts to translate the message in a way that speaks to Muslims. He replaces references to God as *Father*, changing them to Allah, *Rabb*, *Waliy*, *al-Aziz*, *Amri*, *Ruh Allah*. We appreciate the difficulty in communicating the fatherhood of God in a Muslim context. The goal is to use meaningful terms for your audience, even if they are Muslim-compliant.

Assessment: It is legitimate to contextualize the Bible for the audience. This is a normally accepted translation practice. The difficulty arises when the text is changed for the sake of the reader's sensibilities, so that the author no longer says what he intended. This practice is not exegesis, but eisegesis. In the Gospels and Acts, Mallouhi replaces references to the Son (*huios*, usually translated in Arabic as *ibn*), to *Habib* (Beloved) or *Sayyid al*

---

[8] This anecdote is in my notes as well as those taken by two other missiologists at the conference, both with over 25 years experience in the Islamic world.

[9] Phil Parshall, "Danger! New Directions in Contextualization." *EMQ* 34(4): 406.

[10] The story of Cain and Abel (Q5:31-2), and the story of the Raven (31) are taken from the *Targum of Jonathan-ben-Uzziah*; the blood (32) comes from *Mishnah Sanhedrin* 4:5. Abraham and the smashed idols and the fiery pit (Q21:51-71) are found in *Midrash Rabah*. Solomon and Sheba (Q27:17-44) and the hoopoe bird is found in *II Targum of Esther*. The story of Mary, Imran, and Zachariah (Q3:35-7) is borrowed from *Protoevangelion of James the Lesser*. Jesus and the palm tree (Q19:22-6) comes from *The Lost Books of the Bible*. Jesus talking as a baby (Q19:29-33) is from *The First Gospel of the Infancy of Jesus Christ*. Jesus creating birds from clay (Q3:49) is borrowed from *Thomas' Gospel of the Infancy of Jesus Christ*.

Bashir (Master of Men). Jesus as the *Son of God* is replaced with *Messiah*, or *Son who comes from God*, which demotes Jesus to nothing more than a prophet, and no longer divine.

If this were not bad enough, how will we then explain the relationship between the first two persons of the Godhead with such changes? How will we use the relational aspect of the Godhead as a model for our relationships within the family, community, fellowship, and Church, once the model for this relationship is excised from the text?

Lastly, how will we answer the accusation that we change the text of the Bible? How far should we go in being compliant? Perhaps our next Bible versions should have no references condemning homosexuality (viz., Rom 1:26-7). Do we need a gay compliant translation, or perhaps an atheist or Mormon compliant translation?

As one long term missionary in a Muslim country recently stated, "[Muslim-compliant Translations (MCT)] have caused a huge amount of headaches here . . . especially when displacing terms such as *Son of God* with Representative of God." Another missionary friend in a large Muslim country said that things seemed to have started off well, but now the advocates of MCT (mostly Western missionaries) are fighting publicly with those using traditional translations. They have decided to go ahead with their translation over the traditional churches' objections, not realizing the indigenous church will have to bear the consequences for the missionaries' actions.

Biblical Exegesis

a) Gen 16:12 = Ishmael "against" everyone, changed to "with" everyone to accept Ishmael's line.

    Explanation: "Against" is one of 21 possible meanings of the preposition *b-*.

    The most commonly understood translation of *b-* is "in."

b) Gen 17:18-21 = "Ishmael's blessing" proved his inclusion with Isaac as the chosen race.

Explanation:

    -Isaac received the blessing of the covenant.

    -Ishmael received the promise of a blessing .

    -Isaac and his descendants are destined to be the agents of God's work.

    -Ishmael and his descendants are destined to be unique recipients of God's work.

c) 1 Cor 7 = "Stay like" means Muslims stay in the condition that Christ met them, i.e., as Muslims.

    Explanation: Culturally they remain, transformed by the Holy Spirit into their new nature, yet in their old Muslim culture.

d) 1 Cor 9 = Missionaries "become like" means to be like Muslims.

    Explanation: To "become like" as culturally as possible, but we are not insiders.

We do not teach that Christian background folks should become Muslims. We strongly discourage missionaries from becoming Muslims, or from pretending to be Muslims.

Assessment: A common criticism of the IM concerns their usage and application of Scripture, especially when they use a text to validate their paradigm. Here are some examples:

a) Genesis 16:12. To say Ishmael will be *with* instead of *against* his brothers seems highly improbable. I am not a Hebrew scholar, but I wonder why no other popular translations agree with the MCT's rendering? We probably need the Hebrew scholars to help us here. The right understanding of authorial intent for *brother* is possibly found in Deuteronomy 17:15. Here a brother is an Israelite, precluding Ishmael and his descendants.

b) Genesis 17:18-21. If the IM proponents believe Ishmael is equally blessed with Isaac, that there is no Scripture that keeps him from Isaac's promises, I suggest looking a few chapters later (Gen 22:2,12,16). Three times God refers to Abraham's one and only son, Isaac. God knows Abraham has two sons, suggesting He considers Isaac the unique son of the promise. They should also consider Paul's eloquent comparison and contrast of the two covenants (Gal 4:23-5, 28-31). He stipulates we are part of the free woman's (Sarah's) covenant, and to have nothing to do with the slave woman's son (i.e., Ishmael). Ironically, borrowing the IM paradigm, this means that we are to have nothing to do with Muslims, who they believe are of Ishmael's lineage.

c) 1 Corinthians 7:17-24. The problem with *staying like* or *remaining in* Islam is that Islam is both a religion and a culture. Staying in Islam means to take on all the religious connotations, as well as its spiritual power. In these verses Paul does not suggest Gentiles stay as pagan worshippers in their local temples, but he does speak specifically of newlyweds staying in their station in which Christ found them.

d) 1 Corinthians 9:19-23. I believe IM has interpreted this correctly. They state they themselves should not become like or even pretend to be like Muslims; however, later they indicate some of their missionaries do become like Muslims (borrowing Muslim forms). I trust they do not publicly claim to be Muslims. There will be a problem when Muslims or new believers ask these missionaries, "Who are you?" If they do not claim to be Muslims, yet ask their Muslim believers to remain and call themselves Muslims, will not this seem odd or confusing, or possibly disingenuous?

In Atlanta very few attendees questioned these interpretations of Scripture, possibly because there was no platform to do so, or because they did not know Scripture that well. If IM proponents want credibility, they must allow these interpretations to be publically discussed. I suggest they write up their interpretations of these verses in journals where bona fide biblical scholars can assess whether they are indeed interpreting these Scriptures correctly. My impression is that they come to the Scriptures with an agenda: looking for verses that may substantiate their own views. This is not helpful, perhaps even dishonest. Many cults operate on this principle with disastrous effects. I hope this is not the case for IM.

Muhammad

New believers, under the leading of the Holy Spirit, are given the freedom to come to their own conclusions concerning the role that Muhammad played in their lives.

Assessment: In this statement IM admits the possibility of concluding Muhammad is a prophet. The *CG* workbook goes even further: "My own judgment is that I see Muhammad as an authentic prophet of God, even though like other prophets after the time of our Lord, neither morally perfect nor doctrinally infallible."

Here is another case of saying one thing at the conference and in a hand-out, then pulling back to a more neutral stance when held accountable. Public admission to Muhammad's prophet-hood is in agreement with the *shahada*. The creed is often used as a litmus test for one's allegiance to Islam. It is an identity marker for all Muslims. Many Christians can repeat the first part of the *shahada*: "There is no God but God [Allah]." The second half is problematic: "and Muhammad is the prophet of Allah." This is the confession made by all converts to Islam, and repeated by every Muslim before entering Mecca for the *hajj*.

Suggesting Muhammad is a legitimate prophet opens IM to a host of questions. Affirming the *shahada* embraces Muhammad's life, while affirming the godliness of the man. Yet Muhammad opposed, even hated the cross, denied the deity of Christ, and advocated many biblically immoral acts. To affirm his prophet-hood is to spiritually submit to his example, while endorsing his rejection of Christ's divinity.

Confusions concerning Christ are found throughout the Qur'an, Muhammad's supposed revelation. The Qur'an (Q4:171) tells us Jesus is only a messenger, not the Son of God, and presents the confused notion that Jesus and Mary should not be worshipped alongside God (Q5:116), that Christians believe God had a wife (Q6:101), and that God cannot eat (Q5:75). But probably the greatest confusion is that Jesus did not die on the cross and that Allah gave Jesus' image to another (Q4:157). What true prophet, in one sentence, denies the greatest act in the history of mankind, and by doing so, condemns mankind for eternity? If Muhammad doubted Jesus' divinity (as every Muslim exegete for 1400 years agrees), denied both the crucifixion and the atonement, how can IM proponents suggest he is a prophet?[11] IM imposes its own interpretation on qur'anic texts to support these dubious conclusions.

Christian Forms

Christian traditions and creeds **are** accretions by definition. Yet, the Western expression of the Church with "creeds and structures, baptism and the word Trinity" is just as valid as any other form that God is using to reconcile people to himself through Christ. However, where extra-biblical forms create a barrier, which is keeping people away from reconciliation with God, they should be considered optional. The point is not that Christian traditions and creeds can or should be simply replaced with Muslim ones. The point is that the Bible is our standard—not the traditions. Let the Bible be the creed and source of theology, rather than extra-biblical terms like Trinity, which are part of Christian denominations. Muslims don't have to go through Christianity, but Christ alone.

Assessment: There is a growing desire in Western Christianity to move away from the traditions of the Church and return to a purer biblical paradigm. The emergent church is reflective of this; I recognize the attraction. The IM seems to borrow from this new tradition.

Is the desire to return to the fundamentals—jettisoning nearly 2000 years of experience and tradition based primarily on Scripture—modeled on Christ's example and motivated by the Holy Spirit? In one generation, will we move away from the creeds of the Church, belittle the need for baptism, or suggest the word *Trinity* is unhelpful? It seems naïve to jettison Christian forms, impregnated with biblical meanings, and replace them with spiritual terms and concepts from a religion that is anti-Christianity at its core.

Muslim Forms

Muslim forms [Mosque, the prayers, the *Ramadan* fast, the Qur'an] with transformed meaning can become ways of practically living out Jesus'

---

[11] We must be honest about the negative aspects of Muhammad's life: his convenient revelations, aggressive wars, the treatment of the Jews in Medina, and the numerous caravan attacks (Q9:1-5; 9:29; 8:39, as well as the *Maghazi* documents or battle campaigns within the *sirah* tradition). What should we do with Muhammad's multiple wives (Q33:50) in contrast to the qur'anic allowance of only four (Q4:3), or his suggestion that Zayd, his adopted son, divorce his beautiful wife Zaynab so that he could then marry her himself (Q33:36-37)? The list could go on.

More problematic from a biblical perspective is that Muhammad does not qualify as a biblical prophet: one, he was not a descendent from Isaac, the prophetic line; two, he performed no miracles; three, his revelations contradicted biblical revelations; and finally, he did not know the personal name of the God he was supposedly representing (Yahweh).

Moses said it clearly: "A prophet who presumes to speak in my name anything I have not commanded him to say, or a prophet who speaks in the name of other gods, must be put to death" (Deut 18:20).

commands to wholeheartedly love God and selflessly love one another. As the perfect insider, Jesus used some of his culture and religion; he transformed the meaning of aspects of his culture and religion, and he threw some out. We should not quickly condemn nor absolve a particular form but we need to test it in its context to see its true nature. The *CG* team has always been very involved in spiritual warfare, deliverance, and freedom in Christ issues. When the meaning of forms is transformed by the Spirit of God, they can become helpful and empowering. Some insider missionaries have become like Muslims (i.e., dress, vocabulary, lifestyle, even going to the mosque). They can continue using forms meaningful to them.

Assessment: Following on from the discussion above, in an attempt to divorce themselves from an accretion of 2,000 years of *Christian* forms, the *CG* and IM (Insider Movement) people have decided it perfectly acceptable to adopt and adapt an accretion of 1400 years of *Muslim* forms, which even they accept are neither Qur'anic, nor reflective of the prophet Muhammad's example. Why reject one set of forms, which I would suggest are modeled on a biblical understanding of Christ's example, yet, deemed insufficient by *CG* proponents, and then turn around and adopt another set of even more inadequate forms? At least the Christian forms are an attempt to be faithful to the Bible. The Islamic forms are anti-biblical, anti-Jewish, and anti-Christian. Jesus proved himself the perfect insider because he applied the real meanings to the forms. The same cannot be said of Islamic forms.

The Islamic forms that the IM would borrow are not easily given new meanings. Can we identify ourselves as Muslims, attending the mosque and hoping real Muslims accept our new interpretation of Islamic forms? Can we expect Muslims to accept us as Muslims? How is this different from a Muslim calling himself a Christian, attending Church, reading the Bible, and expecting real Christians to accept him as a Christian? Once Muslims understand this deceit, they will consider it a threat to their identity. Outsiders cannot recreate the meaning of Muslim forms anymore than we allow non-Christians to define us. This is arrogance coupled with Western intellectual imperialism.

Finally, IM proponents suggest some IM missionaries have become like Muslims. Are they endorsing this practice? Previously they seemed to repudiate the notion. We need clarity. If extraction is not biblical, how can it be biblical for missionaries to be extracted from their *oikos* and thrust into Islam? If everyone were to remain an insider there would be no mission. If the early church remained an IM—a Jewish sect—there would have been no world Christianity.

Spiritual Power
There is no intrinsic spiritual power imbued in Islamic forms (the Mosque, ritual prayers, fast, etc.). We would underline intrinsic. Similar

to meat sacrificed to idols, the spiritual power, which is present in Islamic forms is dependent upon the faith/belief/conscience of the practitioner. This can be glorifying to God or maintain a bondage to demons. As in any forms in any religion (including Christianity), there can be demonic bondage.

Assessment: After more than a quarter century working with Muslims, I am convinced that there is a spiritual control pervading this religion. I believe its forms are filled with power, manifested by an absolute conviction to the religion. What other religion creates such utter fanaticism for its cause, sending so many to their deaths? At the center of this growing religion sits the mosque, the ritualistic prayers, the fast, even the public reading of qur'anic verses, all of which have not changed in 1400 years. I believe these forms must not be adopted but resisted, even abolished, because of the spiritual control they have those inside.

Ask believers from a Muslim background whether they ought to retain their former Muslim forms, and they cringe. They understand something I believe most of us in the West do not; that many of these forms are imbued with spiritual power. The forms have an evil and controlling influence, which stretches back for generations, often requiring much prayer to be released. We should therefore be careful when we suggest these forms are simply benign, unwittingly trivializing something few of us outside of Islam have experienced.

Contextualization

See 1 Cor 15:3-4. This is the way in which the Gospel is presented. We allow meaning of forms to be transformed to bring them into accord with the rule and reign of Christ (under the law of Christ, 1 Cor 9:21). We are not afraid of participation in some Muslim religious forms. Our principle is to follow Christ's example (1 Thess 2:3). In practice, some insider missionaries do this . . . some do not.

Assessment: I commend the *CG* people for contextualizing the Gospel. What I caution is the prevailing *CG* view that all Muslim cultures are completely Islamic, assuming the culture cannot be separated from the religion (i.e., to be a Southeast Asian is to be Muslim). While Islam has dominated some of these cultures for 1400 years, there was a previously existing Christian culture, which predated Islam by 600 years, and still exists today. We may be jumping too quickly to contextualize Muslim forms without first investigating whether existing Christian forms are already practiced. Have not indigenous Christians adapted what they believe is Christ's example within their own culture for over 2000 years? Should they not be first consulted before adopting forms deemed by them synonymous with a faith that persecuted them for 1400 years?

CG proponents claim they follow Christ's example as an insider, in that he stayed within Judaism and Jewish culture. If they are following His example then there should be no contextualization. If it is wrong for non-Western believers to take on Western traditions, how can it be right for Westerners like the IM leaders to take on Islamic traditions? You cannot have it both ways and be intellectually honest.

Kingdom of God

This is the central theme and message of Jesus Christ in the New Testament: the good news of the kingdom of God. Our commitment is to bring an unencumbered, pure Gospel to Muslims. All men seek it first and enter it without any reference to a religious form or denominational creed. The rule and reign of God is broader than religious labels. Salvation is through Christ and entering his kingdom, and not through the joining of a particular religion.

Figure 12. Kingdom of God in relation to the religions of Christianity and Islam.

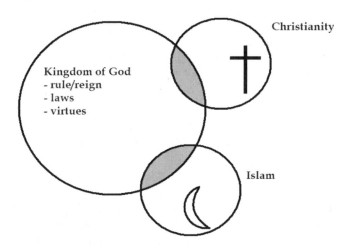

Assessment: I like the idea of coming directly to the kingdom unfettered with any cultural or religious overlay. I have difficulty, however, believing that Christianity and Islam are equally inadequate interpretations of that kingdom (Figure 12). How can anyone compare Islam's history with Christianity's? Islam has a history of violence toward other faiths, women and minorities, all of which is found in their primary revelations, and modeled by the prophet Muhammad. Christianity (not to be confused with the state, which borrowed the Christian label) has a history of peace towards its enemies, the care shown for the widows and orphans, and charity to the poor, the oppressed, and the strangers. All of these actions are found in our primary revelation and modeled by Jesus Christ himself. Have we become so cynical and apologetic that we believe the witness and testimony of the Church around the world is no better than that of Islam?

While recognizing that there may be unbelievers within the visible church who do not witness the Gospel correctly, there are no grounds for condemning the entire visible church as being as ungodly, unbiblical, and equally distant from the kingdom of God as Islam. Furthermore, what do *CG* and IM proponents suggest is this kingdom of God, a kingdom, which is greater than the Church? Have they discovered in the last twenty years what 2000 years of Church theologians, pastors, priests and practitioners have not? I find this attitude toward the twenty-first century Church disturbing. It suggests gross political correctness based on a strong postmodern critique that increasingly infects the American church.

Once this cynical view of Christianity sets in, it is a simple step to willingly replace it with a romanticized paradigm of Islam. Yet, the cynicism that created this mistrust is hopelessly incapable of guarding us from its dangers, so that soon Islam, not Christianity, becomes their new kingdom of God. The messengers of this kingdom are naïve in their fervor. Traditional Christians and Muslims will not know with whom they are engaging; resulting in a new sect: **Chrislam**? Is this the kingdom of God for the proponents of the insider movement?

What about intergenerational transmission, the passing of the faith to the next generation? It is documented that after the Islamic conquests in the seventh and eight centuries, some Christian communities gained permission to convert to Islam as insiders—Christian followers of Islam—by simply repeating the *shahada*. In time these communities disappeared as the children were trained by imams, inevitably losing contact with their former communities. What have the IM proponents put in place as their intergenerational strategy to keep this from happening with the new believers?

Water Baptism

Confession of our relationship to Christ is central to the faith of the new believer. Water baptism and circumcision were both rituals in the Jewish community. Circumcision proved to be a tremendous barrier to the natural expansion of the Gospel, and was internalized to be *circumcision of the heart*. What decision would the early church have reached had the Gentile revulsion been against water immersion instead of circumcision?

Assessment: The analogy with circumcision is incorrect. Circumcision was a public Jewish identity marker that was no longer needed in the first century Church, due to its fulfillment in Christ Jesus. Christ introduced water baptism (Mt 28:19) as the new public identity marker. Baptism is a public statement: the believer dies to his old life and rises with Christ. There are some missionaries who toy with dynamic equivalents that would be more adaptable for their environments. I support their efforts.

What disturbs me is that *CG* and pro-IMers seem to renounce a primary Christian sacrament of the Church. They jettison baptism as a barrier to the Gospel. If public baptism brings persecution—and it will—I must assume the *CG* solution is to discard it along with the other. What are they suggesting as a replacement?

Credal Statement

The focus of the new *ekklesia* is to congregate together for fellowship, and obey Jesus Christ, trusting Jesus as Lord and Savior. *Jam'at*s may simply be the people of God living and interacting together in community for prayer and reading the word, and not for just once a week meetings.

Assessment: While I have little difficulty dropping the name Church and replacing it with *Jam'at* or any name deemed appropriate—providing Muslims understand who we are by this name—I question the criterion for qualification in the *Jam'at*: a simple confession that Jesus is "Lord and Savior."

Muslims I know consider a Lord as an authority, and all prophets are saviors to some extent. This is hardly mentioned in any *CG* materials. I prefer a clear pronouncement that Jesus is God incarnate, co-existent with God the Father and God the Spirit. The Romans 10:9-10 passage demands that we recognize Jesus as Lord, yet in that context, lordship definitely includes divinity. There must be a clear public recognition that Jesus is God. For me, that is the *shibboleth* delineating the believer's belief in the Jesus of the Bible, and not the *Isa* of the Qur'an.

Conversion

Proselytos only refers to Gentiles becoming Jews. *Epistrophe* (Acts 15:3) literally means to turn towards and *aparche* literally means first fruit. Neither necessarily implies changing one's religion. Our point is that the English translation falsely gives the impression that faith in Christ is connected with conversion (changing religion or denomination) and has an inflammatory implication for those of a Muslim background who are considering becoming followers of Christ.

Assessment: Whether one changes from Gentile to Jew, from Islam to Christianity, this is a change of allegiance from one set of beliefs and practices to another. Call it conversion or reversion; a mind and heart change is required. To deny the change because it is inflammatory to Muslims misses the point. Conversion to any belief or faith is inflammatory. To divorce Christian conversion from the visible Christian community separates what God has joined together.

If conversion does not mean changing one's religion, why bother with missions? Why not simply leave people in their religious traditions? No, witness is about calling people out (Rom 10:14-15). When one is called, the response means answering the call. Becoming a Christian does not necessarily mean being extracted from one's family, but it is a call to become part of a bigger, extended spiritual family. Paul ends v. 15 saying, "How beautiful are the feet of those who bring the good news." May we all walk proudly with beautiful feet.

Quarantine

New Muslim believers are guarded from those western traditions that have nothing to do with the message of Jesus. We guard the new Muslim believer from those who "trouble those turning to God" and who "make trial of God by putting a yoke upon the neck of the new disciples" (Acts 15). If the unbelieving community brands the new believer Christian, the label, not the message, becomes the primary obstacle for spreading of the Gospel. It is therefore important to keep people separated for a period of time.

Assessment: There is wisdom in initially keeping the new convert hidden as a secret believer, a practice common to many missionaries in Muslim lands due to the persecution that will come if they announce their belief in Christ too quickly. This idea of guarding them from unhealthy Western traditions, however, is simple political correctness, unnecessarily driving a wedge between the new believers and the indigenous churches. It will lead to isolation and eventually, and if not controlled adequately, to syncretism and possible heresy. How will the local Church recognize them as fellow believers when they have been isolated from them for so long? If the believers are quarantined, has not IM created a sect of Chrislam within Islam?

How are the proponents of IM guarding new believers from spurious Western traditions? Do they mean these traditions have nothing to do with the message of Jesus, or that they are merely Western? If they have nothing to do with the message of Jesus, then what do Islamic traditions have to do with the message of Jesus? Islam is not a context that promotes long-term spiritual health and growth.[12] IM proponents pretend to be champions of local culture, and therefore champions of contextualization, while simultaneously demonizing their own culture.

Persecution

We believe persecution is biblical, necessary and helpful. One's commitment to Christ and the cross should be the source of persecution. Jesus said we must love him more than any family member. (Luke 14:26) This applies in all cultures, including America.

---

[12] Miriam Adeney (2002). *Daughters Of Islam: Building Bridges with Muslim Women* (76-82). Downers Grove, IL: InterVarsity.

But loving Christ more does not always imply becoming a traitor to family members, or offending them. On the contrary, we are taught to honor all men (1 Pet 2:17), including our parents. If persecution is because we desire to live a godly life in Christ (2 Tim 3:12) then so be it. If persecution is because of our rudeness, dishonoring of parents, etc., then it is not persecution for Christ.

Assessment: This is a difficult discussion for two reasons. Every IM proponent I meet bristles at the suggestion this movement is designed to stave off persecution. They emphasize the motive of the paradigm is to prevent extraction, not to sidestep persecution. There is fear of persecution within the Church when dealing with Islam. Let us admit it and move on. This may be a subtle motivation for the IM paradigm, though I may be publicly castigated for the suggestion.

A real problem is the orthodox Muslims' reaction to IM once they discover what is happening to their religion, to their Scriptures, to their god, and to their prophet. I am not speaking of benign Muslims, but the Muslims I work with in the U.K.: those who passionately and publicly define themselves by the identity codes adopted by the IM.[13] I believe traditional Muslims will feel deceived, possibly threatened, and certainly angered. Can we blame them? How would Christians feel if Muslims similarly posed as Christians?

Finally, I remind the proponents of the IM of an oft-repeated accusation we level at many Muslim apologists today: you, like they, practice dissimulation or *taqiyya*, concealing or disguising one's beliefs. Is this not what IMers ask new believers to practice? Is this how we want the world to know us? Does *taqiyya* model the example of Jesus?

There is also the question of accountability. Advocates of IM are not accurately sharing this methodology as it applies on the field. IMers argue this is for the sake of security. I am surprised just how little the Church knows about this movement. Churches are funding the insider movements out of ignorance.

Conclusions

I am deeply troubled by the beliefs and practices of many IM proponents. I still have many questions left unanswered.[14] Advocates of insider movements desire to incarnate themselves too deeply within an Islamic context. This unnecessarily elevates Islam's foundational identity markers beyond prudence. There is spiritual power in Islam which most of us do not understand. When we tinker with these forms, orthodox Muslims will react. I feel somewhat relieved, however, that there are a few

---

[13] The identity codes: attending the mosque, but not worshiping Allah as assumed by Muslims, performing *salat*, yet not praying to the qur'anic Allah, but to *Isa*—each is an aberration to Muslims.

[14] See Appendix 3.

who know of the danger of such a practice, and have forwarded, a healthier model by quickly bringing the searcher home to the safety and sanctity of Jesus and his Gospel.

I conclude with an anecdote for what I believe happened at the Atlanta *CG* conference. It may give us the reason why IM is catching on so fast, primarily in the U.S. As I listened to the well-developed and eloquent speeches of the leaders at the conference, I looked around at the hundreds of young faces, many of whom were students in Bible schools and seminaries. I was told most were heading to the Muslim world. It was obvious they were beginning to revel in the possibilities of the IM paradigm. I began to desire the same thing; when IM proponents began naming the large increase of new insider believers around the world and the large number of *Jam'ats* being created I, like those around me, got caught up in the euphoria. I wanted to belong to a success story. Who would not?

I started doubting what I had been taught all my life concerning what the Gospel was, what the Church represents, and even the call to missions. I began believing that maybe my parents and my grandparents before them, all missionaries, were wrong. Maybe conversion to Christ within the Church was not the answer, and possibly these eloquent men and women knew something that no one up to this time knew. Maybe Islam really was not so bad; God could have used Muhammad. His revelation could be adapted to bring people to know the Muslim *Isa*, not the Western Jesus, in a new and invigorating way. I remember leaving the sanctuary one evening wondering how I was going to break the news to my wife and to my colleagues in England, to say nothing of my mission board.

When I got back to the hotel I realized that I had been seduced by the numbers game and the alleged success of this movement; it was truly seductive. I would love to tell Muslims they did not have to be extracted from their family in order to follow Christ; that they remain in their religion, follow their creeds, observe the *Ramadan* fast, and perform the *salat*. For someone who has seen only a handful of people come to Christ, I could now point to over 100,000 who now believed. I began to see the possibilities, the acclaim, and with it the downfall of Islam in my lifetime. It all seemed too good—**in fact, it was.**

6.2 Can Christians Be Muslims?

David Cook

David Cook is professor of religious studies at Rice University. Author of many articles, chapters and five books, including *Understanding Jihad* and *Martyrdom in Islam*, he also contributed the chapter on "The Role of Islam as a Motivating Factor in Usama b. Ladin's Appeal with the Muslim World" in *The McGraw-Hill Handbook for Homeland Security*. David's contribution to the critique of insider movements is welcome and insightful.

Introduction

The dangers presented by the insider movements today are immense to Christians. It is clear to me as a scholar that more and more contemporary Christians are being seduced by the idea that Christians and Muslims can co-exist in some type of an ecumenical existence based upon the *Common Word* document or upon the idea that Christians can live as Muslims and gradually come to convert Muslims to a belief in Jesus.[1] Both of these ideas are extremely dangerous and need to be recognized as such by the Christian community. This does not mean that we need to demonize Muslims at all, but that we need to recognize that being a Christian is a choice between a number of different possible belief systems and that those belief systems, the most obvious and dominant one of which is Islam, are incompatible with orthodox Christianity. While it is perfectly possible for Christians to live as minorities and in some cases as crypto-Christians for a period of time, maybe even for the duration of years, it is fundamentally dishonest and dishonoring to the Gospel of Jesus Christ for the policy of his evangelists to be one of deliberate dishonesty in that they blur the lines between Christianity and Islam.

The basis for the ecumenical dialogue between contemporary Christians and Muslims is the so-called *Common Word* document issued in 2007 at the behest of a wide range of international Muslim leaders. It was the result of what they perceived as the demonization of Muslims in Europe and the United States following multiple terrorist attacks and assaults upon Western cultural values such as the freedom of speech and the freedom of religion. Currently it is easy to see that these attacks and assaults have bred a fund of opposition towards Islam on a political and cultural level that is manifested in the rise of anti-Muslim political parties and attitudes in Europe and elsewhere.

However, the *Common Word* does not touch upon those issues

---

[1] *Common Word* at http://www.acommonword.com/index.php?lang=en&page=option1 (accessed 7/3/11).

precisely; instead it focuses upon the Christian religious leadership as it is understood by the Muslim world—in other words, the range of Christian formal leaders from Roman Catholic, Orthodox, Anglican and Protestant variants of Christianity, and appeals to them to join with Muslims, based upon their common monotheism. The *Common Word* is deeply rooted in Islam, and is based upon the Qur'anic verse 3:64:

> Say: O People of the Book: come to an equitable word between you and us, that we worship none but Allah (God), do not associate anything with Him and do not set up each other as lords besides Allah. If they turn their backs, say: Bear witness that we are Muslims (or submitters to God).[2]

Couched as it is in the language of give-and-take and sweet reason, this verse is one of the most dangerous extant in the Qur'an. It posits three attitudes that should serve as the basis for dialogue. In reality, the verse provides the reasons why the non-Muslim should become a Muslim. The idea that we all worship none but Allah (or God) is superficially seductive, but in reality the god described by the Qur'an as Allah, while bearing the name of God, has few characteristics in common with the God of the Bible.

Secondly, the idea that we all should not associate anything with God, while placing the dialogue within the framework of monotheism, again presupposes Muslim strictures upon that belief in one God that preclude acceptance of the Trinity. Consider sura 5:17 and 73:

> Unbelievers are those who say: Allah is the Messiah, the son of Mary. . . . Unbelievers too are those who have said that Allah is the third of three. For there is no god except the one God, and if they will not refrain from what they say, those of them who have disbelieved will be severely punished.

There are many additional verses in the Qur'an that specifically oppose the doctrine of the Trinity and characterize it as polytheism.

Lastly, the phrase "set up each other as lords besides Allah," which sounds so odd to a non-Muslim, means that rule and dominion belong exclusively to a Muslim political system ruled (hypothetically) by Allah. The *Common Word* document describes this (citing al-Tabari, the medieval commentator) as "'that none of us should obey in disobedience to what to what God has commanded, nor glorify them by prostrating to them in the same way as they prostrate to God.' In other words, the *Common Word* document elucidates "Muslims, Christians and Jews should be free to each

---

[2] Translation from Majid Fakhry (1997). *The Qur'an: A Modern English Version*. London: Garnett.

follow what God commanded them, and not to have to prostrate before kings and the like." One should note that immediately following this apparently ecumenical statement, there is a curious caveat: "As Muslims, we say to Christians that we are not against them, and that Islam is not against them—so long as they do not wage war against Muslims on account of their religion and drive them out of their homes." Curiously, Muslims allow themselves the privilege of fighting when they believe their religion is attacked. The same privilege is not afforded to Christians in the *Common Word* document. It is clear that ultimately Muslims can arrogate to themselves the definition of what constitutes justice and right throughout the world, and enforce it with violence. So, too, in the Qur'anic verse with regard to the setting up each other as lords, this is a phrase that is one of the bases for the political thought of radical Islam.

The Qur'an

The basic problems that a Christian has with masquerading as a Muslim are located within the text of the Qur'an. It bears recalling and re-emphasizing again, the Qur'an **cannot** be dismissed as just another text; for Muslims it is the **very words of God.** Although it is perfectly true that one of the weaknesses of contemporary Islam globally, is that Muslims are profoundly ignorant of the Qur'an, and those that know it, usually do not actually read it with understanding, but recite it by rote. Nevertheless, it is impossible to get around the sense of authority the Qur'an conveys to Muslims or the fact that its message permeates every aspect of Islamic society consciously or unconsciously. It is a vast mistake to underestimate the power of the Qur'an within Islam, which is essentially what the insider movements are doing.

Fundamentally the issues with regard to the Qur'an can be grouped into three: one, the incompatibility of the Allah of the Qur'an with the God of the Bible; two, the incompatibility of the person and function of Jesus in the Qur'an and the Bible; and three, the rejection of the Bible as an authoritative and binding document in favor of the Qur'an. While there are other things that one can bring forth from the text of the Qur'an that are problematic for the Christian, the theological issues are the most important.

One needs to recognize that the Allah of the Qur'an is not the same as the God of the Bible. Although he is said to be "merciful and compassionate," what the Qur'anic text conveys is his vengefulness, his capriciousness and arbitrary judgments, and most of all his distance and inapproachability. Orders that are given are without reason. The best example is the order for the angels to bow down to the created Adam (Q2:74, 7:11, 18:50, 2:116). This directly contradicts all Islamic teaching, including the *Common Word* cited above. Allah of the Qur'an is an oriental despot, who must be placated because of his temper tantrums, inexplicable rages, and reason-defying commands. One would have to ask whether Allah is in fact a just god at all.

For the Christian, the person and role of Jesus that differs between the Bible and the Qur'an is the most obvious. Insider movements need to carefully think over their position. Jesus is lauded highly inside the Qur'an. He is said to be "a Word from him [God]" (Q3:45) and given superlative titles, such as the Messiah (*al-masih*) and others; however, his function is completely different and devoid of any salvific aspect. The doctrine of the crucifixion is specifically rejected in Q4:157:

> And their [the Jews'] saying: "We have killed the Messiah, Jesus, son of Mary and the apostle of Allah." They neither killed nor crucified him; but it was made to appear so unto them. Indeed, those who differ about him are in doubt about it. Their knowledge does not go beyond conjecture and they did kill him for certain.

How could this possibly be reconciled with 1 Corinthians 1:23 ("but we preach Christ crucified")? Even if one were to grant the possibility that the crucifixion was not literal—accomplished by denying substantial sections of the New Testament and almost the entirety of Christian theology—what then is the significance of Jesus' ministry? In the words of C. S. Lewis, he becomes another good man in the line of Socrates, Buddha or Gandhi. It is impossible to believe in the Jesus of the Qur'an and the Jesus of the Bible at the same time; their personalities are simply incompatible.

Indeed, the Qur'an does position Jesus to be just another figure in the line of prophets and messengers by stating in Q4:171:

> O People of the Book, do not exceed the bounds of your religion, nor say about Allah except the truth. The Messiah, Jesus, son of Mary, is only Allah's apostle and His Word, which He imparted to Mary, and is a spirit from him. So believe in Allah and His apostles, and do not say 'three' [gods]. Refrain, it is better for you. Allah is truly one God. How—glory be to him—could he have a son?

Although the terms that are given here for Jesus have a striking similarity to words of the Bible (cf. John 1:1), the content of Jesus' ministry is denuded of significance, and his relationship with God as a God-man bridge between the divine and humanity is rejected. It is difficult to see that there is anything left.

There is one function left for Jesus in order to make him stand out from other prophets: he must proclaim the coming of Muhammad. As it says in Q61: 6: "And when Jesus, son of Mary, said: O Children of Israel, I am Allah's messenger to you, confirming what came before me of the Torah, and announcing to you the news of a messenger who will come after me whose name is Ahmad [Muhammad]." No such proclamation can be found in the New Testament—other than the Muslim claim that John

14:16-17 and 15:26-7 is such an annunciation—so Muslims must make the bizarre claim that both Jews and Christians conspired together in order to change their Scriptures with the goal of deleting any references to Muhammad. This doctrine, known as *tahrif* or *tabdil*, quite aside from its historical improbability, effectively reduces the Bible to nothing but a paste-job stitched together by Jews and Christians, presumably during the few periods when the two groups were not murdering each other. Looking at this doctrine, it is easy to see the reasons why conspiracy theories have such prevalence in the Muslim world today. If one can accept the doctrine of *tahrif*, it is not difficult to believe the Jews control the world and other absurdities heard in *Dar al-Islam*.

The Bible promotes a different conception of humanity and its relationship with God than does the Qur'an. The Bible promotes a historical view of humanity, in which even the greatest prophets and apostles, are sinners. The Qur'an takes the opposite tack: each prophet is carefully denuded of his humanity and recreated as a perfect vessel for the reception of God-given knowledge. The Qur'anic perception of humanity is that knowledge only comes from God, and that people are unable to think for themselves. For instance, Adam, who in the biblical account names the animals out of his own accord (Gen 2:19), in the Qur'anic story receives the names from God (Q2:30). David composes the Psalms as praise to God (Ps 34:1-2), but the Qur'an says he received them from God (Q4:163). Many other examples could be adduced as well. All of this is in addition to the substantial historical mistakes contained within the text of the Qur'an, such as the idea that Jews have believed that Ezra was the son of God (Q9:30) or that the sun sets in a pool of muddy water (Q18:86). It is important to remember that Islamic society is autocratic, ahistorical, given to endless conspiracy theories, and a society in which personal agency is absent, is the direct result of the Qur'an's influence.

Islamic Dogma

The Muslim confession of faith, the *shahada*, recited by every Muslim as part of the five daily prayers, states, "There is no god but Allah and Muhammad is His Messenger." This confession of faith stands in direct contradiction to John 14:6, "Jesus said: I am the way and the truth and the life. No one comes to the Father except through me." The *shahada* presupposes the Gospels are incomplete and cannot be completed until the appearance of Muhammad.

It is impossible for a Christian to believe in the prophecy of Muhammad and remain a Christian. The type of messenger that is promoted by belief in Muhammad, again as with the type of God that is promoted by the text of the Qur'an, is fundamentally different from that of the Bible. Muhammad's early career does have some parallels with the manner in which a biblical prophet should act, but his later career is mostly characterized by jihad and violence. It is possible to draw some comparisons between the career of Muhammad and that of Joshua for example, but that type of conquering, dominating biblical figure is clearly superseded by the message of Jesus, who preached love and compassion.

This function of the aggressive spread of Islam inherent in the first conquests (AD 634-730), then later through the Ottoman period, and with accompanying jihads in Africa and India, these conquests are exemplified by the following tradition ascribed to Muhammad:

> I was sent with a sword so that they would worship Allah alone, who has no partner, and my daily sustenance was placed beneath the shadow of my spear—humiliation and contempt were placed upon those oppose me, and whoever likens himself to a group becomes one of them.[3]

This is an important methodological statement that affirms the importance that power and domination play within the spread of Islam, even in cases not carried out by actual military violence. The final phrase, "whoever becomes like to another group becomes one of them," should be carefully considered by the insider movements, as such a likening is precisely what they mean to accomplish. One should also consider the fact that a high percentage of contemporary Muslims are in fact descended from groups that were historically Christian and were persecuted to the point of conversion.

The figure of Muhammad is normative for all Muslims, whether Sunni or Shi`i. Consider this creedal statement of al-Tahawi, who states:

> [We assert] that Muhammad is his chosen servant, his selected prophet, his approved messenger, the seal of the prophets, the imam of the pious, the beloved of the Lord of Worlds . . . He is the one sent to the generality of the jinn and the entirety of humankind, the one sent with truth and guidance, with light and radiance."[4]

Since it is a major doctrine in Islam to believe that Muhammad is the Seal of the Prophets (cf. Q33:30), it is impossible to avoid the emphasis placed upon the figure of Muhammad within Islam. This is the statement inside al-Bukhari affirming this doctrine:

> I was given five qualities not given to anyone previous to me. I was aided by a terror at the distance of a month's journey, the earth was made for me to be a worshipping ground in its purity . . . spoils were permitted to me that were not permitted to anyone previous to me, I

---

[3] Ahmad b. Hanbal, *Musnad*, ii: 50, 92.
[4] W. Montgomery Watt (trans.) (1914). *Islamic Creeds* (419, no.4). Edinburgh: Edinburgh Press.

was given intercession, and while other prophets were sent to their peoples specifically I was sent to all people generally.[5]

There is no room within this statement—and the many others like it—for the Gospel of Jesus. It specifically stands in opposition to the Great Commission (Mt 28:16-20).

As IM would be hypothetically masquerading within Muslim cultures as Muslims, it is reasonable to ask: how do you intend to deal with the figure of Muhammad? The values promoted by the constant adulation of Muhammad in Muslim society are fundamentally different from those that are promoted by the Gospels, and yet you believe that somehow you will be insulated from these Islamic values, and instead be able to gradually change the discourse into one that is Christian in content, if not in form? Does it not seem much more likely that you yourselves will be transformed by the constant pressure and need to conform from the Islamic society all around you?

While one can legitimately say that Islam, especially in its Sunni form, is not a credally based religion and that many Muslims remain ignorant of the fundamentals of their faith, it equally true that these fundamentals are taught through example—*the way of the Prophet*, based upon the *usawa al-hasana* of Q33:4—and by adducing the manner in which Muhammad acted in a given situation or by citation of a tradition associated with him. These teachings are the methods by which Islam, in the broadest sense, is propagated. Islam does not rely for conversions merely upon broad, flashy people movements, but subtle, slow social transformations, in which both the person and the broader society are effectively Muslim almost before their actual conversion.

Issues between Christians and Muslims

Traditionally Islam's relationship towards Christianity has been characterized by supercessionism and a sense of triumphalism: "It is He who sent his apostle with the guidance and the true religion in order to make it triumph over every religion, even if the polytheists should resent it" (Q9:33). It should be remembered that Muslims define Christians, because of the doctrine of the Trinity, as polytheists, associating with Christians and Christianity the Qur'anic language originally addressed to the polytheists of the Arabian Peninsula. These facts have led to the establishment of a system of discrimination, designed to demonstrate from an outward perspective, that Islam is triumphant and dominant inside the society in which it is located. Non-believers have historically primarily meant Jews and Christians, but additionally Hindus, and today Bahais and Ahmadis. Non-believers must be tolerated, but humiliated.

For this purpose, Q9:29 ("Fight those among the People of the Book

---

[5] Sahih Al-Bukhari, i, p. 100 (no. 335).

who do not believe in Allah and the Last Day, do not forbid what Allah and His Apostle have forbidden, till they pay the poll-tax out of hand and submissively") is significant. While the traditional payment of the poll-tax or *jizya* has lapsed in all but radical Muslim countries, Christians are subject to second-class status in the Muslim world. The apostasy laws are still in effect, if not always actually on the books as they are in Iran, Libya, Algeria and other countries. They are practiced on a popular level with the authorities turning their backs, as in Pakistan, Afghanistan and Nigeria. Even Christians who are recognized by the state as legitimate, including the Copts of Egypt and other Christians of the Middle East, have found that *de facto* the discriminatory laws concerning apostasy and the building of new churches are still in effect. Again, this is a triumphalistic issue: Muslims can build new mosques because according to Islamic doctrine Islam is the future, but Christians must suffice with decrepit old buildings because Christianity is the past. It is important on a systematic level for Christians and Christianity to be humiliated and insulted while Islam is exalted and magnified.

It is easy to see the danger this presents for a missionary group such as the insider movements. Forced at every point to conceal what they truly believe all around them the society will be beckoning their converts to return to normative Islam. While it is important for the Christian believer not to be seduced by the temptations of this world, when he himself is living a lie, as the insider movements promote, it is difficult to know where and how one would draw the boundaries between lying to save one's skin (*taqiyya*) and merely lying for the sake of lying.

Today Muslims claim that they have freedom of religion, and indeed the *Common Word* document proclaims this. But the verse they cite in evidence for this, Q2:256 ("There is no compulsion in religion"), does not actually promise true freedom of religion. Islam demands from non-believers on a practical level, conformity with its norms—while simultaneously not allowing for such conformity when it is in the minority, as in Europe, or reciprocating any of the benefits conferred upon it by non-Muslims. For example, just recently two Algerian Christians were put on trial for eating, even discreetly, during the Muslim fasting month of Ramadan.[6] It is this type of situation that raises questions about whether there can ever be any religious freedom in a Muslim society of the type that would be meaningful to non-Muslims, and whether it is a good idea for Christians to participate willingly in such a repressive and dominating religion while gaining converts.

Importance of the issue from a historical point of view

So, in short the answer to the question of whether Christians can be Muslims is yes, they can be Muslims. They can just become Muslims. Both

---

[6] http://www.alarabiya.net/articles/2010/09/21/119915.html (accessed 7/3/11).

from a theological point of view and from a historical point of view, it is clear that Christians who sought to blur the lines between Christianity and Islam have only gone in one direction: they became actual Muslims. Perhaps that is because of the complete domination on the part of Islam of its own societies that Christians who have taken this route have been lured time and time again into the fallacy that they can extricate themselves or co-exist with the compromises they have to make in order to *live* as Muslims. In actuality, they cannot.

It is, of course, historically true that Christians during the first centuries of Islam, as were Jews, were able at certain times to recite the first part of the *shahada*—There is no god but Allah—as a confession of monotheistic belief. However, it is worth noting these people and their descendents **eventually became Muslims.** Because Islam is not merely a religion, but an entire civilization that controls the social and cultural patterns of the people within it, eventually it will come to dominate all of those who remain under its domination. Muslims historically have taken a much longer view of ultimate conversion than have Christians, realizing that over the period of centuries people will gradually enter Islam. Due to the laws against apostasy and the social norms that Islam dictates, those who are at first reluctant converts will eventually—either personally or through their descendents—become true Muslims. As it is not possible for even marginal Muslims who might otherwise be converted to Christianity to leave Islam, eventually Islam comes to dominate a given area. All of this happens because Christians systematically refuse to see the dangers inherent in Islam, instead seeing an attractive spiritual alternative.

It is clear to me that the insider movements are playing into this historical pattern of slow conversion to Islam, and by allowing its missionaries to masquerade as Muslims, for its new Christians to continue to pose as Muslims (while believing in Jesus), this movement will merely facilitate the growth of global Islam. Subscription to the *Common Word* document is merely the first step in this process. Insider movements make such theological penetration by Islam of Christianity into a formal reality, but subverting its missionaries into a false and dangerously ecumenical paradigm.

Study of Islam from a scholarly point of view, as well as from a Christian point of view, leads one to see that Islam is a strong contender for humanity's spiritual attention. Islam has the capacity to subvert even committed Christians to its core tenets. Islam cannot exist as a belief system in tandem with Christianity if either faith is taken seriously. Usually the default position, if there is some type of ecumenism, is that of Islam, not that of Christianity. The Bible and the Qur'an are two fundamentally different documents and in many of their core teachings cannot be reconciled, despite the fact that both Christianity and Islam are monotheisms and hearken back to the biblical tradition. The personality of Muhammad is central to Islam in all of its variants and cannot be reconciled with core Christian teachings. It is, therefore, my conclusion that it is extremely dangerous and unwise for groups of Christians to pretend to be Muslims in order to gain converts to Christianity, as well as being dishonest towards both faiths.

6.3 A Word to Secret Believers[1]

Samuel Zwemer

The great apostle to Islam was keenly aware of the issues facing the mission to Muslims displayed by the IM of today. He speaks prophetically, passionately, yet compassionately to those who would compromise the proclamation of the Gospel. He calls us to the courage of our convictions, the honor of the Gospel, and to a life of sacrificial service [eds.].

There are secret believers in Jesus Christ who never are bold enough to confess Him before men. There are Nicodemus disciples who come to see Jesus by night because they are afraid of men. There is a belief that never comes to utterance. Faith in the heart, but lips that are silent. Love for the truth but it always stops short of confession. Opinions that are the result of investigation but do not crystallize into deep convictions. Light but no fire. There is a kind of easy approval of Christ's teaching and an admiration of His life, which never registers itself in confession. It is like a hothouse plant grown up in sheltered seclusion and unable to stand the winds and cold of publicity. Such a plant is never strong but always artificial and tender because it needs more air and more ventilation and deeper root. Christians who try to be so secretly are always anemic. They remain puny and never get beyond spiritual babyhood. Belief which is never oxygenated by open confession can never produce vigorous and exhilarating life.

Christ came that we might have life abundant and redundant. The confession of our faith starts its fountain of influence and power. "With the mouth confession is made into salvation". A Kafir, that is, one who covers the truth, becomes a Moslem by confessing the short creed of two words. So it was in the early days of Islam. These two short words expressed faith, conviction, desire to join the company of believers at any cost. So Abu Bakr, Omar and the rest became Moslems. It was the same in the early days of Christianity; only the conditions were far more difficult. Matthew heard the call and forsook all to follow Christ. Peter confessed that Christ was the Son of the Living God and this confession became as it were the bedrock of his apostleship and ministry. Saul, the persecutor, boldly confessed Christ in Damascus and in Jerusalem where men knew him. He did not try to escape to some place where no one knew his antecedents. It was Paul himself who afterwards wrote to the Christians in the great pagan capital, Rome:

If thou shalt confess with thy mouth Jesus as Lord and shalt believe in

---

[1] Originally published in *Orient & Occident* 23(10): 313-6.

thine heart that God raised him from the dead thou shalt he be saved. For with the heart man believeth unto righteousness and with the mouth confession is made unto salvation.

Such confession is the one means to moral health, the one condition of spiritual growth. Confession in the early days of Christianity meant risk, a venture which exposed the life, even to the shedding of blood. It meant a frank defiance of the world and an eager challenge of the devil. It gave the soul the joy of a great decision. It was like the conduct of soldiers who burn their bridges behind them and leave no way open for retreat.

Such decisions are muscle for the soul, strength for the will, joy for the emotions and peace to the heart. Those who confess Christ before men go from strength to strength and from glory to glory. Those who are timid and draw back, go from weakness to weakness nay often from being ashamed to shame.

My brother, art thou secretly ashamed of that which thou knowest to be the purest and truest and strongest fact of human history-Jesus Christ? Art thou afraid of man's opinion and man's judgment when in the secret chambers of thy soul thou hast found Christ all and man nothing? Why art thou driven about and tossed by every wind of public favor like the weather vane? Hast thou not found, tell me, the true Pole Star of joy and hope in One whom thou dost secretly love but art afraid to confess before men? Then let the magnet of thy soul turn always and instantly to Him so wilt thou be a guide to all who are perplexed.

How long halt you between two opinions? If Islam is the final religion and the hope of humanity then follow Islam—all its teachings, all its requirements to the letter. Have the courage of your convictions. But if Christ, then Christ, with all your heart, with your lips, with your life.

The Arab proverb says that the hand cannot hold two watermelons. The heart cannot hold two religions. Jesus showed His knowledge of human nature when He challenged His disciples to forsake all, to endure hardship, carry their cross, brave it out at all costs. The man whom Jesus despised above all others and consigned to the outermost darkness was the man who said, "I was afraid." He buried his talent and his life in a napkin because he was a coward.

Over the gates of heaven it is written that not only "the unbelieving and abominable and murderers and liars" but first of all that "the fearful," that is, the timid, may not enter (Rev 21:8).

Why are men ashamed of Jesus and of his teaching? There are many in Egypt who tell us that they accept Jesus Christ as their Savior but hesitate to confess Him. I have met them even in the Azhar [the most famous Sunni theological institution located in Cairo].

Religious liberty is a plant that best grows when watered with blood. The martyrs for the faith were also the pioneers of the Kingdom. No battle was ever won by secret soldiers. Moral courage is not obtained by majority votes or by parliament sanctions. Moral freedom is the gift of God. As long as we are afraid to express openly our deepest convictions on any subject we are slaves to ourselves in that realm of thought. To be ashamed of the truth is to linger in the dungeon of error.

To know the truth is to grasp the key; to confess it turns the lock and sets us free forever.

Jesus I my cross have taken
All to leave and follow Thee
Destitute, despised, forsaken,
Thou from hence my all shalt be.

Perish every fond ambition,
All I've sought, and hoped, and known;
Yet how rich is my condition!
God and heaven are still my own.

Let the world despise and leave me,
They have left my Savior too;
Human hearts and looks deceive me;
Thou art not, like man untrue.

Appendixes

Appendix 1. A letter to Lausanne Leadership

The influence and preponderance of insider movements' voices in the global Evangelical community is growing. It is not an insignificant blip on missions' radar screen; it is real, has weight, and is persuasively making its case as the major paradigm for the Church to reach Muslims. [eds.]

September 20, 2010
Dear Program Directors of the Lausanne Congress,

Greetings to all of you in the name of Christ! We want to sincerely thank all of you for your vision and leadership of this truly global congress on world evangelization.

We are writing this letter as a group of Muslim background believers with certain concerns that have developed among us over the course of the conference. After a meeting today with each other with the gracious presence of Rev. Henri Aoun, we have decided to express our concerns to you for your prayerful consideration.

We believe that there is a large number of believers and especially MBBs in this conference who are very uncomfortable with the "Insider Movement" and the "C5" methodology of Muslim evangelism, but they are not given venues for an honest, open, respectful and authentic discussion of these important issues.

Many of us MBBs feel hurt and betrayed by the lack of freedom that we have sensed in various contexts of this congress to express our views or to report adequately about our experiences of ministry among our own Muslim people groups. We feel that our voices are not heard.

We feel that much of the discussions about the Middle East and North Africa are dictated by a limited group of Middle Eastern church leaders who speak from a very particular and different context than other countries and ministries in those regions. Thus the agendas and the messages about this region do not reflect the wide and complex realities of the whole region.

We believe that much of the intellectual support and zeal for the promotion of the "Insider Movements" among evangelicals, are coming from the West or at least Eastern non-MBBs who are mostly speaking from an outsider perspective about an "Insider Movement."

We truly hope that in the future, MBBs who are passionate about and active in the robust evangelism of Muslims can feel welcomed and celebrated by the leadership of the Lausanne Movement.
Your co-laborers in Christ,

A Group of Muslim Background Participants at Cape Town, 2010

Appendix 2. My experience with *Common Ground*:

Hilki Berisha[1]

Having a Muslim background, it was quite impressive to me [the] first time I encountered the *Common Ground* approach. It was so attractive, very different from the usual Christian perspective on reaching Muslims. I felt like I really had a new enlightenment. I started calling myself [a] follower of Jesus instead of Christian and considered even attending a mosque once again. But that was very difficult since I was already known as [a] convert from Islam to Christianity and by going back to mosque I feared they would think I renounced my new Christian faith. I changed my personal Christian terminology while sharing with Muslims and started using qur'anic verses pointing to Jesus as bridge to his true identity and salvation from the Bible.

On few occasions that worked out, but in most of the cases people would ask me to use my terminology as a Christian because it seemed to them I was trying to deceive them. People I was talking to were asking me not to use verses from Quran so as not to distort its original meanings. It was like I was trying to teach them what Quran taught and that was not [an] honest thing to do at all. I had some other big problems too. Every time I would ask what the *Common Ground* movement thought about Muhammad and Quran, I never had a clear answer. Was Muhammad a true or a false prophet? What was [the] Quran considered to be? The Holy Spirit will confirm [it to] you, they say! I have never seen within this movement a clear division between the truth and falsehood, between darkness and light. Muhammad is considered a pre-evangelistic tool to bring people to Christ, but I never them say he was a false prophet.

One time I saw a Christian fasting during the Ramadan month. I knew he was taught the *Common Ground* approach. I asked him what his motive

---

[1] The author is a Christian from a Muslim background from Kosova. He came to Christ in 1998 after Jesus appeared to him in a vision. Read his full testimony online: http://answering-islam.org/testimonies/ibrahim_kosovo.html.

Since he came to Christ, Hilki has been interested in reaching Muslims. He has read extensively on Islam. God has made it possible for him to start and manage the Albanian section of the Answering Islam website. God has used the site in the last two years to bring the Gospel to thousands of Albanian Muslims. Now an average of 100 visit the site each day. It is perhaps the only webpage in Albanian language that deals with Islam. It is reaching out to Albanians in Kosova, Albania and around the world. In addition to his work with Answering Islam, Hilki is deeply involved with his local church, serving as a member of the church's council. God has been speaking to him lately about possible missionary work in Turkey. He just graduated in dentistry, and with his wife and son, is planning to take up a residency program in Turkey, one of the largest unreached countries in the Middle East. [The editors have taken the liberty to edit the article for the sake of clarity.]

behind the fasting was. I assumed he was going to respond that he was fasting due to his Muslims friends. But that wasn't the case. I got a troubled understanding from him: he was fasting for his own sake and not just for Muslims. The fasting during the Ramadan month was a good opportunity for him to grow spiritually. I sensed he was so confused and somehow he was trying to perform duties of both religions. Biblical fasting is supposed to be a very personal practice and not publicly professing to anyone. Obviously, not forsaking Islam brings confusion as to where do our hearts stand. Do we truly believe that Jesus is the only way, truth and the life or there is still some room and fondness in our hearts for Mohammad, too?

My father is a practicing Muslim and I met him once with a *Common Ground* missionary believing they could talk to him and share the truth from the Gospel. He asked my father [about] the Quran and [then the missionary] started explaining the verses from the Quran in relation to Jesus Christ. My father was honestly stating that he would have to confirm that [the new interpretation of the Qur'an] with his Imam. They discussed for hours and at the end my father accepted [the missionary] even praying for him. I was astonished that finally there was someone to talk to my father about Jesus Christ. He agreed that he was going to read the Bible.

But the situation turned the opposite after he consulted with Imam. He told him that nothing of what he heard from the Christian missionary was true and that it was only a way to change his mind. My father got so upset and told me he was even worse than the other Christians who honestly share their Christian faith from their biblical perspective. He [the missionary] is more dangerous he said, and as a result he never read the Bible. I felt so bad after this incident because instead of helping my father, I made the situation worse.

After some years in closeness with the *Common Ground*, I still had a lot of unresolved questions within myself! Should MBBs continue to attend mosque; would that be helpful for them? If so, what happens after the Islamic congregation understands there are some different Muslims in their congregation? Will they tolerate, expel or persecute them? Where will they get their true spiritual nourishment? Perhaps they will meet in home groups in addition to attending mosque, but for how long will that situation last? What about Church planting, since they are supposed to stay within the Islamic culture and religion? Will it be established at some point [by] the Christian community or [is] such a thing not necessary? What about their identity—is it Christian with Christians and Muslims with Muslims? Who are going to be their true brothers and sisters, Muslims or Christians or both of them?

I personally believe today there is a compromise of biblical truth within this approach. Bringing Muslims to the point of accepting Jesus as being crucified and risen without leaving and forsaking Islam is definitely not a biblical thing. Mohammed is a prophet, but definitely a false one. While we should be committed to loving Muslims, we should expose the false teachings of Islam. Mohammed openly rejected Jesus' divinity and distorted biblical truth, and as such he cannot carry the true message. If there are confusions regarding these truths, then one did not come to understand God's only way of salvation as found in the Bible. The confusion will inevitably come into lives of these believers and at some point they will no longer know who their true Master is!

Appendix 3. Questions for *Common Ground* leadership

This is a list of the questions is from Jay Smith who asks, "Will they be answered?"

Does not the true family of Christ take precedence over our biological family?

Are we not challenged by Matthew 5:15 to confront the darkness within our biological Muslim family, rather than to acquiesce to it?

When we do challenge, should we not expect and even welcome the resulting persecution that has emboldened the Church for the last 2000 years?

Should we expect new believers to be the best agents for reaching out to their families, especially while they are such babes in Christ and therefore the most vulnerable to Islam's pernicious spiritual power and control?

In giving undue credit to the Qur'an, will we not find it difficult to move away from its authority?

Considering the many ways the Qur'an has borrowed from other religions, should we assume it is nearly equivalent to our own Scriptures?

What advantage is gained by MCTs that do injustice to authorial intent, giving rise to the accusation that we change the Bible?

If we remove 'God as father' and the 'sonship of Jesus Christ' from the Bible, how do we explain the unique modeling of fatherhood and sonship we now enjoy within the Christian family?

In their attempt to include the sons of Ishmael within a covenant uniquely reserved for the sons of Isaac, do not IMers eisegete certain Scriptures, torturing the text and leading to greater problems?

Please reconsider the exegesis of your scriptural basis for staying like (1 Cor 7:17-24). Do not so many other Scriptures refute the IM agenda?

If we ask the believers to remain in Islam, yet choosing not to do likewise, does that not create confusion for both new believers and the larger Muslim community?

How can we suggest that Muhammad is a legitimate prophet when his example diametrically contradicts the examples of the biblical prophets and Jesus?

Since Muhammad does not fulfill the four criteria of prophethood stipulated in the Old Testament, how can we accept him as one?

How, for the sake of our Muslim brother's sensibilities, can we so easily jettison 2000 years of questioning, debating, and coming to conclusions on how best to live out the Gospel of Jesus Christ, and then quickly and simplistically replace Christian forms with Muslim forms that not only contradict these traditions, but in some cases stand in direct opposition to the Gospel message?

If we believe that Christian forms are examples of later Western cultural accretions, is it wise to simply adopt equally later cultural Muslim accretions as adequate substitutes?

Is it right for those of us in the West to dismiss the intrinsic spiritual power of Muslim forms knowing that our BMB brothers warn us of the spiritual power behind these forms?

In our haste to adapt Muslim forms, might we be neglecting better and more dynamically acceptable Christian cultural forms that already exist in those cultures?

Should we be so cynical to suggest that traditional Islam and traditional Christianity are equally inadequate representations of the kingdom of God?

Where are the models of this kingdom of God of which the *CG* and IM proponents propose: Minneapolis, Atlanta, or the Southeast Asian Jam'at?

When jettisoning water baptism and other Christian institutions for the sake of slowing possible hostile Muslim response, do the *CG* and IM proponents have biblically acceptable alternatives with which to replace them?

How is a simple reference to Jesus as Lord and Savior sufficient for identification as a Christian? Since both terms are easily applied to the prophets of Islam. What is the clear IM equivalent?

Why should we fear the public rejection of one set of beliefs for that of another (i.e., conversion) if indeed the other belief turns out to be the better and more biblically truthful?

Should we spend our energies and finances creating a sect within Islam that remains under its control (i.e., Chrislam), or should we spend our time bringing Muslim friends into the worldwide family of Christian believers?

Since fear of Islam is so widespread within the Church, could this not also be a motivation for IM proponents keeping the new believer within their Muslim environment?

If we fear persecution, how much more should we fear the future persecution by Muslim leaders once they discover we have adapted sacred Muslim identity codes (i.e., Muslim forms) for our own purposes?

Is the IM paradigm nothing more than an act of deceit (taqiyya)?

Selected Bibliography: Advocates of Insider Movements

Accad, Fouad Elias (1997). *Building Bridges: Christianity and Islam.* Colorado Springs, CO: NavPress.

[Accad's book is not thoroughly IM, but it does provide some impetus for basic premises held by proponents and advocates of IM.]

Brown, Rick. "'The Son of God': Understanding the Messianic Titles of Jesus." *IJFM* 17(1): http://www.ijfm.org/PDFs_IJFM/17_1_PDFs/Son_of_God.pdf

_____. "What Must One Believe about Jesus for Salvation?" *IJFM* 17(4): http://www.ijfm.org/PDFs_IJFM/17_4_PDFs/02_Brown_Beliefs_hw.pdf

_____. "Presenting the Deity of Christ from the Bible" *IJFM* 19(1): 20-7.

_____. "Explaining the Biblical Term 'Son(s) of God' in Muslim Contexts." *IJFM* 22(3): 91-6.

_____. "Translating the Biblical Term 'Son(s) of God' in Muslim Contexts." *IJFM* 22(4): 135-45.

_____. "Brother Jacob and Master Isaac: How One Insider Movement Began." *IJFM* 24(1): 41-2.

_____. "Biblical Muslims." *IJFM* 24(2): 65-74.

_____. "Why Muslims Are Repelled by the Term Son of God." *EMQ* 43(4): 422-9.

Brown, Rick, John Penny and Leith Gray. "Muslim-Idiom Bible Translation: Claims and Facts." *SFM* 5(6): 87-105.

Caldwell, Stuart. "Jesus in Samaria: a Paradigm for Church Planting Among Muslims." *IJFM* 17(1): http://www.ijfm.org/PDFs_IJFM/17_1_PDFs/Jesus_in_Samaria.pdf

Chandler, Paul-Gordon. "Resurrecting the Middle Eastern Christ." *IJFM* 25(3): 143-50.

Culver, Jonathan. "The Ishmael Promise and Contextualization Among Muslims" *IJFM* 17(1): 61-70.

Decker, Frank. "When Christian Does Not Translate." *MF* (September-October 2005): 8.

Dutch, Bernard. "Should Muslims Become Christians?" *IJFM* 17(1): http://www.ijfm.org/PDFs_IJFM/17_1_PDFs/Muslims_as_Christians.pdf

Greeson, Kevin (2007). *The Camel: How Muslims are Coming to Christ*. Arkadelphia, AR: WIGTake Resources.

Harling, Mack. "De-Westernizing Doctrine and Developing Appropriate Theology in Mission." *IJFM* 22(4):159-166.

Higgins, Kevin. "The Key to Insider Movements: The 'Devoteds' in Acts." *IJFM* 21(4): 155-65.

_____. "Acts 15 and Insider Movements Among Muslims: Questions, Process, and Conclusions." *IJFM* 24(1): 29-39.

_____. "Identity, Integrity and Insider Movements: A Brief Paper Inspired by Timothy Tennent's Critique of C-5 Thinking." *IJFM* 23(3): 117-23.

_____. "Inside What? Church, Culture, Religion, and Culture in Biblical Perspective." *SFM* 5(4): 74-91.

_____. "Beyond Christianity." *MF* (July-August 2010): 12-13.

_____. "Muhammad, Islam, and the Qur'an." n.d. (Internet only).

Jameson, Richard and Nick Scalevich. "First Century Jews and Twentieth Century Muslims." *IJFM* 17(1): http://www.ijfm.org/PDFs_IJFM/17_1_PDFs/Jews_and_Muslims.pdf

Kim, John. "The Anotoc Story Continued, the Role of Group Dynamics in Insider Movements." *IJFM* 27(2): 97-104.

Kraft, Charles H. (1996). *Anthropology for Christian Witness*. NY: Orbis.

_____ (Ed.). *Appropriate Christianity*. Pasadena, CA: William Carey Library.
[While the book is not an IM piece, Kraft is one of the early architects of IM methodologies based on his views of culture and dynamic equivlancies.]

Lewis, Rebecca. "Sharing the Gospel through Open Networks." *MF* (January-February 2006): 22-3.

_____. "Promoting Movements to Christ within Natural Communities." *IJFM* 24(2): 75-6.

_____. "Insider Movements: Honoring God-Given Identity and Community." *IJFM* 26(1): 16-19.

_____. "Integrity of the Gospel and Insider Movements." *IJFM* 27(1): 41-8.

Mallouhi, Mazhar. "Comments on the Insider Movement." *SFM* 5(5): 3-14.

Massey, Joshua. "Planting the Church Underground in Muslim Contexts." *IJFM* 13(3): 139-53.

_____. "God's Amazing Diversity in Drawing Muslims to Christ." *IJFM* 17(1): http://www.ijfm.org/PDFs_IJFM/17_1_PDFs/Drawing_Muslims.pdf

_____. "Part I: Living Like Jesus, a Torah-Observant Jew: Delighting in God's Law for Incarnational Witness to Muslims." *IJFM* 41(1): 13-22.

_____. "Part II: Living Like Jesus, a Torah-Observant Jew: Delighting in God's Law for Incarnational Witness to Muslims." *IJFM* 41(2): 55-71.

_____. "Misunderstanding C5: His Ways Are Not Our Orthodoxy." *EMQ* 40(3): 296-304.

Medearis, Carl (2008). *Muslims, Christians, and Jesus: Gaining Understanding and Building Relationships.* Minneapolis, MN: Bethany House.

_____. *Speaking of Jesus: the art of not-evangelism* (2011). Colorado Springs, CO: David C. Cook.

Petersen, Brian K. "Foreigners, Pharisees and Foreskins: The Controversy Over Changing 'Community Identity' in the Book of Acts." *IJFM* 24:2 (web only): 21pp.

_____. "The Possibility of a 'Hindu Christ-Follower:' Hans Staffner Proposal for the Dual Identity of Disciples of Christ within High Caste Hindu Communities." *IJFM* 24(2): 87-97.

Ridgway, John. "Insider Movements in the Gospels and Acts." *IJFM* 2492): 77-88.

Talman, Harley. "Comprehensive Contextualization." *IJFM* 21(1): 6-12.

Timmons, Tim. "Christianity Isn't the Way – Jesus Is." *IJFM* 23(5): 157-60.

Travis, John. "The C1 to C6 Spectrum." *EMQ* 34(4): 407-8.

_____. "Messianic Muslim Followers of *Isa*: A Closer Look at C5 Believers and Congregations." *IJFM* 17.1 (Spring 2000): http://www.ijfm.org/PDFs_IJFM/17_1_PDFs/Followers_of_Isa.pdf

_____. "Must All Muslims Leave 'Islam' to Follow Jesus?" *EMQ* 34(4): 411-15.

_____. "Producing and Using Meaningful Translations of the Taurat, Zabur and *Injil*." *IJFM* 23(2): 73-7.

Travis, John and Anna (2005). "Appropriate Approaches in Muslim Contexts" (394-414). In Charles H. Kraft (Ed.). *Appropriate Christianity*. Pasadena, CA: William Carey Library.

_____. "Contextualization Among Muslims, Hindus, and Buddhists: A Focus on Insider Movements." *MF* (September-October 2005): 12-15.

_____. "Maximizing the Bible!: Glimpses From Our Context." *MF* January-February 2006: 22.

Travis, John and J. Dudley Woodberry. "When God's Kingdom Grows Like Yeast: Frequently Asked Questions About Jesus Movements Within Muslim Communities." *MF* (July-August 2010): 24-30.

Wiarda, Timothy. "The Jerusalem Council and the Theological Task." *JETS* 46.2 (June 2003): 233-48.

Winship, Jamie. "From Bandung to Baghdad: A Journey to the Inside." *IJFM* 25(4): 193-8.

Winter, Ralph. "Editorial comment." *MF* September-October 2005:5.

Woodberry, J. Dudley. "Contextualization Among Muslims: Reusing Common Pillars." *IJFM* 13(4): 171-186.

_____. "To the Muslim I Became a Muslim?" *IJFM* 24(1): 23-8.

IM Websites and Blogs

Blue Passport
Operated by R.G. Lewis, he offers mostly cross-cultural advice and teaching, though he dabbles in writing about IM.
http://bluepassport.blogspot.com/2005/09/insider-movements.html

Carl Medearis
Very well done website with good resources for those interested in Medearis and the IM approach.
www.carlmedearis.com

Common Ground
"Building Bridges of Trust that Bear the Weight of Truth"
www.comgro.org

Common Path Alliance
Operated by Congressional District Programs, this is an organization initiating peace dialogues between Christians and Muslims. "The Common Path Alliance seeks to continue building bridges of unity based on our common belief in loving God and loving our neighbor."
http://commonpathalliance.org/

A Common Word
Not specifically an IM site, nevertheless the sentiment is present in this Muslim attempt (aided by Christian dhimmitude) to Islamicize Christianity and Jesus: "...despite their differences, Islam and Christianity not only share the same Divine Origin and the same Abrahamic heritage, but the same two *greatest commandments*."
www.acommonword.com

Global Teams
This small international mission is decidedly IM. Their homepage appears to redefine insider movements as God moving in a culture, people, clan or tribe and "as new communities of believers are formed and new disciples are made, they too seek to live like 'the Word made flesh' and 'live among' the people -their people - and cultures as light and salt and yeast." *GT*'s International Director is Kevin Higgins.
www.global-teams.net

Insiders
This is a Korean mission organization fully ensconced within the IM family. At the bottom of the site you will notice two interesting comments in English from Mark Harlan (Christar, USCWF, ISFM, professor) and Kevin

Higgins (Global Teams).
>   http://www.insiders.or.kr/bbs/view.php?id=mnotice&no=19
>   Home page: http://www.insiders.or.kr

Jesus in the Qur'an
Headed by Jamie Winship and housed by Grace Fellowship in Atlanta, GA, *JIQ* is "an entirely new paradigm and, in other ways, an ancient one dating back to the days of Jesus." The site is filled with resources for those interested in IM, though interestingly the term is never used on their website.
>   www.jesusinthequran.org

Al Kalima
"Al Kalima publishes and distributes books which help Muslims understand Christ, to build bridges of understanding between Muslims and Christians." This is Mazhar Mallouhi's business website. The translation project with which he is associated is discussed.
>   http://www.al-kalima.com/index.html

Messianic Muslims
A very simple site, but one that encourages Muslims to follow Jesus yet remain Muslims. In their "7 Principles" they cite equally from the Tawrat, Zabur, *Injil*, and Qur'an to make their plea for Muslims to follow Jesus. "The testimony of all the holy writings [this includes the Qur'an]…" leads to Jesus. The site gives the Qur'an's teachings about itself, the Bible and Christ.
>   http://Messianicmuslims.com/

Messianic Muslims – Facebook
This seems to be a lone ranger operated site with few posts or interactions. Read the info page to see what it is about, disregarding the misspellings.
>   http://www.facebook.com/pages/Messianic-Muslims/131212510234104

Missiological Blogger
Adam Hoffman operates this blog that offers links to many of the IM articles mentioned in the bibliography. It seems more neutral than IM or Historical in presentation.
>   http://adamhoffman.wordpress.com/tag/insider-movement

The Navigators U.S. Metro Ministries – Detroit
John Ridgway writes an article on IM housed at this site. It seems to be the only IM article at the site.

>   http://navigatorsdetroit.com/Paper%207%20-%20Essential

Northern Thai Missions
The goal of this mission is to see every northern Thai city, town and village be engaged with a church planting effort. Seems to have been started by two South Africans, Gerhard Groenewald and Rynier Kruger, both one-time members of YWAM.
    http://thaimissions.com/thai-insider-movement

TOAG
Training Ordinary Apprentices to Go offers a ten-month program of insider movements' theology and methodology, feeding many of its graduates into Frontiers. Nathan D'Jiim (pseudonym) is the director.
    http://toag.net/

The People of the Book
This website is run by one of the Navigators' personnel, but it not officially affiliated with the organization. From home page, go to STRATEGY for rationale and support for IM.
    http://www.ThePeopleOfTheBook.org

Perspectives
The content of the Perspectives classes leans to IM; however, there is nothing on the website that indicates this.
    http://www.perspectives.org

Sabeel Media
Christian Arabic language materials, but purveyors of *The Stories of the Prophets* and operated by Wycliffe.
    http://www.sabeelmedia.com/ar/node/392

Ummah al Masih
"As Believing Muslims in *Isa* Al–Masih (Jesus the Messiah), we join the great Ummah or nation of Muslims in reciting a creed, though, as Muslims who have experienced Allah´s mercy firsthand, through Al–Masih, our creed goes beyond the traditional submission to Allah´s sovereignty. Our realization that true Islam, such as was foreseen by the Sayyidna Ibrahim and the Prophets must include an expression of the Compassion and Mercy of our Lord."
    http://www.ummahalmasih.com/index.php?option=com_content&task=view&id=39&Itemid=58

YWAM CP Coaches

This YWAM affiliated site lists as one of its three lead articles Rebecca Lewis's "Honoring God-Given Identity and Community." No comments are made about it, but the presence of the article without critique implies acceptance.

    http://www.duncanmultimedia.com/~cpcoaches

Also *YWAM among Hindus*
    http://www.hindustudy.com/about-us

Selected Bibliography: Historical Perspective

Carson, D.A. "The Emerging Church." *Modern Reformation Magazine* 14:4 (July-August 2005): http://www.modernreformation.org/default.php?page=articledispl ay&var1=ArtRead&var2=128&var3=authorbio&var4=AutRes&va r5=238.

Coleman, M. and P. Verster. "Contextualisation of the Gospel among Muslims." *Acta Theologica* 2006(2): 94-115.
http://www.stfrancismagazine.info/ja/contextualisation%20of%th e gospel%20among%20muslims1).pdf.
[Written from an Adventist perspective, the authors present a sound argument for looking beyond simple contextualization to a holistic presentation of the Gospel, perhaps solving—at least for them—the IM problems.]

Corwin, Gary. "Insider Movements and Outsider Missiology." *EMQ* 42(1): 10-11.
_____. "A Humble Appeal to C5/Insider Movement Muslim Ministry Advocates to Consider Ten Questions." *IJFM* 24(1): 5-20.
_____. "Issues of Identity in a Muslim Context: *Common Ground?*" *EMQ* 44(1): 8-9.

Dixon, Roger. "The Major Model of Muslim Ministry." *Missiology* 30(4): 443-54.
_____. "Identity Theft: Retheologizing the Son of God" *EMQ* 43(2): 220-6.

Nichols, Laurie Fortunak and Gary Corwin (Eds.) (2010). *Envisioning Effective Ministry: Evangelism in a Muslim Context.* Wheaton, IL: EMIS.
[A very balanced presentation of both insider and non-insider perspectives; take special note of Corwin's epilogue.]

Grafas, Basil. "Insider Movements: An Evangelical Assessment." *Invision* (August 2006).
http://www2.mtw.org/home/site/templates/mtw_invision.asp?_r esolutionfile=templatespath%7Cmtw_invision.asp&area_2=public /Resources/Invision/2006/08/InsiderMovements.
_____. "Evaluation of scriptural Support for Insider Movements: Critique of John Ridgeway's "The Movement of the Gospel in New

Testament Times with special reference to insider movements." *SFM* 4:2 (March 2007): http://www.stfrancismagazine.info/ja/pdf/2007/2007-3_3.pdf.

Heldenbrand, Richard L. (1999). *Christianity and New Evangelical Philosophies* (3rd ed.). Middletown, CT: Words of Life.

Hiebert, Paul (1994). *Anthropological Reflections on Missiological Issues*. Grand Rapids, MI: Baker.

Houssney, Georges (2010). *Engaging Islam*. Boulder, CO: Treeline.

Morton, Jeff. "Narrative and Questions: Exploring the Scriptures with Muslims." *EMQ* 40(2): 172-6.
_____. (2011). *Two Messiahs*. Colorado Springs, CO: Biblica.
_____. "The Trial: a cautionary tale for Crypto-Christians." *SFM* 7:2 (April 2011): 174-94

Muller, Roland (2000). *Tools for Muslim Evangelism*. Belleville, ON: Essence.

Nikides, Bill. "Evaluating 'Insider Movements': C5 (Messianic Muslims)." *SFM* 4 (March 2006) http://www.stfrancismagazine.info/ja/pdf/2006/2006-3_2.pdf.
_____. "Special Translations of the Bible for Muslims? Contemporary Trends in Evangelical Mission." *SFM* 4 (March 2006) http://www.stfrancismagazine.info/ja/pdf/2006/2006-3_6.pdf.
_____. "A Response to Kevin Higgins's 'Inside What? Church, Culture, Religion, and Insider Movements in Biblical Perspective." *SFM* 5:4 (August 2009): 92-113.

Oksnevad, Roy and Dotsey Welliver (Eds.) (2001). *The Gospel for Islam: Reaching Muslims in North America*. Wheaton, IL: EMIS.

Parshall, Phil. "Danger! New Directions in Contextualisation." *EMQ* 34(4): 404-17.

Rommen, Edward and Gary Corwin (Eds.) (1996). *Missiology and the Social Sciences: Contributions, Cautions and Conclusions*. EMS Series #4. Pasadena, CA: William Carey Library.

Schlorff, Sam. "The Translation Model for Mission in Resistant Muslim Society." *Missiology* 28:3 (2000): 305-28.

Span, John. "Jesus the Ultimate Insider? A Response to the Proponents of the Insider Movement that Jesus is the 'Ultimate Insider' and the Ultimate Justification for the Methodology." *SFM* 5:5 (October 2009): 41-8.

Span, John and Ann. "Report on the *Common Ground* Consultants Meeting, Snellville (Georgia)." *SFM* 5:4 (August 2005): 52-73.

Tennent, Timothy. "The Challenge of Churchless Christianity: An Evangelical Assessment." *International Bulletin of Missionary Research*, Vol. 29(4) (October 2005): 171-7.

_____. "Followers of Jesus (*Isa*) in Islamic Mosques: A Closer Examination of C-5 'High Spectrum' Contextualization." *IJFM* 23:3 (Fall 2006): 101-15.

Woods, Scott. "A Biblical Look at C5 Muslim Evangelism." *EMQ* 39(2): 188-95.

Historical Perspective Websites

Biblical Missiology
A place for discussion among those involved in the Historical method of Muslim evangelism as well as the occasional IMer who shows up.
>www.biblicalmissiology.org

Gospel for Muslims
This is a ministry located in Texas and founded by Abraham and Amie Starker.
>www.gospelforMuslims.org

Jesus for Muslims
A network of non-profit organizations located in NYC with the express purpose of mobilizing and helping the church reach the more than one million Muslims of the greater metropolitan area.
>www.jesusformuslims.org

Insider Movements
Site to purchase DVDs and mp3s of the *IM: a Critical Assessment* conferences.
>www.insidersmovements.org
>www.i2ministries.org

Saint Francis Magazine
SFM, a joint effort of Interserve and AWM, is an e-zine that speaks clearly about a broad spectrum of missions issues in addition to IM.
>www.stfrancismagazine.org/info/ja

Index

Accad, Fouad Elias *202, 212*

Bailey, Patricia *32*

Bangladesh *173-4, 180, 230ff, 252, 254-5, 258-60, 262*
   number of insiders, *239, 254*

Bible (Scripture)
   inerrancy of *95*
   Islamic teachings align with *96*
   Islamic view of *137*
   Islamization of *156, 221, 264*
   Reconciled with Islamic teachings *96*

Brown, Rick *12-13, 20, 28, 32-3, 35, 38-41, 157-8, 201-6, 220*

Caldwell, Stuart *16*

Camel method *145ff, 236, 265*
   elevates Qur'an *148*

Christian(s)
   bounded-set *35*
   centered-set *35*
   Christian Muslim *33, 263*
   changed Scripture *137-8, 157, 159, 203, 207, 210, 237, 242, 286-7, 303, 317*
   cultural *25*
   dogmatic *20*
   from Muslim background *27, 74, 124, 206, 230, 235, 237-8, 264, 267, 280, 282, 284, 292, 295*
   identity and tradition *83*
   Jewish-background *64*
   Masihiyyoo (Christians of North Africa) *270, 274*
   mosque attendance *16, 74, 283*
   re-converting converted Christians *258*
   religious identity *35*
   sham *54*
   sub- *93, 260*
   traditional *35-6*
   understanding of Islam *124-5*

Christianity
   as Christendom *36, 86*
   fulfillment of Judaism *119*
   global *8, 57, 117*
   individualistic *144*
   Islamic view of *121-2, 125, 134*
   Islamization of *147*
   man-made religion *83, 85, 135*
   pitted against the Kingdom *82*
   sect of Islam *255*
   socio-religious system *83, 129*
   socio-religious-political category *36*
   unifying with Islam *97*

Church
   community of believers *17, 81, 100, 108, 133, 144, 160*
   definition *36*
   JIQ meanings of *223*
   little local kingdoms *30*
   not sole proprietor of Christ *6*
   persecuted *153, 235-6, 250, 257, 284*
   relation to kingdom *30, 77ff*
   so-called *130*
   stumbling block to Muslims *135*

Common Ground (CG) *82, 122, 201, 212, 280*
   Seven signs *222fn, 285*

Common Word 299-301, 306-7

contextualization *6, 48, 51, 53, 55, 64, 72-3, 89-90, 92-3, 127-8, 140-1, 146, 148, 173-4, 179, 264-7, 280, 286, 292-3, 296*
   decontextualize *23, 73*

continuity *116, 118-9, 120*
   between Islam and Christianity

conversion *16, 22, 28-9, 36, 47-8, 53, 66, 68-9, 135, 153, 158, 253-4, 256, 270-2, 274, 277-8, 295, 298, 304-5, 307, 318*
    change of allegiance *26, 29, 67, 132, 135, 157, 295*
    cultural *19, 48*
    discouraged *71*
    not changing religions *26, 140, 295*
    obstacles of *86*
    replaced by conversation *161*
    re-conversion into Islam *258, 260, 263*
    socio-religious *36*
    traditional paradigms *82*

covenant *52-8, 102-6, 114-5, 121, 123, 129, 131-2, 135, 138, 159, 175-7, 201, 212, 287-8, 317*
    in Qur'an *121*
    non-covenant Abrahamic nations *14*
    non-covenantal religion *52, 55*

C-Spectrum *88ff*
    C5 *8, 22, 24, 26, 37, 89-90, 93-9, 146, 199, 231, 267, 278, 311*
    C5 and Bible translation *96*
    C5 believers *16, 19, 33, 37, 286*
    C5 exegesis *94*
    C5 is an attempt to create concept without a text *94*
    C5 methodology *96, 98, 311*
    C5 not accepted by Christians or Muslims *90*
    C5 philosophy *96*
    C5 theology *96*

Coe, Doug *212*

culture
    as identity *28*
    and Church *78, 98*
    Bible and *142*
    Christian *25, 83*
    corrected by Gospel *21*
    darkness of *49*
    defined by Qur'an *147*
    God designed *22, 49*
    Islamic *24, 136, 140-1, 292*
    Islamic view of *315*
    neutral *140, 143*
    not everything in it is good *20*
    prison of disobedience *144*
    sensitivity to *107, 114*
    transformation of *72*

Culver, Jonathan *14*

Decker, Frank *24*

divergence *116, 118*
    between Islam and Christianity *124*

Dutch, Bernard *21, 27, 35, 49, 50*

emergent church *2-8, 127, 161, 290*

extraction *17, 24, 140-1, 283-4, 291, 297*

Gray, Leith *38fn, 39fn*

Greeson, Kevin *145ff*

Gustafson, Kim *82, 200*

habib (Allah) 286

Harling, Mack (see Harley Talman) *82fn*

hermeneutic(s)
    experience as *51*
    gymnastics *147*
    of IM *43ff*
    postmodern literary *156, 161, 269*

Higgins, Kevin *15-16, 20-2, 24-5, 28-30, 33, 36, 46-9, 53, 55, 60, 94, 116-8*

Historical perspective *2, 85, 118, 122*

identity *3, 17, 24, 29-30, 49-50, 53, 60, 65-7, 69-70, 83, 130, 136, 254, 265, 294, 297, 315*
   Christian *35, 83*
   change *35, 69*
   codes *278, 295, 316*
   dual *6, 36, 53*
   ethnic *66, 68-9*
   in Christ *9, 72, 81, 144, 179, 263, 265, 280*
   Islamic *240, 280*
   Muslim *18, 28-9, 33-4, 85, 142, 233, 241, 246ff, 280, 289, 291, 297, 318*
   of Isa *136, 149, 159, 261,265, 278, 295, 298*
   religio-cultural *250*
   socio-religious *30, 36, 84*
   spiritual *19, 24-5, 27, 30, 83*

insider movements (IM)
   accommodates Muslim prejudices *126, 130-1, 156, 160, 206, 215*
   advocated by Western missionaries *1-2, 38, 96, 116, 126, 219, 223, 227, 285, 287*
   allows theological penetration of Christianity *307*
   believe Bible and Qur'an *35fn, 263*
   biblical support for *14-22*
   compared with emergent church *2-8*
   definition *23-4, 36, 240*
   methodological model of evangelism *280*
   missiology *97, 132, 136, 140, 274*
   Muslim Replacement Theology *126-9*
   Navigators *201-2, 210-13, 227*
   pray the *shahada 96*
   numbers *227*
   prevents persecution *71, 236, 240, 251, 255-6, 297*
   ten premises of *26*
   underestimates power of the Qur'an *301*

Isai (Isahi) 147, 238, 260-1

Islam
   anti-Christianity *139, 211fn, 290-1*
   compared to Judaism *29, 34*
   divine involvement in remote origins of *14*
   dhimmitude *126-7*
   equal to Christianity *84-5, 293*
   folk practices *31*
   forms *23, 29, 31, 36, 74, 140, 142, 291-2, 297, 317-8*
   forms borrowed from Jews and Christians *31*
   forms given new meaning *29, 141-3*
   heritage *24, 28-9, 243*
   mixture of culture and religion *140*
   new kingdom of God *294*
   pillars *29, 31, 34, 281*
   practices in keeping with Word of God *26, 132*
   redefining *96*
   religion of death, chains, blindness, pride *143*
   religio-cultural phenomenon *140*
   revealed through Jesus *27*
   socio-religious system *268*
   truth in *49*
   way of life *267*

Jabbour, Nabil *83-4, 211*

Jameson, Richard *29, 32, 34, 60*

Jesus in the Qur'an (JIQ) 200fn, 201, 222-6

journals
   pro-IM journals *269*
   neutral journals *2*

kingdom of God *23, 26, 29-31, 77-86, 98, 132-3, 135, 144, 195, 197, 285, 293-4, 318*

Kosova *314f*

Kraft, Charles *8, 26, 29, 31, 48, 132, 140, 142-4*

Lewis, Rebecca *17, 19, 24-5, 27, 30, 35-7, 49, 83, 85, 126*

Livingstone, Greg *214*

Love, Rick *664, 146fn, 214fn*

Mallouhi, Mazhar *24, 27-8, 32, 37, 163, 213-222, 226, 286*

Mannan, Timothy *234fn*

Massey, Joshua *18, 20-1, 92-8*

Medearis, Carl *214fn*

Messiah (*al masih*)
   in the Qur'an *33, 96, 137, 139, 149, 159, 181, 300, 302, 325*
   sonless *170*
   substitution for Son of God *38-49, 174, 203, 205*
   supracultural *6*

missiology (missiologists) *35, 38, 40, 46, 56, 58, 81, 89, 91-3, 96-8, 101, 145-6, 148, 173-4, 180, 230, 247, 269, 274*
   defined *23, 132*
   Paul's *71-2*
   inappropriate *132*

Muhammad *27, 31, 33, 98, 121, 127, 137-9, 141-4, 146, 149-51, 171, 206, 209-10, 222-4, 230, 239-42, 259, 284, 287-8, 296, 300-3, 312, 315*

Muslim(s)
   accepting Christ *35*
   background believers (MBB and BMB) *27, 74, 124, 206, 235, 237-8, 265, 270, 274, 280, 282, 284*

biblical *32*
Christian becoming a *232, 300*
-compliant translation (MCT) *156-7, 159, 286-7*
cultural *38*
definition *62, 146, 223-6, 261*
descendents of Ishmael *14*
embrace Jesus *6*
emerging believing community *29*
follower of Christ (*Isa*, Jesus) *19, 25, 28-9, 95-6, 135*
follower of the Straight Way *29*
for *Isa 14*
forms *290-2*
-friendly translations *216, 219-221*
heart-and-soul followers of Jesus Christ *34*
-idiom translations *156, 200*
insider *37*
Messianic *8, 33, 96, 260*
nominal (marginal) *27, 307*
objections to biblical language *38-9*
pure *258, 260*
re-converted *260*
remaining *15, 27, 36, 47, 52-3, 55, 83, 96, 283, 288*
seekers *236*
true *258, 260, 263, 307*
view of Christianity *35, 121, 159, 173, 181, 305*
worship the true God *47*

namaz (see *salat*) *10, 255-6, 263*

oikos 280-2, 289

People of the Book *24, 44, 121, 137, 300, 302, 306*

persecution *70-1, 153, 234-5, 239-40, 249-51, 254-6, 263, 267-8, 282-4, 292, 295-7*

Petersen, Brian K. *53, 60*

postmodern(-ism) *4, 5, 8, 80, 95,*

127, 156, 161, 269, 277, 294

Qur'an(-ic) *1, 7, 29, 210, 222, 224-6, 236, 240ff, 256, 258, 263-4, 267, 276-8, 285, 300-1, 303*
   Adam(a) *125, 149*
   Allah *123, 150, 173, 261, 265, 300-2*
   biblical revelation encompasses *122*
   Christian reinterpretation of *202, 225, 277, 288-9*
   Christianizing the *151*
   confirms previous revelation *137*
   continuity with biblical revelation 122
   divinely inspired *201, 221*
   -equivalent words *265, 285, 317*
   God's names in *122*
   Gospel in *32, 137, 148, 151, 265, 286*
   high regard for *147-8*
   Holy Spirit in *124, 151*
   inspiration of *128, 285-6*
   is the word of Yahweh *122-3*
   Jesus (*Isa*) in *33, 123, 138-9, 146, 149-51, 157, 173, 181, 259, 262, 265, 278, 285, 289, 295*
   missionaries recite from *74*
   Muhammad *146, 201, 235, 312*
   on the Bible *95, 121, 137-8, 300*
   on Christians *121*
   on of People of the Book *121*
   on the Trinity *276, 299-304*
   points to Jesus *32, 225*
   powerful apologetic *95*
   rejected by Muslims *254*
   stepping-stone or candle *284*
   teaches followers of *Isa* are Muslim *29*
   tool to reach Muslims *32, 147*
   worldview *97*

religion
   Abrahamic *17, 321*
   biblical worldview of *59, 86, 100, 104*
   cultural sub-system *25*
   devil uses *80*
   Durkheimian view of *136*
   false *84, 104, 135*
   fingerprints of God in *21*
   IM understanding of *23-32, 289*
   no need to change *19, 26, 135, 277, 294*
   of Jesus *26, 135-6*
   of Judaism *19, 21, 27, 34, 36, 59, 132-3*
   of Samaritans *9, 16-7, 47, 49, 135*

Ridgway, John *48, 83, 85*

salat, salah (see *namaz*) *10, 142, 290, 282, 297*

sawm (fasting) *29, 133, 266, 273, 305, 313-4*

Scalevich, Nick *29, 32, 34, 60*

Scott, Waldron *211*

shahada (confession of faith, creed) *32-3, 96, 127, 133, 136, 143, 239, 288, 293, 297, 302, 306, 308*

Son of God
   Christ sent from God *39*
   cultural wall *39*
   equivalent to Messiah *40*
   God's only beloved *182*
   in non gender format *38*
   Islamic rejection of *156*
   linguistic stumbling block *38, 99, 205*
   offends Muslims *28, 157-8, 160*
   not equivalent to Messiah *174, 202*
   substitute with Messiah *13, 39, 173, 181, 202*
   removal of *157, 159, 162, 218*
   retheologize *196*
   stumbling block *38, 41, 184, 219*
   troublesome term *40*

Stallsmith, John *223-5*

Stockholm syndrome *126ff*

syncretism *5, 24, 48, 97, 158, 210, 239, 245-6, 248, 294*

Talman, Harley (see Mack Harling) *14*

taqiyya 134, 295, 305, 316

theology of religions (TR) *7, 57, 116ff*
    exclusivism *116-7*
    inclusivism *67, 117*
    pluralism *15, 118*

Timmons, Tim *30*

translation(s) and translator(s)
    Arabic *163-68; 215-8*
    Bengali *164-68*
    C5 Bible *96*
    demoted Jesus from deity *159*
    dynamic equivalence *297*
    insider Bible *234, 237*
    Kitab Suci Injil 98
    Malay (Shellabear) *168-171*
    Muslim-compliant (MCT) *156-7, 159, 163ff, 284-5*
    Muslim friendly *215, 218-20*
    Muslim-idiom *156, 199*
    principles of *161ff, 218*
    reconstruct identity of Jesus *88*
    rejected by church *235*
    remove offensive terms *41*
    thought-for-thought *97*
    word-for-word *38, 97*

Travis, John *8, 16, 19, 24-5, 28, 30, 35, 9-91, 93-6, 98, 146, 279-80*

Travis, John and Anna *26-7, 31, 33-4, 37, 97, 132, 136, 138, 140-1*

Trinity *13-14, 40, 95, 139, 156, 174, 182, 185-8, 190, 195, 240, 245, 259, 275, 288, 290, 303*

Wiarda, Timothy *19, 54*

Winship, Jamie *31-2, 199-200, 221, 223-5*

Winter, Ralph *34, 146fn*

Wycliffe (WBT/SIL) *163fn, 199, 209, 219-221*

Woodberry, Dudley *18, 25, 28, 30-1, 33, 35, 60*

zakat (almsgiving) *29*

Scripture References

Genesis
2:19, *301*
12:3, *37*
15:6, *135*
15:16, *102, 104*
16:12, *285-6*
Ch 17, *14*
17:18-21, *285-6*
17:20, *14*
21:13, *14*
21:20, *14*
22:2, *286*
22:12, *286*
22:16, *3286*
28:14, *37*
42:6, *135*

Exodus
4:22-3, *177*
23:23, *101*
23:30, *129*
23:32-3, *129*
34:11, *101, 104*
34:11-12, *129*
40:34-5, *18*

Leviticus
18:24-5, *102*
18:26-30, *102fn*
18:27, *102*
19:1-18, *200*
19:17, *200*

Numbers
Chs 22-24, *15, 52*
22:8, *52*
22:18, *52*
23:1, *15*
31:16, *52*
35:34, *102*

Deuteronomy
Chs 2-3, *101*
4:9-10, *106*
4:38, *129*
5:15, *106*
6:12, *106*
6:13, *106*
6:20, *106*
7:1, *101*
7:1-11, *101*
7:2, *101*
7:3-4, *102*
7:6, *109, 131*
7:8-9, *104*
7:17-18, *106*
8:2, *106fn*
8:11-20, *106*
9:5, *104*
9:7, *106*
11:22, *129*
11:23, *129*
12:29-30, *129*
13:12-18, *103fn*
17:15, *286*
18:20, *288fn*
20:10-18, *101*
20:17, *101*
20:18, *103*
26:16-18, *101*

Joshua
6:17-19, *101*
6:21, *101*
8:1-29, *101*
10:28, *101*
10:30, *101*
10:32-5, *101*
10:37, *101*
10:39-41, *101*
11:8, *101*
11:11-12, *101*
11:18-20, *101*
Ch 13, *106*

13:13, *101*
Ch 16, *106*
16:10, *101*

Judges
1:1-2:9, *106*
1:17, *101*
6:13, *106*
Ch 17-21, *106*

2 Samuel
14:7, *189*

2 Kings
Ch 5, *15-16, 52*
5:1-14, *118*
5:15, *94*
5:18, *16*
5:19, *16, 47*

2 Chronicles
20:30, *77*

Esther
3:6, *77*

Psalms
Ch 2 *189*
11:3, *156*
16:4, *106*
72:9-11, *15*
103:19, *77*
Ch 107, *107*
115:8, *107*
145:11, *77*
145:13, *77*

Proverbs
14:15, *226fn*
15:8, *84*
18:1, *88*
27:5-6, *215fn*
28:23, *226*

Isaiah
7:14, *275*
9:6, *275*
42:1, *189*
55:10-11, *158*
60:6-7, *14-15*

Jeremiah
2:5, *107*
2:19, *107*
7:25, *106*
10:7, *77*
31:31ff, *135fn*

Ezekiel
3:17-21, *200fn*
18:32, *226fn*
33:11, *226fn*

Daniel
9:1, *77*
11:9, *77*

Amos
5:26-7, *106*

Joel
1:13f, *135*

Jonah
Ch 1, *16, 53*

Zechariah
14:9, *78*

Matthew
1:21, *138*
Ch 2, *14*
2:1-12, *14*
2:11, *15*
3:8, *214*
3:17, *162, 191*
4:3ff, *191, 198*
4:16-17, *132*
5:11-12, *255*
5:13, *103*
5:13-16, *100, 103, 107*
5:14-15, *107*
5:15, *280-2, 315*
5:16, *163, 281*
5:17, *133*
5:18-19, *133*
5:21-32, *212*
5:23-24, *133*
5:43-7, *112*
5:45, *163, 215*
5:48, *163, 215*
6:1ff, *133*
6:2-4, *29*
6:5-7, *29*
6:10, *77*
6:16-18, *29, 133*
7:12, *275*
8:27, *193*
10:17-23, *281*
10:35-7, *281*
11:2-3, *193*
11:27, *192, 197*
11:29-30, *115*
12:23, *193*
12:46-50, *280*
13:56, *192*
14:33, *191*
16:16, *193*
16:18, *133*
17:5, *162, 191*
18:15-20, *191*
18:17, *112*
21:10, *193*
21:12ff, *133*
22:34-40, *200*
22:42, *193*
24:4-5, *210fn*
24:36, *192*
26:62-6, *159*
27:40, *191*
27:54, *191*
28:16-20, *303*
28:17, *203*
28:18-20, *100*
28:19, *186-7, 190, 192, 209, 292*

Mark
1:1, *219fn*
1:1-2, *238fn*
1:14, *132*
3:11, *191, 193*
5:7, *193*
8:34-8, *281fn*
12:28-31, *200*
12:34, *226fn*
14:36, *178*
14:61, *194*
15:39, *2193*

Luke
1:32, *132, 188, 194*
1:35, *188, 194*
3:8, *241*
4:3, *194*
4:9, *194*
6:36, *177, 182, 220*
8:28, *194*
9:23, *157*
9:26,
9:35, *194*
Ch 10, *151fn*
11:2, *209*
11:13,
11:52, *201*
14:26, *294*
14:27, *157*
21:12-13, *248*
21:16-18, *248*
22:28-30,
22:42,
22:70,
23:34,
23:46,

Luke (cont.)
24:24-52, *152-3*
24:27, *153*
24:34, *153*
24:49,

John
1:1, *139, 300*
1:14, *18*
2:13ff, *133*
2:20-5, *261*
3:1ff, *132*
3:3, *132*
3:16, *198*
Ch 4, *16-17, 47*
4:1-3, *261*
4:19-24, *17*
4:22, *17*
4:23, *135*
4:42, *17*
5:16-18, *203*
5:17-23, *204*
5:21, *197*
6:40, *197*
8:36, *197*
8:58, *243*
10:25-33, *203*
10:30, *183*
10:30-9, *204*
12:23,
13:13-18, *217-18*
13:34, *110*
14:6, *259, 301*
14:9, *262*
14:16-17, *301*
Ch 15, *225*
15:26-7, *301*
Ch 17, *17-18*
17:1-2, *197*
17:5, *197*
17:21, *18, 197*
17:22-3, *18, 197*
18:36, *132*
19:25-7, *150fn*
20:20, *243*
20:31, *156, 190, 195*

Acts
4:10, *150*
4:12, *259*
5:17-40, *251*
Ch 8, *17*
8:14-17, *18, 49*
9:15-16, *70*
Chs 10-11, *49*
11:26, *147fn*
14:21-8, *36*
Ch 15, *18-20, 30, 48, 53-4, 56, 66, 294*
15:3, *293*
15:8, *18*
15:11, *19*
15:19ff, *19*
15:28, *19*
Ch 16, *67*
16:3, *66, 68*
Ch 17, *20-1, 55*
17:16-34, *94*
17:20, *70*
17:22-31, *94*
17:23, *20-1*
17:30, *264*
17:32, *55*
18:1-18, *65*
18:2, *72*
18:9, *71*
18:24-5, *65*
20:24-32, *112*
20:28, *113*
21:39, *65*
Ch 26, *151fn*
26:18, *136*
26:20, *20*
26:28, *147fn*

Romans
1:3-4, *174, 179, 191fn*
1:16, *70*
1:26-7, *285*
2:28-9, *65*
5:5, *226fn*
5:10, *196*
Ch 8, *178*
8:1-3, *178*
8:2, *191fn*
8:5-8, *107*
8:10-11, *178*
8:12-15, *178*
8:14-17, *197*
8:15, *178*
8:16-17, *255*
8:17, *178*
8:23, *178*
8:29, *179, 197*
8:29-30, *178*
8:31-9:3, *177*
8:32, *179, 91fn, 196-7*
9:1-2, *177*
9:4-5, *177*
9:5, *95, 177*
9:6, *65*
9:22-4, *177*
10:9-10, *293*
10:14-15, *294*
12:1ff, *28*
13:9, *200fn*

1 Corinthians
1:17, *70*
1:17-18, *158*
1:18, *71, 272*
1:21, *272*
1:22-3, *70*
1:24-5, *71*
1:26-31, *115*
2:1, *71*
2:2, *70*
3:6, *71*
5:1-5, *112*
6:14-18, *281fn*
Ch 7, *2, 285*
7:17-20, *21*
7:17-24, *286*
7:19, *68*
7:24, *98*
Ch 8-10, *22, 63*
8:1-3, *73*
8:4, *72fn*
8:7, *72*
8:9, *73*
8:11, *74*
8:13, *73*
Ch 9, *285*

1 Corinthians (cont.)
9:15, *76*
9:19-23, *62ff, 286*
9:21, *2290*
9:22, *69*
10:19-20, *73*
10:21, *74*
10:23, *74*
10:28, *76*
10:31, *75*
10:32, *75*
13:6, *215fn*
15:3-4, *290*

2 Corinthians
2:17, *258*
3:18, *72*
4:1-2, *213fn, 226fn*
4:2, *75*
5:13-21, *226fn*
5:17, *71, 152*
6:14, *136*
6:14-18, *115*

Galatians
1:6-9, *226fn*
1:10, *75*
1:16, *191fn*
Ch 2, *69*
2:3, *67*
2:4, *54*
2:11-13, *68, 200fn*
2:20, *291fn, 198*
3:7-9, *177*
3:10, *66*
3:22, *177*
3:24, *177*
3:26, *177*
3:29, *177*
Ch 4, *177*
4:4, *191fn*
4:4-5, *197*
4:4-6, *197*
4:4-7, *177*
4:5, *177*
4:6, *178, 197*

4:23-5, *286*
4:28-31, *286*
5:6, *68*
5:12, *20*
5:14, *200fn*
5:18, *66*

Ephesians
1:3-6, *176*
1:6, *176*
1:13-14, *178*
2:8-10, *36*
3:14-15, *182*
4:1, *153*
4:4-6, *59, 185*
4:15, *99*
4:24, *72*
5:8, *83, 136*
6:19-20, *72*

Philippians
1:12, *72*
1:12-14, *248*
1:29-30, *248*
2:9-11, *171*
3:5, *69*
3:8, *70, 247*
4:20, *205*

Colossians
1:13, *84, 196*
1:13-14, *197*
1:15, *196, 262*
1:15-20, *196*
1:18, *114*
1:24-29, *89*
1:27, *197*
1:28, *104, 114*
1:28-9, *107*
3:1, *103*
3:1-4, *107*
3:9-11, *72*

1 Thessalonians
2:3, *290*
5:5, *136*

1 Timothy
1:5, *213fn*
1:18-19, *213fn*
1:20, *200fn*
3:9, *213fn*
5:22, *200fn*

2 Timothy
3:10-12, *247*
3:12, *295*
4:2, *103, 226*
4:2-4, *215fn*
4:3, *71fn*
4:6-8, *111*
4:10, *200fn*
4:14, *200fn*

Titus
1:11, *250*

Hebrews
1:1-2, *197*
1:1-4, *174*
2:10, *197*
2:11, *197*
4:12, *158*
4:14, *197*
7:25-8, *197*
9:11, *184*
9:23, *184*
13:18, *213fn*

James
2:8, *20fn*

1 Peter
1:1, *109*
1:9, *153*
2:9, *136*

1 Peter (cont.)
2:17, *295*
3:16, *213fn*
3:21, *213fn*
4:12-17 *255*
4:16, *147fn*
5:1, *108*

2 Peter
2:1-3, *257*
2:15, *52*
3:9, *226fn*
4:12-17, *255*

1 John
1:1-3, *110-11*
1:5, *105*
1:6-7, *109*
2:3, *110*
2:6, *109*
2:7-8, *110*
2:15, *103*
4:1, *126*
4:2-3, *110*
4:9-10, *197*
5:2-3, *110*
5:21 *105fn*

2 John,
108-12

3 John
9, *200fn*

Jude
11, *52*

Revelation
Chs 2-3, *84, 110-1*
2:2, *110*
2:6, *110*
2:9-10, *110*
2:14, *110*
2:15, *110*
2:18, *162*
2:20, *110*
2:23, *265*
2:24, *110*
3:1, *111*
3:4-5, *226fn*
3:18, *226*
3:19, *215fn*
7:9, *226fn*
7:9-10, *226fn*
7:13-14, *226fn*
11:15, *81*
19:14, *226fn*
21:8, *81*
22:18-19, *162*

Qur'anic References

Al Fatihah (The
  Opening)
1:7, *265*

Al Baqarah (The
  Heifer)
2:29ff, *123fn*
2:30, *301*
2:74, *299*
2:87, *151*
2:106, *225*
2:113, *121*
2:116, *299*
2:120, *121*
2:135, *121*
2:256, *304*
2:177, *159*

Al Imran (Family
  of Imran)
3:35-7, *284fn*
3:42-55, *146, 148,
  151*
3:45, *151, 300*
3:45-7, *146*
3:46, *151*
3:46-9, *284*
3:47, *151*
3:49, *149, 151*
3:51, *149*
3:52, *152*
3:56, *150*
3:57, *150, 122*
3:59, *151, 243*
3:64, *298*
3:78, *147fn*
3:85, *245*

Al Nisa (The
  Women)
4:3, *288fn*
4:136, *284*
4:145, *264fn*
4:157, *150, 243, 287,
  300*
4:163, *301*
4:165, *181*
4:171, *123fn, 149,
  243, 287, 300*

Al Ma'idah (The
  Repast)
5:14, *121*
5:17, *298*
5:18, *121, 181*
5:31-2, *284fn*
5:45-6, *284*
5:46-9, *242, 284*
5:48, *242*
5:51, *264fn*
5:68, *284*
5:73, *398*
5:75, *387*
5:85, *264*
5:111, *29, 280*
5:116, *243, 287*
5:156-9, *125fn*

Al An`um (The
  Cattle)
6:101, *181, 287*

Al A`raf (The
  Heights)
7:11, *299*
7:11ff, *123fn*
7:20-4, *125fn*
7:178, *264fn*

Al Anfal (Spoils of
  War)
8:39, *288fn*

Al Tawbah
  (Repentance)
9:1-5, *288fn*
9:29, *288fn*
9:30, *181*
9:33, *304*

Yunus (Prophet
  Jonah)
10:15-16, *146fn*
10:37, *137*
10:94, *3284*

Hud (Prophet
  Hud)
11:12-14, *146fn*

Al Ra`d (The
  Thunder)
13:20-5, *123fn*
13:27, *264fn*

Al Hijr (Rocky
  Tract)
15:26ff, *130fn*
15:29, *159*

Al Nahl (The
  Bees)
16:17, *123fn*
16:93, *264fn*
16:102, *124fn*

Al Isra' (The
    Night Journey)
17:111, *181*

Al Kahf (The
    Cave)
18:50, *299*
18:86, *301*
18:110, *146fn*

Maryam (Mary)
19:19-20, *284*
19:21, *138*
19:22-6, *3284fn*
19:29-33, *384fn*
19:35, *173,181*
19:88-92, *181*

TaHa
20:115ff, *123fn*

Al Anbiya' (The
    Prophets)
21:7, *284*
21:51-71, *284fn*

Al Hajj (The
    Pilgrimage)
22:16, *123fn*

Al Naml (The
    Ants)
27:17-44, *284fn*

Al Qasas (The
    Narrations)
28:77, *123fn*

Al `Ankabut (The
    Spider)
29:49, *284*

Al Sajdah (The
    Prostration)
32:13, *264fn*

Al Ahzab (The
    Confederates)
33:4, *303*
33:21, *146fn*
33:30, *302*
33:36-7, *288fn*
33:50, *288fn*

Al Shura (The
    Consultation)
42:52, *149*

Qaf
50:16, *123fn*

Al Saff (The Battle
    Array)
61:6, *146fn, 300*

Al Muddaththir
    (One Wrapped
    Up)
74:31, *264fn*

i2 Ministries: Who are we and what do we do?

i2 Ministries provides intensive classes on video in Muslim Ministry and Islamic Studies from the leading experts in the field. We believe the solution to global, radicalized Islam is found in a well-trained, mobilized, and Spirit-led Church, equipped in biblical theology, spiritual warfare, missiology, apologetics, and Islamics. It is our goal to facilitate the Church as she endeavors to finish the Great Commission among Muslims.

Islam's Issues, Agendas & The Great Commission

Why Care About Muslims?

Mission Muslim World University
Module 0: Orientation
Course 1

8 Disk Course
In this presentation, Joshua Lingel gives an introduction to the Muslim Worldview and the unique challenges it presents to Global Christianity today. His challenge to the Church is to consider its role in the Great Commission, especially in regards to the Islamic World.

Featuring
Prof. Joshua Lingel
i2 Ministries, Inc.

Disk 1 Why Care About Muslims
Disk 2 How Muslims Come to Christ
Disk 3 How Islam is Changing the World
Disk 4 Introduction to Islam
Disk 5 Everything You Need to Know About Radical Islam
Disk 6 Jesus In Islam and Christianity
Disk 7 Insider Movements: A Critical Assessment
Disk 8 Finishing the Great Commission Among Muslims

For more information on this and other courses offered by i2 Ministries to equip your church to reach Muslims with the Gospel, visit us on the web at
www.i2ministries.org
or email info@i2ministries.org

Christian Apologetics to Islam

Mission Muslim World University
Module 1: Muslim Ministry & Islamic Studies Foundations
Course 2

13 Disk Course
The aim of this course is to equip the Christian to effectively engage in evangelism with Muslims through a deeper understanding of the Islamic Worldview, and to answer the polemical questions often raised by Muslims in regard to the Bible, the nature of Jesus, and the origins and development of Christianity.

Featuring
Prof. Joshua Lingel
i2 Ministries, Inc.

- Disk 1   Why Care About Muslims
- Disk 2   How Muslims Come to Christ
- Disk 3-4   Biography of Muhammad, Part 1 & 2
- Disk 5   Muhammad's Prophethood & Moral Character
- Disk 6   Historical Critique of the Sources for the Life of Muhammad
- Disk 7   Shariah Law & Society
- Disk 8-10   Qur'an Critique Part 1, 2 & 3
- Disk 11   Textual Criticism of the Qur'an
- Disk 12   Isa in Islam or Jesus in Christianity?
- Disk 13   A Guide to Finishing the Great Commission

For more information on this and other courses offered by i2 Ministries to equip your church to reach Muslims with the Gospel, visit us on the web at
www.i2ministries.org
or email info@i2ministries.org

Radical Evangelism to Muslims
Introduction to Muslim Evangelim

Mission Muslim World University
Module 1: Muslim Ministry & Islamic Studies Foundations
Course 3

11 Disk Course
Radical Evangelism to Muslims means to love Muslims enough to be a faithful witness to the gospel to them in our modern day. Christian apologist Jay Smith communicates the reality of resurgent Islam and its impact on the Church's witness to the Muslim World.

Featuring
Prof. Jay Smith
Brethren in Christ World Mission

Disk 1   Introduction to Muslim Evangelism
Disk 2   Understanding Islam's Beliefs & Practices
Disk 3   Islam & Christianity Compared - "Hermeneutical Key"
Disk 4   Muhammad - A Christian Critique
Disk 5   The Bible - A Christian Apologetic
Disk 6   Confident Christianity: In 7 Areas vs. Islam
Disk 7   Khilafah vs. Kingdom of God
Disk 8   Which is the Religion of Peace, Islam or Chrisitianity? The Question Post 9/11 & 7/7
Disk 9   Frequently Asked Questions (FAQ's)
Disk 10 The Attraction of Islam
Disk 11 Missiological Methodologies Post 9/11

For more information on this and other courses offered by i2 Ministries to equip your church to reach Muslims with the Gospel, visit us on the web at
www.i2ministries.org
or email info@i2ministries.org

Christian & Islamic Theological Issues

Introduction to Christian & Islamic Theological Issues

Mission Muslim World University
Module 1: Muslim Ministry & Islamic Studies Foundations
Course 4

11 Disk Course

Dr. Tavassoli compares the concepts of God, Man, Christ, and the Scriptures in each worldview and explains how these differences can be confronted when speaking with Muslim neighbors.

Featuring Prof. Sasan Tavassoli

- Disk 1 Introduction to Christian & Islamic Theological Differences
- Disk 2-6 The Doctrine of the Trinity Part 1-5
- Disk 7-8 The Doctrine of Man Part 1 & 2
- Disk 9 Islamic View of Jesus
- Disk 10 Christian Response to the Islamic View of Jesus
- Disk 11 Islam's Challenge to the Scriptures

For more information on this and other courses offered by i2 Ministries to equip your church to reach Muslims with the Gospel, visit us on the web at
www.i2ministries.org
or email info@i2ministries.org

Loving God with All Your Mind

Conversion to Jesus and Being a Disciple: Personal Reflections

Mission Muslim World University
Module 2: Apologetics 1
Course 5

9 Disk Course

J.P. Moreland presents a logical case for the role of the mind in spiritual transformation. He challenges us to develop a Christian mind and to use our intellect to further God's Kingdom through evangelism, apologetics, worship, and vocation.
In this up-to-date series, Dr. Moreland addresses such issues as: Anti-Intellectualism vs. the thinking Christian, Jesus the greatest intellectual in history, Atheism, Secular Humanism, Post-Modernism and their impact on Western and global culture.

Featuring Prof. J.P. Moreland

Disk 1	Conversion to Jesus & Being a Disciple: Personal Reflections
Disk 2	Emergence of the Modern Secular Worldview
Disk 3	Faith & Reason
Disk 4	Evidence Against Scientific Naturalism & Evidence For God
Disk 5	Postmodernism and Its Impact on Western Culture
Disk 6	The Search for God: How Does One Select a Religion in a Rational Way?
Disk 7	Hell: Fact or Fiction?
Disk 8	Jesus Christ: The Only Way to God
Disk 9	The Problem of Evil and God

Evidence that Demands a Verdict

The Bible Part 1

Mission Muslim World University
Module 2: Apologetics 1
Course 6

13 Disk Course
Based upon the book of the same title, this course addresses the trustworthiness of the Bible and offers historical evidence and supporting attestations for Jesus' claim to divintiy. This is a powerfully influential course on apologetics from one of the most prolific apologists of this generation.

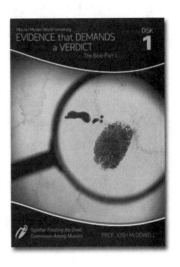

Featuring
Prof. Josh McDowell
Josh McDowell Ministries

Disks 1-4	The Bible Part s1-4
Disks 5-9	Resurrection Factor Parts 1-5
Disks 10-11	Attributes of God Parts 1 & 2
Disks 12-13	Bible: Fact or Fiction Parts 1 & 2

For more information on this and other courses offered by i2 Ministries to equip your church to reach Muslims with the Gospel, visit us on the web at:
www.i2ministries.org
or email info@i2ministries.org

The Master Plan of Evangelism

The Great Commission Lifestyle: Incarnation

Mission Muslim World University
Module 2: Apologetics 1
Course 7

9 Disk Course

For more than 40 years this classic, biblical look at evangelism has challenged and instructed over 3 million readers. Now repackaged on video for our contemporary challenges, The Master Plan of Evangelism is as fresh and relevant as ever. Join the movement and discover how you can minister to the people God brings in to your life.

Featuring
Dr. Robert Coleman

Disk 1   The Great Commission Lifestyle: Incarnation
Disk 2   The Great Commission Lifestyle: Selection
Disk 3   The Great Commission Lifestyle: Association
Disk 4   The Great Commission Lifestyle: Consecration
Disk 5   The Great Commission Lifestyle: Demonstration
Disk 6   The Great Commission Lifestyle: Delegation
Disk 7   The Great Commission Lifestyle: Supervision
Disk 8   The Great Commission Lifestyle: Reproduction
Disk 9   The Great Commission Lifestyle: Impartation

For more information on this and other courses offered by i2 Ministries to equip your church to reach Muslims with the Gospel, visit us on the web at:
www.i2ministries.org
or email info@i2ministries.org